Religion, Media, and Marginality in Modern Africa

CAMBRIDGE CENTRE OF AFRICAN STUDIES SERIES

Series editors: Derek R. Peterson, Harri Englund, and Christopher Warnes

The University of Cambridge is home to one of the world's leading centers of African studies. It organizes conferences, runs a weekly seminar series, hosts a specialist library, coordinates advanced graduate studies, and facilitates research by Cambridge- and Africa-based academics. The Cambridge Centre of African Studies Series publishes work that emanates from this rich intellectual life. The series fosters dialogue across a broad range of disciplines in African studies and between scholars based in Africa and elsewhere.

Derek R. Peterson, ed.
Abolitionism and Imperialism in Britain, Africa, and the Atlantic

Harri Englund, ed.
Christianity and Public Culture in Africa

Devon Curtis and Gwinyayi A. Dzinesa, eds.
Peacebuilding, Power, and Politics in Africa

Ruth J. Prince and Rebecca Marsland, eds.
Making Public Health in Africa: Ethnographic and Historical Perspectives

Emma Hunter, ed.
Citizenship, Belonging, and Political Community in Africa: Dialogues between Past and Present

Felicitas Becker, Joel Cabrita, and Marie Rodet, eds.
Religion, Media, and Marginality in Modern Africa

Religion, Media, and Marginality in Modern Africa

Edited by Felicitas Becker,
Joel Cabrita,
and Marie Rodet

Ohio University Press • Athens

Ohio University Press, Athens, Ohio 45701
ohioswallow.com

Printed in the United States of America
Ohio University Press books are printed on acid-free paper ∞ ™

28 27 26 25 24 23 22 21 20 19 18 5 4 3 2 1

Library of Congress Cataloging-in-Publication Data

Names: Becker, Felicitas, 1971- editor, writer of introduction. | Cabrita, Joel, 1980- editor, writer of introduction. | Rodet, Marie, editor.
Title: Religion, media, and marginality in modern Africa / edited by Felicitas Becker, Joel Cabrita, and Marie Rodet.
Other titles: Cambridge Centre of African Studies series.
Description: Athens : Ohio University Press, 2017. | Series: Cambridge Centre of African Studies series | Includes bibliographical references and index.
Identifiers: LCCN 2017053678| ISBN 9780821423035 (hardcover ; alk. paper) | ISBN 0821423037 (hardcover ; alk. paper) | ISBN 9780821446249 (pdf)
Subjects: LCSH: Mass media in religion--Africa. | Christianity in mass media. | Islam in mass media. | Digital media--Africa. | Digital media--Religious aspects. | Social media--Africa. | Social media--Religious aspects. | Marginality, Social--Africa. | Marginality, Social--Religious aspects.
Classification: LCC BV652.97.A35 R45 2017 | DDC 261.52096--dc23
LC record available at https://lccn.loc.gov/2017053678

Contents

Acknowledgments

The origins of this edited collection lie in a conference organized by the three editors and held at SOAS, University of London, in March 2013. We are grateful to all the participants—many of whom are represented in the present volume—for their rich papers. The conference was funded by an Arts and Humanities Research Council Research Networking Award (held by Becker and Cabrita). We are also grateful to the Faculty of Arts and Humanities at SOAS for their generous support. Our thanks also to the editors of the Cambridge Centre of African Studies Series for their support of the volume, as well as to Gillian Berchowitz, the director and editor in chief of Ohio University Press. Finally, we are grateful to the anonymous reviewers who offered valuable feedback on earlier iterations of this volume.

Introduction

Religion, Media, and Marginality in Modern Africa

FELICITAS BECKER AND JOEL CABRITA

THE PRESENT COLLECTION ENTERS AN ALREADY LIVELY FIELD, AS the role of media in Africa's ebullient religious activism has engaged the attention of scholars for the last couple of decades. And for good reason: a salient feature of Islamic revivals and expanding Pentecostal churches alike is the use of TV, video, mobile phones, and the internet and the claiming of audible and visible space through loudspeakers and billboards.[1] Part of the aim of this collection, though, is to go beyond the most attention-grabbing and public forms of media use and to include such relatively low-key examples as handwritten religious scripture circulating only among a small group of believers, pamphlets with similarly limited circulation, and registration forms. The objects just enumerated already point to another intention of this volume—namely, to examine "old" media, such as handwriting and print, and "new" media, such as video and the internet, in the same frame, thereby avoiding an evolutionary distinction.

Although with a few important exceptions recent literature has defined "media" in this context as new electronic and digital media,[2] here we also consider print culture—perhaps the still most heavily used media form in contemporary Africa—alongside them. We seek to situate recent "new media" phenomena within a longer history of Muslims' and Christians' use of older media forms, including both print and penned manuscripts, not least among them their sacred scriptures. Studies of religion and media in Africa typically treat new electronic and digital media in isolation from a well-established scholarship on print and manuscript culture in Africa. "Old" and "new" media tend to be positioned as different moments in time, with digital and electronic media frequently represented as succeeding print media in a linear, chronological fashion. By contrast, this volume considers the manner in which old and new media coexist on a single spectrum of media practice in Africa. Written texts—just as much as recent social media—have contributed to the formation of new forms of public life in Africa.[3]

There are two main reasons for doing so. First, the variety of processes and outcomes traceable across these media, combined with the similarities between outcomes involving media of different generations, enable us to challenge a tendency that appears occasionally in the literature—namely, to assume a kind of evolutionary progression, where different generations of media are associated with different social processes and outcomes. Broadly speaking, written media, and especially print media, tend to be associated with bringing people together, developing national publics, and expanding religious congregations. Conversely, in much of the literature on new electronic and digital media, the dominant theme concerns the fragmentation of audiences, especially national ones, that were formerly relatively homogeneous. This is seen in the development of niche audiences and diverse, competing religious claims, even as the new congregations thus established strive for overseas contacts and see themselves within a global frame of reference.[4]

Of course, these associations are undeniable in some ways. Clearly, in Africa, the mid-twentieth century was an era of popular nationalism as well as of expanding reading publics, epistolary networks, and radio audiences.[5] Conversely, the period since the 1990s is associated with the breakdown of monolithic political structures—one-party states in particular—and with the diversification of religious communities, political associations, and, last but not least, electronic media forms.[6] We think that it is important, though, not to take these associations too readily as evidence of causality. Granted, mass-circulation newspapers are bound to have a homogenizing effect on the knowledge and opinion of their reading publics, and there is no denying that communication via the internet supports the development of very specific subcultures whose members would otherwise find it much harder to connect. But mass-circulation newspapers can fall out of favor and end up minoritarian, while websites, too, can serve mass audiences.

In what follows, we seek to pay attention to how contingent and variable the effects of all media forms are. "Marginality," in this pursuit, serves us as a means to bring the variation into focus. Literally understood, a medium is a means; more specifically, it is a means for connecting or bringing together the people interacting with it. In this sense, all media mitigate their users' marginality relative to those they are enabled to reach. But each act of inclusion implies an act of exclusion; each public and audience has its margins. In Africa, the state of marginality can be taken as a shorthand for the challenges faced by people coping with pervasive poverty, lack of opportunity, and instable, sometimes conflict-ridden social and political environments. The present collection explores how some mediatized congregations or communities exist on the margins of others (say, national ones) and how media are used not only to reach out to others but also to close off some avenues (of communication or argumentation) by reaching out for others.

Given the intensity of social change in Africa since the colonial period, the fluidity of social borders as well as their sometimes quite sudden rigidity in situations of conflict, and the multitudes of people facing and seeking to mitigate one or another form of marginalization, it seems to us that addressing, mitigating, or conversely establishing marginality is an important thing media do.[7] As will be seen, both old and new, paper-based or electronic, media can operate at a great variety of scales; in the bid to consolidate an existing audience, they can foreground either outreach and inclusion or marginalization and exclusion of outsiders. The existing literature on media also makes very clear that media do much more than merely channel or convey communication or information. Media forms address and hail their audiences—readers, listeners, viewers—in highly particular ways, encouraging the formation of certain dispositions and attitudes. In so doing, they play a key role in constituting new ways of self-knowledge, collective being, and relating to wider social worlds. Keeping this in mind, we seek to contextualize recent transformations in media use within a long-standing history of religious practitioners in Africa using technologies of communication, as well as the resources of their religious traditions, to articulate identities and build communities.

Given the volume editors' specializations in Southern African Christianity, East African Islam, and West African postslavery societies, we feel well-placed to offer a comparative historical perspective. Too often, the large and lively bodies of literature on Islam and Christianity in

Africa exist in isolation from each other.[8] Here, we make an initial attempt at bringing aspects of these two scholarships into comparative dialogue. We are aware that the spectrum of religions to be considered could, and ideally should, be increased further. There are long-standing Hindu communities and growing Buddhist ones in Africa, and Islam, Christianity, and (especially) indigenous African religion have many more expressions than we consider here. But in offering the selection that we do, we hope to at least open a vista on an enormous, delicately patterned variety. Later in this introduction, we examine the different ways Christianity and Islam in Africa have been thought to make contributions to the formation of the public sphere. But first, we turn to a discussion of media and the formation of publics.

Media, Publics, and Politics

There has been considerable debate in recent years about the role of media in constituting and shaping what is variously called the "public sphere," "public culture," or simply "publics," and likewise about the role of religion (that is, religious organizations, attitudes, beliefs, and practices) in the same context.[9] This debate responds to a palpable sense that major change is afoot with the recent efflorescence of "new" electronic media, a category that typically encompasses mobile telephony and internet-based media and may also refer to video recordings and TV broadcasts not under state control, such as those of Pentecostal churches. The debate takes place in all parts of the globe, but it continues to be arranged around a story that focuses on Europe. In what follows, we examine the narrative concerning media and the public sphere and how African experiences fit into it, specifically drawing on case studies from the chapters collected in the present volume. Drawing on scholarship on media in Africa and elsewhere, we trace how our authors demonstrate that the work media do in society is driven both by specific cultures and institutional contexts of usage and by the aims and motivations of geographically and historically located actors.

The standard account of the history of media in Europe has itself been recognized to carry with it as many questions as consensual claims. Based on Jürgen Habermas's foundational work, it asserts that the democratic public sphere arose alongside the European bourgeoisie in the nineteenth century. At that time, the public was in essence a reading public, drawing on the ever-expanding dissemination of "print capitalism" in newspapers and books.[10] It was also, in this telling, an increasingly enlightened, self-emancipating public, forming a counterweight to hereditary rulers and increasingly encroaching on their rights. The twentieth century then saw the dawning of the era of mass media, with broadcasting, and especially radio, taking the lead over print. Responding to Europe's recent experience, Habermas and many other members of the Frankfurt school viewed the rise of broadcasting in much more ambivalent terms than that of print, emphasizing the possibilities of domination inherent in it over those of enlightened discourse.[11] Radio in particular was the medium of state propaganda, including the totalitarian variety, and it was epitomized in the widespread provision of radios and the effective use of radio speeches in Nazi Germany. This means that these authors ended up placing the period when media use in the public sphere was at its most emancipatory in a time when women, as well as colonized people, did not have the vote, let alone equal access to the public sphere. Conversely, demand-driven, consumer-oriented entertainment broadcasting was suspected of being opium for the masses. Taking these contradictions into account, it becomes harder to be sure that any media-constituted public sphere was ever unambiguously enlightened or emancipatory. When it became in Habermas's telling more inclusive, it also became at least potentially more repressive.

While this story obviously does not translate wholesale to the colonial world, it has its counterparts there. Benedict Anderson has asserted the crucial role of the spread of vernacular-language print media in establishing the "imagined communities" of anticolonial nationalists since at least the early twentieth century, providing something of a symmetry with Habermas's European story.[12] African Christians in the nineteenth century and the first half of the twentieth century, by virtue of their access to missionary-sponsored education, became increasingly well-positioned to establish themselves as a progressive elite at the vanguard of the formation of national imagined communities. These individuals differed in many ways across the continent but were everywhere united in their aspiration to attain Western cultural capital—above all, education. To take two examples, they became known in South Africa as the *amakholwa*, or "believers," and as *wasomi*, "the learners" or "readers," in Kenya.

A large recent literature has focused on how many of these African converts worked intensively with European missionaries to translate

Christian texts into a variety of languages, often codifying languages in writing for the first time. Terence Ranger showed us how missionaries in colonial Zimbabwe—seeking a common language to communicate with their converts—began creating standardized grammar books, dictionaries, and Bible translations.[13] Further, in the process of translating the word, many Christians discerned important equivalences between indigenous concepts of God and the newly received Christian missionary vocabulary. Translating sacred texts thus gave voice and shape to religious concepts that were thought to have long existed in African traditions.[14] The political implications of this Christian vernacular linguistic work were profound. In the context of colonial rule, the written codification of vernacular languages shaped African intellectuals' political imagination, providing a unified medium to imagine and argue over the black "nation" and to knit together far-flung individuals into coherent linguistic constituencies and reading publics that challenged the hegemony of white rule in the continent.[15] Across the continent, these mission-educated elites produced a profusion of print—newspapers, autobiographies, nonfiction, novels, pamphlets—that experimented with new forms of address, prompting their readerships to imagine themselves members of a single shared form of public life increasingly known as the "nation,"[16] although often encompassing more expansive ideas of pan-Africanism as well as fixed territorial units.[17]

Reading publics were clearly essential to the history of African nationalism; the multitude of literate activists, often mission educated, were at the forefront of anticolonial activism.[18] Yet there are at least as many qualifications to be offered in the African case as with Europe. Beyond urban centers and the tiny educated elite, reading publics remained diminutive until decades after the end of colonialism. For example, in South Africa in 1911, the first national census calculated that only 6.8 percent of all Africans could read.[19] Moreover, an exclusive focus on the connection between print and nationalist activists and intellectuals runs the risk of obscuring the vast amount of literate work carried out by nonelites, far from the spotlight of national politics. Along these lines, a seminal collection on "tin-trunk literacy" has eschewed the written work of political and academic African elites in favor of the "waged labourers, clerks, village headmasters, traders and artisans [who] read, wrote and hoarded texts of many kinds."[20] One recent study has dubbed this profusion of nonelite African intellectuals "homespun scholars."[21] Their tools were not always the formally printed book and newspaper.

Grassroots authors across the continent turned to genres as diverse as handwritten diaries, letters, and religious liturgies, many composed with the assistance of scribes, who greatly increased the potency and reach of literacy in the areas they worked in.[22] What was crucial is that these texts often addressed—and thereby constituted—audiences that sat at odd angles to the national audience of literate elites, providing examples of the work print could accomplish beyond or between Anderson's egalitarian and enlightened national imaginaries.

African writers, then, did not always imagine themselves addressing audiences constituted by Anderson's sense of "deep, horizontal comradeship"; self-professedly democratic national publics were not the inevitable outcome of print work.[23] One example of the rich range of counternationalisms generated by the creation and use of texts is found in David Gordon's chapter in this volume. Gordon complicates the narrative of the development of horizontal, anonymous, national print-reading publics by emphasizing the persistence of handwritten textual cultures, often characterized by highly uneven access to information and power. Gordon's focus is on the penned manuscripts of the Zambian Lumpa Church, whose members were primarily loyal to the memory of their charismatic church founder Alice Lenshina rather than the Zambian nation. Members of the church responded to a long history of exile and persecution from both European missionaries and African nationalists by creating a series of handwritten narratives, hymns, and ritual instructions for correct worship that constituted themselves as a chosen people, marginalized by earthly powers yet close to God. While type and print were on occasion used to strategically represent the church community to outsiders in a bureaucratic register (for example, through the creation of printed church membership cards and typed letters to colonial officials), handwritten documents were especially prized for their spiritual value and the possibilities they afforded of articulating internal church politics and identity. Gordon shows how Lumpa reading publics were hierarchically organized into dense clusters of loyalty to regional deacons who alone owned the communities' handwritten sacred texts and had the power to read and interpret them to the broader community. These, then, were not "open" texts; rather, they were closely guarded by custodians who carefully regulated access to them, thereby establishing new nodes of social authority in twentieth-century Zambia. Text, in Gordon's telling, did not always entail equal access to its riches and could call into being highly uneven imaginaries, worlds away from the transparent and egalitarian reading publics of Habermas and Anderson.

Gordon's example illuminates the continued importance of handwritten manuscript cultures in Africa; it is also worth remembering that print audiences in modern Africa were highly diverse, consisting of many more participants than early black nationalists and intellectuals. In many parts of the continent, a vibrant European settler press existed, often linked to imperial news outlets such as Reuters. While many accounts of newspapers in Africa have cast them as vehicles of anticolonial nationalism,[24] Jörg Haustein's chapter in this volume illuminates the potential of newspapers to marginalize Africans from discourses concerning their futures. Focusing on German-language newspaper debates on Islam in German East Africa, Haustein argues that newspapers here, by their very print form, created an echo chamber that excluded the people (Muslims) being discussed. German colonialists in East Africa used newspapers as a platform from which to debate Islam as a cultural, administrative, and potential security problem. Some colonialists, missionaries in particular, sought to portray Muslims as "foreign" Arab settlers, blameworthy for their involvement in slave trading and deserving marginalization. Others, focused more on bureaucratic governance, depicted Islam as a harmless instance of folkloric culture, emphasizing the suitability of Islam for an innately "superstitious" African population. Through such acts of misrepresentation, colonial newspapers were simultaneously constructing arguments for the self-evidently beneficial nature of European rule in the continent, drawing together and consolidating a German settler public in self-satisfaction while silencing the people under discussion.

Liz Gunner's chapter, by contrast, focuses on African newspaper readers and emphasizes that religion was often a prominent and popular topic within the imaginary of the nation as constituted and discussed by newspapers. While the classic theorists have construed the nation normatively as a rational and enlightened sphere free of the influence of hereditary rulers or religious priests, religious figures and institutions played, and continue to play, a key role in African nation-states, however self-consciously "modern" the latter position themselves as. Gunner's chapter focuses on several years of coverage of a large South African organization, the Nazaretha Church, by the *Sowetan*, a leading daily with historical associations to Black Consciousness. Gunner shows how the paper's charting of complex leadership disputes within the church was also a commentary on the precarious state of the national public at a particularly unsettled moment in the country's political life. The large Nazaretha Church has long occupied a prominent place in the country's national imaginary, casting itself as something of a repository of black identity for its citizens. Gunner's analysis casts the newspaper as a type of midwife to the still-new South African nation-state, anxiously charting the tensions and fragmentations of the church as a type of barometer of national health. This popular newspaper constantly reminds its readership that a key part of South African national identity is the legacy of its historic black-led churches such as the Nazaretha.

Clearly, as Haustein's example shows, Muslim reading publics are hard to fit into these narratives. Whereas Christians across the continent were shaped by exposure to Western education—and their consequent adoption of written genres such as newspapers, pamphlets, and magazines—Muslims often faced the new forms of education from a defensive position. They struggled with participation in colonial education in ways that were clearly conditioned by Muslim scholars' competing claims to truth and to learned authority, on the one hand, and by missionaries and colonial schoolmasters, on the other. Overall, Muslim participation in formal education was consistently lower than that of Christians, and there was little of the synergy between formal education and successful cash cropping that is so striking in, for instance, highland Kenya or the Tanzanian Kilimanjaro region or the arable Highveld of South Africa.[25] Despite the symbiotic political relationships that developed between Muslim elites and colonialists in places as diverse as Senegal, Sudan, Northern Nigeria, and Zanzibar, Muslim scholarly milieus retained a sense of unease about their position under Christian rule, even if relations between colonial officials and Muslim clerics could be quite friendly.[26]

But as several writers show, scholars in places such as Northern Nigeria, Zanzibar, and Mauritania conducted an ongoing debate on how to sustain Muslim moral and legal practice under colonial rule.[27] The development of colonial education also inspired innovation in Muslim schooling. Moreover, the impetus behind these innovations was not purely defensive—not everything was all about "keeping up" with growing Christian communities. Rather, Muslims experimented with far-reaching reformulations of the meaning of citizenship in Islamic communities, of the criteria for learnedness, and of the means to transmit learning. Sean Hanretta's chapter in this volume shows how a type of print document not even meant to communicate publicly—that is, marriage registration forms—could become involved in these kinds of negotiations, both during the colonial and the postcolonial period, and in a process to which Muslims and state authorities contributed actively. Moreover, while the circulation of printed matter remained much more limited than with Christian congregations, single copies of, for example, a popular *maulid* poem reached a great many ears and memories, and scholars corresponded in a variety of languages, most often written in Arabic script. To some extent, then, Muslim congregations had their own publics. For recent years, Hirschkind has traced out a related phenomenon around the use of cassette sermons in Egypt, which he describes as "counter-public."[28] Perhaps a more appropriate term for this would be "parallel public" since it avoids making assumptions about the participants' political dispositions, which were quite varied and complex despite the shared anxiety about colonialism.

Unlike the narrative of progress toward integrated, often emancipatory reading publics, a narrative that dominates the understanding of the history of print, discussion of the history of broadcast media is more likely to focus on their connection to repression and propaganda—that is, their ability to marginalize groups whom those in power would rather were kept silenced. Radio was often the medium of choice of populist, activist leaders, most famously perhaps in the broadcasts connected to the Bandung conference in 1955.[29] While Bandung served an anticolonial agenda, tight state control of media was implicated in the shift of many newly independent countries to one-party states.[30] In the words of one commentator of the African media scene in the postcolonial period, "while media had played a role of promoting democratization in the years before independence, it did not take long for the same media to become strangled by the very masters they had helped to power."[31]

Scholars have charted how recently independent African states started to make strategic use of media for repressive ends, aimed at consolidating state hegemony and fostering national imaginaries that countenanced little dissent. In postindependence Cameroon, for example, the mass media was tightly controlled by state president Ahmadou Ahidjo in order to forestall any popular criticism of the regime. Radio broadcasting in particular became a key tool for political propaganda, often promoting ideological visions of national identity.[32] And in Jerry Rawlings's Ghana, television programming stressed the importance of Ghanaian "cultural heritage" and addressed top-down aims of "enlightenment, national integration and cultural roots."[33] Egypt, too, has mirrored northern experiences with totalitarian media use fairly closely (and, not coincidentally, also came to embody the "new media" challenge to this hegemony during the Arab Spring). Since Nasser's ascent to power in 1952, successive military regimes here have kept a firm hold on print and broadcast media alike.[34]

Yet, as with the case of print media, there are many qualifications to this portrayal of mass broadcast media as an instrument of hegemony. For a start, the history of Mao's "Little Red Book"[35] throughout the 1950s and '60s shows that print media, too, were amenable to this kind of use; in Africa, newspapers such as *L'Essor* in Mali or *The Nationalist* were part of the hegemonic project quite as much as radio.[36] In the case of Egypt, the flip side of state domination of the media was the contribution of Egyptian radio to anticolonial broadcasting in Africa south of the Sahara.[37] In this part of the continent, too, radio broadcasts have marked significant historical moments, delicately perched between insurgent and repressive. Patrice Lumumba's speeches and their role in precipitating Belgian interference come to mind, as well as Julius Nyerere's radio announcement concerning forcible villagization in 1973.[38] Moreover, lack of access to receivers, electricity, batteries, or spare parts meant that participation in the consumption of propagandistic broadcasts was curtailed by Africa's chronic poverty.

Even with these logistical considerations bracketed, though, the "mass-media" potential of radio broadcasts does not necessarily translate into large-scale reach. While national state radio broadcasts aspired to transform disparate and diverse individuals into obedient subjects, Bruce Hall's chapter in this volume instead focuses on a local radio station that broadcasts in a minority language called Western Songhay, which is predominantly spoken in a limited area of northern Mali, along the western half of the Niger bend. Rather than a media form that enjoys national stature, Hall's example illustrates the highly fragmentary reach of small, local radio stations throughout the continent. Furthermore, what is particularly striking in Hall's telling is that an originally oral storytelling tradition concerned with the legitimacy of chiefly privilege (and by extension, with legitimate political authority in Mali) gains very little by way of broader saliency or popularity through its transferal to FM radio. The medium does not supply the elite narrators of this nostalgic tale of chiefly authority with an effective platform for claiming popular legitimacy, illustrating that mass media cannot simply create an audience for all types of claims, regardless of their content.

Given the relatively limited nature of mass media in Africa, an observer might consider the continent to be, as so often, a straggler and relatively marginal to a historical process with many global refractions. Africanists' weariness with this kind of marginality perhaps fed into the excitement when, around the turn of the twenty-first century, the continent appeared for a change to be at the forefront of the development of new forms of media use. The years after the end of the Cold War saw renewed interest in the role of civil society in challenging state power, while the new paradigm of globalization suggested that the power of nation states was on the wane compared with that of networked organizations, media or otherwise, spanning national territories.[39] In an influential treatment, Manuel Castells characterized these developments as the rise of the network society in the information age.[40] Whereas studies had previously emphasized that elites used media in top-down ways to instill loyalty and obedience in passive subjects, now attention was directed to the active construction of meaning by ordinary people via the media technologies at their disposal. One instantiation of this approach focused on a perceived link between democratization and media in the Middle East. Dale Eickelman and Jon Anderson pioneered this shift from viewing mass media as states' "vehicles of consolidation and standardization" to instead stressing the participatory, destabilizing, and subversive capacity of "new media" such as video, audio cassettes, faxes, and desktop publishing. They identified this capacity in a series of movements for change across the Middle East, especially in Iran.[41] In distinction from traditional media forms, these new "small media" were supposed to be above all "participatory, public phenomena, controlled neither by big states nor big corporations. . . . [They] focus on popular involvement, on horizontal communication, and on active participation."[42] They were hailed as forms of media able to bypass state scrutiny, censorship, and regulation.

In Africa, these paradigms seemed eminently applicable. Africanists soon detected parallel processes whereby "small media" helped bring into being alternative visions to that of the formal state, which in any case in many regions was suffering a crisis of popular legitimacy.[43] It was certainly a time when nation states appeared weakened, not only by internal challenges but also by the growing influence of international financial institutions and their agendas, often characterized, albeit problematically, as neoliberal.[44] The weakness of state-run media infrastructure gave an edge to the providers of private video and television. Later in the first decade of the century, that advantage extended to providers of mobile telephony and, increasingly, to those providing internet access. Many argued that new, privately owned and controlled electronic and digital media had the power to hold governments to account[45] and to offer on national and local events a more grassroots, bottom-up perspective unconstrained by the "official" version circulated by the older state broadcasts. The popularity of the term "radio trottoir" or "sidewalk radio"—which did not necessarily take technological form and referred to orally transmitted rumor—is telling. This talk medium provided "people who would otherwise lack the opportunity to influence opinion the satisfaction of doing so."[46]

Although print and radio have often been assumed to inaugurate potentially repressive visions of the nation state, many recent studies have emphasized how new media offer platforms for diverse interests neither reducible to nor necessarily compatible with national publics. Examples range from the expression of queer identities on social media sites in contemporary Kenya[47] to the use of mobile phones by female entrepreneurs in Nairobi to break into a largely male-dominated economy[48] to the mobilization of internet sites by the Ogoni people in Nigeria to protest against the environmental and economic effects of Shell oil drilling in their region.[49] These instances of activism tend to be depicted as possessing a kind of cultural authenticity, despite their use of Western-derived technology.[50] Some have argued that subversive media practices in Africa gained their potency and popularity by building on older indigenous categories of oral expression, successfully intermingling local myths, folklore, and oral history traditions with cutting-edge technology; in one recent characterization, mobile phones were dubbed the "new talking drums of Africa."[51] The common factor is that these new digital and electronic media forms are seen as having the potential to fracture once-unitary national publics by introducing a diversity of previously little-heard voices and competing claims.

And yet in 2016 this narrative, despite the sound empirical observations that back up much of these observations, is clearly in need of significant qualification. International financial institutions in Africa have accepted the need to "bring the state back in" and are as likely to actively support as to challenge national governments.[52] Notwithstanding the protracted crises in some states, many have weathered the transition to multiparty electoral politics. At the same time, the rise of nativist politics in Europe and America in response to increasing economic stratification and migration makes nation states here look more solid and relevant than they did ten years ago. Contrary to predictions that nations are on an inevitable trajectory toward fragmentation and internal multiplicity, national idioms have remained or become highly salient. And while the increase in global connectedness heralded by, for example, Pentecostal churches remains observable, national borders and loyalties do not therefore appear to be losing their importance—even for Pentecostal churches, as Katrien Pype's chapter in this volume will show. It is also clear from recent events in the Middle East and North Africa that the subversive powers of new social media forms such as Facebook and Twitter are more limited than they appeared during the Arab Spring. Despite unprecedented high levels of internet usage in countries such as Tunisia and Egypt, the capacity of governments to curtail and restrict not only internet usage but also internal dissent has become very evident, with all the violent repertoires of state power at their disposal.[53]

The perceived subversive effects of new media are also frequently noted within the context of religious institutions. Echoing aspects of the aforementioned political narrative, Christians' and Muslims' use of media has been said to have a democratizing effect on historic religious organizations—often themselves in strategic alliance with state officials. In this context, the use of electronic and digital media can facilitate the rise of charismatic individuals—often from outside the pool of those traditionally holding leadership positions—who claim new forms of spiritual legitimacy, frequently challenging older centers of religious power.[54] Thus it has recently been argued that new media offered women and the uneducated possibilities of prominence in religious sphere long dominated by elites that excluded them. Dorothea Schulz shows how new media technologies—primarily taped cassette sermons—empowered women in Mali to assume unaccustomed roles as authoritative preachers, while also facilitating the stellar rise to prominence of religious mavericks and outsiders with little formal religious training, such as Sharif Haidara.[55] Indeed, Haidara is the focus of one of the chapters in the present volume. André Chappatte's analysis shows how much of Haidara's popularity with Muslim youth in present-day

Mali is generated through the circulation of recordings, radio broadcasts, and telephone ringtones featuring Haidara's performance of the religious musical genre of *zikiri,* translated literally as "remembrance [of the name of God]." Through the popularity of these recorded *zikiri,* Haidara has become one of West Africa's most prominent religious celebrities, bypassing traditional routes to religious authority. That he is particularly popular with Muslim youth—themselves disenchanted with both state and religious elites—further underscores how in this instance new media has bolstered a charismatic individual against the clerical mainstream.

Yet, as with instances of mediated dissent within nation states, the power of new media to subvert religious organizations and clerical elites should not be exaggerated. Chappatte's analysis shows us that many of the followers Haidara has gained via new media usage are loyal to Haidara in only the loosest possible way. Attention to Haidara via electronically recorded sermons or *zikiri* produces nothing like the intense devotion of face-to-face tutelage between a Sufi leader and disciple; many sympathizers of Haidara never meet him personally nor experience anything like a strong bond. Chappatte emphasizes the "loose and uneven influence" of electronically mediated religious leaders in Mali on devotees, highlighting here not only the possibilities for religious outsiders generated by new media but also the limits they encounter owing to the very properties of these media forms. Chappatte's analysis is valuable not only in charting the fact that new types of religious authority are made possible through new media but also for its in-depth exploration of the exact nature and quality of believers' mediated affiliations to these new figures.

Similar qualifications apply in the case of Christianity. Much has been made of the democratizing effect of new media on hierarchical organizations such as the Roman Catholic Church; a recent study has shown how communicating with priests via mobile phones considerably levels clerical authority.[56] Focusing on recent debates among Catholics in Kinshasa, Katrien Pype's chapter in the present volume charts the conflict between those who position themselves as guardians of orthodoxy, on the one hand, and those who offer alternative routes to spiritual help or power, on the other. The protagonist in this story is Brother Raphael, a devout lay Catholic who bypasses the official hierarchies of the organized church and claims to offer his followers privileged access to the petitionary prayers of the Virgin Mary. The use of both "new" and "small" media has been central to this conflict. While the Catholic Church has mobilized its state connections to block Brother Raphael's access to broadcast media such as TV and radio, Brother Raphael has used photographs, pamphlets, and the internet to contest the hegemony of religious officialdom in Kinshasa. But while aspects of Pype's narrative echo the usual depiction of small media as undermining hegemonic positions, her chapter offers much-needed nuance to this somewhat deterministic narrative. In recent years, Brother Raphael's following has declined, and his influence as a religious leader in the city waned. This is due to the declining appeal of his religious message, especially given the fundamental ambiguity attached to the Virgin Mary in the strongly Pentecostal climate of the city. Thus, Pype's analysis underscores the open-endedness of media usage in Africa: the use of the internet does not guarantee successful contestation of religious orthodoxy on the part of outsiders, and factors quite independent of the technologies involved contribute to the outcome of a challenge to the Catholic hierarchy. Pype's story is also a timely reminder of the continuing power of mass media ownership. Despite the increasing visibility of online religious forums, Brother Raphael's downfall has been in part due to his lack of skill at using these influential media platforms.

Thus, while the rise of new currents of Pentecostal Christianity and Reformist Islam, heavily invested in new media usage, poses a challenge to older and more centralized religious organizations, much evidence suggests that historic organizations and denominations invested in clearly discernible hierarchical structures have retained much of their power. The historian of Christianity in Africa David Maxwell has commented that "the historic churches [in Africa] remain enormously influential, still staffed by expatriate missionaries who work in tandem with and usually under the authority of African clerics."[57] In this volume, too, Pype's story similarly demonstrates the enduring presence of organized Catholicism in a region more usually celebrated for the emergence of decentralized new Pentecostal churches.

The present volume therefore highlights that despite the appearances produced by references to "new media," the changes observable are not driven simply by technological change. Nor is the succession of stages in the history of media use—from state-run mass broadcasting and national publics to private new media use to fragmented, networked publics—all that unidirectional and clear. For one, the term "new media" itself is ambiguous. The only truly technologically new media of recent decades are mobiles and internet-based media, but the term is often used to include cassette and video tapes, DVDs, and privately run TV channels. What is new here is not the technology itself, but rather the forms (or lack thereof) of political regulation—of access and ownership—that the technology is subject to. This observation further calls into question the frequently acclaimed emancipatory qualities of new media, highlighting that it is not technological innovation that precipitates empowerment for those who are positioned or position themselves as marginalized, but rather highly contingent, political, and context-specific circumstances.

This point has been made briefly by a number of scholars writing on the topic, but it has never been dwelt on at any length. Nor has it seemed to have much impact on the overwhelmingly positive assessment of new media as a route to liberation and communal and self-improvement.[58] Yet examples abound not only of the limitations of powerful media technologies such as the internet but also of highly conservative or repressive effects that can result from individuals' and communities' use of new media. Take as examples the marginalization of "African Traditional Religion" via the heightened public media presence of a particular, exclusionary type of Pentecostal-Charismatic Christianity in Ghana;[59] the continued ability and will of states to patrol and censor the airwaves (for example, the Nigerian government's censoring of "unverified [Pentecostal] miracles" that receive airtime);[60] and the use of new electronic media by the Rwandan government to ever tighten its control over the lives of ordinary citizens.[61]

Users of new media, moreover, can quite simply disengage from larger political questions. While celebrated as vehicles of the revolution in the case of the Arab Spring, the platforms of new social media sites such as Facebook and Twitter can at the same time serve as insular echo chambers (here invoking the German-language colonial newspapers of Haustein's chapter) that facilitate only internal conversations amongst the like-minded. This is a point that has repeatedly been made in the aftermath of the recent political elections in the United States; rather than heralding the advent of Castell's "networked" society, Facebook seems to have served only to cement the homogenous, monocultural quality of the social circles of many of its users. Echoing many of these themes, Maria Frahm-Arp's chapter in this volume shows that three of Johannesburg's largest and most influential new Pentecostal churches extensively use Facebook and Twitter to mediate new forms of religiosity. Leaders' and laity's postings on these sites, however, tend to shy away from any criticism of or commentary on government corruption or the socioeconomic inequalities that increasingly characterize modern South Africa. In the context of South African Pentecostalism, then, new social media, far from being agents of egalitarianism, instead stabilize and codify entrenched norms of religious practice and piety within congregations that are largely detached from explicit engagement with the broader society.

Our point here is not to simply replace one paradigm (new small media "liberates") with another (new small media "disempowers") but rather to emphasize the limited usefulness of any variant of technological determinism. No single media form is capable, on its own, of instigating social change. Instead, change in Africa—as elsewhere in the world—occurs through interlocking technical, social, political, cultural, and economic processes. In this respect, we are indebted to an important article by Karin Barber, who argues that the human consumers of media—whom Barber broadly identifies as "audiences"—are profoundly historical and situated phenomena, prompted into being and made possible "only by existing ways of being in society."[62] Rather than assuming that new modes of sociality—emancipatory or repressive—are catalyzed by new media technologies, Barber argues that we need to take cognizance of historically and culturally specific ways of audience reception and interpretation, and of how they condition the reach and influence of media technologies. Along with the authors contributing to this volume, we seek in this spirit to avoid the trap of "communication essentialism" or of decontextualizing media technologies.[63]

This is not to deny that texts, both sacred and otherwise, can have great motivating power. But texts, the sacred ones especially, are always there, whereas the ways in which people seek to live up to and interact with them change constantly. Thus, we need to pay attention to how text is activated, performed, and deployed in particular contexts. This point, moreover, applies to any form of media. Given the momentous development of electronic media since the second half of the twentieth century, and the manifest role of radio, tapes, DVDs, Twitter, and so on in spreading religious points of view, there is no denying the importance of new media to religious change. But it would be misleading to assume that the introduction of new media on its own drives religious change. It catalyzes and enables, but any media are what people make of them for reasons not solely contained within the technologies. A medium, after all, is literally a *means.* It does not carry its end in itself.

Although one of the key arguments of this introduction is that the contrast between "old" and "new" media should be softened, we also call for attention to the range and diversity of media forms involved in religious life in Africa. Hence the inclusion of two chapters on photography in religious congregations—both Muslim and Christian—in the present volume. Whereas earlier analyses of photography from and in Africa were dominated by the idea that control over the shutter ensured control over the ways Africans were represented by European photographers,[64] a more recent body of work nuances this view of what is in effect white control over photographic production. It shows instead how vernacular practices of photography invested the medium with new and occasionally subversive layers of meaning.[65] Heike Behrend's chapter explores the ambivalence of photographic cultures in Africa, showing that photography could both be the medium of colonial governance as well as a means to articulate very different subjectivities on the part of the Africans colonized. Moreover, also in this volume, Asonzeh Ukah's focus on photographs in the sacred spaces of the large Pentecostal Nigerian Redeemed Christian Church of God (RCCG) offers an instance of photography in Africa that occurs in a postcolonial context, entirely unmoored from any association with regimes of colonial governance or European knowledge production.

Furthermore, the two chapters on photography in this volume also show that much like texts in their various mediated instantiations, photographic images can play a vital role in enabling new forms of religiously constituted selfhood and sociability. Behrend examines photographic practices on the East African coast among a predominantly Muslim population. She shows that the colonial state's imposition of bureaucratic photography for identity documents was experienced by many as intrusive and humiliating, with an added resonance of both defying Islam's interdiction on figurative images and—in the case of pious women—demanding they show their faces unveiled. Yet Behrend shows how some people subject to this intrusion transformed the bureaucratic images into idealized family portraits or worked them into collages where individuals appeared modestly garbed. In this way, the photographs became treasured possession for their subjects' descendants. Her chapter shows us how East African Muslims took acts of photographic self-representation into their own hands.[66] In a very different context,

Ukah's chapter also focuses on how religious subjects use photographic resources to imagine and represent themselves in novel ways. He focuses on the religious practices of Pentecostal Christians within the precincts of the RCCG "Redemption Camp." In particular, his chapter highlights the large photographic picture boards around the camp that display glossy, inflated photographs of successful believers accompanied by scriptural quotations affirming that the faithful will be rewarded by material blessings in the here and now. In Ukah's analysis, these images become vital props in the practical outworking of the "prosperity gospel" teachings of the RCCG: believers meditate on, emulate, aspire to, and debate these stylized depictions of the successful Pentecostal life, imaginatively mobilizing these photographs in their own personal pursuit of flourishing and security.

What is evident from the diverse case studies elaborated above is that all the old and new varieties of media at work can "work"—that is, constitute publics, include or marginalize—at a variety of scales. In both Ukah's and Behrend's chapters, the scale is the microlevel of the self and the small-scale networks of relationships—such as family, for example—constituted around persons. However, seen from the national scale long implicitly considered normative, all of these media effects can be either unifying or fragmenting, inclusionary or marginalizing, and can be so at different historical conjunctures. Take for example the diminutive reading public, very much in tension with the nation, established by the texts of the Zambian Lumpa Church, or the persistence of nationwide collective broadcast events in the present, for example, around international sporting competitions. We do not claim to be the first to have noticed this. The terminological transitions toward less monolithic terms such as "public culture" or "publics" (in the plural) in the debate on what used to be called the public sphere indicate observers' well-established wariness of any normative notion of the public and evolutionary progress toward it.[67] But it is worth emphasizing this indeterminacy in the face of a palpable sense that media are currently self-propelled agents of change, in Africa in particular. Of course, they are: mobile phones, and smartphones in particular, make information travel with totally unprecedented ease. But the effects of this ease are likely to be multiple and contradictory rather than unambiguously emancipatory or its opposite. This proviso becomes particularly important when considering the interaction between religion, secularization, and politics.

Religion, Politics, and Secularization

When it comes to the interaction between these multiply constituted publics and newly emergent forms of mediated religious expression, we encounter a rare instance of fairly uncontroversial consensus among academic observers—namely, that this salience of religion undermines the claims about the changing relationship between religion and public life in the modern era long known as the secularization hypothesis.[68] With the establishment of secular public spheres in modern societies, religion was supposed to retreat into the privacy of home, family, and place of worship. The hypothesis draws heavily on sociologist Max Weber: with the "disenchantment of the world" and the entrenchment of "rational" bureaucracies in power, religious institutions and practices would lose their role in politics. That this hasn't happened is only too evident, with the role of evangelicalism in American politics, the rise of political Islam, the growing role of religious difference in the politics of various African states, and so on.[69]

There is no consensus, though, on how exactly the secularization hypothesis was wrong. For example, did religion in the West reemerge in public life, or had it never really gone away? Occasionally, there is a hint of triumphalism about the dismissal of secularization as a mirage pursued by naïve, pseudoscientific atheists. Moreover, as the anthropologist Harri Englund points out, there is a temptation to merely invert the understanding of the relationship between religion and public life contained in secularization theory: where formerly the former was considered a separate and subordinate subsystem of the latter, observers may instead treat religious commitments as the prime movers and public life as their extension, fundamentally structured by religious commitments.[70]

This is what appears to happen in one of the strongest statements about Africa as a case study in "nonsecular" public life: Stephen Ellis and Gerrie ter Haar's *Worlds of Power: Religious Thought and Political Practice in Africa.*[71] According to Ellis and Ter Haar, concern with a particular kind of religious force, what they call the occult, is pervasive in African politics and public life and colors practically all interpretations of public events. From this point of view, Africa is at the forefront of things to come because it has never been "modern" in the sense of "secular." Although it offers a perceptive reading of many rumors and urban myths current in contemporary Africa (what the authors, with Congolese audiences, call *radio trottoir*), the book has attracted considerable criticism for its sweeping claims and vague use of terms relating to religious belief and expression, such as "the occult" and "invisible worlds." But it addresses perceptions that are clearly widespread, both in scholarly work and in popular everyday perception. Terence Ranger's sobering account of press coverage of supposed "ritual killings" taking place in West African Pentecostal communities in the United Kingdom reveals the mixture of racism, incredulity, and ignorance at play in depictions of West Africans supposedly mired in "occultism."[72] Recent discussions of "radical Islam" in Africa and the Middle East lean heavily on the notion that it is religion itself—in this case, Islam—that possesses its own intrinsic properties that drives adherents toward violence and the espousal of social structures portrayed by detractors as repressive and patriarchal. In these readings, then, "religion"—whether Christianity, Islam, or so-called African traditional religion in the form of the occult—drives politics.

Ironically, this view of the relationship of religion and public life appears as the inversion of the view taken in much earlier literature. As Terence Ranger noted as long ago as 1986, historians of Africa looking for evidence of popular protest and resistance under colonialism tended to turn to religious movements as a substitute of sorts for more explicitly political, secular protest movements.[73] A famous example of this was the study of Zionist Christians in apartheid-era Southern Africa by Jean Comaroff, who analyzed in great detail Zionists' religious dress as symbolic protests against South Africa's capitalized mining industry, which drew in large numbers of Zionists as migrant labor.[74] In Comaroff's reading, Zionists' rituals, as well as their religious uniforms, were best understood in light of "politico-economic processes of colonial domination."[75] Of course, this substitution was not entirely random: movements like John Chilembwe's in Malawi clearly did address political concerns in religious terms.[76] But Ranger pinpointed an increasingly widespread unease with a tendency to reduce religion to politics by treating the religious elements as incidental to the political message.

A more recent instantiation of this tendency to read political intent into religious pursuits is the current fascination with Pentecostal-Charismatic churches in Africa, which have been interpreted by some not only as a product but also a critique of neoliberal globalized capitalism. By highlighting believers' confidence in the promise of the Holy Spirit to steer believers through treacherous economic waters, as well as the egalitarian aspects of Pentecostal communities, some commentators have cast Pentecostalism in Africa as an emancipatory, grassroots critique of global neoliberalism.[77] At the same time, others—echoing older Marxist critiques of religion—express anxiety that the prosperity-gospel teachings of Pentecostal-Charismatic Christianity constitute "false consciousness," distracting Africans from the real-world search for improved material conditions and equitable economic structures.[78] Such observations are often well-grounded in empirical reality. As Asonzeh Ukah's chapter in this volume shows, a lively pictorial culture consisting of visual representations of biblical verses on church walls quite literally draws the gaze of members of the Nigerian Redeemed Christian Church of God away from the stark contrasts between luxury real estate owned by elites (both religious and political) and the impoverished living conditions of ordinary members. Yet what concerns us here is that such assessments, whether critical or positive, are two sides of the same coin: both construe the importance of religious activities in Africa in terms of their political effects.

By making religious expression a function of politics rather than the other way around, our concern is the opposite of the concern many have raised about Ellis and Ter Haar's approach. Caricaturing only slightly, one could say that while religious and political concerns were and are closely imbricated in many African societies, it is difficult for academic observers to think about these intersections without dissolving one side into the other. Holding them in balance has been a constant challenge. It can be done, as evidenced, for example, by the excellent work on central African religion-cum-protest movements, but it involves making choices that tend to flatten out or overshadow some aspects of the picture.[79]

To mitigate these unwanted effects, it is helpful to take a closer look at the notion of religion itself. Ellis and Ter Haar's definition is reasonably representative of many definitions at play in accounts of religion in Africa. They hold that religion expresses "a belief in the existence of an invisible world, often thought to be inhabited by spirits that are believed to affect people's lives in the material world."[80] However, there is a good deal of evidence that the treatment of something called "religion" as a discrete realm of human activity, focused on humans' relationship with (for want of a better word) spiritual powers and structured by its own institutions and hierarchies, is historically quite specific and had no clear complement in many historical African societies.[81] The category "religion" as used today, then, lumps together many things—life-cycle rituals, healing, the management of witchcraft, and more—that arguably were quite discrete before the category of "religion" became available and that at times are still treated as such. The impression given by Ellis and Ter Haar—that Africans are hopelessly, obsessively religious—arises partly from this lumping together.

The aim in making this observation is not to introduce another African exceptionalism. The notion of "religion" arguably can do with denaturalizing everywhere. It is worth noting that in Europe, religion acquired the status of a freestanding category in the course of drawn-out conflicts between its representatives and those of alternative approaches to the world.[82] Thus, we read there the long-standing narratives of how science and secularism gradually emancipated themselves from its hold. In this sense, the notion of religion is a product of the particular history of religious institutions and their place in the political realm in Europe; above all, the unusual coherence, political power, and longevity of the Catholic Church and its replication, if less ambitiously, in Protestant ones. From this vantage point, Europe presents an extreme, and Africa is probably closer to the center of a global spectrum of institutional, ritual, and social arrangements for addressing the concerns we know as religious.

All of the chapters contained in the present volume offer divergent and context-specific elaborations of the highly varied meanings of being Muslim and being Christian in modern Africa. In doing so they implicitly challenge any fixed notion of "religion" as a stable descriptive category with predetermined attributes. Although Ellis and Ter Haar were sure that religion involved belief in an "invisible world" of spirits, in Ukah's analysis of Pentecostal practice in contemporary Lagos, it is visibility—rather than invisibility—that looms large. Pentecostal piety is predicated on what can be seen, touched, heard, felt, and grasped in material, tangible ways; what is at stake in Pentecostals' this-worldly spirituality is very much the visible world, driven by believers' anticipation of God's promises realized in the here and now.

And while the Holy Spirit doubtless overshadows the world of Pentecostals—both in Africa and elsewhere—other forms of piety on the continent place far more weight on practices of administration and paperwork than on the "invisible spirits" so frequently seen in scholarly and popular accounts of religion in Africa. Although Weber differentiated between charisma and bureaucracy, much counterevidence throughout the continent points instead to the imbrication of the two. Often, piety emerged through the disciplines of reading and writing rather than being crafted in a nonliterate realm.[83] Sean Hanretta's chapter in this volume shows how standardizing paperwork (in particular, the British colonial state's insistence on recording marriages in documentary form) was used by Muslim elites in what became present-day Ghana to configure new forms of religious authority. Not only is Hanretta's chapter a detailed study of how religion was quite literally written into existence throughout this period via administrative practices, it is also a refreshing account of overlapping processes driven by both colonial Britons and Gold Coast Muslims. Far from treating religion in Africa as somehow exceptional, Hanretta instead highlights how the emergence of a Muslim identity was the fruit of a long process of "convergence and translation," as both parties drew on the possibilities of bureaucratic marriage records to stabilize a new meaning of being Muslim—although to very different ends.

Of course, treating the category "religion" as something that is put together very differently in different contexts and moments has its own problems. The people pursuing one or another religious allegiance may find this approach dismissive; it has to guard against a similar kind of reductionism as the approaches Ranger reviewed. Nevertheless, thinking of religion as composed from a subset of implicit attitudes, explicit claims, practices, norms, and institutions makes clear that the place of any particular instantiation of religion in public life must be context-bound and historically and spatially specific and changeable. Whether "religion" or "politics" appears as the prime mover, then, depends on how the observer is positioned relative to the particular instantiation of this complex they are dealing with. The same public, moreover, may invoke religious categories, as well as quite unrelated (to the observer's mind) ones.

This also means that Africans didn't first have to learn to be religious in order to then be able to be secular. The existing literature makes clear that the terms "Christianity" or "Islam" do not function straightforwardly as analytical concepts but are better understood as normative terms offered by practitioners (and scholars) as legitimating arguments for specific projects of social positioning and self-definition. "Secularism," too, would benefit from a context-specific understanding. A recent article on the debates surrounding religious adherence and secularism in present-day Egypt has argued that the term is best understood as "essentially open," by which the author means the sense in which practitioners use the term as a rhetorical argument for particular visions of an ideal society in which certain types of pious spirituality are regulated by the state: it is "used both aggressively and defensively in advancing and supporting diverse positions. . . . No final agreement on the meaning of the concept can be achieved."[84] In this reading of the secular, the term is intrinsically intertwined with its opposite; by its invocations, its users are explicitly or implicitly contrasting it against the religious. This again makes clear that we can expect no tidy linear progressions from normatively religious to secular configurations of the public.

In the present volume, we observe such rhetorical, argumentative processes whereby historical actors invoke secularism as components of various self-legitimating projects. For example, we discern a comparable dynamic in the Zambian state's repression of Lenshina's Lumpa Church—grounding its repression on the claim that religious allegiance disrupts the project of civic secular nationalism (see Gordon's chapter), the state nevertheless simultaneously draws on the legacy of Christian mission education to cement the postindependence state. Another example of the slippery and contested nature of the term, as well as its rhetorical proximity to the religious, is found in Behrend's discussion of state-sponsored colonial identity photography and its refashioning into Islamic practices of self-formation and communal identity. At times, Behrend's coastal Muslim subjects have rejected photography as an unwelcome intrusion of the foreign "secular," yet at other moments they have been willing to co-opt these technologies into their religious practices. At the same time, Hanretta shows how slippery the state's claims to secular status could become when it sought to define a religious practice, in his case, Muslim marriage. The point here is not merely that the "religious" and the "secular" are categories that continually infiltrate and permeate the other (as has usefully been stated in recent literature).[85] Rather, these examples show that the contrast made between the "secular" and the "religious" is a "peculiar kind of practice that serves a purpose for particular types of people."[86] Pointing to certain types of people as excessively religious, or marking out others as advocates for an ungodly secularism, are acts deeply embedded in social topographies. The nature of these practices and their manifold purposes are as endlessly varied as history, geography, and circumstance allow.

To be clear, we do not argue for replacing all discussion of religion and the secular, or religion and the public sphere, with a series or awkward circumlocutions. The terms commonly used in European contexts, such as "religion," "the secular," "Christianity," and "Islam," have their place also in Africa (and arguably they can do with questioning as much in Europe as Africa). There are well-established aspects of the history of religious congregations in Africa that can readily be discussed within the existing terms, such as the role of mission students in establishing reading publics and mobilizing them for independence; its obverse, the conflicts around the limitations on access to higher education that Muslims have experienced; or the role of both churches and Muslim congregations in challenging or supporting postcolonial regimes. Much the same could be said of studies of secularism in several postindependence states, such as Nyerere's Tanzania.[87] But where the distinctions become cumbersome, it is well to remember that they are a heuristic device with normative overtones, rather than a statement of facts.

The changing and sometimes hard-to-discern shape of the things called "religious" also serves as a reminder that the distinction between what is public and what is private has been made in many ways by religious practitioners in Africa. While now-outmoded theories of the supposedly secular public sphere relegated religious practice to the realm of the private, in fact many religious concerns in Africa and elsewhere, such as healing, life-cycle transitions, and the commemoration of the dead, clearly straddle the divide between public and private. This fluidity of the border between the public and the private is also seen in the diverse performances of media-savvy Muslim preachers, whose registers range from the explicitly political to the tone of intimate, private conversations made available publicly. And with regard to Christianity, the private experience of reading the Bible informed public politics; the congregations of faith healers are often small and present very private problems, yet healing prophets and witchcraft cleaners still position their work as "public service." Moreover, while media clearly can be and are used to claim public space—to fill it with sound and image—they are present also on the other side of the divide, as evident for instance in the intimate commemorative practices involving photography and painting that Behrend discusses. This also serves as a caution against taking the most salient, visually in-your-face, loudest aspects of media practice, such as those associated with the prosperity gospel, as the most important.

Each one of the chapters presented here, then, presents a specific configuration of the "religious" and "secular" concerns and media use that occur at a particular conjuncture of public and private. These configurations are implicated in the processes of social positioning through which people seek to avoid or address their marginality. While some marginalizing or integrating, repressive or enabling effects are very clearly discernible, often there is a combination of both, and which aspect predominates may be a matter of personal disposition or individual perspective: Lenshina's followers marginalized themselves from the Zambian nation, but in the process, they held, they came close to God. The radio narrators Bruce Hall examines similarly claim a very specific, bounded, and situated space, oblivious of other religious congregations' claims to global reach. There is no clear evolutionary timeline along which these cases could be ordered. But they all display some of the endless possibilities that make the encounter of religion, media, and their publics so productive.

The rich literature referred to above is testament to the excellent work being done in the field of religion and media. Our aim in calling for the avoidance of technological determinism and the assumption of evolutionary progression is not to reject what has been achieved. Rather, setting these assumptions aside brings out the creativity involved in the use of media, and the resulting diversity, even more clearly. Nor do we set out to insist that every single encounter between religious pursuits and media must be studied entirely in its own terms. For us, marginality, the efforts to address, mitigate, or impose marginality in mediatized religious activity, the different scales at which marginality operates and the way it can arise unintended, have all served as a lens on this diversity. Surely there are many others. One notable effect of the use of this lens has been to draw attention back to the large-scale political and societal context. For example, "small media" could do the work they did in the 1990s not only because they were media but also because they were operating at a moment when many formerly fairly monolithic regimes in the global south were showing signs of exhaustion. It is not the case, then, that there are no patterns, correlations, and regularities to be found. Rather, similar patterns may occur in different media and at different points in time, as when the aristocratic self-assertion that Hall examines in Western Songhay radio appears to parallel quite closely earlier face-to-face storytelling. To be clear, these recurrences are not particularly African. We finished this introduction in the middle of a social media storm in the United Kingdom over the effects of a nationalist vote, and over how much of its occurrence is attributable to the influence of what was supposed to be a declining media form: the print newspaper. By the time we are submitting the final manuscript, Twitter, a medium once thought of as enabling horizontal networking and free-floating niche publics, is emerging as another nationalist's chosen bully pulpit, similar in function to mid-twentieth century radio. In Africa and elsewhere, the permutations appear endless.

Outline of the Book

The following ten chapters are arranged into three sections. The first section—"Engagements with State Power in the Colonial Period and Beyond"—examines how Muslim and Christian practitioners in the colonial and postcolonial periods used a variety of media forms, including bureaucratic marriage records, handwritten manuscripts, and photographs, to negotiate and occasionally contest the marginalizing effects of colonial power. Sean Hanretta's chapter shows how the fill-in-the-blank marriage registration forms disseminated by British administrators were appropriated by Ghanaian Muslims as a new means to reconfigure religious identity and spiritual authority. His chapter thus reveals the unexpected ways African subjects made use of new colonial media forms to serve their own purposes. Jörg Haustein's chapter adopts a different perspective in discussing the German-language press of white colonial settlers in German East Africa from the late nineteenth century to the First World War. It shows that the publics constituted by and addressed in this press were less the members of a discursive public sphere than a cacophonous series of echo chambers. By ignoring voices from among the country's Muslim congregations and routinely drawing on racist as well as civilizational stereotypes, the press effectively marginalized Muslims in the colony. At the same time, though, it also shut itself off from any meaningful engagement with and understanding of the social and historical complexities of Islam in the colony.

The next two chapters in this section straddle the colonial and postcolonial periods. David Gordon's chapter on the Lumpa Church in the Chiponya village of northern Zambia shows how barely literate and disempowered individuals specialized in oral religious performances but wrote a "tin-trunk bible" to engage with colonial and postcolonial regimes of literacy and print media. The handwritten texts of the church helped forge a local community in the face of prejudice, shaping the identities of this marginal community cast out from mainstream ethnic, religious, and national groups. Heike Behrend's chapter reveals a similarly creative and ingenious appropriation of the media technologies of the colonial state. Her chapter emphasizes that colonial state photography did not define photography as a whole; whereas early twentieth-century anthropologists "were the only ones who owned a camera and took pictures . . . today most subjects of ethnography have access to modern media and make use of photographic cameras." In this vein, she examines local traditions of studio photography in the mid-twentieth century as key practices in Muslim rites of passage such as weddings, showing how the production, circulation, and remembrance of these images constituted a new "technique of the self" or means for individuals to articulate idealized aspirations for wealth, virtue, and status.

The second section of this book is entitled "Claims to Tradition and Particular Identities in the Shadow of the State." The three chapters included here emphasize how religious practitioners' use of a range of media forms enabled the articulation of new and distinct identities—often only loosely in conversation with the national identities encouraged by state authorities since independence. Frequently, these new identities used media forms to more powerfully invoke idioms of "tradition" and "culture." Thus Bruce Hall's chapter discusses how vernacular storytelling in present-day Mali is now mediated through tape cassettes and their broadcasts on private radio stations. Hall shows how this "self-consciously folkloric" media form invokes so-called traditional values, thereby continuing to place issues of slavery and aristocracy at the heart of contemporary Muslim identity in Mali. Liz Gunner's chapter shows how the popular South African daily newspaper, the *Sowetan,* similarly riffs on tropes of indigeneity and "African" identity in exploring the role of the large Zulu-speaking Nazaretha Church within the South African nation-state. State and church exist in an uneasy relationship within this print-mediated discourse; the church is alternatively presented as the salvation of the troubled nation, yet at the same time, its conflicted internal affairs are held up as a mirror image of a flailing state. The final chapter in this section examines the mediated creation, not of a folkloric identity, but of the new community of pious Nigerian Pentecostals who belong to the large Redeemed Christian Church of God (RCCG). RCCG members construct themselves as modern, aspirational, and successful Christians—in part through their ability to both invoke and better what the Nigerian state can offer to its citizens. The church's large Redemption City is an improved version of the metropolis of Lagos, and its official ethos of probity and self-discipline promises believers the God-given ability to rise above personal obstacles and economic inequalities.

The final section—"Religious Community Building on the Margins"—zeroes in on how Christians and Muslims use media forms to negotiate issues of orthodoxy, hierarchy, and innovation within their religious communities. Katrien Pype's chapter focuses on a popular Catholic figure in the Congo, Brother Raphael Minga Kwete, who claims to have received messages from the Virgin Mary, Jesus, and other Christian figures since 1986. Pype shows how the opposition of the Catholic Church—including an informal media ban—was countered by Brother Raphael's use of a range of "small media" to assert his visions; this tussle over media platforms emerged within a larger field of competition between orthodox Catholicism and more popular forms of engagement with Catholic spirits. André Chappatte's chapter similarly focuses on the subversive power of media to carve out new spheres of spiritual influence and authority. He documents the controversy over the "*zikiri*" (a religious musical genre) in the provincial town of Bougouni, Mali, in the light of the new civic liberties and expanding media use that characterize public life in the Third Republic of Mali. Through their reception of these songs, and their commitment to their best-known promoter, Cherif Ousmane Madane Häidara, Muslim youth undermine their traditional marginalization as "bad Muslims" by coming to the fore of public debate about Islam. The final chapter is by Maria Frahm-Arp, who emphasizes how mediated religiosity can be used to present idealized representations and self-representations of the lives of people existing as insecure and aspirational individuals on the margins of the fragile new black middle class in South Africa. The Pentecostal Facebook and Twitter users she discusses use new media to affirm their values of personal ambition and attainment. The result is a highly stylized representation of church members' experience and lifeworlds, especially poignant given that many of them are not, in fact, economically secure.

Notes

1. For example, Paul Gifford, *Ghana's New Christianity* (Bloomington: Indiana University Press, 2004); Birgit Meyer and Annelies Moors, eds., *Religion, Media, and the Public Sphere* (Bloomington: Indiana University Press, 2005); Harri Englund, ed., *Christianity and Public Culture in Africa* (Athens: Ohio University Press, 2011); Birgit Meyer, "'Praise the Lord': Popular Cinema and Pentecostalite Style in Ghana's New Public Sphere," *American Ethnologist*

31, no. 1 (2004): 92–110; Charles Hirschkind, *The Ethical Soundscape: Cassette Sermons and Islamic Counterpublics* (New York: Columbia University Press, 2006).

2. Francis B. Nyamnjoh, "Global and Local Trends in Media Ownership and Control: Implications for Cultural Creativity in Africa," in *Situating Globality: African Agency in the Appropriation of Global Culture,* ed. Wim van Binsbergen and Rijk van Dijk (Leiden: Brill, 2004), 59.

3. Karin Barber, *The Anthropology of Texts, Persons and Publics* (Cambridge: Cambridge University Press, 2007).

4. See especially Birgit Meyer and Annelies Moors, introduction to *Religion, Media, and the Public Sphere.*

5. James R. Brennan, "Radio Cairo and the Decolonization of East Africa," in *Making a World after Empire: The Bandung Moment and Its Political Afterlives,* ed. Christopher Lee (Athens: Ohio University Press, 2010), 173–95; Derek Peterson, *Ethnic Patriotism and the East African Revival: A History of Dissent, c. 1935–1972* (Cambridge: Cambridge University Press, 2012).

6. Frederick Cooper, *Africa since 1940: The Past of the Present* (Cambridge: Cambridge University Press, 2002); Bruce Berman, Dickson Eyoh and Will Kymlicka, eds., *Ethnicity and Democracy in Africa* (Athens: Ohio University Press, 2004); Paul Nugent, *Africa since Independence: A Comparative History* (London: Palgrave Macmillan, 2012).

7. For studies of Africans coping with marginalization in the nineteenth and twentieth centuries, see for example Marcia Wright, *Strategies of Slaves and Women: Life-Stories from East/Central Africa* (New York: Lilian Barber, 1993).

8. Although see Benjamin Soares, ed., *Muslim-Christian Encounters in Africa* (Leiden: Brill, 2006).

9. For example, Manuel Castells, *The Rise of the Network Society* (Oxford: Blackwell, 2000); Meyer and Moors, *Religion, Media, and the Public Sphere;* Englund, *Christianity and Public Culture.*

10. Jürgen Habermas, *The Structural Transformation of the Public Sphere: An Enquiry into the Category of Bourgeois Society* (Cambridge, MA: MIT Press, 1991).

11. Herbert Marcuse, *One-Dimensional Man: Studies in the Ideology of Advanced Industrial Society* (London: Sphere Books, 1968); Max Horkheimer and Theodor Adorno, *Dialectic of Enlightenment* (London: Verso, 1986).

12. Benedict Anderson, *Imagined Communities: Reflections on the Origin and Spread of Nationalism* (London: Verso, 1991).

13. Terence Ranger, "Missionaries, Migrants and the Manyika: The Invention of Ethnicity in Zimbabwe," in *Creation of Tribalism in Southern Africa,* ed. Leroy Vail (Berkeley: University of California Press, 1991), 118–50; J. D. Y. Peel, *Religious Encounter and the Making of the Yoruba* (Bloomington: Indiana University Press, 2000); Derek Peterson, *Creative Writing: Translation, Bookkeeping and the Work of the Imagination in Colonial Kenya* (Portsmouth, NH: Heinemann, 2004).

14. David Chidester, *Savage Systems: Colonialism and Comparative Religion in South Africa* (Charlottesville: University of Virginia Press, 1996).

15. Peel, *Religious Encounter*, especially 278–309; see also Peterson, *Creative Writing*, 7.

16. See Hlonipha Mokoena, *Magema Fuze: The Making of a Kholwa Intellectual* (Scottsville: University of KwaZulu-Natal Press, 2011); Wangari Muoria-Sal, Bodil Folke Frederiksen, John Lonsdale, and Derek Peterson, eds., *Writing for Kenya: The Life and Works of Henry Muoria* (Leiden: Brill, 2009).

17. Karin Barber, *The Anthropology of Texts, Persons and Publics: Oral and Written Culture in Africa and Beyond* (Cambridge: Cambridge University Press, 2007), 155–58.

18. Cooper, *Africa since 1940*.

19. Union of South Africa, *Union Statistics for Fifty Years, 1910–1960* (Pretoria: Bureau of Census and Statistics, 1960), table A-22.

20. Karin Barber, "Introduction: Hidden Innovators in Africa," in *Africa's Hidden Histories: Everyday Literacy and Making the Self*, ed. Karin Barber (Bloomington: Indiana University Press, 2006), 1.

21. Derek Peterson and Giacomo Macola, "Homespun Historiography and the Academic Profession," in *Recasting the Past: History Writing and Political Work in Modern Africa*, ed. Derek Peterson and Giacomo Macola (Athens: Ohio University Press, 2009), 5.

22. Joel Cabrita, *Text and Authority in the South African Nazaretha Church* (Cambridge: Cambridge University Press, 2014), chapter 4.

23. Anderson, *Imagined Communities*, 7.

24. Although for a complicating narrative, see Derek Peterson, Emma Hunter, and Stephanie Newell, eds., *African Print Cultures: Newspapers and Their Publics in the Twentieth Century* (Ann Arbor: University of Michigan Press, 2016).

25. Peterson, *Creative Writing*; John Iliffe, *A Modern History of Tanganyika* (Cambridge: Cambridge University Press, 1979); for the longer-term development of civic discourse in a society distinguished by far above-average access to favorable markets and mission schooling, see Emma Hunter, *Political Thought and the Public Sphere in Tanzania: Freedom, Democracy and Citizenship in the Era of Decolonization* (Cambridge: Cambridge University Press, 2015).

26. Muhammad S. Umar, *Islam and Colonialism: Intellectual Responses of Muslims of Northern Nigeria to British Colonial Rule* (Leiden: Brill, 2006); Roman Loimeier, *Between Social Skills and Marketable Skills: The Politics of Islamic Education in Twentieth-Century Zanzibar* (Leiden: Brill, 2009).

27. Louis Brenner, *Controlling Knowledge: Religion, Power and Schooling in a West African Muslim Society* (Bloomington: Indiana University Press, 2001); Scott S. Reese, *The Transmission of Learning in Islamic Africa* (Leiden: Brill, 2004); Rudolph T. Ware, *The Walking Qur'an: Islamic Education, Embodied Knowledge and History in West Africa* (Chapel Hill: University of North Carolina Press, 2014).

28. Hirschkind, *Ethical Soundscape*.

29. Lee, *Making a World after Empire*.

30. Achille Mbembe, *On the Postcolony* (Berkeley: University of California Press, 2001).

31. Göran Hydén, Michael Leslie, and Folu F. Ogundimu, eds., *Media and Democracy in Africa* (New Brunswick, NJ: Transaction Publishers, 2002), 39.

32. Hamadou Adama, "Islamic Communication and Mass Media in Cameroon," in *New Media and Religious Transformations in Africa,* ed. Rosalind I. J. Hackett and Benjamin Soares (Bloomington: Indiana University Press, 2015), 138.

33. Meyer, "'Praise the Lord,'" 93.

34. For this context, see Patrick Gaffney, *The Prophet's Pulpit: Islamic Preaching in Contemporary Egypt* (Berkeley: University of California Press, 1994); Hirschkind, *Ethical Soundscape.*

35. Alexander C. Cook, ed., *Mao's Little Red Book: A Global History* (Cambridge: Cambridge University Press, 2014).

36. See Martin Sturmer, *The Media History of Tanzania* (Ndanda: Ndanda Mission Press, 1998).

37. Brennan, "Radio Cairo,"173–95.

38. On Lumumba, see Nugent, *Africa since Independence,* chapter 1; and Johannes Fabian, *Remembering the Present: Painting and Popular History in Zaire* (Berkeley: University of California Press, 1996). On Nyerere's radio presence, see Sturmer, *The Media History of Tanzania* (Ndanda: Ndanda Mission Press, 1998); Felicitas Becker, "Remembering Nyerere: Political Rhetoric and Dissent in Contemporary Tanzania," *African Affairs* 112 (2013): 238–61.

39. For influential treatments, see Anthony Giddens, *Runaway World: How Globalization Is Reshaping Our Lives* (London: Profile, 1999); Saskia Sassen, ed., *Global Networks, Linked Cities* (London: Routledge, 2002).

40. Castells, *Network Society.*

41. Dale F. Eickelman and Jon W. Anderson, "Redefining Muslim Publics," in *New Media in the Muslim World: The Emerging Public Sphere,* ed. Dale F. Eickelman and Jon W. Anderson (Bloomington: Indiana University Press, 2003), 3.

42. Annabelle Sreberny-Mohammadi and Ali Mohammadi, "Small Media and Revolutionary Change: A New Model," in *Media in Global Context: A Reader,* ed. Annabelle Sreberny-Mohammadi, Dwayne Winseck, Jim McKenna, and Oliver Boyd-Barrett (London: Arnold, 1997), 221.

43. Susanne Hoeber Rudolph and James Piscatori, eds., *Transnational Religion and Fading States* (Oxford: Westview Press, 1997).

44. David Harvey, *A Brief History of Neoliberalism* (Oxford: Oxford University Press, 2005); for a recent critique, see James Ferguson, *Global Shadows: Africa in the Neoliberal World Order* (Durham, NC: Duke University Press, 2006).

45. Hydén, Leslie, and Ogundimu, *Media and Democracy,* 12.

46. Ibid., 24. On the emancipatory, grassroots effects of radio, see also Japhet Mchakula, "Youth Participation in Radio Listening Clubs in Malawi," *Journal of Southern African Studies* 33, no. 2 (2007): 251–65.

47. Evan Mwangi, "Queer Agency in Kenya's Digital Media," *African Studies Review* 57, no. 2 (2014): 93–113.

48. Alice Wanjira Munyua, "Women Entrepreneurs in Nairobi: Examining and Contextualizing Women's Choices," in *African Women and ICTs,* ed. Ineke Buskens and Anne Webb (London: Zed Books, 2009), 119–32.

49. Debra Spitulnik, "Alternative Small Media and Communicative Spaces," in *Media and Democracy in Africa,* ed. Göran Hydén, Michael Leslie, and Folu F. Ogundimu (New Brunswick, NJ: Transaction Publishers, 2002), 190.

50. Faye Ginsburg, Lila Abu-Lughod, and Brian Larkin, eds., *Media Worlds: Anthropology on New Terrain* (Berkeley: University of California Press, 2002), 7.

51. Mirjam de Bruijn, Francis Nyanmjoh, and Inge Brinkman, eds., *Mobile Phones: The New Talking Drums of Everyday Africa* (Bamenda: Langaa RPCIG, 2009). See also Peter Geschiere, "Sorcery and the State: Popular Modes of Action among the Maka of Southeast Cameroon," *Critique of Anthropology* 8, no. 1 (1988): 35–63.

52. Anthony Hopkins, "The New Economic History of Africa," *Journal of African History* 50 (2009): 155–77.

53. Hanan Badr, "Limitations of the Social Media Euphoria in Communication Studies," *Egypte/Monde Arabe* 12 (2015): 177–93.

54. Beth Buggenhagen, "Islam and the Media of Devotion in and out of Senegal," *Visual Anthropology Review* 26, no. 2 (2010): 81–95. For a similar example in Cameroon, see Adama, "Islamic Communication," 138–48.

55. Dorothea Schulz, *Muslims and New Media in West Africa: Pathways to God* (Bloomington: Indiana University Press, 2012), 15 and Dorothea Schulz, "'Charisma and Brotherhood' Revisited: Mass-Mediated Forms of Spirituality in Urban Mali," *Journal of Religion in Africa* 33, no. 2 (2003): 146–71. See also Marloes Janson, *Islam, Youth, and Modernity in the Gambia: The Tablighi Jama'at* (Cambridge: Cambridge University Press, 2013).

56. Castor Goliama, *Where Are You Africa? Church and Society in the Mobile Phone Age* (Bamenda: Langaa RPCIG, 2010).

57. David Maxwell, introduction to *Christianity and the African Imagination: Essays in Honour of Adrian Hastings,* ed. David Maxwell, with Ingrid Lawrie (Leiden: Brill, 2002), 21.

58. Nyamnjoh, "Global and Local Trends," 59; Patrick Eisenlohr, "Media and Religious Diversity," *Annual Review of Anthropology* 41 (2012): 41.

59. Marleen de Witte, "Media Afrikania: Styles and Strategies of Representing 'Afrikan Traditional Religion' in Ghana," in Hackett and Soares, *Religious Transformations in Africa,* 207–26.

60. Asonzeh Ukah, "Managing Miracles: Law, Authority and the Regulation of Religious Broadcasting in Nigeria," in Hackett and Soares, *Religious Transformations in Africa,* 245–65.

61. Danielle de Lame, "Flows and Forces: Once Contained, Now Detained? On Connections, Past and Present in Rwanda," in *The Social Life of Connectivity in Africa,* ed. Mirjam de Bruijn and Rijk van Dikj (London: Palgrave Macmillan, 2012), 21–44.

62. Karin Barber, "Preliminary Notes on Audiences in Africa," *Africa: Journal of the International African Institute* 67, no. 3 (1997): 348.

63. Mirjam de Bruijn, Francis Nyanmjoh, and Inge Brinkman, "Introduction: Mobile Communication and New Social Spaces in Africa," in Bruijn, Nyanmjoh, and Brinkman, *Mobile Phones,* 11.

64. Christopher Morton and Elizabeth Edwards, eds., *Photography, Anthropology and History: Expanding the Frame* (London: Ashgate, 2009).

65. For example, Wolfram Hartman, Jeremy Silvester, and Patricia Hayes, eds., *The Colonizing Camera: Photographs in the Making of Namibian History* (Cape Town: University of Cape Town Press, 1998). For comparative examples, see Karen Strassler, *Refracted Visions: Popular Photography and National Modernity in Java* (Durham, NC: Duke University Press, 2010).

66. See also Jean-François Werner, "Photographies and Modernities in Africa," *Visual Anthropology Review* 14, no. 3 (2001): 241–42.

67. On this point, see especially the discussion in the introduction to Englund, *Christianity and Public Culture.*

68. Again, see Englund, introduction to *Christianity and Public Culture;* see also Meyer and Moors, introduction to *Religion, Media, and the Public Sphere.*

69. For one of many treatments of this observation, see Gilles Kepel, *The Revenge of God: The Resurgence of Islam, Christianity and Judaism in the Modern World* (Cambridge: Polity Press, 1994).

70. Englund, introduction to *Christianity and Public Culture.*

71. Stephen Ellis and Gerrie ter Haar, *Worlds of Power: Religious Thought and Political Practice in Africa* (London: C. Hurst, 2004).

72. Terence Ranger, "Scotland Yard in the Bush: Medicine Murders, Child Witches and the Construction of the Occult: A Literature Review," *AFRICA* 77, no. 2 (2007): 272–83.

73. Terence Ranger, "Religious Movements and Politics in Sub-Saharan Africa," *African Studies Review* 29, no. 2 (1986): 1–69.

74. Jean Comaroff, *Body of Power, Spirit of Resistance: The Culture and History of a South African People* (Chicago: University of Chicago Press, 1985).

75. Ranger, "Religious Movements," 12.

76. On Chilembwe, see Landeg White, *Magomero: Portrait of an African Village* (Cambridge: Cambridge University Press, 1997).

77. Jean Comaroff and John L. Comaroff, "Millennial Capitalism: First Thoughts on a Second Coming," *Public Culture* 12, no. 2 (2000): 291–343; Elsie Lewison, "Pentecostal Power and the Holy Spirit of Capitalism: Re-Imagining Modernity in the Charismatic Cosmology," *Symposia* 3, no. 1 (2011): 31–54.

78. Gifford, *Ghana's New Christianity,* 196–97.

79. White, *Magomero;* Karen Fields, *Revival and Rebellion in Colonial Central Africa* (Princeton, NJ: Princeton University Press, 1985).

80. Ellis and Ter Haar, *Worlds of Power,* 3.

81. Paul Landau, "'Religion' and Christian Conversion in African History: A New Model," *Journal of Religious History* 23, no. 1 (1999): 8–30.

82. Talal Asad, *Formations of the Secular: Christianity, Islam, Modernity* (Stanford: Stanford University Press, 2003).

83. Thomas G. Kirsch, *Spirits and Letters: Reading, Writing and Charisma in African Christianity* (New York: Berghahn, 2008).

84. Gregory Starrett, "The Varieties of Secular Experience," *Comparative Studies in Society and History* 52, no. 3 (2010): 635.

85. Christopher Dole, *Healing Secular Life: Loss and Devotion in Turkey* (Philadelphia: University of Pennsylvania Press, 2012); Courtney Bender and Ann Taves, eds., *What Matters? Ethnographies of Value in a Not So Secular Age* (New York: Columbia University Press, 2012).

86. Starrett, "Secular Experience," 646.

87. On which see David Westerlund, *Ujamaa na Dini: A Study of Some Aspects of Society and Religion in Tanzania, 1961–1977* (Stockholm: Almquist and Wiksell International, 1980).

ONE

Formal Care

Islam and Bureaucratic Paperwork in the Gold Coast/Ghana

SEAN HANRETTA

SCHOLARS ARE INCREASINGLY AWARE THAT THE MODERNIST PROJECTS of eighteenth-, nineteenth- and twentieth-century Europe were part of a broader family of transformations in culture, ideas, and social relations that took a myriad of different forms in many parts of the world.[1] While the question of the possible shared roots of these changes remains a very open and controversial one, it is nonetheless important to note the ways that certain social transformations that are often thought of as being distinctively European had, in fact, parallels in other regions. The emerging picture of the early-modern and modern world, particularly in its imperial spaces, is one in which various practices with preexisting resemblances became knit together in distinct-yet-convergent ways over the course of a few centuries. Accompanying these new constructions was a complex process of intertranslation during which, of course, the asymmetry of Western colonialism and capitalism proved highly significant. This translational asymmetry ensured that local practices could be made "intelligible" within the framework of Europe's distinctive modernity but also often created the illusion that the similarities that made translation possible were imposed.

"Religion" is one of the phenomena that emerged out of this process of convergence and translation. The various projects of religious modernization undertaken by diverse groups thus share a family resemblance, having multiple points of similarity as well as of difference.

Certain technologies—including new media and discursive tropes, alphabetization, and transportation and communication infrastructure—interacted dialectically with these projects. Nourished by modernism, such technologies could also make certain forms of modernization easier while raising the costs of others; they thus accelerated the convergence of projects while reinforcing the asymmetries in their mutual articulations. One particular technology, the written document, has long been recognized as a crucial player in the drama of both Christian and Muslim religious reform.[2] But documents come in many genres with many different conventions and social properties. This essay explores the role of an often-unheralded genre—the bureaucratic form—in the emergence of new configurations of religious authority among Muslims in what is now Ghana. More than other kinds of texts, bureaucratic forms have the advantage of putting their formal properties front and center—that is, their material attributes are an acknowledged aspect of their function. While this is true to an extent with all documents, the form of forms is readily graspable and thus particularly conducive to what, following Weber, we could call the "routinization" of the kinds of expertise that involve their use—removing them from exclusive association with the authority of an exemplary, unusual figure and making them available in configurations more suitable to everyday use.[3] Their emergence as common aspects of daily religious life thus reflects, I argue, an identifiable and identifiably similar moment in the movement toward the reification of "religion" as a distinct aspect of sociality. In the case of Ghana, the efforts by the British colonial state to create records of Muslim marriages (along with other bureaucratic campaigns) converged with a similar "formal" turn in the exercise of professional duties by Muslim scholars. These projects were pulled together into an asymmetrical bond by their shared property of expressing themselves through the circulation of standardized paperwork.

The Marriage of Muslims versus Muslim Marriage

During the early years of British administration in the colony of the Gold Coast and the protectorates north of it, no ordinances regulated marriages outside the established churches. It was only gradually—first in response to pressure to recognize non-Anglican marriages, then to pressures created by African converts to Christianity—that marriage law became a robust feature of Native Affairs governance. The first

"Marriage of Mohammedans" ordinance in what is now Ghana was issued in 1907. It was explicitly motivated by the need to define the situations in which divorce, inheritance, and child custody proceedings would be heard in accordance to (administrative understandings of) Islamic law versus those in which they would be referred instead to "customary" (i.e., chiefly) authority. The idea itself was not new—the ordinance was modeled on the laws established in South and Southeast Asia and in East Africa—but its particular shape and timing reflected some discomfort on the part of colonial officials with the very idea of a significant Muslim presence in the region. Administrators in places like Northern Nigeria, Sudan, and Uganda were accustomed to thinking about Muslim subjects; but the Gold Coast had long been established within the colonial imaginary as a non-Muslim space, facts on the ground notwithstanding.

In 1925, administrators in the Ashanti District and Northern Territories began a campaign to encourage the licensing of imams to officiate at Muslim weddings and to register marriages so conducted. Previously, only Christian religious leaders had been granted such licenses, reflecting the position that Muslim marriages were essentially a form of customary marriage. But the growing formalization of British interpretations of Islamic law and the desire to "modernize" native authority courts required a mechanism for deciding which marriages had to be treated according to "sharīʿa" principles. The British had no clear sense of what Muslim weddings entailed in these regions; instead, they extrapolated from Anglican and Catholic models in which the person presiding over the legal statements of consent and witnessing also had sacramental powers. Recognized "officiants" were thus formally known as "licensed Mohammedan priests," despite the fact that British specialists in Islam knew full well there was no office in Islam analogous to that of a priest. Though initially developed to facilitate the resolution of disputes, the licensing of Muslim "priests" was quickly put to another use: to formalize control over religious institutions by establishing a direct hierarchy between district officers, the chiefs of individual Muslim communities, and the imams licensed to officiate within those communities.

In a 1927 Gold Coast Supreme Court ruling on inheritance and subsequently in a celebrated child custody case in Tamale in 1932, courts and administrators made it clear that a Muslim ("Mohammedan") wedding was not a wedding between two Muslims, regardless of the religious beliefs of the couple, but rather one that had been officially registered.[4] In the absence of a certificate issued by a licensed imam, a marriage defaulted to "customary law," which could be adjudicated according to principles completely anathema to the parties concerned. Thus, there was no necessary relationship between the official status of an individual and his or her own beliefs, nor did the customary rules according to which a couple's marriage were to be adjudicated necessarily reflect their or their community's own normative practices. The same principle was later upheld in matters of divorce and adultery by a joint decision on the part of the Asante Confederacy Council and the regional commissioner.

These events have attracted the attention of historians since the 1970s and have helped illustrate some important features of colonial rule in Africa.[5] Efforts to require registration were fitful, unrealistic, and underfunded; they failed to take into account the structure of Muslim communities, the varieties of marriage practices, and the particular role of writing and documents in social life; and they reflected a misunderstanding of the nature of wedding celebrations, reducing them to the moment of ratification of a contract (in ways that, as we shall see, ironically coincided with emerging ideas about weddings among some Muslim reformists). Nonetheless, there remain a few interesting questions about both British rule and Islamic practice during the era that can be usefully explored through the traces that the registration drive left behind.

Mervyn Hiskett, in his groundbreaking contribution to this topic, considered the policy to have been an almost universal failure. To be sure, it does not appear that registration was ever widespread or consistent. Still, it is hard to know exactly how successful the efforts to register Muslim marriages were in any location at any moment. Around two hundred certificates have survived from the areas around Tamale and Yendi between 1931 and 1939 alone (the vast majority from 1933 to 1938).[6] Judging by the numbers of people licensed to register marriages in other districts and in other decades—and the struggles among chiefs and headmen to appoint "Mohammedan priests" or to recommend them for appointment—it is clear these two hundred are only a portion (how small a fraction may be unknowable) of the total certificates issued.[7]

Hiskett himself recognized the possibilities for abuse that the system had created. Insofar as the ordinance served local interests, they were those of Hausa-speaking (and often Hausaland-trained) "malams" (in Arabic *'ulamā'*, denoting scholars with specialized knowledge of Islamic law) and chiefs who sought to impose a particular form of Islam on other Muslims in the region. Once licensed as a Mohammedan priest, a *malam* could collect fees for officiating at a wedding with the backing of the state and, more generally, could claim that his status as one of the most important religious figures in the community had been recognized by the government. As a result, this status became something to be competed for and a source of patronage for chiefs who were often asked to vouch for the status of an aspirant licensed priest. Because the British generally appointed Hausa-speaking men to serve as chiefs or headmen of Muslim communities, usually regardless of the heterogeneity or actual composition of the majority of the group, networks of Hausa scholars and their chiefly patrons quickly dominated recognized registrations. These networks were not, however, without contestation, and the registration drive created endless problems for both the administration and ordinary people. Chiefs sought to use their role in advising British officers on the suitability of a particular imam for licensing as a way to bolster their local authority, while rival imams frequently fought over the privilege and the fees that came with it. This continued to be a source of tension right through the 1950s and even past independence.[8]

The chaos within the bureaucracy meant that the certificates themselves were, in most cases, worse than useless. In Yendi in 1937, for example, a divorced woman who had originally married under the Marriage of Mohammedans Ordinance sought to remarry and to have this new marriage also recognized by the state. In order to do so she needed to formally register the divorce of the first marriage, but she was unable to do so for some time because the local district commissioner lacked the necessary form. In other cases, the law was simply ignored by administrators. When, in 1940, the district commissioner in Prang reported that a large number of women were approaching the Native Authority courts seeking divorce from their husbands, the result was characteristically ad hoc. The local Native Authority had decided, apparently on the basis of the provision in Maliki law that failure on the part of husbands to provide for their wives can be grounds for divorce, that all the women involved should be granted divorces in exchange for payment of a fixed sum to their former husbands. But in many ways this in fact departed from the "official" understanding of Islamic law that registration had been established to help enforce: the specific conditions in Maliki law for divorce do not appear to have always been met, not all divorces in Maliki law required the return of marital payments (*mahr*), and the amount paid by the wife seems to have been fixed instead of reflecting the amount of the original *mahr*. Women whose cases did not meet the (unstated) criteria of the Native Authority and who were thus not granted divorce instead often simply left their marital homes. In response, the Native Authority ordered them to return and the district commissioner sought authorization to use governmental force to compel them to do so. But the chief commissioner in Tamale attempted (unsuccessfully, it appears) to refer the cases to an Islamic judge for further scrutiny. At no point in all this drama was the question of the jurisdictional effect of registration under the Marriage of Mohammedans Ordinance ever raised.[9]

An Ethnographic 'Ulamā': Devotional Orthopraxis as Index of Piety

There is good reason, then, for seeing the registration of Muslim marriages in the Gold Coast as a classic case of colonial bureaucratic malfeasance. At the same time, however, the impulses driving administrators' desire to register marriages responded to a deep current within modernist thought, one that was not exclusive to European colonial rulers. Above all, the British saw registration as the best way to standardize what it meant to be an Islamically married couple as distinct from a Muslim couple married under customary law; this implied a distinction between an Islamic ritual as such and a ritual practiced by Muslims, which in turn depended on conceptualizing Islam as something distinct from what Muslims do—a normative vision of the religion. Creating such a definition was crucial to the rationalizing of legal jurisdictions within the colonies even as it reflected the attitude that, although "pure" Islamic marriages surely existed somewhere out in the world, they were not typical of most West Africa Muslims. In the explicit formulation of the assistant district commissioner of Kumasi in 1925, registration could thus have "considerable educational value."[10] Moreover, it depended on understanding a wedding as the moment in which a marriage—understood administratively as a legal status—came into existence. This contractual and event-oriented approach connected the filling out of a piece of paper (and its legal witnessing) with the coming into existence of a specific state that bound together the marital couple as well as those otherwise touched on by the contract.[11] These two fundamental assumptions—that registration helped resolve the question of who was and was not a Muslim, thereby mobilizing a normative definition of Islam, and that the process of filling out the paperwork itself had what we could call a "disciplining" effect—were equally shared by many Muslim reformists operating within Ghana at the time.

Such reformists grew out of what was by then a century-old movement that had seen a seismic shift take place in the nature of religious authority and the attention paid to orthopraxis—correct practice of rituals and other devotional activities—in the daily lives of many Muslims in West Africa. Even a sketch of the broad outlines of this movement are beyond the scope of this essay, but in general what emerged was a greater degree of interest in the piety and practices of the "ordinary Muslim," as states that founded their legitimacy on their religiosity depended on and cultivated mass piety as a source of authority. Efforts to reform popular practice reflected a shift in the gaze of the pious away from scrutinizing rulers and one another for "venal" practices and toward a community constituency to whom they owed guidance and spiritual support. One manifestation of this interest was a change in the amount and nature of written devotional texts that circulated through the region. The nineteenth century had seen an increase in the copying, distribution, and standardization of devotional materials across many parts of West Africa, including the areas in the orbit of the "Sokoto Caliphate" based in what is now northern Nigeria.[12] What was crucial in this was not necessarily the content—sometimes it reflected radical changes, but just as often much of the theological, spiritual, and pedagogical fundamentals received little modification from older texts—but rather the form of many of these documents. The overall consequence of these processes was a kind of routinization of spiritual authority born out of a quest for uniformity and a belief in the importance of the quality of popular religious practice. A wide range of activities that sat at the intersection of religious doctrine and daily life became subject to new forms of scrutiny and regularization, with documents playing an increasing role in mediating between authority and behavior. Although the main thrusts of this movement focused on events such as funerals and forms of worship, marriage was certainly part of the complex of social life that came within view of the reformist project.

The major devotional and legal sources used by Muslims in West Africa and elsewhere had always made it clear that marriage was a contract (*'aqd*). But alongside this ran a concurrent stream of thought that emphasized that marriage was also an act of worship (*'ibāda*). This view not only lingered on the ethical and psychological dimensions of marriage but highlighted the importance of the celebratory and social activities surrounding the entering into the marital contract, such as feasting (*walīma*), the playing of drums (*dufūf*), and announcing the marriage to the community (*i'lān* or *iẓhār*).[13] The services provided by the local 'ulamā' during these events were intertwined with what later generations (and some scholars elsewhere) would distinguish as the religious and cultural aspects of weddings.[14] But it appears that weddings were not, in general, of much great interest to the learned before the nineteenth century. In his major compendium of religious practices, the great twelfth-century Islamic synthesizer, Abu Hamid al-Ghazali, discussed weddings in a way that offered little of interest for the spiritual virtuoso in the form of opportunity for self-discipline or enlightenment, nor did the issue involve such doctrinally explosive issues that it generated sharp polemics. Ghazali himself classified it as one of the "customs" (*'ādāt*), as compared to events like death and burial, which figured among the "means of salvation" (*munajjiyāt*).

By the late nineteenth century, however, weddings and their performance had begun attracting somewhat more attention. The reasons for the transformation in interest in weddings should probably be sought in the changing social role of the 'ulamā' rather than from any specific alteration in the attitude toward marriage among the pious. Studies on Islamic law in other parts of the Muslim world have noted that whereas the distinction between 'ādāt and religion (*dīn*) is very old in Islamic scholarship, its practical deployment is historically contingent. Wael B. Hallaq and Michael Peletz identified an increasing interest in the distinction among scholars in the decades of the nineteenth century that preceded European colonial occupation.[15] In one famous example, the Damascene scholar Muḥammad Ibn 'Ābidīn al-Shāmī insisted in the 1820s—before the Ottoman *tanẓīmāt* centralizing reforms—that judges "must not stubbornly adhere to the opinions transmitted in *ẓāhir al-riwāya* [the apparent meaning of legal rulings]" but "must follow custom."[16] It is worth noting here that Ibn 'Ābidīn did not oppose custom to sharī'a but rather to the "apparent meaning" of legal texts; law itself was understood to encompass and reflect custom. As the étatisation of the law proceeded in the next decades, custom became more clearly distinguished, and of course a more self-conscious justification of the taking into account of customs implied the obligation of the learned to familiarize themselves with such practices.[17] It was a small if crucial and contingent step from there to the subordination of custom to the written corpus of law.

In Ghana, the increasing rigidity of the law and the growing distinction between religion and custom were closely associated with the Hausa trading diaspora. Before British occupation, the Hausa-speaking regions of West Africa had begun to routinize religious care, and the role of the local scholar or holy man in marriages shifted as part of this broader "professionalization." Some of these changes likely grew out of the struggles over authority and credentialing associated with the arrival of new legal texts, new approaches to the study of the Arabic language, and the changing political and economic landscape of the Sokoto Caliphate. Kano was the center of a new devotional and scholarly effort, one closely identified with perceptions of an improvement in religious knowledge, the refinement of practice, and the rejection of "traditional" scholarly authority. The preeminent figure of the era was the Kano scholar Muhammad Salgha (1871/2–1939).[18] During the 1920s and 1930s, reformists associated with Salgha actively condemned a whole series of practices, particularly those associated with funerals. Roman Loimeier has demonstrated that the intellectual activity of Salgha and his students was closely entangled with shifting class and political identities. Most of these scholars were connected with Hausa merchants and embraced an insurgent agenda that targeted both the local aristocracy and "collaboration" with the British. By contrast, those who defended existing customs "represented the traditional establishment . . . supported the policy of modernization initiated by the British, and . . . defended the position of the [Hausa] emir [of Kano]."[19]

Ironically, however, the underlying intellectual assumptions of the group around Salgha were ultimately quite compatible with the logic of colonial "modernization." Their hostility to colonial modernisms can thus be seen as a critique of style and rationale from a position of deeper consonance. This was not an isolated development. Various researchers—Peletz writing on Malaysia, Muhammad Qasim Zaman on South Asia, John Bowen on Indonesia, and Felicitas Becker and Loimeier on East Africa—all noted how scholarly interest in distinguishing religion and custom converged with British imperial needs and how this convergence facilitated an increased deployment of the distinction among nonelite circles.[20] The case in Ghana perhaps most closely resembles that of

Malaysia in that the British were eager to clarify jurisdictional lines so that Islamic law was not applied to non-Muslims or to "nominal" Muslims. In contrast to India, where the British felt a need to reign in what they saw as a tendentious judiciary and to discipline judges according to their own understandings of Islamic law,[21] administrators in Ghana generally had much less familiarity with Islam. In most cases it was the judgment of a chief or other notable that sufficed to vet a prospective licensed Mohammedan priest. If Ghana's malams felt threatened by this process, it was more because of the increasing role of chiefs in authorizing their spiritual roles than to any intellectual limiting of their legal discretion.

The small piece of this larger process that is relevant here is the effect reformists had on the day-to-day organizing of some of the devotional activities carried out by the rank-and-file 'ulamā', an effect that can be summarized as the routinization of spiritual services. Two documents—one from Ghana, one from Nigeria—offer some insight into the consequences for individuals. The first (figure 1), is a single-leaf draft of a sermon (*khuṭba*) for use in blessing a wedding (*nikāḥ*), taken from the collection of 'Umar Falke, a Tijani student of Muhammad Salgha and a key member of the Hausa scholarly and merchant diaspora linking Kano with Ghana and points further west.[22] The blessing itself is rather unremarkable; it is rather the form of the text itself that is of interest.[23] A loose leaf that could be easily carried around for use whenever a malam had to attend a wedding, the sheet constituted a literal template into which the specifics of the marriage to be blessed could be inserted. After the standard Qur'anic verses, the text provides placeholders for the names of the groom (*fulān*, literally a male so-and-so) and bride (*fulāna*, female so-and-so) and for the amount (*kadhā*, literally such-and-such an amount) of the marital payment (*ṣadāq*), including the amount paid in cash (*naqad*) and the amount outstanding (*ajal*). These are standard pieces of information comprising the marital contract and are often recorded by anyone who officiates at a wedding. Having specific prompts for each provided for great precision even on the part of someone without deep training in Islamic marital law. The text was clearly meant to be read aloud during the wedding itself, as it includes a direct exhortation to those gathered to witness the information about the *nikāḥ* that the malam is intoning: "ayuhā al-nās ashhadū 'alā dhālik," or "oh people, witness this."

More stage directions were provided in a text associated with the very prominent Ghanaian scholar, al-Hajj 'Umar of Kete-Krachi. Designed to assist those who were called on to pray for the recently deceased, the text begins "if it happens that you visit a grave" and then provides detailed instructions for actions and prayers.[24] Umar's prestige in northern and central Ghana—and indeed in northwest Nigeria—was great enough that having his imprimatur on such a guide would have granted it almost unquestioned legitimacy. Such texts, we can deduce, appealed to those who valued precise and authoritative guidance in the performance of their community duties but who were anxious about their own knowledge. They also suggest that the learned scholars who composed the guides felt that those who had only partial training in the Islamic sciences were in danger of being misled by the easy availability of complex theological writings and sophisticated spiritual practices. Significantly different from other genres of scholarly guidance provided to the 'ulamā', such as reference compendia of *fiqh*, *fatwas* or prayers, these single-leaf, single-purpose, easily usable "scripts" constituted exactly the kind of field manual needed at a time when concern for popular orthopraxis outstripped the institutional capacity of the "well-trained" to provide for the needs of the masses.

There were various precedents for this genre, perhaps the most important of which was the epistolary handbook. This was an ancient form that provided guidance for malams—often the only literate members of their communities—who were called on to write formal letters on behalf of others. Collections of these, known as *wathā'iq*, could range from the very technical discussions that guided jurists in expressing legal opinions to more eloquent and rhetorical forms for lay usage. The more technical kinds of *wathā'iq* emerged out of the specialization of contract law and legal pronunciations, and they served to integrate the world of abstract theory and daily courtroom practice.[25] Some such works that circulated in the Maghribi Islamic world (into which West Africa was highly integrated) made use of the same "fill-in-the-blank" templates such as we see in figures 1 and 2.[26] Charles Stewart and Bruce S. Hall have noted that at least one important work in this tradition, Ibn Salmūn al-Kinānī's *al-'Iqd al-munaẓẓam*, circulated in West Africa,[27] and Hunwick discovered a version in the collection of papers that had belonged to 'Umar Falke.[28] Al-Hajj 'Umar of Kete-Krachi himself composed one, which itself serves as an interesting source for understanding the changing nature of religious authority at the time. Two of the twelve sample letters he provided involved problems within a marriage caused by the prolonged geographic separation of the couple.

In one a husband writes to thank his wife for her patience and promises to be more attentive; in another a wife informs her husband that his extended absence and failure to provide material support has created a general consensus that she may divorce him and marry another.[29]

But by their nature such handbooks focused on written style and the explicitly discursive qualities of a document, whereas objects such as figure 1 and figure 2 reflected instead a concern with the precision of act and expression and with the relationship between trace and event. The documents in figures 1 and 2 can thus be thought of as the result of a process of simplification and popularization of the techniques for transmitting knowledge to less esteemed (or less confident) members of the 'ulamā', thereby bureaucratizing the authority of the original author and making it available to those in possession of the guiding text. The development and circulation of such genres of text thus reveal quite a bit both about the changing nature of scholarly authority in Muslim West Africa at the time and about the growing demand for authoritative guidance by larger numbers of Muslims. Routinization and the popularization of reformist ideas about orthopraxis thus reinforced one another dialectically.

While we have no direct evidence (that I am aware of) as to why individual malams sought to become "licensed Mohammedan priests" or why Muslim couples sought to have their marriages certified, I would suggest that the motivations behind the production of such documents were not as alien to local Muslim practice as they may at first seem. To be sure, the kind of authority that derived from the possession of a document that was considered to be a copy of a text written by a prestigious scholar like al-Hajj 'Umar of Kete-Krachi was certainly different from the authority that the British attributed to a marriage certificate. All the same, the possession of a license to issue marriage certificates allowed malams to engage in the practices crucial to their quotidian authority with (at least in theory) state and chiefly backing. Moreover, the formal consonance between the properties of figures 1 and 3 *as forms* established an exact correspondence in the way at least some aspects of that authority was exercised: the filling-in of blanks. The infrastructure that could have made government efforts at systemic registration logistically practicable was lacking—malams and new couples alike complained about difficulties in traveling to a district office to submit marriage paperwork, the hardships in getting the paperwork in the first place, and the processes for licensing officiants—but the basic ideas motivating registration were broadly consistent with the reform objectives of many late-nineteenth- and early-twentieth-century Muslim leaders.

Language, Ethnicity, and Gender: Paperwork as a Space for Negotiation

Seen in this context, the story of the efforts of British colonial officers to codify Muslim marriage practices through the production and dissemination of standardized texts takes on a different meaning from the ones typically accorded to it by studies of colonial rule or theories of the "power" of the archive or the bureaucratic form. Recent theories for thinking about the connections between archives and governance have brought very sophisticated techniques to bear on the reading of colonial-era documents. Rather than seeing them as passive records of practices—or even as heavily biased, underinformed records—we have become accustomed to seeing in them the sinews of the state itself. It was through investigation, the recording of information, and the consulting of archives that states came to embody a very modern form of power. At the same time, however, the apparent coherence of the "grain" of an archival system—the visible workings of power within its organization and its very existence—can disguise the results of local struggles over information, both its production and its use.[30] Although colonial bureaucratic systems operated under the sign of "modernization," overstating the degree of coherence within both their documentary procedures and their exercise of power risks mistaking this often-incantatory sign for an actual residue of effective, rational power.[31]

This is not to say that the institutions of the colonial state in the Gold Coast and its protectorates were not sources of struggle, but rather that at least some of the struggle was among colonial subjects with different attitudes toward the relationship between authority and religious practice. Control of the state apparatus for nominating and recognizing Muslim "headmen," for vetting "Mohammedan priests," and for regulating the collection of administrative marriage fees gave power to privileged intermediaries to define the practices that could create official "Muslim marriages." The abstract version of a wedding enabled by the process of certification and the reformist rhetoric of contract and formula was, of course, hardly culturally "neutral": insofar as it reflected certain individuals' sense of what the event should be, it allowed particular versions of Muslim culture to stand in for Islam as a whole. Struggles over how to celebrate a marriage thus connected directly to struggles over the political control of the right to represent Muslims and thereby define Muslimness; this was primarily an intra-Muslim struggle, not one between Muslims and the British state.[32] In 1934, to give one example, Gonja elders in Kumasi (represented by Mallam Sani Salga) petitioned the Asantehene—whose court stood as the highest "customary" legal body in the region—reiterating an old request to be allowed to select a "Gwanja [Gonja] headman." The reason they gave, at least in this instance, was to facilitate the performance of

> a marriage according to Gwanja custom in the house of the woman's father, as was performed in the days of the late Mallam Usuman. . . . [T]he reason of the stoppage of such [Gwanja] Mahamadan custom in Kumasi was due to the Ex-Sarikin Zongo [chief] Mallam Sallao having acquired a Tribunal became tyrant and put a stop to such Mahamadan legal custom and adopted that of his own contrary to the pleasure of all the . . . community which was one of the subjects of the [1932] riot [in Kumasi] but we are not here for that as such is against our wishes, therefore we wish to exempt ourselves from any different community to avoid any misunderstanding.[33]

Marriage registration represented a useful resource in these struggles. Awareness of what a bureaucracy expects on a form can shape how people organize, record, and make sense of their own documentable practices. This can provide an occasion for the internalization or "subjectification" of various forms of domination.[34] At the same time, however, the actual day-to-day functioning of a bureaucracy gives documents certain opportunities to evade the expectations of the state. The obvious fact that forms such as the "Marriage of Mohammedans" certificates were filled out before being submitted meant that such disciplining was always imperfect and subject to challenge. Furthermore, by forcing into the open questions of who was *really* married as a Muslim, the certificates helped those resisting versions that aspired to hegemony articulate the nature of their grievances. It was possible—then as now (though computerized forms may reduce such possibilities)—to fill out a form "incorrectly" in a consequential, or at least revealing, manner. One clear example of this is visible in the

"Bride's Wali" space on the registry form reproduced as figure 3. Typically this space was intended for the name of the bride's father or other male guardian (often called *walī* or *wakīl*). In this instance, however, a woman's name, Maryam, appears. It is possible, of course, that the person filling out the form inadvertently switched the name for the "walī" with that for the bride's "witness"—given on this certificate as Sulayman. However, most interpretations of Maliki law would also not permit a woman to serve as a witness to a marriage contract. In either case, what seems clear is that the parties filling out the form considered it appropriate—or at least plausible—to have a woman serve in one of these two roles. Whether the British officer who received the form agreed (or noticed) is anyone's guess. Other copies of certificates listed more than the required two witnesses, allowing the forms to reflect in some way the much larger, more complicated social rituals that most weddings involved.[35] By filling out the forms in this way, the people who used them turned a tool that was designed to correspond to the idea of a marriage as a contract and of a wedding as its ratification into an object that bore witness to a more socially complex conception of the ritual.

Furthermore, the history of Muslim marriage registration in Ghana suggests it is possible to mobilize bureaucratic logic against the logic of governance. The reification of a state ideology in the form of a form can serve as the grounds for a kind of resistance. A beautiful example of this is the campaign waged by Ahmadi Muslims in the Gold Coast to have a range of languages besides Arabic and Hausa recognized by the British administration as official "Islamic" languages. The Ahmadiyya movement grew out of a South Asian Islamic context in the late nineteenth century and saw perhaps its greatest global success in the Gold Coast. Particularly in the southern portions of the colony, many people from ethnic groups that were not traditionally Muslim converted to Islam under the auspices of the Ahmadiyya, and few of these spoke Hausa or Arabic. Ahmadi schools did not typically emphasize the teaching of Arabic, considering translations of the Qur'an as acceptable vehicles for spiritual development.[36] Yet to have a marriage registered under the Marriage of Mohammedans Ordinance, one had to have both a licensed Mohammedan priest—that is to say, a malam recognized as such by the state—and the required form, typically filled out by the licensed priest both in English and in either Hausa or Arabic (see figure 3). These corresponded to the languages of British administration and of "Islam," respectively. Both requirements were difficult for Ahmadi Muslims to meet since typically their leaders were not recognized by other Muslims as "true" Muslims (and therefore could not receive the recommendations necessary to become "licensed priests"), nor could they usually write either Arabic or Hausa.

This would seem to be a clear case of the role of a piece of paperwork in defining Muslimness and thereby excluding an entire group of people from official membership.[37] But members of the Ahmadiyya refused to simply acquiesce to this bureaucratic affront. In 1931, Maulvi Nazir Ahmad, the head of the Ahmadiyya movement in the Cape Colony, petitioned to have the Ahmadi Imam of Saltpond licensed to register marriages under the ordinance. In addition, he requested that, rather than requiring officiants to fill out the first column of the marriage certificate in either Arabic or Hausa, the ordinance be amended to allow the imam, who himself was not literate in Arabic, to enter the relevant information in Twi or Fanti instead.[38]

Rarely were the racial and civilizational assumptions embedded in British Islamic policy clearer than in the internal debates over how to respond to the Ahmadis' request, revealing yet another layer of the kinds of struggles that could be touched off by paperwork. Instinctively upset by the idea, the commissioner of the Western Province argued that "the Arabic language (including cognate languages and script) is essentially the language of Islam, in Africa at any rate, and it is difficult to understand how a convert can be raised to the dignity of a Priest competent to perform marriages, before he has acquired the little knowledge of the language and script necessary to fill in the particulars in a marriage or divorce certificate." Perhaps most striking here is the way the category of "cognate languages" (not generally a frequent feature of British colonial administration in Africa) was invoked to account for and defend the uniqueness of Hausa's acceptability for the filling out of the form. By taking what had initially been a bureaucratic convenience—reflecting the fact that many Ghanaian Muslims did not write Arabic and that the British generally favored Hausa speakers for leadership roles among Muslims—and transforming it into an inherent phylogenetic feature of the language itself, the commissioner's logic "naturalized" administrative practice and bolstered the claims of Hausa speakers to authority over religious matters.[39]

But since, from an administrative perspective, it was the English column on the form that mattered, the commissioner was forced to confess to having "no great objection to the certificates being written in Twi or Fanti, or Moshi, or Dagomba for that matter, though I think this would be a pity." But he urged that "extreme caution . . . be exercised in the issue of licenses to converts." Opening the ethnic and linguistic floodgates—and with them, it was implied, the intellectual floodgates—risked "cheapening an ancient and, in some respects, noble religion." As a compromise, the administrator proposed instead that a special ordinance be created distinctly for Ahmadis that would not include the language restriction—creating, that is, yet another form of Muslim marriage so that "customary," "Mohammedan," and "Ahmadi" would all effectively have distinct legal status. Equally revealing was the approach of the attorney general, which ended up prevailing. He felt that the privileged role of Hausa and Arabic properly reflected the fact that these were "'written languages' . . . which the pagan vernaculars are not." He therefore proposed amending the ordinance so that Ahmadi officiants could simply record marriage information in English and skip the first column entirely. This sidestepped the question of whether Arabic and Hausa had a special religious authority while also avoiding elevating Twi and other languages to equal status. Though it did not, perhaps, achieve the outcome that Maulvi Nazir Ahmad had hoped for, the Ahmadi protest highlights the way that the simple existence of a form to be filled out could generated questions about how it was to be filled out, which could in turn reach into the conceptual foundations of state policy and public religious identity.[40]

A Formal Legacy

Although it was true, then, as Hiskett argued, that in the 1930s the bureaucratization of marriages was consonant with a "Hausafication" project pursued jointly by malams, chiefs, and colonial officials, it also became a way to challenge Hausa practices and became part of an ethical orientation that was picked up by, and in some ways perfected by, non-Hausa scholars. It was, on its deepest level, an effort to abstract religion from culture, and in this it dovetailed—not seamlessly, but effectively—with the approach of the British administration and some postcolonial Muslim elites. This helps explain why so much reformist energy in the last few decades has (often intentionally) served to weaken Hausa hegemony over religious authority in Ghana.[41]

To be sure, the legacy of colonial Muslim marriage registration has been contradictory. Memories of the push to register marriages have largely faded. Although many individuals kept and keep their own private notes about the marriages they have blessed or attended, in over a dozen interviews with malams and Muslim chiefs—the very people whose fathers and grandfathers were at the center of the administrative push to register marriages—only one person had any recollection or awareness of these earlier registrations. Everyone else insisted that although it was a good idea and a possibility for the future, state registration had never been attempted. Indeed, modernist rhetoric imposes a strict temporality on such practices: to the extent that recording and registering is interpreted as modern, routinized, standardized, and rationalized, most Ghanaian Muslims assume it could be only a new development, a movement away from the more personal, informal, and socially embedded (and thus cultural) forms of practice in the past and toward those informed by today's more legalistic, "universal" approach to Islam. This form of what Mudimbe has called "retrodiction" is quite sincere but clearly can obscure the contradictions and complexities of the historical record.[42]

The seductions of such a false chronology should be a warning for scholars as well not to draw the lines too sharply between different kinds of knowledge "economies." The use of forms and registries in the 1920s and the 1930s was embedded in nontextual social life, and the same is true today. Two of the major "reformist" Muslim organizations in Ghana—the Islamic Research and Reformation Center (popularly often called simply "Research") and Ahl al-Sunna wa Jamaʿa—were issuing their own marriage certificates in the middle of the first decade of this century, and indeed they had done so for over a decade. I was privileged to be provided with a detailed discussion of Research's procedures and to be given samples of both their application form for a marriage certificate and a certificate itself. Cognizant of the power such forms embody, Research is eager to protect against abuses. They thus take pains to independently investigate the claims of those applying for certification, including sending representatives to the couple's neighborhood to discretely ask questions. The issuing of certificates also provides an opportunity for engagement with the norms of practice: whereas, for instance, Research's "Application for Marriage Certificate" requires the signatures of the bride's *wakīl* and of an "officiator" (codifying the role of officiant just as the British had done), the marriage certificate itself prominently feature spaces for the signatures of "bridegroom" and "bride" (and in keeping with assumptions about Muslim women's literacy, there is the option for the bride's right thumbprint instead).

The staff at Research and most Muslim elites with whom I spoke about these independent certificates explained them as an effort to remedy a defect in the legal protections offered to Ghanaian Muslims by the state, a defect caused by the failure of the state to respect or attend to Muslim marital law. Since Ghana's independence in 1957, the state has drifted deeper and deeper into an informal Christo-centrism. Whereas the British imperial state made some effort at making good on its official neutrality in religious affairs (even as the administration in the Gold Coast frequently revealed its bias against Muslims), the Ghanaian state has often elided the existence of Muslims entirely.

Indeed, a series of legal reforms enacted in 1985 dramatically changed the landscape for Muslim marriage registration. The Customary Marriage and Divorce (Registration) Law and the Intestate Succession Law together reflected an effort by the state to shed what urban, Christian elites had come to see as undesirable legacies of colonial rule and to resolve definitively the status of matrilineal succession (commonly practiced among Akan peoples in Ghana) and polygamy. British colonial law had created special protections for the offspring of a union registered under the (non-Muslim, monogamous) Marriage Ordinance, giving them (complex, often convoluted) rights against the matrilineal kin group that would have otherwise had the dominant claim on inheritance via "customary law." While such marriages had, in the early colonial period, been rather rare, by the time Ghana became independent it was widely desired that the primary marriage ordinance and registration legislation should reflect the practices and needs of the majority of the population. At the same time, matrilineal succession had become less desirable for many wealthy Akan households, and so "customary law" was similarly seen to be out of alignment with social realities. The 1985 reforms (and smaller reforms promulgated in 1979) attempted to resolve these tensions by creating a unified system for the distribution of intestate property in which the bulk would be allocated to a (single) spouse, to children, and to any surviving parents, with only a portion dispersed according to the individual's "customary law." In the process, all provisions for a distinct "Islamic" system of inheritance, such as had been established by the

Marriage of Mohammedans Ordinance, were swept aside. Muslim marriages were, in effect, returned uniformly to the category of customary marriages.[43]

This was less a question of the particular targeting of Muslim marriages for delegitimization than of the consequences of the social and political marginalization of Muslims in Ghana and, thus, the lack of concern for the effects of such reforms on their lives. In theory all "customary" marriages were to be registered, but in fact the Ghanaian state has consistently failed to enforce this provision or to maintain any organized registry for this purpose. As a consequence, unless a Muslim executes a will—a very uncommon practice in Ghana—their property cannot (legally) be disposed of in keeping with whatever understanding of sharī'a they or their family may have.[44] Since the registration of a marriage would, even in principle, have little effect on this—the "customary" portion of the inheritance can never exceed one quarter—and since in practice it is impossible to register such a marriage, the entire system of registration has completely collapsed. Furthermore, by defining Muslim marriages as customary rather than statutory, it reopens the question of whose version of custom should count as Islamic.

A 2002 survey carried out by the Legal Resources Center (LRC) in Accra (an organization that, among other things, defends the rights of Muslim minorities in Ghana) indicated that many elite Ghanaian Muslim spokespeople felt that the lack of state-recognized marriage registration was a distinct liability. Fearing the effects of a creeping informality in the status of Muslim marriages, the difficulties in substantiating marital claims in court, and the potential chaos involved in defining customary norms, these elites came down strongly in favor of legal reform to buttress registration (and indeed for a registration system for Muslims as individuals!). By contrast, when the LRC surveyed five hundred Muslims, most respondents indicated they did not want the state to be involved in the registering of mosques or the licensing of officiants. Ninety-nine percent noted that community authority figures (chiefs, imams, respected elders) would, in fact, recognize a marriage regardless of whether it was registered, and 72.8 percent believed that they should do so.[45]

These results suggest that although Muslim elites are clearly attentive to the forms of authority generated by registration, in terms of social reality the lack of official registration of marriages has had little concrete effect. This has not, however, apparently reduced the attraction for many of possessing such a certificate, whether because of its informal value or simply its symbolism. Certainly the modernity signaled by possession of this piece of paper is not simply an abstract one: it also serves as a proxy for the full citizenship rights granted to Christian Ghanaians whose marriages are directly recognized by the state. To this extent, then, in an echo of what has happened with Islamic education in many Sahelian states, the failure of the state to create a public space for Islam has been met with ad hoc action on the part of nonstate actors.[46] At the same time, in the case of certificates issued by Research, the involvement of the organization in community life and even the activities of the investigators who verify the propriety of a couple seeking to have their marriage certified somewhat ensure that documents continue to reflect social relationships rather than depersonalized institutions.

It remains the case, then, that much energy is devoted to managing the relationship between the Islamic in the abstract and the customary, a distinction that is produced and reproduced even as it is scrutinized and debated. As a recent manual on Islamic marriage published in Ghana put it, "The purpose of stating some of the African traditional practices is to reveal some of the practices that are in conflict with the teachings of Islam and also to draw a clear distinction between the Islamic requirements and the traditional demands. Some people cannot distinguish between customary demand and Islamic requirements."[47]

Conclusions

The British Gold Coast's "Marriage of Mohammedans" certificates have ceased to circulate as physical objects—only these nearly two hundred seem to have survived and they lie neglected in archives—and have also almost vanished from living memory. Although colonial officials may have imagined that these papers could stabilize what it meant to be a Muslim in a juridical, if not intellectual sense, whatever effects they achieved likely came from the deep logic they shared with processes of social transformation at work among Ghanaian Muslims themselves. That the new version of being Muslim promoted by the British and reformists alike could cut deeply into the intimate spaces of peoples' lives is not in doubt. But in this case, at least, the medium provided a kind of screen onto which social dynamics were occasionally and distortedly projected, even as its very form gave rise to opportunities to subvert, redirect, and even challenge the logic that inspired it.

As a medium, paperwork complicates the relationship between documents as texts and as material culture. The forces that call for, produce, and consume paperwork are a major portion of the forces that structure what scholars have come to call "the archive." But as I have argued elsewhere, such structures do not achieve total control over the production of knowledge, much less over the processes by which knowledge can circulate or be taken up. Archives do not possess coherent grains against which or along which one can read.[48] To imagine that they do is, in some ways, to replicate the error Marx decried in Hegel: to accept the bureaucracy's own image of itself.[49] At least two things disrupt the easy relationship between the mechanisms of governance and the constitution of the archive. One is the assumption that the bureaucratic apparatus of the colonial state was *the* archive of the colonial period. As Mervyn Hiskett's analysis implied, the British bureaucratization of Muslim personal life (as opposed to the bureaucratization of political authority) in Ghana was so fitful and ultimately so feeble that its mechanisms held little exclusionary power. There were undoubtedly other pieces of paper generated by the British colonial state in Ghana that were far worse to be without than the Marriage of Mohammedans certificates. The more significant transformation, one that did a much better job of using paper to create selves than the colonial state could, was the rise of practical literacy among the lower ranks of Muslim scholars themselves and the concurrent development of textual genres that could standardize and broaden the scope of their religious activities among their communities. This process left behind an archive, but it is one that is scattered and is only beginning to be assembled.

The relationship between the mechanisms of governance and the constitution of the archive is also troubled by the polysemic nature of the very papers that mediate between the two. To be sure, the grid of the form exercises a disciplining function on those who fill it out, and the colonial project certainly had managerial aspirations.[50] As Nancy Hunt has noted for colonial-era birth certificates, official documents conferred status by reflecting "contact with official . . . spaces,"[51] and it is clear that the relatively wealthy families who sought to have their unions recognized by the British state—or those who seek to have them recognized by contemporary organizations like the Islamic Research and Reformation Center—altered their status by doing so. At the same time, the form externalizes and objectifies social relationships, allowing them to work differently than they otherwise could. The "blank" spots on the page—whether the empty cells of the colonial certificate or the *fulān* "so-and-so" of figure 1—were indexical ruptures in the texts that enabled a much more active approach to writing in general. This power was not lost on Ghanaian Muslims who, to the extent they could, sought to turn it to their own purposes, allowing it to structure their actions on a different level. The efforts of Ahmadi Muslims to force the administration to recognize paperwork filled out in languages it did not recognize as "Islamic" ones represented efforts to seize the power of that technology for themselves, even as the technology gave them a new way to articulate the ways they were being excluded from both the Muslim community and the colonial state's networks of authority.

As with any technology that lowers the costs of some actions but not others, paper forms in colonial Ghana provided a powerful force for pulling together practices of religious reform that had a deep family resemblance. In the end, the distinct trajectories of those movements of transformation, and their very separate roots, reflected distinct social processes that came to be entangled. The similarities between them facilitated the selective uptake of new media forms that were themselves similar and that then further pulled the practices into consonance. The role of the technology was significant but depended on other underlying forces. Ivan Illich has argued that rather than emphasizing the role of the printing press in the transformation of knowledge in early modern Europe, historians should instead highlight earlier changes in medieval scribal practices that, by reimagining what a book was, "created the object which, three hundred years later, was fit for print."[52] In the early twentieth century, Ghanaian Muslims began making intellectual and social shifts in religious practice that made a formal system for the standardization of spiritual care attractive. The people whose practices changed most in this shift were the malams, who shaped their devotional acts to match the forms. But it was not until at least the 1980s that many nonscholars seem to have begun taking advantage of the form's properties within their own religious practices. This disjuncture suggests there remains much to understand both about the shifting nature of religious authority in mid-twentieth-century Ghana and about the social and intellectual forces that shaped this authority's relationship with media.

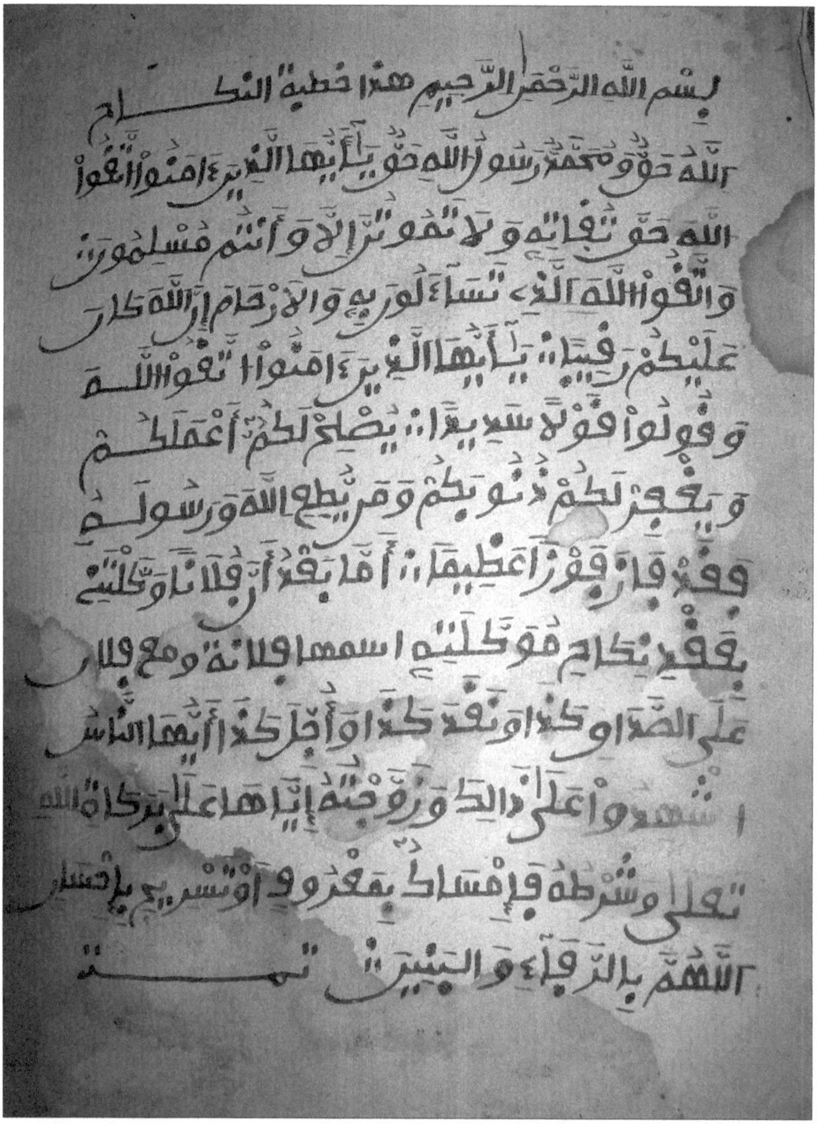

بسم الله الرحمن الرحيم هذا خطبة النكاح

الله حق ومحمد رسول الله حق يا أيها الذين آمنوا اتقوا

الله حق تقاته ولا تموتن إلا وأنتم مسلمون

واتقوا الله الذي تساءلون به والأرحام إن الله كان

عليكم رقيبا يا أيها الذين آمنوا اتقوا الله

وقولوا قولا سديدا يصلح لكم أعمالكم

ويغفر لكم ذنوبكم ومن يطع الله ورسوله

فقد فاز فوزا عظيما أما بعد فإن فلانا وكلني

بعقد نكاح موكلته اسمها فلانة ومع فلان

على الصداق كذا ونقد كذا وأجل كذا أيها الناس

اشهدوا على ذلك وزوجته إياها على بركة الله

تعالى وشرطه فإمساك بمعروف أو تسريح بإحسان

اللهم بالرفاء والبنين تمت

FIGURE 1. "Khuṭba al-nikāḥ," unpublished MS. Courtesy Herskovits Library, Arabic Manuscripts Collection, Umar Falke Collection #2776, Northwestern University.

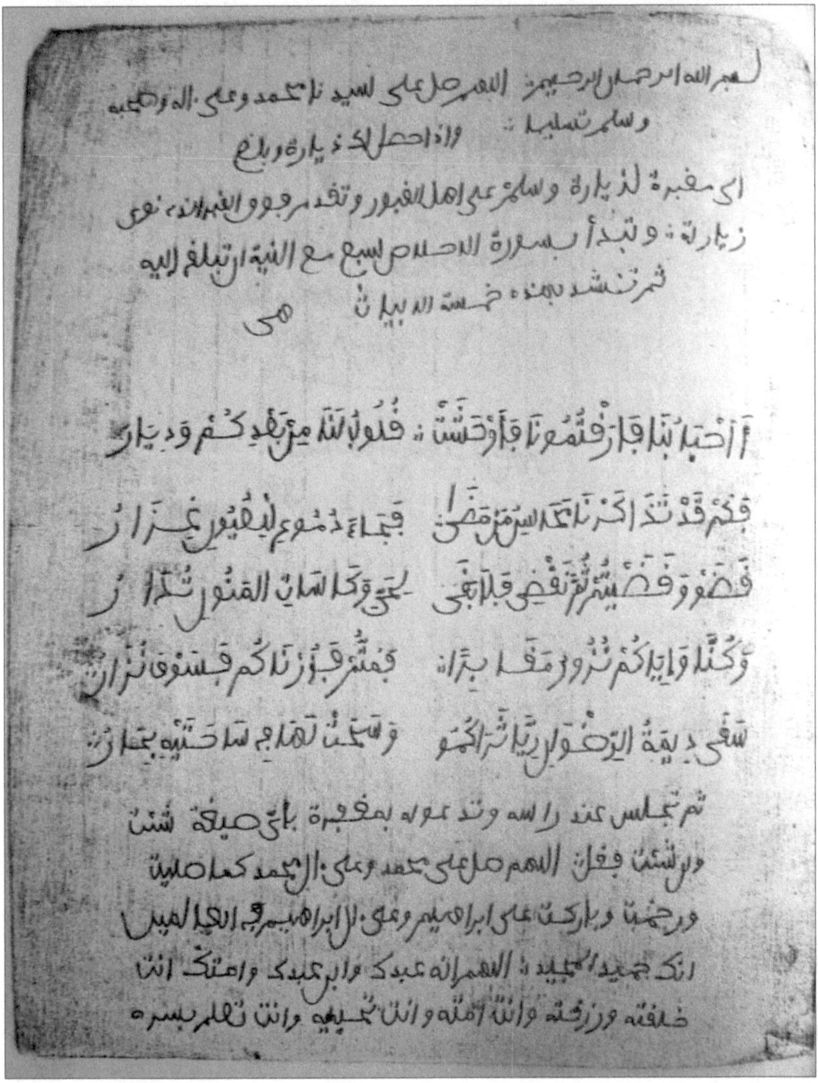

بسم الله الرحمن الرحيم اللهم صل على سيدنا محمد وعلى اله وصحبه
وسلم تسليما :: واذا حصل لك زيارة وبلغ
الى مقبرة لزيارة وسلم على اهل القبور وتقدم وجوه القبر [illegible]
زيارة :: وتبدأ بسورة الاخلاص سبع مع النية ان تبلغ اليه
ثم تنشد بهذه خمسة الابيات هي

أأحبابنا [illegible] :: فلولا الله من بعدكم [illegible]
[illegible]
[illegible]
[illegible]
[illegible]

ثم تجلس عند راسه وتدعو له بمقبرة باي صيغة شئت
وان شئت فقل اللهم صل على محمد وعلى ال محمد كما صليت
ورحمت وباركت على ابراهيم وعلى ال ابراهيم في العالمين
انك حميد مجيد :: اللهم انه عبدك وابن عبدك وابن امتك انت
خلقته ورزقته وانت امته وانت تحييه وانت تعلم بسره

FIGURE 2. "Idhā ḥaṣala laka ziyāratun," unpublished MS, University of Ghana Institute for African Studies Arabic Text 219. Courtesy Herskovits Library, Arabic Manuscripts Collection, Ghana Collection #219, Northwestern University.

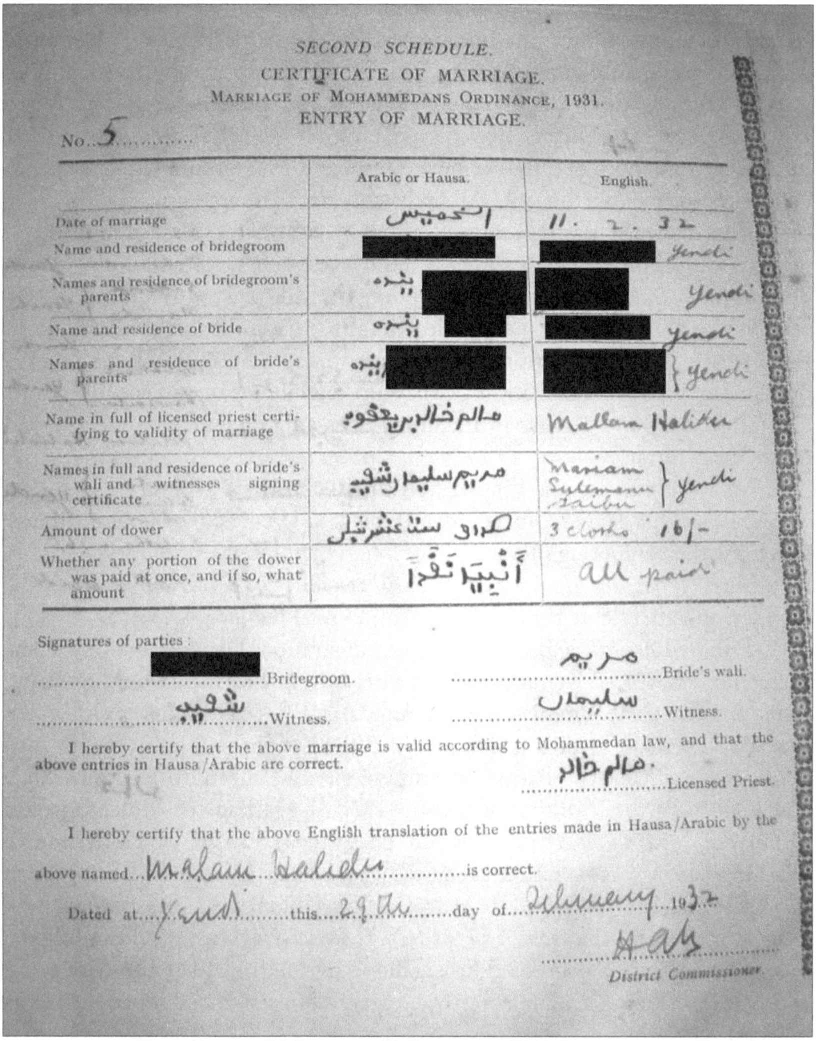

SECOND SCHEDULE.
CERTIFICATE OF MARRIAGE.
MARRIAGE OF MOHAMMEDANS ORDINANCE, 1931.
ENTRY OF MARRIAGE.

No. 5

	Arabic or Hausa.	English.
Date of marriage	الخميس	11. 2. 32
Name and residence of bridegroom		Yendi
Names and residence of bridegroom's parents		Yendi
Name and residence of bride		Yendi
Names and residence of bride's parents		Yendi
Name in full of licensed priest certifying to validity of marriage	مالم خالد بن يعقوب	Mallam Halidu
Names in full and residence of bride's wali and witnesses signing certificate	مريم سليمان شعيب	Mariam Sulemanu Saibu } Yendi
Amount of dower		3 cloths 16/-
Whether any portion of the dower was paid at once, and if so, what amount		All paid

Signatures of parties:

..................Bridegroom. مريم ....Bride's wali.

شعيب ....Witness. سليمان ....Witness.

I hereby certify that the above marriage is valid according to Mohammedan law, and that the above entries in Hausa/Arabic are correct.

مالم خالد ....Licensed Priest.

I hereby certify that the above English translation of the entries made in Hausa/Arabic by the above named...Malam Halidu...is correct.

Dated at...Yendi...this...29th...day of...February...1932.

....
District Commissioner.

FIGURE 3. Certificate of Marriage (Marriage of Mohammedans Ordinance), 28 Feb 1932 [identifying information redacted]. Courtesy of the Public Records and Archives Administration Department, Accra, Ghana, ADM 67/5/7.

Notes

Archivists in Ghana and at the Herskovits Library at Northwestern University were indispensable in providing access to source material (Hafiz Mohammed Shees's contributions went well beyond those of archivist); Bruce Hall provided crucial bibliographic references; staff at the Islamic Research and Reformation Center in Nima, Accra, and the Legal Resources Center in Mamobi, Accra, were generous with both time and information, as were other interviewees; colleagues and patient audiences at numerous talks provided valuable feedback. Felicitas Becker's penetrating questions were particularly helpful, as were those of Ohio's anonymous reviewers. Stanford University provided support for this research. All faults and errors are my own.

1. This makes it particularly fraught to venture to offer a definition of modernization projects, but some of the frequent characteristics of the family members include a sense of temporal rupture or suturing, an effort to establish explicit formal rules for legitimating authority, an acceleration in the dialectic of differentiation and dedifferentiation in consumption and production, and the generalization of virtuoso techniques of subject formation, all clustered around a sense of incompleteness, an anxiety about spatial and temporal deferral.

2. My approach here is shaped by Ivan Illich, *In the Vineyard of the Text: A Commentary to Hugh's* Didascalicon (Chicago: University of Chicago Press, 1993), but the competing literature is beyond voluminous.

3. Max Weber, *The Theory of Social and Economic Organizations,* trans. A. M. Henderson and Talcott Parsons (New York: Free Press, 1947), 363–72.

4. Public Records and Archives Administration Department of Ghana (hereafter PRAAD), Kumasi, ARG 3/1/26 D89/4: Provincial Commissioner Ashanti to District Commissioners, 21 June 1927; PRAAD, Tamale, NRG 2/6/1.

5. Two excellent studies, which provided the jumping-off point for my own reflections, are Mervyn Hiskett, "Commissioner of Police v. Musa Kommanda and Aspects of the Working of the Gold Coast Marriage of Mohammedans Ordinance," *Journal of African Law* 20, no. 2 (1976): 127–46, which deals with Muslim marriage registration specifically, and Sean Hawkins, "'The Woman in Question': Marriage and Identity in the Colonial Courts of Northern Ghana, 1907–1954," in *Women in African Colonial Histories,* ed. Jean Allman, Susan Geiger, and Nakanyike Musisi (Bloomington: Indiana University Press, 2002), 116–43, which explores marriage registration for (mostly) non-Muslims in Northern Ghana.

6. The two main collections are PRAAD, Accra, ADM 56/1/178 (for Tamale) and ADM 67/5/7 (for Yendi and Gushiago).

7. See, as samples from a surprisingly large corpus, PRAAD, Accra, CSO 21/8/63, CSO 5/1/391, CSO 5/1/597, CSO 18/12/74; PRAAD, Cape Coast, ADM 23/1/548, ADM 23/1/506; PRAAD, Kumasi, ARG 1/26/1/28 E140a/2, ARG 1/30/2/36 D86/7, ARG 1/30/2/45 D87/1, ARG 3/1/32 D89/5; PRAAD, Tamale, NRG 8/19/4, NRG 8/19/16; as well as the supporting documentation

accompanying the certificates themselves in PRAAD, Accra, ADM 56/1/178 and ADM 67/5/7. As a sample, when the CRO for the Northern Region sent around a request in September 1957 for currently active licensed Mohammedan priests, responses indicated there were four in Tamale, three in Bawku, two in Kusasi, one in Wa, one in Salaga, and none in Navrongo, Lawra, Tumu, Zuarungu, Gambaga, and other locations. After some delay to research the question, the district commissioner in Yendi reported back that "although there are many Mohammedan Priests practicing in this area, none are licensed." Still, over twenty years after the last serious administrative push to license officiants, there were still eleven who held active licenses. Furthermore, the circular itself seems to have prompted another round of registrations. Government Agent, Yendi, to Secretary to the Regional Commissioner, Tamale, 28 November 1957, PRAAD, Tamale, NRG 8/19/16.

8. See, for example, PRAAD, Kumasi, ARG 2/2/123 J265/2.

9. PRAAD, Accra, ADM 56/1/178, Mohammedan Laws of Marriage, 1913–1930. See also ADM 56/1/146 and 181.

10. Assistant District Commissioner, Kumasi, to Commissioner Northern Province, Kumasi, 2 September 1925, PRAAD, Kumasi, ARG 1/26/1/28 E140a/2. This was, of course, a motif of colonial rule in Africa more generally, and not just among the British. For a general overview see Talal Asad, "Two European Images of Non-European Rule," *Economy and Society* 2, no. 3 (1973): 263–77; and, in the French context, see Christopher Harrison, *France and Islam in West Africa, 1860–1960* (Cambridge: Cambridge University Press, 1988) and David Robinson and Jean-Louis Triaud, eds., *Le temps des marabouts: Itinéraires et stratégies islamiques en Afrique occidentale française, v. 1880–1960* (Paris: Karthala, 1997).

11. See, for instance, the discussion on an Indian case in National Archives of the United Kingdom, RG 48/1667, Proposed Marriage—Divorced Mohammedan, 1944.

12. Inter alia, Charles C. Stewart, "Southern Saharan Scholarship and the Bilad al-Sudan," *Journal of African History* 17, no. 1 (1976): 73–93; Charles C. Stewart and Bruce S. Hall, "The 'Core Curriculum' and Book Market in West Africa," in *The Trans-Saharan Book Trade: Manuscript Culture, Arabic Literacy and Intellectual History in Muslim Africa,* ed. Graziano Krätli and Ghislaine Lydon (Leiden: Brill, 2011), and Mervyn Hiskett, *A History of Hausa Islamic Verse* (London: SOAS, 1975).

13. For example, Abū Ḥāmid al-Ghazālī, "Kitāb ādāb al-nikāḥ," *Iḥyā' 'ulūm al-dīn* (Cairo: Lajnat Nashr al-Thaqāfa al-Islāmiyya 1937), 1:681–752. For an effort to revive such ideas among a more popular (Western-oriented) audience, see the useful overview in Jane Fatima Casewit, "The Spiritual Significance of Marriage in Islam," in *Voices of Islam,* ed. Vincent Cornell and Virginia Gray Henry-Blakemore, vol. 3, *Voices of Life: Family, Home, and Society* (Westport, CT: Greenwood Publishing, 2007), 77–92.

14. As I try to make clear below, the greatest danger is in anachronistically assuming such a distinction was always present and in the same way.

15. Wael B. Hallaq, *Sharīʿa: Theory, Practice, Transformations* (Cambridge: Cambridge University Press, 2009), 368–70, and Michael G. Peletz, *Islamic Modern: Religious Courts and Cultural Politics in Malaysia* (Princeton: Princeton University Press, 2002).

16. Wael B. Hallaq, *Authority, Continuity, and Change in Islamic Law* (Cambridge: Cambridge University Press, 2001), 219–35, esp. 230–31, and Haim Gerber, *Islamic Law and Culture, 1600–1840* (Leiden: Brill, 1999), chapter 6.

17. Hallaq, *Authority,* 230.

18. Roman Loimeier, *Islamic Reform and Political Change in Northern Nigeria* (Evanston, IL: Northwestern University Press, 1997), 20–32; David Robinson, "The Umarian Emigration of the Late Nineteenth Century," *International Journal of African Historical Studies* 20, no. 2 (1987): 245–70; John N. Paden, *Religion and Political Culture in Kano* (Berkeley: University of California Press, 1973), 73–83, 86–90; Adamu Mohammed Fika, *The Kano Civil War and British Over-Rule, 1882–1940* (Ibadan: Oxford University Press, 1978), chapters 5 and 6; M. G. Smith, *Government in Kano, 1350–1950* (Boulder, CO: Westview Press, 1997), 457–59.

19. See John O. Hunwick, *Arabic Literature in Africa,* vol. 2, *Writings of Central Sudanic Africa* (Leiden: Brill, 1995), 262–70. Many of these polemics were collected in Shaykh Sharif Ibrahim Salih, "Kitāb al istidhkār li-mā li-ʿulamāʾ Kanim-Barnu," unpublished MS, Northwestern University Arabic Manuscripts from West Africa (hereafter NUA), John Hunwick Collection, #209. See also Paden, *Political Culture,* 101, and, on the strength of these sentiments, 202; Muhammad S. Umar, *Islam and Colonialism: Intellectual Responses of Muslims of Northern Nigeria to British Colonial Rule* (Leiden: Brill, 2006), 36–38; John Weir Chamberlin, "The Development of Islamic Education in Kano City, Nigeria, with Emphasis on Legal Education in the 19th and 20th Centuries" (PhD diss., Columbia University, 1975), 175–99; Loimeier, *Islamic Reform,* 31–32.

20. Peletz, *Islamic Modern;* Muhammad Qasim Zaman, *The Ulama in Contemporary Islam: Custodians of Change* (Princeton: Princeton University Press, 2002); John Bowen, *Islam, Law and Equality in Indonesia: An Anthropology of Public Reasoning* (Cambridge: Cambridge University Press, 2003); Roman Loimeier, *Between Social Skills and Marketable Skills: The Politics of Islamic Education in Twentieth-Century Zanzibar* (Leiden: Brill, 2009); Felicitas Becker, *Becoming Muslim in Mainland Tanzania, 1890–2000* (Oxford: Oxford University Press, 2008).

21. Zaman, *Ulama,* 21–31.

22. Anonymous, "Khutba al-nikāh," unpublished MS, NUA, ʿUmar Falke Collection, #2776. See Paden, *Political Culture,* 101–2.

23. The specific Qur'anic verses recommended for a *khutba al-nikāh* seem to have been remarkably consistent in the Muslim world at the time, even across vast distances and across the various legal schools. They typically included 3:101–2, 4:1, and 33:70–71. See, for instance, C. Vreede-de Stuers, "Churi: The Fragile Position of Women in Muslim Marriage in North India," *Bijdragen tot de Taal-, Land- en Volkenkunde* 148, no. 2 (1992): 274.

24. Unpublished MS, University of Ghana Institute for African Studies Arabic (hereafter IAS/AR), Text 219. The exact authorship of the text is unclear.

25. My interpretation here is indebted to Wael B. Hallaq, "Model *Shurūṭ* Works and the Dialectic of Doctrine and Practice," *Islamic Law and Society* 2, no. 2 (1995): 109–34, who rejects the older, Schachtian tradition that saw such documents as consistently subordinated in theory to oral testimony.

26. For example, Amalia Zomeño, "Abandoned Wives and Their Possibility for Divorce in al-Andalus: The Evidence of the *Wathā'iq* Works," trans. Harry J. Bone, in *Writing the Feminine: Women in Arab Sources,* ed. Manuela Marin and Randi Deguilhem (London: I. B. Tauris, 2002), 111–26.

27. Stewart and Hall, "Core Curriculum," 170.

28. John O. Hunwick, "Falkeiana III: The Kitāb al-Tarsīl, An Anonymous Manual of Epistolatory and Notary Style," *Sudanic Africa* 5 (1994): 179–84. Hunwick tells us that this text also contained a sample letter "from a man to his wife, and *vice versa,*" but Hunwick himself focused on what the manual could reveal about the history of slavery (180).

29. Al-Imam Al-Hajj 'Umar, "Kitāb al-sarha al-warīqa fī 'ilm al-wathīqa," unpublished MS, IAS/AR Text #313, also reprinted in Idriss Abdul-Razak, "Alhaj Umar of Kete-Krachi: A Muslim Leader a Teacher a Poet and a Social Commentator of His Time" (M.Phil thesis, University of Ghana-Legon, 1996), 246–54; see the discussion of these by Razak, 122–23. For background on Umar, see Douglas E. Ferguson, "Nineteenth-Century Hausaland: Being a Description by Imam Imoru of the Land, Economy and Society of His People," (PhD diss., University of California, Los Angeles, 1973), 32; Hunwick, *Writings of Central Sudanic Africa;* J. A. Braimah and J. R. Goody, *Salaga: The Struggle for Power* (London: Longmans, 1967).

30. See Ann Laura Stoler, "Colonial Archives and the Arts of Governance: On the Content in the Form," in *Refiguring the Archive,* ed. Carolyn Hamilton, Verne Harris, Jane Taylor, Michele Pickover, Graeme Reid, and Razia Saleh (Cape Town: Kluwer, 2002), 82–101; Sean Hanretta, *Islam and Social Change in French West Africa: History of an Emancipatory Community* (Cambridge: Cambridge University Press, 2009), chapter 4.

31. Pace Stoler, see Sean Hawkins, *Writing and Colonialism in Northern Ghana: The Encounter between the LoDagaa and the "World of Paper"* (Toronto: University of Toronto Press, 2002), and others.

32. A point that was recognized, at least in part, early on by Hiskett, "Marriage of Mohammedans Ordinance."

33. Petition, 3 Aug 1934, Manhyia Palace Archives, Kumasi [hereafter MPA], MAG 1/2/28C, pp. 8754–5. Similar petitions were filed that year by Yardigah elders, and in 1938 the Asantehene recognized the ritual autonomy of Asante Nkramo (Twi-speaking Muslims): MPA, MAG 1/2/28C, pp. 8756–7; MAG 1/1/28, pp. 8689–8691; etc.

34. The study of the cultural politics of bureaucracy, from which I have drawn inspiration, has developed considerably in recent years. Inter alia, see Matthew S. Hull, "Documents and Bureaucracy," *Annual Review of Anthropology* 41

(2012): 251–67; Akhil Gupta, "Blurred Boundaries: The Discourse of Corruption, the Culture of Politics, and the Imagined State," *American Ethnologist* 22, no. 2 (1995): 375–402.

35. This speaks, to some degree, to Sean Hawkins's concerns about the collapsing or eliding of actual wedding practices through registration. See his "Woman in Question."

36. On the Ahmadiyya, see Humphrey J. Fisher, *Ahmadiyyah: A Study in Contemporary Islam on the West African Coast* (London: Oxford University Press for the Nigerian Institute of Social Research, 1963) and John H. Hanson, "Modernity, Religion and Development in Ghana: The Example of the Ahmadiyya Muslim Community," *Ghana Studies* 12–13 (2009–10): 55–75.

37. See Hiskett's discussion of this issue in "Marriage of Mohammedans Ordinance."

38. PRAAD, Accra, CSO 18/12/74, Native Customary Marriages.

39. Quotation from ibid. To my knowledge, this attitude toward Hausa was somewhat unusual among British administrators (and Christian missionaries) at the time. The more typical approach was to promote Hausa as a "safer" alternative to Arabic and either as more practical than English or less likely to lead to "over-education." See John Edward Philips, *Spurious Arabic: Hausa and Colonial Nigeria* (Madison: University of Wisconsin Press, 2000), 31–35; for a good overview of how linguistic cognates came to be folded into racial ideologies, see Martin Lewis, "The Vexatious History of Indo-European Studies," *GeoCurrents*, 11–17 December 2013, http://www.geocurrents.info/indo-european-origins/vexatious-history-indo-european-studies-part (accessed 4 September 2014); the situation with the "Afro-Asiatic" and "Semitic" groupings was, of course, even more vexed.

40. All quotations from PRAAD, Accra, CSO 18/12/74, Native Customary Marriages.

41. See, for example, Ousman Murzik Kobo, *Unveiling Modernity in Twentieth-Century West African Islamic Reforms* (Leiden: Brill, 2012).

42. Although in contrast to the version he identifies among inculturation-minded African Christians, it is a kind of "negative" retrodiction. V. Y. Mudimbe, *Tales of Faith: Religion as Political Performance in Central Africa* (London: Athlone Press, 1997), 13–14.

43. William E. Offei, *Family Law in Ghana* (Accra: Sebewie Publishers, 1998); Gordon R. Woodman, "Ghana Reforms the Law of Intestate Succession," *Journal of African Law* 29, no. 2 (1985): 118–28.

44. The question of who benefits from one particular inheritance scheme or another is beyond the scope of this paper, but it is in general more complex than most caricatures of Islamic law typically allow. For an introductory discussion, see J. Fenrich and T. E. Higgins, "Promise Unfulfilled: Law, Culture and Women's Inheritance Rights in Ghana," *Fordham International Law Journal* 25 (2001): 259–341.

45. The Legal Resources Centre-Ghana (LRC), "Report on Muslim Family Law Conference Held on 27th November, 2004, at Miklin Hotel, Accra," January 2005.

46. Inter alia, Louis Brenner, *Controlling Knowledge: Religion, Power, and Schooling in a Muslim Society* (Bloomington: Indiana University Press, 2001); Leonardo A. Villalón, "Rethinking Education in the Sahel: Democracy, Religious Change, and the Politics of Reform," in *Governing Africa's Changing Societies: Dynamics of Reform,* ed. Ellen Lust and Stephen Ndegwa (Boulder, CO: Westview Press, 2012).

47. Mustapha Ibrahim, *Islamic Law of Marriage: With Reference to Quran and Hadith and Special Mention of Some African Marital Practices Part One,* 5th ed. (Accra: Islamic Council for Development and Humanitarian Services, 2003), 16.

48. Hanretta, *Islam and Social Change,* chapter 4.

49. "The highest point entrusts the understanding of particulars to the lower echelons, whereas these, on the other hand, credit the highest with an understanding in regard to the universal; and thus they deceive one another." Karl Marx, *Critique of Hegel's "Philosophy of Right,"* trans. Annette Jolin and Joseph O'Malley (Cambridge: Cambridge University Press, 1970), 47.

50. The pioneering description of the importance of paperwork to management and of management to control was provided by Joanne Yates, *Control through Communication: The Rise of System in American Management,* rev. ed. (Baltimore: Johns Hopkins University Press, 1993); see also Cornelia Vismann, *Files: Law and Media Technology,* trans. Geoffrey Winthrop-Young (Stanford: Stanford University Press, 2008).

51. Nancy Rose Hunt, "Bicycles, Birth Certificates, and Clysters: Colonial Objects as Reproductive Debris in Mobutu's Zaire," in *Commodification: Things, Agency, and Identities: (The Social Life of Things Revisited),* ed. Wim M. J. van Binsbergen and Peter Geschiere (Münster: LIT Verlag, 2005), 123–41, quoting from page 124.

52. Illich, *Vineyard,* 116.

TWO

Provincializing Representation

East African Islam in the German Colonial Press

JÖRG HAUSTEIN

Colonial newspapers were an important part of the colonial project overall. Next to a variety of practical information in the form of announcements, advertisements, and reports, they provided an essential platform for mobilizing and influencing public opinion through ideological debates, the repetition of stereotypes, and the exclusion of certain voices, especially the colonized themselves. As such, the colonial press presents a peculiar type of historical source. It can hardly be trusted to reflect adequately the conditions and dynamics in the colonies, but at the same time it is quite representative of the debates and attitudes that influenced colonial perception and practice. In other words, the echo chamber of the colonial press usefully highlights the hiatus of colonization itself.

The case presented here will explore this colonial hiatus in the representation of Islam in German colonial newspapers. Though Islam was anything but marginal in German East Africa and increasingly became an index and catalyst of modernization,[1] the debates in the colonial press did not properly reflect its role, nor did they convey an adequate picture of its dynamic plurality in the German Empire's largest protectorate. To most contributors, be they colonial advocates, missionaries, settlers, or politicians, Islam was an exotic and unfamiliar religion. This unfamiliarity left them unable to account for Islam's notoriously complex configurations in Tanganyika and its entanglement with the "struggles for citizenship"[2] that had characterized the late precolonial Swahili coast. Instead, contributors to the debate tended to address the religion as a monolithic and inherently "Arab" entity, focusing on whatever of its "traits" were deemed useful in assessing its nature and place in the colonial fiction of "Greater Germany." In effect, this approach marginalized Muslims (and Muslim voices) in their political and religious agency by weighing them only in terms of their utility or threat to the colonial project. And yet, wherever Islam was discussed, it became a projection screen for all sorts of colonial aims and ideologies, and the most fierce debates about colonial strategy coalesced around this religion and its significance in the German colonial enterprise. Though factually marginalized, Islam—or certain images of Islam—was of peculiar centrality to the German East African colonial debate overall.

The following sections explore these debates in the German colonial press in a chronological fashion, from the establishment of the colony to the First World War. The analysis is centered on German newspapers that endeavored to serve as outlets for the broader public interested in colonial affairs. This excludes missionary periodicals and the emerging Swahili press (published by various missions and the German government school in Tanga), which catered to more specific constituencies and contained less controversy and debate, especially with regard to Islam. However, since the makers of these papers participated in the wider debate as well, their views and to some extent articles flowed into the broader colonial press and form a substantial part of the debates analyzed below.

Conquest: Saving Africans from "Arab Rule"

In 1885, colonial advocates formed the German East Africa Company, based on the imperial charter that the notorious explorer and colonial advocate Carl Peters had secured for his treaties with chiefs of the coastal hinterland. However, this brief phase of charter colonialism was replaced by conquest only three years later. In 1888, Bismarck pressured the sultan of Zanzibar to lease the coast to the company, opening the way for a political and economic takeover of the Tanganyikan interior. However, the company's efforts to enforce the lease immediately sparked militant resistance in parts of the coastal population, led by the merchant and planter al-Bushiri ibn-Salim al-Harthi. The company lacked the financial and logistic capabilities to subdue the population and appealed to the German Empire for help. This appeal eventually led to the formation of the Protectorate Force (*Schutztruppe*) under Herman von Wissmann and the full conquest of the coast and, gradually, the hinterland. The German Empire then secured its gains in further treaties with the sultan and with Britain before finally taking over operations from the German East Africa Company on New Year's Day 1891.

The establishment of colonial interest groups and their press paralleled these events. In 1887 a merger of different colonial associations resulted in the foundation of the German Colonial Society (Deutsche Kolonialgesellschaft),[3] and from January 1888 the society published the weekly paper *Deutsche Kolonialzeitung*.[4] It reached a print run of nineteen thousand copies by the end of 1891, and thirty thousand at the turn of the century. These numbers roughly aligned with the society's membership figures, which is indicative of its primary readership.[5] Altogether, the German Colonial Society was an endeavor of the upper and upper-middle class. Half of its membership consisted of businessmen and merchants, and another third was made up of government officials, military officers, judicial professionals, teachers, and ministers.[6] Therefore, although the society sought to mobilize the wider public for the colonial enterprise, it is clear that most of its actors belonged to those with an economic or political interest in colonialism.

It is hardly surprising then, that the narratives about the East African coast paralleled the conquest endeavors by the German East Africa Company, mostly by envisioning a necessary end to "Arab" rule of East Africa, which included strongly hostile tones against Islam as well. The first such article in the *Deutsche Kolonialzeitung* appeared in its second month (new edition) and was penned by the editor of the paper, Gustav Meinecke. He incorporated excerpts from a racially charged lecture by the Egyptologist Heinrich Karl Brugsch,[7] who contended that after a long period of Hamitic societies in Africa, Semites had now taken control in the form of Arabs and needed to be replaced. Meinecke quotes him as follows:

> Now the hour has come, in which Japheth commences his cultural mission. This is the spirit of the colonial endeavors of our time. Still the Semites, the Arabs, have great power. They know the land, all roads, and footpaths, they are familiar with the Negroes, they are merchants, soldiers, and missionaries all at once, who together with Islam also spread the hate against Christians and Europeans. The battle will not be easy, and the war requires the joint powers of all. But the task is a noble one, worthy of the best, worthy also of German blood, even though it pains us to see it poured out.[8]

Meinecke then takes Brugsch's racial sentiments to their colonial-political conclusions: he points to the ubiquitous presence of "Arabism" in Africa, diagnoses a rising tide of "Mohammedan fanaticism," and contends that East Africa would be strategically well-placed for curbing Arab rule over the whole continent while rescuing "Negroes" from slavery and gradually "nurturing" them into Christian civilization.

Similar articles followed. In September 1888, the *Deutsche Kolonialzeitung* printed an article by Hermann von Wissmann arguing for the importance of a planned expedition into Equatoria to "rescue" the (originally German) governor of the Egyptian province, Eduard Schnitzler, alias Emin Pasha, from the pressures of Mahdist forces, which at the time were perceived as the pinnacle of a violent, expansionist Islam.[9] Wissmann, who soon would be tasked by the German Empire with suppressing the "Arab Revolt" on the East African coast, painted a dramatic geopolitical picture. "If Emin Pasha falls, the Arabs of the South and the Mahdists will shake hands. The Sudan, together with the lakes region and the Eastern Congo state will become a massive territory under Arab rule."[10] This connection, he envisioned, would result in an influx of ammunition, increased ivory exports, massive slave hunting, and an interior inaccessible to Europeans because "a combination of religion and common interests would create cohesion among the rulers of the vast lands, the Arabs."

This geopolitical notion of "Arabdom" and its conflation with Islam also allowed for the incorporation of missionary voices in a common project aimed at supplanting Muslim hegemony. Several articles followed Cardinal Lavigerie's proposition to form a band of Christian mercenaries to contest Arab control and battle slave trade in Africa.[11] On the Protestant side, the inspector of the Berlin Missionary Society, Alexander Merensky, took the Mahdi Uprising, the predicaments of Emin Pascha, and an Arab attack on Scottish missionaries near Lake Malawi as signs of a "Mohammedan counter-thrust against Christian civilization" and concluded that "the real enemy of Christian culture in Africa is the tyrannical and violent Mohammedanism."[12] It is noteworthy that even missionaries framed the Christian-Muslim conflict in terms of political control rather than religious adherence, arguing not for conversion efforts but military actions. Significantly, none of the articles mentions Muslim converts among Africans; rather, they point out that "Arabs loot, murder, and scorch" but do not make converts because "a population turned Muhammadan does not provide slaves anymore."[13]

Once the news had emerged about the resistance on the coast, this narrative only needed extension. Articles now projected a "psychological connection" between the "Arab Uprising" against the Germans, the Sudanese Mahdi, and the slave raider Tippu Tipp, contending that a "great Arab movement" was "pressing for the decision, whether the cross or crescent should rule over the black continent."[14] Even less militant observers, who were advocating an alliance with the "Arab element," did not contest this notion of a monolithic Arab rule and influence in Africa.[15]

This nexus of geopolitics, Christian-Muslim antagonism, and racism was extremely useful for the colonial conquest narrative, especially for pressuring a reluctant German government into military action. Friedrich Fabri, who was a former mission inspector, a prime architect of the colonial movement, and an intermittent editor of the *Deutsche Kolonialzeitung*, built the short-lived German antislavery movement around these sentiments, establishing a broad coalition of politicians, military officers, industrialists, merchants, Protestant and Catholic clergy, as well as a wider public audience. This effort was flanked by the *Deutsche Kolonialzeitung*[16] and became part of Fabri's strategic pitch to Bismarck to use the antislavery coalition to end the Kulturkampf and move the (Catholic) Center Party, the main opposition in the Reichstag, to support colonial causes.[17] Fabri's maneuvers were successful, and the Center Party introduced a resolution into the Reichstag calling on the emperor to act and pledging full parliamentary support. The resolution passed with a large majority and provided a fig leaf for the government to request resources and prepare conquest.

Although this broad platform, built on the conflation of Arab rule, slavery eradication efforts, Christian-Muslim antagonism, and geopolitical calculations, proved politically instrumental for colonial advocates, it was also a wholly inadequate reading of the situation at stake in that it relied on entirely fictional notions of Islam and "Arabdom." There was no connection, "psychological" or otherwise, between the Mahdi and the Omani networks of East Africa. There certainly was no common ground between them in Islam. The eschatological claims of the Mahdi were scorned by the religious establishment in Egypt and elsewhere, and there is no indication of them being accepted by the predominately Shāfiʿī population of littoral East Africa. Furthermore, their Omani rulers were Ibāḍī Muslims and cultivated their religious distinction from Sunni Islam, not even accepting converts. Similarly, by dubbing al-Bushiri's military resistance the "Arab Uprising," the Germans completely misread the political dynamics beneath the opposition they faced. In the decades prior to the arrival of the Germans, Tanganyika had seen a progressive encroachment of Omani military and administrative power, which altered the established trading networks and socioeconomic relations between Shirazi patricians, Indian merchants, and Arab traders of various origins (Hadramaut, Comoro, Zanzibar). As Glassman pointed out, the German colonizers were tolerated as long as they were seen as challenging Omani domination. However, with the treaty of 1888, Germans were perceived as clients of the sultan, and now their former allies turned against them, simultaneously contesting German and Omani authority over the coast.[18] The uprising, in other words, indicated the precariousness of Omani Arab hegemony, rather than "Arab" leadership, and was rooted in a social contest that pitted diverse religious and ethnic identities—Ibāḍī, Shāfiʿī, Sufi, Swahili, Arab—against each other. These political and economic dynamics were not lost on all contemporary observers, as Rochus Schmidt's account from 1892 reveals.[19] However, such an analysis did not find an echo in the colonial press during the conquest years.

It is clear that at this point the *Deutsche Kolonialzeitung* was part of a larger mobilizing platform that transcended the confines of colonial interest groups. The most important tool for building this platform was the conflation of geopolitical, economic, humanitarian (antislavery), and religious causes, based on the inverse projection of an Arab, Muslim, slave-trading rule in Africa. This narrative certainly attributed much political significance to Islam but misread its religious capacity. This monolithic notion of Islam as an anti-European power and threat left no room for its plurality and fragmented nature, nor for exploring its multifarious connections with people's livelihood, practices, and interests. Interestingly, this monochromatic notion of Islam and its conflation with racism and geopolitical calculations would persist, whereas the broad conquest coalition soon broke apart over conflicting strategic ideas of how to integrate Islam in colonial governance.

Governance: Controlling and Integrating Islam

The progress of the German military conquest in 1889 and the delimitation of interest spheres in the Anglo-German Agreement of 1890 entailed a gradual shift in the colonial press away from conquest narratives and toward issues of colonial governance. In 1890, the government also commenced publication of its colonial gazette *Deutsches Kolonialblatt.* Each issue consisted of an official and nonofficial part, with the former containing laws, decrees, and other administrative business, and the latter providing news, travel reports, literature reviews, and similar material. The *Deutsches Kolonialblatt* also published the colonies' annual reports in separate issues. Overall, it professed the German government's rationale of a gradual, well-planned, and carefully executed process. Islam is only mentioned in passing in a few articles and typically portrayed as a facet of a multicultural colony under "just and fair" German rule.[20] The more ideological debates about Islam and the governing philosophies were left to the *Deutsche Kolonialzeitung.*

The gradual turn toward issues of governance did not immediately displace the earlier opinions about "Arab rule" and Islam. Some of the geopolitical ideas about the need to curb Arab influence lingered on, initially in connection with the expansion of colonial control into the interior,[21] and later emanating mostly from missionary circles.[22] However, the majority of articles soon were concerned with how best to govern the "Arab element." The erstwhile and now-defeated competitor for hegemony over the region was now repositioned as a potential intermediary of government, an "element" to be made useful rather than marginalized. Missionaries tended to disagree.

Significantly, this entailed a change of focus from geopolitics to religious creed and observance, while retaining the monolithic, totalizing notion of Islam. An example of this can be found in an exchange about Muslim "fatalism." In 1890, the *Deutsche Kolonialzeitung* published a letter by the botanist and explorer Georg Schweinfurth, who reacted to an earlier article advocating cooperation with Arabs. Whereas Schweinfurth contended that one must "stop Arabdom with weapons," he nevertheless saw a governing option in the "exaggerated Monotheism" of Islam, "paralyzing all of man's self-determination and willpower."[23] One must avoid the "illusion, that we could permanently make Mohammedans our genuine friends," but because of their religious "fatalism," they would gravitate toward the victorious power. Two issues later the Orientalist Leo Hirsch reacted by warning against a derogatory misunderstanding of "Mohammedan fatalism," for as Germans had found out, Muslims will participate in the shaping of history. His recipe of success rather consisted of "strictness, justice, respect for traditions, most of all the religion of Islam and its institutions, friendly relations with respected and educated Mohammedans."[24]

One important reference point for reframing the governance of Islam in terms of religious difference was the institution of law. An article from 1890 asserted that whereas the earlier coastal resistance was geopolitical rather than religious, the German governance of "Arabs" must now be based on the integration of "Islamitic law and its legal concepts."[25] Similarly, an editorial about a government memorandum on East Africa made the criticism that the "religious element" was insufficiently taken into consideration and advocated studying legal precepts to further political integration: "It is questionable whether the Arabs as Muslims will ever fully come to terms with the Christian German rule, but political prudence should prompt us, not to impose our law on them, but define the provincial Shafi'ite law."[26] Even the earlier notions of a cultural clash between "Christian civilization" and "Muhammadan rule" were now rearticulated within this juridical framework. The legal historian Conrad Bornhak opined that German laws could not be applied to Muslims on account of the close connection between religion and legal matters, citing polygamy and inheritance as examples. He concluded that "keeping the Islamitic law for Mohammedans is not a matter of practicability, but one of freedom of religious practice."[27] With many European observers, he thus assumed that religious affiliation unambiguously determined the actions of East African Muslims, leaving little room for the diversity of Muslim practice. Like the earlier geopolitical narrative, this characterization of the Muslim population in terms of religious difference failed to account for the plurality of Islam and the various ethnic, political, and legal terms defining adherence. The press was not alone in this, as the emerging scholarship operated with similar notions. In 1897 the Orientalist Eduard Sachau published his book *Muhammadan Law According to Shafi'ite Teaching,* which was specifically aimed at the situation in East Africa.[28] On the basis of a very thin exploratory survey,[29] Sachau was satisfied that the majority of the East African population was Shāfiʿīite, and rather than collecting and commenting on a plurality of local sources, he based his book on an Egyptian commentary, which was not mentioned in the survey data from East Africa. Sachau thereby exemplified the "scripturalism" of European Islamicists of the period, who assumed that they could understand Muslim precepts and practices from a handful of presumed canonical texts. It was not until later that Carl-Heinrich Becker criticized this approach as being far removed from the legal pluralities and practices on the ground.[30] Meanwhile the German authorities in East

Africa learned the finer lines of Islamic differentiation, such as between Ismāʿīli and Ithnāʿashari Khojas,[31] and some colonial officers drew on legal assessors from multiple Muslim communities when making pronunciations in "indigenous law."[32]

In addition to the failure of the colonial press to account for the plurality of Islam, its tendency to address the governance of Muslims in religious terms was oblivious to the fact that the demarcation of religious identities was hardly a decisive factor in motivating or hindering cooperation. From what the archives contain about the collaboration of local elites—such as the influential planter, tradesman, and politician Sulayman bin Nasr al-Lamki, or the Indian trader and wealthy donor Sewa Haji Paroo—the most important points of convergence and conflict were around matters of real estate, political influence, and economic gains, whereas there is hardly any discussion of religious sensibilities nor any evidence that German efforts to integrate Islam were a decisive factor.[33] The same could be said of upwardly mobile African elites, like Mtoro bin Bakari, the well-known Swahili lecturer and author of *Desturi za Wasuaheli*.[34] Coming from a respected Zaramo Muslim family, he worked for the Germans as a tax collector and from 1900 as a Swahili teacher at the School of Oriental Languages in Berlin. He did not understand the German modernizing project to be in contradiction with Islam; rather, his later conflict with German authorities came on the grounds of racism when, after his marriage to Bertha Hilske in 1904, he was subject to extensive discrimination and simultaneously deprived of his livelihood in Berlin and of the possibility to return to East Africa with his wife.

The German colonial papers did not account for such political complexities of collaboration but rather combined their monolithic notions of Islam with an equally inadequate notion of race. In 1895, the *Deutsche Kolonialzeitung* printed an article titled "Mission or Islam?" criticizing the German geographer Siegfried Passarge, who had argued for relying on the "civilizing endeavors" of Muslims rather than "Christian humanity," which he felt would corrupt Africans. The article countered that Islam would rather inhibit racial development. "In our opinion, the biggest danger in the spread of Islam in our colonies is that it makes the Negro all but unsuitable for developing a higher mental culture."[35] Passarge answered that he considered race to be the fundamental parameter, with religion adapting to racial abilities rather than the other way around. As the "product of the national character of the majority of oriental nations," Islam was more suitable to Africa. Whereas both Christianity and Islam would be "reduced to fetishism in the head of the Negro," only Islam was "able to survive outwardly."[36] Furthermore, Passarge considered Islam easier to control because it would manifest open hostility, whereas "fetish Christianity" was a "hidden enemy." In a short rejoinder, the paper's editor Gustav Meinecke countered that Christianity was still the preferable instrument of control, although the "Christian Negro" would never evolve upward to "Germanic Christianity."

Overall, then, commentators on Islam presented "authentically Muslim Arabs" as if their behavior was determined by their religious adherence, whereas Africans were considered intrinsically unable to become genuine monotheists (Muslim or Christian) in thought or action. In both cases, Islam was considered only in terms of its relation to colonial powers and interests, while the actual complexities of Muslim existence, political allegiance, and cultural transfers were eclipsed by these ideological debates. Interestingly, this produced a kind of marginality of the medium itself on two fronts. First, while the colonial government was learning some of the complexities of Muslim existence, the analyses in the colonial press remained detached from the political realities on the ground and no longer had the kind of impact on policy as before. Second, the ideological debates effected a fragmentation of discourse, especially between the colonial press and missionary circles. This was already visible in the 1890s in heated discussions about the merits of secular government schools, which refrained from teaching religion in order to recruit children of Muslim notables.[37] In the following years, the underlying conflict between the Christian civilizing project and settler colonialism widened and more or less took over the newspaper debates about Islam.

Crisis: Conflicting Aims and "Islamic Danger"

The first decade of the twentieth century was arguably one of crisis for the colonial enterprise. Economically, German East Africa was failing on a large scale, from delayed infrastructure projects to struggling plantations. To make matters worse for planters, the long era of Governor Rechenberg (1906–1912) came with a significant shift in strategy: instead of a settler colony he promoted a trading colony, looking to generate an indigenous economic growth for trading profits. This led to continuous clashes between Rechenberg and the settler associations, who could not solicit the support of the governor for their various schemes for solving the "labor issue" by coercing subsistence farmers into wage-labor relations.[38]

Militarily, these were years of crisis as well. In 1905 the Maji-Maji Uprising caught the government by surprise and was "pacified" by a strategy of scorched earth, leading to a hunger crisis in 1907, which added to the scores of African victims.[39] In 1908, "Mecca letters" emerged in numerous places of the colony, admonishing Muslims for having been unfaithful and warning against collaboration with "unbelievers," thereby playing into a German fear of another uprising.[40] These German East African developments came alongside the more publicized Herero and Nama Uprisings in South-West Africa. These political conflicts led to the dissolution of the German parliament in 1906 and to subsequent elections, thereby cementing the sense of colonial crisis.

For Africans in this period, conversion to either Islam or Christianity increasingly became part of forming new identities in the aftermath of slavery, conquest, and the failure of the Maji-Maji. To missionaries, though, the spread of Islam embodied the real possibility of failure, especially given the fact that they had little or no success in winning converts from Muslims. Settlers, interested in labor only, often found themselves in a conflict of interest with the missions and tended to sneer at their converts as *Hosenneger* (trousered negro). Administrators, meanwhile, were overwhelmingly employing Muslims as government intermediaries and soldiers and cared less about their ethnic and religious affiliations as long as they had the required linguistic and educational background, which Christian converts often lacked. Thus the different European interest groups were pursuing their factional needs, often in conflict with one another, and the evolving role of Islam in the renegotiation of social relations was portrayed in very different ways.

The increasing dissent about colonial governance was accompanied by a pluralization of the press, both in Germany and in the colony. In 1900, the *Koloniale Zeitschrift* emerged, claiming to be an outlet for a rational economic outlook and against any sort of ideological debate. To them, colonies were about economic gains only, not a national or humanitarian cause. Therefore, they opposed anything that would not immediately pay off, including large infrastructure projects such as railways. This outlook put the new paper in direct competition with the *Deutsche Kolonialzeitung*, especially as the former editor of the *Deutsche Kolonialzeitung*, Gustav Meinecke, now served as publisher of the

Koloniale Zeitschrift. Moreover, in 1903 the *Koloniale Zeitschrift* became the mouthpiece of the German Colonial League (*Deutscher Kolonialbund*), which heralded racial supremacy and settler interests and was a rival organization to the older German Colonial Society. In the following years, numerous other print outlets emerged, either related to new colonial organizations or focusing on special interest groups.[41] By the turn of the century, local newspapers began to emerge in East Africa as well. In 1899, the first issue of the *Deutsch-Ostafrikanische Zeitung* was published in Dar es Salaam, owing its financial viability to a substantial print concession from the colonial government. It also distributed the local government gazette, *Amtlicher Anzeiger.* When the paper began to turn against Rechenberg's policy and sided with settlers and planters, the governor founded the rival outlet *Deutsch-Ostafrikanische Rundschau* in 1908. Always in conflict with its rivals, it never reached the popularity of the *Deutsch-Ostafrikanische Zeitung,* which finally bought it up in 1912.[42] In Tanga, the advertising gazette *Anzeigen für Tanga* (published since 1901) was relaunched as the *Usambara-Post* in 1904. It was produced and printed in the government school in Tanga, and as an outlet of settler interests, it similarly ran into conflict with Rechenberg. Both the *Deutsch-Ostafrikanische Zeitung* and the *Usambara-Post* included a number of supplements. The *Usambara-Post* also distributed the monthly Swahili paper *Kiongozi,* which was produced by the German government school in Tanga and had a respectable print run of three thousand copies.

With this proliferation of the print press, the scope of articles relating to Islam increased, especially since the newspapers interacted with one another and with the German daily press. There were also more articles about Muslim customs and festivals, especially in the *Deutsch-Ostafrikanische Zeitung*'s local news. Islam here came into view not as a global foe or an instrument of social control, but as an apolitical part of folklore. Ramadan was mentioned every year, sometimes in colorful descriptions of the festivities, other times in dismissive tones, such as by noting that the feast hardly did justice to the idea of a religious-spiritual purification, or portraying it as a trial of German patience with Muslim servants.[43] Other holidays, like the Eid al-Adha or the Shi'ite Day of Ashura, were mentioned less consistently. The paper also reported on the visits of the Aga Khan, head of the Indian Ismāʿīli Khoja community, initially placing high hopes in his support and later criticizing the substantial financial gifts he collected, which allegedly pushed Indian merchants to the brink of bankruptcy.[44] Altogether, these local articles demonstrated a shift in the perception of the former Arab rule. Whether in commemorating al-Bushiri's defeat, printing excerpts from the autobiography of the former slave trader Tippu Tipp, or reminiscing about the town of Bagamoyo, the articles did not rehash the old geopolitical ideas about "Arabs" and their religion. Rather, they lamented the decline of the "Arab element" and contended that religion had never played a role in the conquest battles.[45]

This, however, did not entail a more nuanced notion of Islam, as can be seen by the extensive debate that ran under the title "Islamic Danger" ("Islamgefahr"). This was a continuous and controversial discussion that—at least for most of the first decade—ran along the fault line between missionaries and settlers. When in 1903 the German newspaper *Tägliche Rundschau* published an article, "The Islamic Danger in East Africa," that projected a pan-Islamic African uprising against Europeans, the *Deutsch-Ostafrikanische Zeitung* reacted with a scathing editorial. It contended that the article came from Catholic missionary circles seeking support for their cause and wanting to dominate, and that the information about Islam in East Africa and the fears of an uprising were unfounded. Instead, the article praised the government's endeavors to raise "useful citizens" without regard for religion and concluded, "At any rate, a so-called Islamic danger can better be prevented by such measures than by one-sided religious efforts, which, as they aim to suppress another faith, only foment hate between the races and cannot even be called Christian."[46] This was followed by an apologetic reply by the Catholic bishop of Dar es Salaam, Cassian Spieß, to which the *Deutsch-Ostafrikanische Zeitung* reacted by printing a number of letters to the editor, refuting Spieß's reply and referring to the Kulturkampf as a similar point of conflict between religious and national interests.[47] These types of exchanges reflected the rising conflicts of interest between missionaries and settlers in these years. Settlers were critical of missionary education because they felt it did not help raise a compliant labor force, while missionaries criticized the settler population for child labor and concubinage. Both sides tended to compete for the same segment of the population, namely, young, able men.

The matter fully escalated when, in the second German Colonial Congress in 1905, missionaries succeeded in passing a resolution that called for the full support of missionary causes in countering the "spread of Islam and Arabic culture." The *Koloniale Zeitschrift* ran several articles against this resolution, ending with a seething declaration by the Colonial

League, titled "Against the New Crusade." The declaration warned of the "vague idea, or better, empty phrase of an Islamic danger, recently raised up on missionary banners"[48] and refuted notions of a spread of Islam and Muslim disloyalty, instead portraying missionaries as the real political danger to the colony. Quoting the Qur'an's sura 60, which asserts that Muslims must remain peaceful when treated justly, the declaration accused missions of inviting Muslim hostility with their "crusade" and concluded that "one could almost label the conduct of missions as politically felonious if it was not all too clear, that they only need the fiction of the political danger of Islâm in order to plausibly justify their existence before the government and donor circles in Germany, as well as to attribute their recent glaring failures to other reasons but their own mistakes."[49] Articles in the *Deutsch-Ostafrikanische Zeitung* as well as in the *Deutsche Kolonialzeitung* offered similar comments. The timing could not have been worse for missionary interests. The Rhenish Mission in German South-West Africa had been accused of siding with the Herero and Nama Uprisings, and the rise of Ethiopian churches in South Africa was cited as proof that revolutionary sentiment would sooner arise from Christian converts than from the spread of Islam. Moreover, the above-cited declaration did not fail to point out that the Maji-Maji Uprising had turned against nearby missions, whereas most Muslim chiefs had remained loyal, together with the Arab population.

Although relations between the colonial press and missions had been strained before, they now turned outright hostile. The *Koloniale Zeitschrift* in particular ran mission-critical articles in almost every issue in 1905 and early 1906. The "labor issue" became part of this debate as well, as missions were accused of not teaching the "Negroes" a proper work ethic and preventing them working on plantations during the hunger crisis. This also coincided with a tendency to downplay slavery, which had been so instrumental in forming the common platform for conquest. The scale of slave raiding was downplayed, and slavery itself praised as a more or less benevolent social institution.[50] The contrast with the years around 1890 is evident: Muslims had turned from foes into allies. What had not changed is the oblique identification of Islam with Arabness.

The earlier common notion of a Christian-Muslim antagonism had become a missionary claim only, whereas settlers vociferously rejected the Christian "civilizing mission." This also affected the racist assessments about religious capabilities of Africans. It was now universally agreed in the colonial press that Islam would be the more suitable religion for the "native" inhabitants of the colony. Since the "Negro" lacked all religious depth, articles contended, both Christianity and Islam would be nothing but a thin outer coating,[51] but the Christian teaching of universal brotherhood would fall on "especially inappropriate ground."[52] Moreover, Islam was deemed closer to the "this-worldly attitude" of the African race, being a "lower" religion than Christianity, but still preferable to "heathendom."[53] Such racist assertions transported a number of derogatory ideas about Islam as well, as the following lecture excerpt, printed in the *Koloniale Zeitschrift*, demonstrates:

> Gentlemen, if you agree with the characterization of the Negro I gave earlier, then you too will have the impression that in his whole predisposition, the Negro is made for Muhammadanism. His passive surrender to nature and its treasures but also horrors, his animosity to actively shape his fate are an unconscious confession to Kismet, an unconscious denial of free will. His rationalism, which asks with each thing: is it edible? lets him see the locust-free and shady paradise of Mohammed as a desirable goal, as the true redemption from the imperfections of life.[54]

However, toward the end of the first decade, the debate on "Islamic danger" began to shift again. This change was embodied perhaps most visibly by the *Koloniale Zeitschrift*, which went from being a vocal outlet of mission criticism to printing a regular missionary column in 1910. This column now contained the kind of articles the paper had railed against before.[55] Furthermore, when the third Colonial Congress of 1910 passed a similar resolution as in 1905, the *Koloniale Zeitschrift* simply reported on this and left the only comment to a missionary letter praising the resolution.[56] The *Deutsch-Ostafrikanische Zeitung* also began to alert its readership to the "Islamic danger" in 1910, at first using it to slight Rechenberg's plans of military reform, and later printing an alarmist article from the *Tägliche Rundschau*, also without editorial criticism.[57]

It is difficult to assess whether this change in perception was due to the noticeable quantitative increase of Muslim affiliation in the colony, the emergence of the "Mecca letters" in 1908, or a stronger missionary lobby. However, it likely reflected the wider public sentiment in Germany, since an increasing "Islamic danger" narrative is also visible in the colonial archives.[58] At any rate, the papers continued to operate with an understanding of Islam that failed to account for its plurality and the central dynamics of its spread in the colony. As Felicitas Becker has shown, the spread of Islam toward the end of the German colonial rule was connected to various socioeconomic and political changes between the coast and the hinterland and should be explained in these local terms.[59] This perspective was already incipient in parts of the German archive. Extensive local reporting, first on the "Mecca letters" in 1908/9 and later in reaction to a proposal to curb the spread of Islam, provided details about a number of local dynamics and concerns, which were not reflected by the discussion in the colonial press.[60] Furthermore, the emergence of the Sufi *ṭuruq* (orders), especially the Qādirīya, challenged the traditional Islamic authorities and created new religious and socioeconomic networks.[61] The Qādirīya, also was instrumental for the spread of the "Mecca letters," but neither the colonial authorities nor the colonial press reflected or even seemed to be aware of this additional layer of Islamic diversity.[62]

Therefore, even in the years of colonial crisis, the colonial press continued to address Islam as a monolithic religious entity, weighing its utility for colonial governance. This was true of both sides of the "Islamic danger" debate and in much of public sentiment. The ideological debates on both sides had little influence on the actual colonial governance, as the vitriolic exchanges of the Rechenberg era indicate. Instead, the fragmentation into various colonial press outlets and interest groups arguably exacerbated the marginal role of the colonial press in its perception of Islam and beyond. If this is the case, then the cessation of the missionary-settler conflict toward 1910 can be seen as a pivot toward a more mainstream and less fragmented perception of Islam, which made concessions to the missionary narrative and reacted to the changing perception of the political potentiality of Islam in the wake of the "Mecca letters."

War: The Return of Geopolitics

The First World War brought serious disruptions to the colonial press. The *Deutsches Kolonialblatt* and the *Deutsche Kolonialzeitung* reduced their publications to one issue per month, and the *Koloniale Zeitschrift* printed only eighteen irregular "war issues" until 1918. The *Deutsch-Ostafrikanische Zeitung* continued to publish two issues per week for about two years, moving production to Morogoro in August 1915 and finally ceasing publication with the capture of the town one year later.

More importantly, the war also led to another shift in the colonial press's portrayal of Islam. The earlier alignment to the "Islamic danger" narrative was replaced by articles weighing the religion's utility for war, lauding the support of Muslims for the Germans or discussing the possibility of a pan-Islamic uprising against the Entente in light of the jihād fatwa of the Ottoman Shaykh al-Islām.[63]

Although the geopolitical fantasies of a pan-Islamic support for Germany did not materialize, the *Koloniale Zeitschrift* contended in a feature article at the end of 1915 that the war would have lasting implications for Christian-Muslim relations in the colony:

> However, the events of this war will necessarily lead to Islam no longer being seen as something hostile, which must be destroyed under all circumstances. It will be reckoned as a brother of Christianity, albeit a stepbrother. . . . The Mohammedans have put up a magnificent fight in this war. . . . Islam has had an impact here that Christian missions cannot have, and perhaps should not have in accordance with their character.[64]

The article called for an end to all criticisms of Islam-friendly German policies and advocated for religious neutrality in the colony. Furthermore, returning to the issue of labor shortage versus personal freedom, it called for finding "a compromise between the Islamitic and Christian world view" on "labor compulsion" for Africans, which would sit somewhere between the passages on slavery in the Qur'an and Christian ideals of liberty.[65]

As in the colonial conquest narrative, these statements interwove the vectors of geopolitics, Christian-Muslim antagonism, and racism, but in a completely inverted manner. Pan-Islamism was now seen as a geopolitical asset, whereas Christianity was deemed not capable of yielding the same mobilizing power. The antagonism between the two religions was to be replaced by neutral relations between "stepbrothers," and some sort of "compromise" between the two seemed necessary for the "cultural elevation" of Africans. Slavery, accordingly, was no longer a cause for intervention but a necessary counterweight to Christian humanitarian causes.

Conclusion: Provincializing Colonial Representation

As the content and the vicissitude of the Islam debate in the colonial newspapers show, the various representations of this religion had very little base in the social and political realities of German East Africa, but rather catered to the echo chambers of German colonial politics. As such, Islam was constantly subjugated to other colonial rationalities, such as garnering support for military conquest, coercion into wage labor, Christianization, or concerns about political stability. No matter how the debate turned, the parameters by which Islam was measured in these contexts quite constantly remained a mix of geopolitics, racism, and Christian-Muslim antagonism. This narrative left little room for more complex readings of Islam or for other modes of Muslim existence, just as the colonial press excluded Muslim voices. In this way, all sides of the argument about Islam in the colonial press rehashed and reinforced stereotypes about Islam, arguably with lasting effects on the German perception of this religion.[66]

These observations allow little direct insight into Muslim practices and identity politics in German East Africa, but they highlight a certain inadequacy or marginality of the German debate itself, the analysis of which may form an important part of postcolonial historiography. As Dipesh Chakrabarty has argued in *Provincializing Europe*, it is "the partly opaque relationship we call 'difference'" that allows historians to produce a more adequate reading of the relationship between "non-Western histories and European thought."[67] Colonial practices and ideologies produce teleological narratives of history, ostensibly necessary histories, which seek to subjugate and assimilate historical elements under their logic. This certainly was the case with the representations of Islam in the German colonial press under the various rubrics of geopolitics, racism, and Christian-Muslim conflict. However, inasmuch as these subjugated elements of history are not inherently forward-looking to the teleological trajectory of such projections and have other historical potentialities, they disrupt and interpunctuate the colonial logic. As the various changes in the colonial debates indicate, Islam was never exhaustively represented by the various media narratives. Moreover, the emergence of "Mecca letters" or the Ottomoan jihād fatwa are clear examples of how German press narratives and debates were disrupted by "incompatible" events.

The exploration of these grounds of historical difference subverts assertions of marginality and centrality in colonial history and brings historians closer to the site of historical struggle. Religions play an important role in this subversion, as is demonstrated by the German failure to adequately capture the dynamics of Islam. Moreover, religions themselves provide narratives of history and contest colonial teleologies, as is exemplified by the following Swahili poem, which subjects the German colonizers to the power of a different historical logic:

Oh God, my Lord, the Glorious who does wonders.

The One who possesses no company. He is the only God, Beneficent.

The One who removes and places, in Heaven and on Earth:

Give strength to the Germans, there should be nobody else.[68]

Notes

1. Felicitas Becker, *Becoming Muslim in Mainland Tanzania, 1890–2000* (Oxford: Oxford University Press, 2008).

2. Felicitas Becker, "Freeborn Villagers: Islam and the Local Uses of Cosmopolitan Connections in the Tanzanian Countryside," in *Cosmopolitans in Muslim Contexts: Perspectives from the Past,* ed. Derryl N. MacLean and Sikeena Karmali Ahmed (Edinburgh: Edinburgh University Press, 2012), 10–30.

3. See Klaus J. Bade, *Friedrich Fabri und der Imperialismus in der Bismarckzeit: Revolution—Depression—Expansion,* 2nd, internet edition (Osnabrück, no publisher [original Atlantis Verlag, Freiburg] 2005), especially 369–512, https://www.imis.uni-osnabrueck.de/fileadmin/4_Publikationen/PDFs/BadeFabri.pdf.

4. The *Deutsche Kolonialzeitung* had originally been founded in 1884 by one of the associations merged in the German Colonial Society. It was then relaunched as the national mouthpiece of colonial interest groups.

5. Bade, *Friedrich Fabri,* 499. In 1891, the Society had roughly 17,700 members; it had 32,200 by 1902.

6. Ibid., 495–96.

7. After his service to the Egyptian government, Heinrich Karl Brugsch (Pascha) lived (and lectured) mostly in Berlin until his death in 1884. He was a founding member of the German Colonial Society and part of its first managing board; see ibid., 293, 298. Cf. also Conrad Weidmann, *Deutsche Männer in Afrika: Lexicon der hervorragendsten deutschen Afrika-Forscher, Missionare etc.* (Lübeck: Verlagsbuchhandlung Bernhard Nöhring, 1894), 20.

8. Gustav Meinecke, "Wandlungen," *Deutsche Kolonialzeitung* 1, no. 7 (18 February 1888): 49.

9. For the expedition, which was beaten by Stanley's effort, see Carl Peters, *Die Deutsche Emin-Pasha-Expedition* (Munich: R. Oldenbourg, 1891).

10. Hermann von Wissmann, "Die Bedeutung der Emin Pascha-Expedition für die Erschließung von Afrika," *Deutsche Kolonialzeitung* 1, no. 39 (29 September 1888): 310.

11. For example, "Aufruf zur Unterstützung der Vorschläge Emin Paschas," *Deutsche Kolonialzeitung* 3, no. 26 (13 December 1890): 307–9; "Das Auftreten des Kardinal Lavigerie und die Araberfrage: II.," *Deutsche Kolonialzeitung* 1, no. 35 (1 September 1888): 274–77; further articles follow until 1889.

12. Alexander Merensky, "Der mohammedanische Gegenstoß gegen christliche Einflüsse in Zentral-Afrika," *Deutsche Kolonialzeitung* 1, no. 17 (28 April 1888): 129.

13. Gustav Meinecke, "Die Lage in Ostafrika und die Araber," *Deutsche Kolonialzeitung* 1, no. 40 (6 October 1888): 317; see also the report of a von Wissmann lecture in "Die Araberfrage und der Sklavenhandel," *Deutsche Kolonialzeitung* 1, no. 43 (3 November 1888): 352–55.

14. Ibid.; "Die Emin Pascha-Bewegung," *Deutsche Kolonialzeitung* 1, no. 44 (10 November 1888): 361–63.

15. "Der Thronwechsel in Sansibar," *Deutsche Kolonialzeitung* 1, no. 15 (14 April 1888): 113–15; Paul Reichard, "Vorschläge zu einer praktisch-kolonisatorischen Inangriffnahme ostafrikanischer Besitzungen (Schluß)," *Deutsche Kolonialzeitung* 2, no. 11 (16 March 1889): 83–85.

16. See the front-page appeal to act against the slave trade, signed by the managing board of the German Colonial Society, "Gegen den Sklavenhandel!" *Deutsche Kolonialzeitung* 2, no. 4 (26 January 1889): 26.

17. See Klaus J. Bade, "Antisklavereibewegung in Deutschland und Kolonialkrieg in Deutsch-Ostafrika 1888–1890: Bismarck und Friedrich Fabri," *Geschichte und Gesellschaft* 3 (1977): 31–58; Klaus J. Bade, *Friedrich Fabri,* 530–48.

18. See Jonathon Glassman, *Feasts and Riot: Revelry, Rebellion, and Popular Consciousness on the Swahili Caost, 1856–1888* (Portsmouth, NH: Heinemann, 1995), 177–97.

19. Rochus Schmidt, *Geschichte des Araberaufstandes in Ost-Afrika* (Frankfurt a. Oder: Verlag der Königlichen Hofdruckerei Trowitsch & Sohn, 1892).

20. For example, "Aus Ost-Afrika," *Deutsches Kolonialblatt* 2, no. 11 (1 June 1891): 241–43; "Ein englisches Urtheil über die Verwaltung von Deutsch-Ostafrika," *Deutsches Kolonialblatt* 5, no. 15 (1 July 1894): 340; "Verwaltung und Rechtspflege in Deutsch-Ostafrika," *Deutsches Kolonialblatt* 5, no. 7 (15 March 1894): 144–45.

21. See for example Paul Reichard, "Die Bedeutung von Tabora für Deutsch-Ostafrika," *Deutsche Kolonialzeitung* 3, no. 6 (15 March 1890): 67–68; "Korrespondenzen," *Deutsche Kolonialzeitung* 3, no. 25 (29 November 1890): 302–3; "Aufruf zur Unterstützung der Vorschläge Emin Paschas," *Deutsche Kolonialzeitung* 3, no. 26 (13 December 1890): 307–9; "Emin und Wißmann," *Deutsche Kolonialzeitung* 3, no. 27 (27 December 1890): 320–22.

22. "Korrespondenzen," *Deutsche Kolonialzeitung* 4, no. 6 (20 May 1891): 79–80; "Rede des Herrn Superintendenten Merensky," *Deutsche Kolonialzeitung* 6, no. 7 (24 June 1893): 87–88; "Mission und Arabertum in Ostafrika," *Deutsches Kolonialblatt* 3, no. 1 (1 January 1893): 16.

23. "Ein Schreiben von Prof. Dr. Schweinfurth," *Deutsche Kolonialzeitung* 3, no. 3 (1 February 1890): 30–31.

24. Leo Hirsch, "Arabische Weltanschauung," *Deutsche Kolonialzeitung* 3, no. 5 (1 March 1890): 55.

25. "Die Araberfrage und Emin Pascha," *Deutsche Kolonialzeitung* 3, no. 6 (15 March 1890): 66–67.

26. "Die Denkschrift über Ostafrika und die Araber," *Deutsche Kolonialzeitung* 6, no. 1 (7 January 1893): 4–5.

27. Conrad Bornhak, "Das Recht der Eingeborenen in den deutschen Schutzgebieten," *Deutsche Kolonialzeitung* 4, no. 11 (17 October 1891): 146. See also Karl von Stengel, "Muhammedanisches Recht," *Deutsche Kolonialzeitung* 11, no. 39 (29 September 1898): 349.

28. Eduard Sachau, *Muhammedanisches Recht nach schafiitischer Lehre*, Lehrbücher des Seminars für orientalische Sprachen zu Berlin, Bd. 17 (Stuttgart: W. Spemann, 1897).

29. Cf. Bundesarchiv, R 1001/5557.

30. Carl Heinrich Becker, "Karstedt's Islampolitische Aufsätze," *Der Islam* 5, no. 2 (1914): 244–47.

31. See documents relating to the visit of the Aga Khan in 1899, Tanzania National Archives (TNA), G 9/39.

32. See Walter von St.Paul-Illaire's report about jurisdiction in Tanga, TNA, G 1/84.

33. On Sulayman, cf. Michael Pesek, "Sulayman B. Nasr Al-Lamki and German Colonial Policies towards Muslim Communities in German East Africa," in *Islam in Africa*, ed. Thomas Bierschenk and Georg Stauth (Münster: Lit Verlag, 2002), 211–29. For a short introduction to Sewa Haji, see A. T. Matson, "Sewa Haji: A Note," *Tanzania Notes and Records* 65 (1966): 91–94.

34. Carl Velten, *Desturi za wasuaheli na khabari za desturi za sheri"a za wasuaheli* (Göttingen: Vandenhoeck & Ruprecht, 1903). For a detailed account of his life, see Ludger Wimmelbücker, *Mtoro Bin Mwinyi Bakari (c. 1869–1927): Swahili Lecturer and Author in Germany* (Dar es Salaam: Mkuku ny Nyota Publishers, 2009).

35. "Mission oder Islam," *Deutsche Kolonialzeitung* 8, no. 45 (9 November 1895): 355–56.

36. Siegfried Passarge, "Mission oder Islam?" *Deutsche Kolonialzeitung* 8, no. 50 (14 December 1895): 394–95.

37. See C. G. Barth, "Die ersten Lebensjahre unserer deutschen Schule in Tanga, Ostafrika," *Deutsche Kolonialzeitung* 8, no. 12 (23 March 1895): 90–93; "Kolonisation und Muttersprache," *Deutsche Kolonialzeitung* 8, no. 35 (31 August 1895): 273–74; "Korrespondenzen: Unsere Muttersprache in den deutschen Kolonialschulen," *Deutsche Kolonialzeitung* 8, no. 37 (14 September 1895): 293; Prof. Dr. Lenz, "Die deutsch-ostafrikanischen Regierungsschulen," *Deutsche Kolonialzeitung* 17, no. 16+17 (1895): 168–69, 177–78.

38. See John Iliffe, *Tanganyika under German Rule 1905–1912* (Cambridge: Cambridge University Press, 1969).

39. See Felicitas Becker and Jigal Beez, eds., *Der Maji-Maji-Krieg in Deutsch-Ostafrika 1905–1907* (Berlin: Ch. Links Verlag, 2005).

40. See Michael Pesek, "Kreuz oder Halbmond: Die deutsche Kolonialpolitik zwischen Pragmatismus und Paranoia in Deutsch-Ostafrika 1908–1914," in *Mission und Gewalt. Der Umgang christlicher Missionen mit Gewalt und die Ausbreitung des Christentums in Afrika und Asien in der Zeit von 1792 bis 1918/19*, ed. Jürgen Becher and Ulrich van der Heyden (Stuttgart: Franz Steiner, 2000), 97–112.

41. For a detailed list, see *Deutsches Kolonial-Lexikon,* ed. Heinrich Schnee (Leipzig: Quelle & Meyer, 1920), s.v. "Presse, koloniale"; Arne Schöfert, "Übersicht der wichtigen Kolonialzeitungen und-Zeitschriften," accessed 12 July 2014, http://www.traditionsverband.de/magazin/kolonialpresse/kolonialpresse.html.

42. For the political conflict, including the infamous "Rechenberg scandal," see Iliffe, *Tanganyika under German Rule,* 121–22; Martin Sturmer, *The Media History of Tanzania*, revised online edition (2008, originally Tanzania: Ndana Mission Press, 1998), 32–37 www.sturmer.at/pdf/themediahistoryoftanzania.pdf. Detlef Bald, *Deutsch-Ostafrika 1900–1914: Eine Studie über Verwaltung, Interessengruppen und Wirtschaftliche Erschließung* (Munich: Weltforum Verlag, 1970), 123–26 shows the relationship of these press organs with settler associations.

43. As examples for each of these tendencies, see "Lokales," *Deutsch-Ostafrikanische Zeitung* 2, no. 1 (6 January 1900): 3; "Festtage unserer mohamedanischen Bevölkerung," *Deutsch-Ostafrikanische Zeitung* 4, no. 3 (18 January 1902): 2; "Aus Daressalam und Umgegend: Das Ramadhan-Fest," *Deutsch-Ostafrikanische Zeitung* 8, no. 43 (27 October 1906): 3.

44. There are a number of articles about his first visit to Dar es Salaam in the September 1899 issues of the *Deutsch-Ostafrikanische Zeitung.* As an example for the latter critcism, see "Lokales: Für Aga Khan," *Deutsch-Ostafrikanische Zeitung* 10, no. 50 (4 July 1908): 2–3.

45. See Georg Richelman, "Wie mir Ostafrika nach langer Trennung erscheint," *Deutsche Kolonialzeitung* 25, no. 41 (10 October 1908): 727–28.

46. "Schreckgespenster," *Deutsch-Ostafrikanische Zeigung* 5, no. 10 (7 March 1903): 1.

47. See "Erwiederung auf unseren Leitartikel in Nr. 10 l. J.," *Deutsch-Ostafrikanische Zeitung* 5, no. 11 (14 March 1903): 1–2; "Verschiedene Stimmen aus unserem Leserkreise," *Deutsch-Ostafrikanische Zeitung* 5, no. 12 (21 March 1903): 1–2.

48. Der Vorstand des Deutschen Kolonialbundes, "Gegen den neuen Kreuzzug," *Koloniale Zeitschrift* 6, no. 25 (1905): 450–52.

49. Ibid., 452. The spelling of "Islâm" is unique, especially as most articles still used the term "Mohammedan."

50. August Leue, "Vor dem Sturm," *Deutsche Kolonialzeitung* 23, no. 42 (20 October 1906): 410–11. Oscar Bongard, "Die Studienreise des Staatsekretärs Dernburg nach Deutsch-Ostafrika (Fortsetzung)," *Deutsche Kolonialzeitung* 24, no. 48 (30 November 1907): 490.

51. For example, Leue, "Vor dem Sturm"; "Einige treffende Ansichten über ostafrikanische Verhältnisse," *Deutsch-Ostafrikanische Zeitung* 9, no. 61 (23 October 1907): 2–3.

52. "Einige treffende Ansichten."

53. "Ueber Christentum und Mohamedanismus in Afrika," *Deutsch-Ostafrikanische Zeitung* 9, no. 73 (4 December 1907): Beiblatt.

54. Hans Zache, "Koloniale Eingeborenenpolitik (Fortsetzung)," *Koloniale Zeitschrift* 6, no. 15 (20 July 1905): 257.

55. For example, Johannes Raum, "Von den Missionsfeldern: Die mohammedanische Gefahr in Deutsch-Ostafrika," *Koloniale Zeitschrift* 11, no. 31 (16 September 1910): 572–74; see also "Zeitungsschau," *Koloniale Zeitschrift* 11, no. 17 (10 June 1910): 348–49.

56. "Vom Missionsfelde (Zuschrift der Berliner Mission)," *Koloniale Zeitschrift* 11, no. 45 (23 December 1910): 890.

57. "Generalissimus von Rechenberg," *Deutsch-Ostafrikanische Zeitung* 12, no. 7/8 (29 January 1910): 1–2; "Die islamitische Gefahr in Deutsch-Ostafrika," *Deutsch-Ostafrikanische Zeitung* 12, no. 11 (9 February 1910): 2.

58. See, for example, documents relating petition by Mr. Zeischold (Halle) in G 9/48, pp. 30–39, TNA, containing an inquiry about the "Islamic danger" by a mission-supporting clerk from Halle, which Berlin forwarded to East Africa for comment.

59. Becker, *Becoming Muslim,* 53–82.

60. See TNA, G9/46–48.

61. See especially August H. Nimtz, *Islam and Politics in East Africa: The Sufi Order in Tanzania* (Minneapolis: University of Minnesota Press, 1980).

62. Cf. Pesek, "Kreuz oder Halbmond."

63. For the instrumentalization of the fatwā in German East Africa, see Michael Pesek, "Für Kaiser und Allah: Ostafrikas Muslime im Großen Krieg für die Zivilisation, 1914–1919," *SGMOIK Bulletin* 19 (2004): 9–18.

64. Wilhelm Förster, "Die christliche Mission und der Islam in den deutschen Kolonien," *Koloniale Zeitschrift* 9, Kriegsausgabe (11 August 1915): 2.

65. Ibid.

66. Cf. Rebekka Habermas, "Debates on Islam in Imperial Germany," in *Islam and the European Empires,* ed. David Motadel (Oxford: Oxford University Press, 2014), 231–53.

67. Dipesh Chakrabarty, *Provincializing Europe: Postcolonial Thought and Historical Difference* (Princeton: Princeton University Press, 2000), 17–18.

68. Muhamadi bana Hasani, "Shairi la Majermani," in *Kala Shairi: German East Africa in Swahili Poems,* ed. Gudrun Miehe, Katrin Bromber, Said Khamis, Ralf Großerhode, and Hilke Meyer-Bahlburd (Cologne: Rüdiger-Köppe-Verlag, 2002), 369–71.

THREE

A Tin-Trunk Bible

The Written Word of an Oral Church

DAVID M. GORDON

Karin Barber coined the phrase "tin-trunk literacy" to refer to everyday and sometimes obscure forms of writing, reading, and archiving.[1] Ordinary texts, kept for years by those who valued them rather than archived by corporate or governmental bodies, not only reveal how individuals or groups perceived the past and valued writing and texts but, in Barber's words, "were linked to the imagining of new kinds of personhood, new ways of being social, and new ways of relating to the world of officialdom."[2] The case considered here is a tin-trunk text kept by a community associated with the Lumpa Church of Alice Lenshina. The church became popular in the northern and eastern parts of colonial Zambia during the 1950s. The Lumpa Church was predominantly an oral movement in the sense that they published no official texts. However, the chief prophets of the church passed on or recited handwritten manuscripts to deacons of different church communities. Although the Lumpa Church is no longer a widespread and popular movement, isolated Lumpa communities still exist and often base their religious and political identities off these handwritten manuscripts. The analysis of this chapter is centered on one such manuscript.

Marginal texts hold special powers. For the Lumpa, who have come to think of themselves as Christian outcasts and martyrs, marginality has become a sign of spiritual power, and their handwritten sacred texts reflect this quality. This chapter considers how one text, a tin-trunk bible that belonged to a Lumpa community living in Chiponya, a small village on the outskirts of the medium-sized Zambian town of Mpika, helped build spiritual significance and communal identity. The text was a product of oral and written memory practices, and it evolved in the context of the Chiponya community's local history and religious ideas.[3]

At least since Benedict Anderson's demonstration of the importance of print capitalism for local forms of nationalism,[4] scholars have examined the formation of identities around textual regimes. Beyond national communities, Africanist historians have shown how subnational and religious identities draw on the dissemination of written languages and sacred texts.[5] The Chiponya manuscript considered in this case exists outside the genre of printed African religious texts, such as the sacred texts of the South African Nazaretha Church.[6] For one, this manuscript is handwritten and unique, not printed. Even though its writers claim to have copied it from other manuscripts and it conforms to general church accounts, there is no evidence of a standardized Lumpa story or text. Nor, however, is it a private autobiographical text that explores personal approaches to the spiritual world, like the revivalist autobiographies examined by Derek Peterson.[7] In the absence of standardized Lumpa texts, this handwritten manuscript created a sense of belonging to a broader Lumpa imagined community, but it also affirmed relationships in an immediate village community located around a patron, a chief deacon who was the reader and possessor of the tin-trunk bible. Such texts were centrifugal and centripetal political forces, contributing to amalgamations and fissures, not unlike other contested politico-religious objects from prior centuries, such as the memory boards (*lukasa*) and staffs of rulers found among Luba peoples to whom followers of the Lumpa Church were loosely related. These objects, like the Chiponya manuscript, were mnemonic devices that catalyzed oral traditions into living sovereignties.[8] Texts and the use of writing were thus part of a longer history of employing physical mnemonics to complement forms of oral memory and identity.

Whereas my previous publications on the Lumpa Church have explored such historical connections, this chapter focuses on what the handwritten text of this particularly marginal community reveals about the intersections between orality and specifically written forms of memorialization, that is literacy, in religious expression.[9] Much ink has been spilled on the topic of orality and literacy in Africanist history and anthropology. The idealized paradigms of oral versus literate developed by Jack Goody and others, with their evolutionist implications, have been critiqued many times. Nowadays, as voice and vision competes with text in African religious communications, from Pentecostal performances to Qur'anic instruction, many of Goody's original formulations seem dated, perhaps attributing too much power to writing.[10] The hybridity of media has replaced the hegemony of writing. Although it is tempting to draw global conclusions from a seemingly heterodox present, the Lumpa emerged at a time when writing, printing, books, and documents implied status and power. The analysis developed here shows how barely literate and disempowered individuals engaged with this regime of writing, including literacy and print media.

This analysis shows how literacy and orality intertwined and infused one another. Previous scholars have pointed to an either linear "retrogressive" retreat into orality or a "progressive" replacement of orality with writing. This analysis of the Lumpa finds that there was neither an "oralizing" of textual regimes, as Patrick Harries and Isabel Hofmeyr have previously shown, nor a replacement of the oral with writing as some interpretations of Goody's work imply (or a replacement of the text with the digital, as is sometimes argued to be the case with contemporary Pentecostalism).[11] In the case of the Lumpa Church, handwriting, printed texts, and orality came to exist together, in distinctive—albeit sometimes overlapping—roles. Printed documents, including church constitutions and church membership cards, came to identify the church's corporate identity in relation to outside authorities; the oral, principally hymns, invoked the spirit for adherents; and handwritten tin-trunk texts, like the Chiponya manuscript, defined a scriptural history for insiders.

The chapter begins with a description of how the Lumpa arose. It then turns to how the Lumpa oral tradition of revelation defined Lumpa beliefs and the orally transmitted hymns invoked the spirit. Books and writing formed a key imaginative theme within these oral forms. This incorporation of text into such oral forms laid a basis for the role of written manuscripts, the Chiponya tin-trunk bible in particular, which is covered in the final and key section of the chapter. Here an exegesis of the Chiponya manuscript reveals how a handwritten manuscript informed the subjective religious and historical identity of an oral spiritual movement.

Who Were the Lumpa?

In 1953, a young woman claimed to have died, gone to heaven, and returned to life, with the intention of saving her people from sinners. She soon became known as "Regina" (Lenshina), and her reputation for healing and removing witchcraft spread across northeastern Zambia. Thousands made a pilgrimage to her Zion, "Sione," where her followers built a huge brick church in 1958, larger than the impressive Catholic mission nearby. Her movement became known as the *Lumpa* Church, which in the ChiBemba vernacular of northern Zambia signified the church that goes beyond.

The insistence of Lenshina's followers on her God-given powers brought them into conflict with the nearby Catholic and Presbyterian missionaries, the colonial chiefs, the colonial administration, and, finally, the nationalists, the United National Independence Party (UNIP). The reasons for the conflicts were numerous and complex: in essence, they revolved around a competition for followers and contestation over the boundaries of sacred and secular sovereignties. Conflict with the nationalist movement culminated in violent raids and counterraids carried out by young men belonging to both UNIP and Lumpa factions. Prior to the formal declaration of independence in October 1964, the acting prime minister, UNIP leader, and future president of Zambia Kenneth Kaunda ordered troops to forcefully disperse Lumpa villages. This resulted in around one thousand deaths, mostly Lumpa but also innocent Zambians in UNIP-dominated villages subjected to Lumpa revenge attacks.[12] Lenshina was captured and detained without trial until her death in 1978. Around twenty thousand Lumpa fled to the Democratic Republic of Congo (DRC), where they sought refuge for the next few decades. In the DRC, they settled around the town of Mokambo, where they formed at least eleven distinct village sections modeled on the villages (the term they used was "*misumba,*" which could be translated as "palaces" or "missions") they had come from in northern Zambia. In the 1970s and through the 1980s, they began to return to Zambia. Upon their return, the Zambian government tried to disperse them by settling them in small family units in remote parts of the country; the Lumpa resisted by recongregating in the larger village units that they had earlier formed in Zambia and in the DRC, and settling in peri-urban areas. The Chiponya community was one such group of returnees.[13]

The Lumpa who returned from the DRC were poor, marginalized, and often despised. Zambian propaganda presented the Lumpa as atavistic savages, as the opposite of the progressive African socialism that Zambia's first president, Kenneth Kaunda (ruled 1964–1991), made into the state philosophy of "Humanism." The Lumpa were pestered and deprived of state resources, even employment. The situation improved in

1991 with the coming to power of the second Zambian president, Frederick Chiluba, an evangelical Christian. Many Zambians, however, were still suspicious of Lumpa communities, and vice versa. The Lumpa kept to themselves; they supported their own communities through patronage networks that extended to the few family members who managed to eke out a decent existence.

Across this history, there were three general shifts in Lumpa religious identity. Immediately after Lenshina's revelations in 1953, many communities across northern Zambia followed the Lumpa Church. Lenshina had far greater success in attracting converts than European missionaries did, and she even converted many who were already mission followers. Lumpa adherents at that time were joyful about the spread of Lenshina's message, her hymns, and the end of witchcraft and jealousy; it was a popular and utopian time. By giving up and admitting to witchcraft and sin, by following the Lumpa commandments, and by recognizing Lenshina as God's agent, a new heavenly order would appear on earth. By the 1960s, confrontations with the missionaries and then with the African nationalist movement and their mission-educated leaders transformed the Lumpa from this utopian community to a confrontational army of warrior Christians who fought to maintain their Christian identity against sinners and witches. They lived in besieged communities and were paranoid of outsiders. Finally, following their violent dispersal by colonial troops commanded by the new nationalist government, the Lumpa became marginalized and isolated communities of suffering, insulted and denigrated by most Zambians, and located in disparate communities across northern Zambia. They thought of themselves as having survived a confrontation with the forces of Satan; their ongoing suffering at the hands of Satan was a sign of the strength of their faith.[14]

The Chiponya Lumpa community lived on the outskirts of a medium-sized and modern town, Mpika, which lies at the junction of the two principal routes northward from the copper mining towns of central Zambia. The Chiponya Lumpa relocated here as refugees. After the violent conflict between the nationalists and the Lumpa Church in 1964, the colonial army burnt down their village. Those who were not killed in the confrontation with the army were detained or fled into the bush. Most then escaped or made their way to the DRC. Around a decade later, after a joint Zambian and Zairian military operation forced their return to Zambia, the Zambian authorities tried to disperse them into distinct communities. While awaiting relocation instructions in the northern Zambian town of Kasama, the chief deacon, William"Kalomba muli Lesa" [Praise in God], allegedly on instructions that Lenshina communicated from detention, secured an opportunity from the government to settle in Chiponya village, Mpika. The relative size of this cosmopolitan town afforded some protection from the persecution that might otherwise be found in rural areas. By the time I came to conduct my research, the community had lived there for around two decades. They had established modest but modern housing and built a large church in 2002.[15]

The maintenance of Lumpa identity in the aftermath of the conflict of 1964, of exile, of return, and of persistent postindependence Zambian government persecution was remarkable. In part the continuation of Lumpa communities in the face of this adversity was due to socioeconomic and psychological necessities. These communities had little choice but to remain together: their best chance for survival, and perhaps some form of prosperity, was within their own communities, apart from their old adversaries. Moreover, most Lumpa had invested their lives in following Lenshina, from their experiences in the anti-Lumpa campaigns of 1964, through their death-defying march across over a thousand miles of central African bush to the DRC, and their final return to Zambia as second-class citizens. A rejection of Lumpa identity would mean a rejection of the purpose and meaning of their historical experiences.

Textual Revelations in Oral Repertoires

Books preceded writing. According to oral traditions, the founding Lumpa prophet Lenshina received two books when she met Jesus in heaven. One book was for black people and the other for white people. She called for baptized Christians to come to her, but since she was born among sinners and witches, the book for black people was swallowed up by the earth before the baptized Christians arrived. Lenshina wrapped the second book, the Book of Life (*ibuku lya Mweo*), in white cloth. Together with her husband and two young girls, she walked to the Scottish Presbyterian Lubwa mission, with which she was affiliated, to tell them of her visions and gift. There, according to the stories, she met with a Scottish Presbyterian missionary, Fergus Macpherson, who took the Book of Life from her and hid it under his shirt while they prayed with their eyes closed. The oral narrative places Lenshina and her followers in this liminal position, between pagan locals and devious missionaries. The books for whites and blacks were the spiritual objects at the center of this narrative.[16]

Followers and antagonists of the Lumpa Church still discuss whether Lenshina lied about these books, whether her followers imagined them, or if they actually existed. Missionaries attached to the Presbyterian Church at Lubwa deny that Lenshina had any books. The missionary concerned, Macpherson, admits to having met Lenshina but denies stealing her book.[17] Eyewitnesses to Lenshina's resurrection insist that there were two books, one of which was stolen by (or given by Lenshina to) Macpherson.[18] Few people actually saw the books, but many insisted on their presence. A Lumpa deacon who was a young man at the time recollected, "They found a book in pure white cloth. It was new cloth straight from Jesus Christ. That white cloth was very nice and it had a book inside—but I didn't see the book myself. No one in the village saw the book. Not even Beneta and Nsofwa who went with Lenshina saw the book. Because it was wrapped in the white cloth. It came like that from heaven—it is difficult to tell the power of Christ."[19] The actual presence of the books, or their putative theft by the missionary, is perhaps less important than their centrality to the narrative of Lenshina's revelations. At the outset, the spiritual imagination centered around books. The question is why would the semiliterate followers of Lenshina insist on these books?

That spiritual power took the form of books was probably the result of how power was conceived and exercised in colonial Zambia. Books and written documents had become markers of identity and authority. The ability to write indicated authority, or at least the potential to navigate the colonial world. The mission church elite rejected Lenshina not only because she was a woman but because she could barely write. Then there were the letters that instructed and exercised power. One such letter from the Presbyterian mission banished Lenshina and her chief followers from their church. Such was the exclusionary and inclusionary powers of writing.[20]

Around the time of Lenshina's revelations, the first completed translations of the bible began to be printed by the Catholics and Presbyterians. Thus, in addition to writing, printed texts were becoming instruments of vernacular religious instruction and sacred power. Lenshina's initial reaction to the appearance of the published bibles was to call them *chibolya,* a deserted village, probably compared to the books that she had received and the followers she had attracted. Her rejection of these published missionary bibles became a major reason for her conflict with mainline missionaries in Zambia—and the principal justification for missionary claims that Lenshina's followers were not true Christians.

In secular life, too, documents confirmed identities and bolstered authority. The colonial government issued identity cards (*fitupa*) that marked identity and restricted mobility; mining companies used booklets, termed "tickets," containing slips in which shift work was noted and wages thereby calculated; and as the nationalist movement gained strength, party cards indicated political allegiances. In part, the Lumpa approach to texts emerged from such acts of "documentary bullying."[21] One of the first conflicts between the Lumpa and the Zambian nationalist movement in 1963, which contributed to the war of 1964, was over political party cards. The Lumpa refused to purchase UNIP cards and even burnt those they had already purchased. For the UNIP such sacrilegious flouting of their documentary authority was tantamount to treason to the nationalist cause and led UNIP youth to attack Lumpa villagers.

As Lenshina's revelation suggests, the Lumpa did not reject books and documents outright in favor of orality but instead sought to establish their own books even within their oral forms. The Lumpa thus engaged with what Isabel Hofmeyr terms the paradoxical nature of documents: "that they are props in the theatre of ruling, policing and dragooning; on the other hand, they betoken enchantment and spiritual authority."[22] In addition to the role of books in the oral tradition, the Lumpa replicated identity and political party cards with their own "passports to heaven"; church communities wrote letters to discuss strategies in the face of opposition; and they sent their "twelve commandments" in a formal letter to the colonial governor.[23] The resources of publication were always beyond them, however. There is no evidence that they rejected publication per se, and a few might have been keen to publish aspects of Lumpa doctrine and music. However, there was frequent distrust of the literate elite, the Protestant and Catholic-trained teachers, who might have pursued such a project of publication. Lumpa leaders accused many members of this literate elite of misappropriating church funds, and eventually they excommunicated them from the church. Books and writing were keys to the imagination of the sacred in a colonial context that proclaimed and acted on the power of writing; yet, initially, for the

Lumpa, writing and texts became part of their oral repertoires rather than replacing them.

Even while the power of writing and of books was everywhere evident and was central to the Lumpa religious imagination, Lumpa spirituality employed an oral mode. Musical performance, in particular, remained at the core of Lumpa religiosity. Hymns that Lenshina had learned while she was dead conjured the spirit. She communicated these hymns to choirs that spread across the countryside of northern Zambia. Such song, often accompanied by drum, dance, and distinctive gesticulations, made the spirit felt. Scholars with a literate bent have tried to use these hymns to identify a type of Lumpa religious dogma available to interpretive exegesis.[24] The literate-centrism of this approach aside, the hymns are tremendously diverse. Moreover, although many hymns have endured (as I witnessed during fieldwork in 2005), it is difficult to identity those that were important in the past. Lenshina and her chief deacons taught many hymns to her followers, so many that it is difficult to garner unified themes from them. Many of them are esoteric, with meanings that are still disputed among the Lumpa. And different communities favored different hymns. At best, a few general patterns emerge: for example, the ideas of "crossing over to the other side," of having ones "heart washed and cleansed," and of the joy in following Jesus prevail.

The literal meaning of these hymns was less significant than the affective power of their music. Regardless of the meaning of the words, performance conjured the spirit—it invoked a soulful sadness that indicated a spiritual presence. For several weeks of each year, the choirs made a pilgrimage to Lenshina's headquarters, where they would learn new hymns. En route, they sang, attracting the attention of many villagers, missionaries, and colonial officials.[25] "Passionate dirge like melodies expressing an intense devotion in a wholly African idiom," according to one missionary. "This is the music a man sings when his heart is nearly mad with sorrow," commented another man upon hearing the hymns.[26] The literal or even symbolic meanings of the hymns were less important than the emotions conjured in those who heard them.

Texts were marginal to this performative repertoire. Hymns were taught by choirmasters who went to Lenshina's headquarters at Zion to learn the hymns and then brought them back to their own communities, singing en route, and thereby attracting new converts. Sometimes older church members, or teachers, tried to write them down. The best example was that Robert Kaunda (Kenneth Kaunda's brother), himself a Lumpa member and keen musician, wrote down many of the hymns. By the time he had done so, however, he had been expelled from the church for allegedly stealing funds; his manuscript lay in the possession of a Catholic missionary rather than informing the standardization of Lumpa hymns.[27] By the time I conducted research among various Lumpa communities across the country in 2005, there were a few particularly popular hymns sung in most churches, but still no standard repertoire of hymns. Choirs always formed the centerpiece of Lumpa services, and the singing of hymns and the dancing gave the services their sacred power.

However, through their remarkable historical experiences, Lumpa identity came to revolve around more than the oral evocation of spiritual power: it developed a historical and scriptural dimension as well. These aspects of Lumpa identity were maintained in handwritten manuscripts, perhaps best thought of as *lieux de memoire,* that revealed the intertwining of communal history, religious belief, and identity. The Chiponya tin-trunk bible is one such example.

The Chiponya Manuscript and Lumpa Identity

Writing and print media did not replace the oral performance of hymn, song, drum, and dance so loved by Lumpa communities. As Thomas Kirsch demonstrates for a southern Zambian church, texts need not be antithetical to charismatic leadership and the spirit.[28] Texts and writing do not exclude orality (or vice versa); they can affirm one another.[29] For the Lumpa media began to play different and complementary roles. Oral performance remained key in invoking the spirit; print was paramount to demonstrate and to defend a corporate identity to the outside world; and handwritten manuscripts began to give shape to a Lumpa consciousness.

After their return from the DRC in the 1970s and 1980s, church members began to use print media to bolster their legitimacy in relation to those secular and religious authorities who invoked the powers of documents. Church members received printed membership cards, termed "church books," which existed alongside their oral "names from heaven," thus giving a printed and public component to their Lumpa identity. The church, renamed as the "Jerusalem Church," adopted a written constitution and registered with the Zambian Registrar of Societies. It also adopted the published Christian bible.

In contrast to the use of the abovementioned documents and print media, handwritten manuscripts were not intended for exposure to the outside world. I first came across the handwritten Chiponya manuscript while interviewing the Chiponya community about their past. Instead of recollecting their personal memories, I noticed that they chose to refer to a book. This book, I was told, belonged to their village church. It had been copied from other books, many of which were destroyed during war and exile. Alfred Kapele, general secretary of the Lumpa church, supposedly wrote the first book. He was the husband of the daughter of Alice Lenshina and leader of the approximately twenty thousand church members who lived in the DRC during the 1960s and 1970s. Apparently, Kapele had taken notes and compiled this testimony, which was then copied by leaders of other mission congregations (*misumba*), such as William "Kalomba muli Lesa," the founder of the Chiponya community. This particular manuscript, according to its owners, was one of the few books that survived the attack on Lumpa, exile, and return to Zambia. The Chiponya community was particularly proud of it.[30]

Given the Lumpa oral records of the white missionary stealing the book from Lenshina, there was a general reluctance to show this book to me. In the end, however, the Lumpa community agreed that their book was significant and should be communicated to the outside world. The manuscript was written in neat longhand in the ChiBemba language on twelve pages of a standard-issue school notebook. It was divided into two main sections, "The Birth of the Queen [Namfumu] Alice Lenshina Mulenga," and "How She Saw the Lord." Both these sections were structured in the form of a narrative of the experience of Lenshina and her followers, interspersed with several hymns and commandments, with some explanations. An epilogue deals with the experiences of the church members during and after the conflict with the Zambian nationalists. The manuscript ends with a few paragraphs of additional testimonies and a final hymn that reflects on the suffering of the people of God.

The first section, "The Birth of the Queen," describes Lenshina's early life. Here, a third-person narrative establishes Lenshina as a respectable woman by demythologizing her and rejecting the demonization of her by the mainstream media and the Zambian government. The book describes a young woman married in a respectable fashion, first to an older man who died, and then to his cousin, according to Bemba tradition. But her village, the manuscript emphasizes, was "difficult" and practiced "sinful behavior," resulting in "misfortunes"—probably a reference to the sin of witchcraft. There was also much cruelty against women: "Many times they severed the breasts of women," we are told.

The manuscript has several calendar dates. Although these dates do not conform to the written records of missionaries and colonial officials, they have helped the Lumpa develop a religious calendar (although oral accounts also emphasize the same dates). According to the manuscript, the miraculous happenings began on October 21, 1953, when Lenshina fell sick. The manuscript emphasizes that she was ill not from magic or madness; rather, she was just sick. She fell into a coma on October 24 and even stopped breastfeeding her young child. The next day, as the community prepared for her funeral, she woke up, blinking her eyes, and cried. She went outside the house, where she died again, but that evening she awoke. Her husband was crying. Lenshina said, "Stop crying." And she told the story of her miraculous death experience.

Thus begins the second main section of the manuscript, "How She [Lenshina] Saw the Lord [*Nashikulu*]." Here the narrative switches from the third person to the first. The effect of this long inner soliloquy is to create the impression of historical veracity—much like the use of direct quotes in popular Western historical composition.

In this section, the content transitions from the parochial concerns of witchcraft and Lenshina's illness to a more universal Christian vision, albeit one that still speaks to a distinctly female Bemba cosmology. At first Lenshina found herself above a valley of blood. She was told that she was there because she had been cursed by her mother and mother's brother. She explained herself to them—and it seems to be a key moment in the narrative when she realizes that to escape this curse she needed to become a Christian: the witchcraft of jealous and unhappy ancestors and family members would give way only with the acceptance of Christianity. The manuscript then has Lenshina waking up and demanding to be among only true Christians—but there were none in her community of sinners. So Lenshina died again, and this time we reach the climax of her experiences and revelations, "her journey to the Christians."

> Where I went you cannot see the end of this huge ocean. Three people came who wore very white clothes and they said you are not supposed to cross to the other side of the righteous. Then, I heard the voice of our lord, Jesus. He told the angels that they should

> throw a chord . . . onto the ocean and immediately the chord came and it touched the rock to which I held. From the other side of the river, they sang a song:
>
> | | |
> |---|---|
> | *Posa ulusale paBemba* | *Throw the chord on the ocean* |
> | *Noushikonke fyakwalesa* | *Those who don't follow God's command* |
> | *Taka buke nakalya* | *Shall not cross at all* |
>
> Then the angels said now cross and go yonder to the place of the righteous. Now I said, "How will I cross?" They said you will cross on the chord. "I will drown." They said, "if you have faith, you will cross and reach the other side." . . . I reached the other side of the ocean where there was a big and beautiful city. This *musumba* [mission/palace] does not exist on earth, there is no comparison on earth in its beauty, size, splendor, and appearance.

The manuscript builds on other texts along with the oral lore of the Bemba past. The above revelation, for example, combines Bemba customs, especially regarding women, with new books and testimonies. The notion of crossing an ocean is core to Bemba cosmology (Bemba means ocean), and it appears in some of the key songs associated with girls' initiation rites (*Chisungu*). On the other hand, this revelatory experience is similar to that which the Christian missionaries were disseminating: in fact, aspects of the narrative resemble that of the *Pilgrim's Progress,* a ChiBemba edition of which had been published and disseminated a few years prior to Lenshina's revelations in 1953.[31]

In the text, Lenshina's experiences and visions are interspersed with hymns, rituals, and "commandments." Commandments are similar to those of the Christian missionaries but emphasize those that affected women—such as marriage, divorce, and prohibitions against drinking and smoking. Rituals are implied in significant actions of Lenshina. For example, upon recovering, Lenshina eats two eggs, perhaps a symbol of rebirth. The Chiponya community followed this annual ritual of eating two eggs, as defined by the manuscript's calendar.

The Chiponya manuscript does not refer directly to Lenshina's receipt of two books from heaven, nor to the disappearance of one and the theft of the other by the Presbyterian missionary Macpherson. It does, however, reference a book toward the end of the manuscript: "We have testimony about the holy book that shows the way, given to the missionaries of Lubwa [i.e., the Presbyterians]." However, the lack of discussion of the book or books given by Jesus, compared to their centrality in oral accounts, is one of the most significant differences of the manuscript to the oral tradition. One plausible explanation is that this manuscript is closer to Lenshina's personal version of her experiences compared to the versions of popular memory, which tend to reinforce the importance of books in response to the secular power of the literate elites such as the missionaries and the colonial and postcolonial administrations. Alternatively, the manuscript could be a sanitized version of the oral tradition.

Regardless of the precise conditions of production, composition, and even the intentions of the producers, how the community came to use the manuscript was distinctive. The text was kept by the chief deacon of the Chiponya church and taken out for selective readings, sometimes to answer questions about the church by inquisitive insiders and outsiders like myself. It was also recited at the most important dates of the church, in particular when Lenshina had her revelations and when government troops attacked the church's headquarters. Although the book was not sacred to the touch, it had to be guarded from those who might steal its words.

This lengthy exegesis and description of the manuscript is necessary to understand the importance of the manuscript for the Chiponya community. This tin-trunk text *functioned* as a sacred narrative, a hymn book, a form of ritual instruction, and a set of commandments. Its presence invoked the memory of the books stolen by the missionary Macpherson (hence the suspicion with which I was treated), even while the book makes no direct mention of the theft. The Chiponya manuscript thereby established the authenticity of Lumpa faith through the authority of books in general. But its material presence did not convey a spiritual power the way a Torah or Qur'an does, nor did its specific content communicate spiritual strength the way the Bible gives strength to a Christian fundamentalist. Rather, the Chiponya manuscript expressed its spiritual power through its performances for audiences attuned to and appreciative of the oral qualities of words.

In addition to its sacred functions, the Chiponya manuscript provides a narrative of truthful events told in the third person that leads to the present—in other words, a *history*. Toward the end of the book, several "testimonies" of significant historical moments are recounted, including the building of Lenshina's Zion Church, the jailing of Lenshina's husband by the colonial administration, and the beginnings of attacks by UNIP. The book thereby imbues the church with historical meaning and significance by inserting Lenshina, her revelations, and the Lumpa community within a narrative of change over time, a teleology beginning with Lenshina's revelations and ending in the revelation of the human experience of suffering. The epilogue of the manuscript reads,

> So this testimony is great and it shows the truth of all things according to the lord Jesus Christ who said that know when those who reject me in the last days because those who reject God are not of this world. They will be put in suffering because I am not of this world. Just as they are not of this world. Those who persevere to do good things to the end will be lucky and will be saved.

The book then concludes with a final hymn:

> I love my children who are courageous
> As Jesus was
> When sinners asked if he was the son of God
> He said yes I am the son of God
> Today we shall do bad things to you.
> He said do it.
> Even if you do bad things to me
> I am with my father
> Suffer, suffer
> That is how the child of the lord suffered
> The child of the lord suffered
> The hatred of this world is like that
> And even you suffer
> That is how the child of God suffered.
> Amen

The Chiponya manuscript is a sacred text kept by a small and marginalized community of Lumpa believers. The history of their suffering as the people of God at the hands of the agents of Satan is recorded in this handwritten notebook. For the Chiponya community, the small and informal, the tin-trunk, is an indication of their special marginality and sacrality. The Lumpa changed from a utopian community of Christians to warriors during the war of 1963–64 to poor and suffering but faithful Christians. This notebook, scruffy and dignified, narrates this history and the corresponding transformation in religious identity.

Conclusions

Writing, print, and the performance of song, drum, and dance came to exist alongside one another, with oral repertoires invoking the spirit, print legitimizing the church, and handwritten manuscripts informing internal aspects of identity. These complementary roles blended into one another. Rather than Goody's "interface," the oral and the written *informed* and *infused* in terms of style, content, and function. Lumpa communities used print to cement and to broadcast their identities to the outside world; they used writing to affirm their distinctive historical and religious experiences. In doing so, they reflected, engaged with, and sometimes subverted wider political and societal views of texts and literacy in general. The Lumpa knew that song invoked the spirit. But they lived through an age in which authority derived from the literate—their letters, documents, and published books. By select incorporation of these objects of power, the Lumpa were able to insist on the agency of nonliterates (or barely literates) in a world that had marginalized them. In the aftermath of their apocalypse, the war of 1964, the Lumpa developed a narrative of suffering, a particular history that would be carefully written and secured in a tin-trunk bible. The manuscript evokes the historical and emotional ties that hold the Chiponya Lumpa together as a spiritual community.

Religious communities engage with media in distinctive ways. Media is not the message, for context and history determine the uses of media, whether writing, print, or oral. For the Lumpa, writing, despite its power, did not take over performance but affirmed it. Unlike the nationalist communities described by Benedict Anderson, Lumpa communities persisted and proliferated in spite of print media rather than because of it. But they did so by writing texts and imagining books that invoked their marginality as a sign of their faith in Lenshina as God's messenger.

Notes

1. Karin Barber, "Introduction: Hidden Innovators in Africa," in *Africa's Hidden Histories: Everyday Literacy and Making the Self*, ed. Karin Barber (Bloomington: Indiana University Press, 2006), 1–24.

2. Barber, "Hidden Innovators," 3–4.

3. The Chiponya manuscript belonged to the Chiponya Lumpa community. They permitted me to photograph and cite it when I visited them in July 2005. My research assistant, Kampamba Mulenga, and I collaborated on a translation based on the photographs of the text. Henceforth, I shall refer to it as the "Chiponya manuscript."

4. Benedict Anderson, *Imagined Communities: Reflections on the Origin and Spread of Nationalism* (London: Verso, 1991)

5. For example, the work of Paul Landau, *The Realm of the Word: Language, Gender and Christianity in a South African Kingdom* (Portsmouth, NH: Heinemann, 1993); Derek Peterson, *Creative Writing: Translation, Bookkeeping and the Work of the Imagination in Colonial Kenya* (Portsmouth, NH: Heinemann, 2004).

6. For analysis of the sacred texts of the Nazaretha Church, see Joel Cabrita, *Text and Authority in the South African Nazaretha Church* (Cambridge: Cambridge University Press, 2014).

7. Derek Peterson, *Ethnic Patriotism and the East African Revival: A History of Dissent, c. 1935–1972* (Cambridge: Cambridge University Press, 2012), 195–216.

8. Lukasa memory boards used carefully arranged beads as mnemonic devices. Luba staffs of rule replicated the patterns of the boards, as well as containing also used iconic figurines. Both referred to the connections of a ruler to political and religious forms of authority, as recorded in oral traditions. See Mary Nooter Roberts and Allen F. Roberts, *Memory: Luba Art and the Making of History* (NY: Museum for African Art, 1996). For an example of the functioning of Luba politico-religious authority, see Thomas Reefe, *The Rainbow and the Kings: A History of the Luba Empire to 1891* (Berkeley: University of California Press, 1981).

9. For more historical context, see especially David M. Gordon, *Invisible Agents: Spirits in a Central African History* (Athens: Ohio University Press, 2012).

10. First in Jack Goody, *The Domestication of the Savage Mind* (Cambridge: Cambridge University Press, 1977), and followed by Goody, *The Interface between Written and the Oral* (Cambridge: Cambridge University Press, 1987).

11. Patrick Harries, "Missionaries, Magic, and Marxists: Power and the Politics of Literacy in South-East Africa," *Journal of Southern African Studies* 27, no. 3 (2001): 405–27; Isabel Hofmeyr, *"We Spend Our Years as a Tale that Is Told": Oral Historical Narrative in a South African Chiefdom* (Portsmouth, NH: Heinemann, 1994), 41–77.

12. David M. Gordon, *Invisible Agents: Spirits in a Central African History* (Athens: Ohio University Press, 2012), 131–57, and Gordon, "Rebellion or Massacre: The UNIP-Lumpa Conflict Revisited," in *One Zambia, Many Histories: Towards a History of Post-Colonial Zambia*, ed. Jan-Bart Gewald, Giacomo Macola, and Marja Hinfelaar (Leiden: Brill, 2008), 45–76. In addition to extensive interview evidence, accounts also draw on government documentation in "Lenshina," Ministry of Home Affairs (MHA) 1/3/10, National Archives of Zambia (NAZ).

13. William "Kalomba muli Lesa," interview by David Gordon, 19 July 2005, Chiponya, Mpika, Zambia. For general accounts from the Zambian government's perspective on the flight of Lumpa to the DRC, see "Lenshina Rehabilitation," Northern Province (NP) 3/12/10, NAZ. For the Zambian government account of the Lumpa in the DRC and joint Zambian-Congolese operations

against them, see "Lumpa," Foreign Affairs (FA) 1/222, 144, NAZ, especially A. G. Zulu, Minister of Home Affairs, "Report to H. E. on Ex-Lumpas at Mokambo," 20 November 1967. For issues around repatriation in the 1970s (although not specifically the Chiponya community), see "Ex-Lumpa," Eastern Province (EP) 1/1/87, NAZ, in particular "Minutes of the Ad hoc Committee of District Governors on the Rehabilitation of Ex-Lumpa, 11 Oct. 1971."

14. For the transformation of the Lumpa, see Gordon, *Invisible Agents*, 131–57, and Gordon, "Community of Suffering: Narratives of War and Exile in the Zambian Lumpa Church," in *Recasting the Past*, ed. Derek Peterson and Giacomo Macola (Athens: Ohio University Press, 2009), 191–209.

15. My account of the history of the Chiponya Lumpa community is from five interviews with the elders of their community—William "Kalomba muli Lesa," Stephenia Nguni, Foster Mubanga Mfula "Kandufyanya," Lewis Mumba, Daniel Sinfunkwe "Nkapitapo"—undertaken in Chiponya, Mpika, on July 19, 2005. These five interviews are part of fifty interviews I conducted with Lumpa members across Zambia in 2005.

16. Dixon Mulenga, interview by David Gordon, 7 July 2005, Chinsali, Zambia; Maggie Nkonde, interview by David Gordon, 9 July 2005, Chandamali, Chinsali. The story of the two books was also recorded by Catholic White Father Pascal Kakokota in 1954. See Letter to L. Oger, and Short Report, Lubushi, 23 February 1962, 1/M/Hi21, White Fathers Archives, Zambia (henceforth WFA).

17. Fergus Macpherson and W. V. Stone, "The Alice Movement in Northern Rhodesia," *Occasional Papers Issued by the Department of Mission Studies, London* (August 1958).

18. For example, Bellita Mutapa, interview by David Gordon, 5 July 2005, Kasomo, Chinsali.

19. Wellington Kapoma, interview by David Gordon, 5 July 2005, Kasomo, Chinsali.

20. Church Elders to BanaKangwa [Alice Lenshina], 25 December 1955, Andrew Roberts Papers. Personal Papers held by Andrew Roberts and consulted with his permission.

21. The phrase comes from Barber, "Hidden Innovators," 6.

22. Isabel Hofmeyr, *The Portable Bunyan: A Transnational History of "The Pilgrim's Progress."* (Princeton, NJ: Princeton University Press, 2004), 143.

23. The first time the "commandments" appear in the archival record is in a letter from Alice Lenshina to the governor of Northern Rhodesia, 18 April 1957, NP, 3/12/3, NAZ. "Passports to heaven," described as such by Lumpa followers, could well have drawn on the "certificate" that granted entry to heaven in *The Pilgrim's Progress*, as described in Hofmeyr, *Portable Bunyan*, 91.

24. In particular, symbolic meanings of select hymns have been explored by Catholic missionaries, first Jean-Loup Calmettes in his thesis, "The Lumpa Sect: Rural Reconstruction, and Conflict," (master's thesis, University of Wales, 1978), and then in the work of Hugo Hinfelaar, *Bemba-Speaking Women of Zambia in a Century of Religious Change* (Leiden: Brill, 1994).

25. Jean-Loup Calmettes, "Church Music in the Chinsali District, 1954–1974," 19, Calmettes Box 3, WFA.

26. Report, "Portrait of a Problem," Acc 7548/B326, National Library of Scotland.

27. No Lumpa members had this hymnal, and the only copy I could find was in the possession of the Catholic White Fathers. J. L. Calmettes and L. Oger, March 1988, Lumpa Hymnal. Reproduction of Original Copy by kindness of Robert Kaunda. Chambalakale, 1974, Calmettes Box 1, WFA.

28. Thomas G. Kirsch, *Spirits and Letters: Reading, Writing and Charisma in African Christianity* (New York and Oxford: Berghahn Books, 2008).

29. As noted by an extensive literature, here, with a pioneering study, Hofmeyr, *"We Spend Our Years."*

30. Mubanga Mfula "Kandufyanya," interview by David Gordon, 19 July 2005, Chiponya, Mpika.

31. See comparable influences of the *Pilgrim's Progress* in Hofmeyr, *Portable Bunyan*. The ChiBemba versions of *The Pilgrim's Progress* were *Ulwendo lwa mwina-Kristu mu cilota* (new ed., Mbeleshi, 1953; first ChiBemba ed., 1925, published by the London Mission at Mbereshi; rev. 1944). The only existing copies I have found are in the Catholic White Father's Archives; see 3/P/R36, WFA.

FOUR

Photography as Unveiling

Muslim Discourses and Practices on the Kenyan Coast

HEIKE BEHREND

Along the East African coast, Muslims—who form a more or less discriminated-against and marginalized minority in the (Christian) postcolonial state of Kenya—have since the 1980s increasingly attempted not only to enter the public domain but also to "Islamize" it by establishing gender segregation and by contesting the public visibility of women. In particular, after the embassy bombings in Nairobi in August 1998 and the repercussions of 9/11 in 2001 in Mombasa, the tensions between Christians and Muslims have increased, and many Muslims had to experience even more discrimination and repression in Kenya.[1] As a response to and a critique of national politics, they have increasingly invoked a moral order that is based on "Swahili tradition" and, above all, on (reformed) Islam.

In the context of the new Islamic Revival, reformed Muslim scholars as well as lay people have increasingly questioned figurative representations. Different and opposing attitudes toward images have gained a new religious-political importance and have become intensely debated and contested. In addition, *purdah,* the ideal of (gendered) modesty, purity, and seclusion—that does not allow women to expose themselves in public—has been explicitly redefined to include photographs of women, videos, tape recordings, and paintings. Interactions and oppositions between different Islamic traditions, as well as interactions with the (Christian) "West" represented by the Kenyan state as well as Europe and the United States, created a more intense awareness of the ways that images (of women) intruded into everyday life, opening up various debates on the "Islamic interdiction of figurative images" and concepts of modesty and piety in relation to visual media.

Although the adaption and creative use of traveling visual media technologies by local actors in the context of globalization processes have been extensively explored, I focus in what follows more on opposite processes of disentanglement, refusal, and withdrawal from global media and the creation of new opacities and secrecies that have been largely ignored by scholars.[2] And whereas it seems as if most scholars take for granted that modern media technologies have gained an undisputed place everywhere in the world and that a counterhistory to the hegemonic spread of mass media on a global scale could not be told (anymore), I will explore specific social spaces on the East African coast in which possibilities of refusal and withdrawal from photography have been created and particular forms of mediation are questioned—even before digital technologies arrived. To better understand the social spaces of refusal as they have been created by Muslims on the coast, I first explore some aspects of the history of (photographic) images on the coast, a history in which highly different attitudes toward images have emerged. Before I do this, I shortly discuss my fieldwork approach and then look at what is generally called the "Islamic interdiction of images" and how it is translated into various local contexts.

Doing Ethnographic Media Research

Ethnography is currently conducted in a globalized world that is increasingly mediated by technical media. The ubiquity and globalization of technical media and media practices also in the peripheries have radically changed the relationship between the ethnographer and his or her subjects of ethnography. Whereas in the old days Malinowski among the Trobiand Islanders or Evans-Pritchard among the Azande were the only ones who owned a camera and took pictures—and the Trobriand Islanders and the Azande did not—today most subjects of ethnography have access to modern media and make use of photographic cameras, camera phones, radio, TV, video, and the internet. Nowadays, ethnographers and the subjects of their research share the same media and participate in a reality that is created by them. Both are confronted with situations, sites, and social relations that are technically mediated; spatial and social distance or closeness, presence, absence, and immediacy often are organized by technical media, and anthropologists have to reflect on these mediations and how they influence and transform ethnographic knowledge.[3]

Since the early 1990s, I have been working with various photographers—ambulant as well as studio photographers—and their customers on the production, circulation, and consumption of photographic images in the towns of Mombasa, Lamu, and Malindi in Kenya and Birmingham in England. Some of the photographers originated from India or Yemen and were Muslims or Hindus, whereas others came from the western and central province of Kenya and were Christians. Some owned prestigious studios and catered for the elite, while others worked as street photographers and took pictures of migrant workers and African tourists.[4]

Although technical media transcend space and time, I decided to study photographic practices in situ, in localized social and cultural contexts. Likewise, I practiced a multilocal ethnographic research. In various places, I participated in photo sessions and festivities (weddings in particular); held long conversations, casual as well as more formal, with photographers and customers; and visited national and private archives. I experimented with various methods to create intercultural feedbacks and interactive engagement by, for example, visiting friends at home and in the diaspora to look at their photo albums together. The latter method often unleashed an astonishing stream of information and stories. It was as though the photos opened fields of knowledge of their own accord, creating ethnographic knowledge I could never have tapped with well-chosen questions alone. In fact, it called on the exploration of possibilities to include photographs themselves in the research process as instruments to generate knowledge.

Through these diverse approaches and with the kind assistance and patience of photographers and customers, I was able to get insights not only into the production, circulation, consumption, and flows of photographs but also into the more negative responses to photography: attempts to create distances, ruptures, and new opacities as well as to withdraw from its regime of visibility.

It is important to clarify that making spaces of refusal the main subject of this contribution is not an attempt to reinstate Orientalism. As Patricia Spyer has shown, resistance to photography was a colonial trope. There was a pervasive European desire to go to all extremes and expose the allegedly primitive (antimodern) refusal to be photographed.[5] However, despite this, we know that in many parts of the world—including the West—photographic subjects experienced severe perturbation and tried to escape the camera, for example, when snapshot photography became possible and produced the "unwilling" subject.[6] I do not intend to reestablish the old opposition that takes the West as a pursuer of visibility, truth, and enlightenment and the Orient (including the East African coast) as prone to concealing and secrecy. As Walter Benjamin suggested, truth is not a matter of exposure that destroys a secret but of revelation that does justice to it.

The Coast and Its Media

Africa is often seen as the continent of figurative icons, of masks, sculptures, bronze castings, and "fetishes," yet, as Jack Goody has suggested, there are large gaps in their distribution. There were and are regions where little or no figurative art was produced or only in restricted contexts.[7] Sometimes people with rich sculptural traditions and those without lived as neighbors, had access to the same resources, and on various levels were in intense contact with each other. Obviously, in certain historical contexts, some people may decide against certain images, maybe in more or less conscious opposition to those who do produce these representations.[8] Thus, not only monotheistic religions have rejected and problematized figurative images and the representability of god; also some polytheistic religions preferred the absence of figurative representation.[9]

It seems that the East African coast was such an area where even in pre-Islamic times we have no evidence of a strong pictorial tradition. And when Islam started to spread along the coast in the eighth century, the (assumed) absence of figurative representations mentioned above may have matched well with Islam's (highly complicated) attitude toward images. Whereas in other parts of Africa the process of Islamization was inimical to African artistry and material culture because Islam (like Christianity) could and would not tolerate "idols" and other figurative representations, it seems highly probable that along the East African coast Islam established itself without iconoclastic acts and without radical rupture; this even more so because Islam's hostility toward and refusal of figurative images seems to be a later development.

Ludwig Krapf, the first CMS (Church Missionary Society) missionary to evangelize the coastal people, mentioned the absence of "idolatry" in his diary (15 December 1848): "In Great Rabbai there is said to be a Kisuka, a little devil, i.e., an image, probably of a saint which the Portuguese left behind them after their expulsion from Mombaz, which is now reverenced by the Wanika as a kind of war-god, and is borne round in procession before the outbreak of a war to rouse the warriors to heroic deeds. This is the only idol I have heard of in Eastern Africa, and it remarkably enough comes from an idolatrous Christian church."[10]

With the exception of the above mentioned *kisuka* "idol"—the statue of Holy Mary, left behind by the Portuguese—we do not know whether the arrival of the Portuguese with their Christian imagery transformed the indifference toward images into a more conscious refusal or whether images continued to not preoccupy Muslim minds. In any case, the material culture that archaeologists have found, such as ceramics, glass, and porcelain, locally produced and imported from China, India, Persia, and Arabia, seems to have followed the aniconic tradition. And coins, most of them probably minted on the coast, were all nonfigural, and with their inscriptions in the Arabic language, they can be classified as Islamic.[11]

Although the production of figurative images (on material support) probably did not take place along the coast, there existed another tradition of visualization that centered on the production of inner images that were given expression in performances of spirit possession. Alien spirits embodied themselves as "living images" in their mediums during possession rituals. In performative visualizations of spirit possession, "living images" of strangers were (and still are) communicated in institutionalized forms. In fact, the absence or marginalization of visual media such as sculpture or figurative painting coincided with complex imaginative practices that centered on embodiment and in the context of spirit possession rituals were externalized so that they could be shared by other people.[12]

Like rituals of spirit possession, the media of scripture and textiles also preceded the medium of photography and intensively shaped the visual economies of recording and processing the visibility, performance, social status, and meaning in photographs.

Textiles and (In)visibilities in the Nineteenth Century

In the nineteenth century along the East African coast, a visual regime dominated that expressed origin and descent, social class and status through the quality and social value of (imported) textiles and by the amount of clothing a person used to cover his or her body. Class and status, as well as sexual difference, manifested themselves within the field of vision by withdrawing women, in particular, from visibility in the public domain. Respectable femininity demanded the veil as a kind of shield against the gaze of unrelated men in public spaces. Whereas slaves went "naked" and wore only the slightest of clothes usually made of the rudest and cheapest material, Omani aristocrats were distinguished by their sophisticated headdress and silk cloth. High-ranking women who were privileged to stay in seclusion would cover their whole bodies in public, including their faces, behind masks, veils, and portable walls, so-called *shiraa,* carried by slaves and later forbidden by the British.[13]

A complex technology of veiling and concealing was made available for extending women's physical seclusion outside their home. Veils in these different forms were movable, flexible, and unstable; as *shiraa,* the wall-like textiles would hide a woman completely, and other forms of veil could take the shape of what they covered, thereby remaining suggestive of what they were hiding.

"Kusitiri," a Swahili term that can be translated as "concealment," has been identified by David Parkin as a "root metaphor," serving as an affective base for social action.[14] In fact, *kusitiri* implies not only the decent concealment of women's and men's heads and bodies with textiles, but also the control of the body, of movement and gestures, and of the affective expression of people, both in speech and in poetry.

It is important to note that a veiled person also gives something to see by creating a secondary image of defacement, thereby challenging the simple binary opposition between revealing and concealing. In fact, the veil makes invisibility very visible; it makes an overt and visual point out of concealment, in the process transforming the private, individual woman into her public representation of a more general kind.[15] The visual power of the veil seems to be rooted in this tension between invisibility and visibility and its intimate relationship with the body. The visible screen that is provided by the veil, hiding and protecting the "inside" from view, produces a strange surplus of desire and energy and lies at the heart of a vast range of social powers and different forms of knowledge.[16]

After the abolition of slavery, men and women of slave origin covered their heads and bodies as one of the first ways they could show their "freedom" and new status.[17] When the *buibui*—a loose black garment that covered the entire body except for face, hands, and feet—was introduced around the 1930s, it was quickly adopted by women of the lower classes and of slave origin to show their respectability, their adherence to Islam, and their modesty.[18]

In the 1960s and 1970s, however, the veil was disappearing in most towns along the coast as unveiling went along with aspirations for independence and modernity. Yet, with the emergence of reformed Islam and its attempts to Islamize public spaces, the veil and new Islamic clothing strongly reappeared, not only to mark (female) Muslim presence but also to erase social and economic differences between wearers. The new Islamic dress imbued women with a kind of moral and religious authority that would discourage harassment and allowed them assertively to enter public spaces.[19]

Although the various technologies of veiling seem to have been able to protect women in particular from being seen (and heard) by others (unrelated men), the introduction of technical media such as photography and video intensely disturbed the existing boundaries between public and private. Because the proliferation of mass media has strongly foregrounded public visuality, new strategies were demanded for the protection of what should not be seen.

When photography arrived in the coastal towns, the foreign medium—when used for figurative representations—met a whole range of different forms of resistance as well as acceptance among Muslims. In the following, I present two photographic genres: identification photography of the colonial and postcolonial state, and wedding photography, a practice of visual recording that connects to administrative image making while at the same time translating photographic documentation into the more private or even intimate domain of family rituals. But before I do so, I discuss the "Islamic interdiction of figurative representations" and give insights into the local debates about photography in the context of the dynamics of reform and piety since the 1980s.

Problematizing Figurative Images

Whereas the God of the Old Testament found it necessary to present the Ten Commandments and among them the interdiction against making images of Himself, this is not necessary in the Qur'an owing to the metaphysical concept of the Islamic God, who is impenetrable and "like nothing else."[20] The God of Islam does not reveal himself in flesh but conceals himself—with the exception of the revelation—and remains constant in form.[21] Muhammad radicalized monotheism by abolishing its pictorial multiplication; he purified godliness from symbolic practice and claimed the position of consistent unity in contrast to Trinitarian Christianity.

Although of the three monotheistic religions, Islam seems to be the most unfavorable toward images, Muslim theologians have hardly shown much interest in images. The Qur'an tells only how Abraham broke the idols of his father Azar. And when the Prophet conquered Mecca in 630, he cleansed the building of idols, whose number is given as 360.[22] It is obvious that three-dimensional objects that throw a shadow are refused here, whereas flat, two-dimensional images are not mentioned at all. It is above all idol-worship that is interdicted, not images as such.

The "Islamic interdiction of images" is based much more on the Hadith, that is, the tradition of the sayings and doings of the Prophet.[23] In the texts of the Hadith—of the Sunni and of the Shia—images are described as impure, like dogs, and therefore that they should not be present during prayer.[24] Whereas aniconic images are allowed, images that depict human beings and animals—creatures with *ruh,* breath or life force—are forbidden because their representation implies an act of hubris, an attempt to do what only God, the Almighty, can do. It follows from the synonymous use of the Arabic word for "to represent" and "to create" that a human being who dares to represent another person is challenging God's privilege and therefore deserves to be punished. On the day of resurrection, God will demand that artists who create human beings or animals in pictures or statues bring to life what they have created. Because they will not be able to give *ruh* to their fabrication, they will be punished in the fires of hell.[25]

Yet, representations of human beings were allowed by some Islamic scholars if the images were not hung on the wall but placed on the ground, for example, on rugs or cushions.[26] Also, images depicting decapitated humans or animals lose the status of being an image and are not forbidden.[27] "If the head of the image (of a human being) is separated, the abjectness is invalid." An image is like a living body. A headless body is no longer alive, and an image of a headless body is no longer an image.[28] This is why some figures were represented with lines separating their heads from the rest of the body to decapitate them and so take their lives.[29] Through these acts, artists made clear that they did not attempt to rival God.

Figures that threw no shadows because they formed part of a two-dimensional space were also understood as already "bereft of life" and were therefore not interdicted.[30] As Hans Belting has suggested, the Islamic image concept identifies body and image in such a way that the fatal damaging of a depicted person, for example, by decapitation, makes the image acceptable because it is no longer an image. It is the negation of a magical concept while likewise recognizing its magical potential in the iconoclastic act through which the power of images is destroyed.[31]

It is important to note that the favoring of aniconism in Islam did not exclude engagement with images. As Oleg Grabar has shown, several Arabic texts dated as early as the tenth century mention the existence of painted portraits of Muhammad, as well as Jesus and other figures of the Old Testament.[32] Yet, it is interesting to note that these portraits were "originally from Christian lands" and thus made by (or for) non-Muslims.[33] When in one of these narratives the Chinese emperor invites Muhammad to China and the Prophet instead sends a portrait of himself, this portrait, so the story goes, is painted so as to disappear after a certain time. This precaution is said to have been inspired by the Prophet's fear that the emperor might be tempted to worship the image.[34]

In contrast to Christian theology, no explicit image theory has been formulated in the Hadith, and for a long time the question of images seems not to have preoccupied Muslim minds.[35] Indeed, the aversion to pictures as expressed in the Hadith may have developed only in the late Umayyad period, probably under Jewish and Christian influence.[36] Perhaps only the confrontation with Christian images made Muslim theologians feel it necessary to mark their own difference and, in opposition to Christian iconography, begin to problematize figurative representations in the Hadith.[37]

However, even then the interdiction of images was never absolute. In the more profane domain of palaces and in the castles of the elites, there were wall paintings and pictorial decorations, especially in Anatolia, where even statues were used. Representations of birds and quadrupeds, as well as of scenes from courtly life or illustrations of various tales, are found on many metal and ceramic objects.[38] Since the ninth century, book illuminations were produced in manuscripts on paper, and these also included portraits of persons; and calligraphy often explored the boundaries between scripture and figurative images by composing a human or animal figure out of letters.[39] Images were prohibited above all in sacred spaces, whereas they were occasionally tolerated in profane buildings. Thus, to speak of an absence of figurative images in the Islamic world before the introduction of modern visual media would be wrong, although in some regions, probably including the East African coast, these images may have been rare.

It seems that of the three monotheistic religions, Christianity has to be seen as an exception because—although never uncontested—it allowed images to become the center of its cult. Yet, interestingly, this happened only after the fifth century, when Christianity had gained the status of a state religion and the images of the emperor had been substituted by the images of Christ.[40]

I would therefore agree with Oleg Grabar that there is nothing inherent in Islam that necessarily rejects or prohibits images. The interdiction of figurative images was formulated owing to specific historical conditions. An attitude of indifference toward images was transformed into a prohibition when Islam had to define its difference from Christianity, which strongly made use of images as a political and religious weapon. The rejection of certain images in certain contexts was then legalized and through jurisdiction gained a moral quality.[41] However, as the proliferation of technical images and all-pervasive image making in the Islamic world—in particular, in the domain of popular religion—for about a hundred years has shown, the interdiction of images was never absolute and may be completely suspended when images are turned into a weapon to serve the cause of Islam. Rather than proclaiming an Islamic prohibition of images, it seems more appropriate to speak of an underlying aniconism in Islamic religious art that, however, in times of religious revival may be actualized into a more radical form of an interdiction of figurative representation.

Debating the "Interdiction of Figurative Images" and Modern Media

Although Islamic practice along the coast is both heterogeneous and contested, the tensions between "custom" (in Swahili *mila*), Muslim authorities, and reformists have grown since the 1980s with the increasing influence of Wahhabism, which Saudi Arabian funding campaigns have established as an integral part of the global community of Muslims, thereby creating various reformist movements and organizations along the East African coast.[42] Reformists have rearticulated forms of piety and the self that put more emphasis on the individual, rationalism, responsibility, and, above all, interiority. For instance, prayer and worship are supposed to have an altering effect and influence one's inner life, one's heart. In addition, reformed Muslim scholars as well as lay people have strongly refocused on the interpretation of the Qur'an, sharia law, and the elimination of what is seen as (un-Islamic) innovations, such as spirit possession and worshipping of saints. As Janet McIntosh and others have observed, many Muslims turn increasingly away from the ostensibly African flavor of certain local Islamic practices and orient themselves toward Middle Eastern affiliations and forms of religiosity.[43] They consider the reformist movement as some sort of enlightenment, a notion that captures its emphasis on the rational, self-governing, and self-responsible individual. And, interestingly, the focus on rationality and introspection is regarded as important even by those who do not consider themselves reformists.[44]

Since the 1980s, in the context of the new Islamic Revival, reformed Muslim scholars as well as lay people have not only actualized the "Islamic interdiction of figurative images" but extended it to modern mass media such as photography and video. In addition, *purdah,* the ideal of (gendered) modesty, purity, and seclusion—that does not allow women to expose themselves in public—has been explicitly redefined to include photographs of women, videos, tape recordings, and paintings. In new Islamic schools called *mahad*—established in Mombasa in the early 1990s—women especially have learned to discuss and problematize their visibility in visual media. What used to be a theological debate among scholars has become an increasingly popularized theme. As mentioned before, not only interactions and oppositions between different Islamic traditions but also oppositions to the (Christian) "West"—represented by the Kenyan state as well as Europe and the United States—created a more intense awareness of the ways that images (of women) intruded into everyday life. Interdictions and moral claims on women's bodies to conform to a particular aesthetics of propriety and piety have translated into new strategies of concealment and veiling also in relation to photography, video, and painting.

Today, among (reformed) Muslims the prohibition to represent human beings and animals is widely accepted; however, the reasons given vary considerably. I met some Islamic scholars who resented photographic portraits because they feared image worship—especially when the picture was hung on a wall—and saw Islamic monotheism endangered, but they accepted video because of its fleeting images that would not allow idolatry. In contrast, other Muslims claimed that photography as a picture medium should not be prohibited because it does not create what it depicts but only reproduces or represents what is already there; therefore, photographers do not violate God's singular capacity of creation. Another scholar argued that only three-dimensional things can become objects of idol worship, whereas two-dimensional pictures of human beings or animals, such as photographs, cannot because they have lost already their lifelike quality. Again, other scholars maintained that the photographic picture is already lifeless; because photography freezes and immobilizes all it captures, an iconoclastic gesture is inherent in it. Since vitality is already annihilated in the photographic image, it cannot be considered as imitating God's creation. And a female Islamic scholar and midwife, Asya Sunkar Salim, held that, since there is no mention in the Qur'an of photographs, the Prophet did not say that photographs should not be taken. For her, photographs of women were, first and foremost, a question of modesty. As long as the photographed women cover their body according to Islamic rules, she had no objections to photographs. For her, the degree of exposure was at issue rather than the portrayal itself.[45]

As demonstrated above, there existed a multitude of competing voices accepting or questioning photographic portraits. These voices covered a spectrum that at one extreme totally refused photographic portraits and at the other included more pragmatic attitudes that allowed the production of photographs in a controlled way. But the problematization of (gendered) figurative images and the actualization of *purdah* did not necessarily function solely in a repressive manner but became also extremely productive, unleashing a creative potential to follow or undermine the interdictions.

Photography as Unveiling

Although one line of argumentation against photographic representations of human beings (and animals) was based on religious discourse and, in particular, on the actualization of the "Islamic interdiction of figurative representation," another line of contestation also existed that was more politically oriented and focused on one specific photographic genre: identification photography. This discourse is connected to state politics, surveillance, and violence and began during colonial times. In the late 1940s, the colonial state in Kenya started to demand photographs—cropped, frontal head-shots—for identification cards to better identify and control its subjects.[46] If somebody wanted to travel, open a bank account, or get a driver's license, a photo ID was needed. Especially in the rural areas, capturing the face for a photo ID was often the first encounter with photography as a gesture of subjection by the (colonial) state.[47]

Although identification photography is a global genre, it nevertheless has accumulated resonances and nuances specific to the East African coast. Here Muslim women's veils formed an obstacle to the sight of the colonial government and its cameras. Veiled women reinforced the impression of inaccessibility. The veil discouraged the colonial photographer's scopic desire and intimated more or less clearly a refusal. Veiling, and in particular veiling the face, was considered equivalent to resistance. And just as for Christians and Westerners the face marked the identity of a person, the veil was not only (mis)understood as a symbol of the oppressed status of women but also as a potentially subversive attempt to hide one's identity. Especially in towns like Mombasa, the colonial administration, as well as colonized husbands and fathers, shared the concern about the control of women who, when wearing the veil, could get "lost" and were hard for the government or relatives to trace.[48] Thus, the veil had to fall and faces, including those of women, had to offer themselves to the bold cameras of the photographers working for the state.

Along the Islamic East African coast, Muslims in particular experienced the imposition of identification photography as a violent act and as humiliating. In colonial as well as postcolonial times, the central government in Kenya lay in the hands of Christians; so measures were interpreted as deliberate infringements of Islam's "interdiction of figurative representations" and as anti-Muslim. I was told many stories about resistance to photography, particularly by pious Muslim women who wanted to go on a pilgrimage to Mecca and therefore needed a passport. They associated photo IDs not only with foreignness, Christianity, and colonization but with the act of forcefully unveiling their face and thereby violating conventions of piety and modesty. Thus, identification photography gained in particular among pious (reformed) Muslims, a negative connotation. The boundaries and divides, such as inside/outside, private/public, female/male, and inclusion/exclusion, that are created by the veil were troubled and disturbed by photography. As the proliferation of mass media has strongly favored public visuality, it conflicted with the already existing boundaries. In fact, photographs were conceived as the opposite of the veil because the camera intruded into a domain conceived as private and because the camera recorded an "excess" of visible details and surfaces that could not be controlled. The mobile medium also provoked anxieties about the easy reproduction, mobility, and circulation of portraits of women among, in particular, (unrelated) men who were not supposed to see them. While veils were used to cover and conceal women's bodies and faces, photographs revealed what should have remained concealed. Strong tensions arose between the global medium of photography, which "unveils" and always gives something "more" to see, and local understandings of the appropriate use of women's visibility. These tensions led to various attempts to withdraw women from visibility and to create new opacities.

In many narratives that were told to me, Muslim women stressed the fact that the photographed person originally had refused to be photographed; only because he or she wanted to go for a pilgrimage to Mecca and therefore needed a passport photograph had he or she finally agreed to have a picture taken. For example, Ahmed Badawy (1898–1939), son of the famous Sheik Habib Saleh (1844–1935), the reformer and founder of the Riyadha mosque in Lamu, refused to be photographed because he did not want to violate the "Islamic interdiction of figurative images," as his great-granddaughter Muzna Ahmed told me. Yet, to be able to go to Mecca he finally allowed a passport photograph to be taken. His cousin, who was an artist, however, secretly painted a full body portrait of him. This together with the passport photograph was brought to the Bakor Studio at Lamu where the owner and photographer Omar Said Bakor produced a wonderful collage out of the passport photograph and the painting, which is still cherished today by Saleh's descendants.

In another conversation I was told about Fatma, the daughter of Sheik Habib Saleh, who also needed a passport photograph to go to Mecca. As a woman, she was even more anxious about unveiling her face to the photographer, because she would thereby violate not only the interdiction of figurative representation but also *purdah,* or women's purity and modesty that is associated with their (partial) invisibility in the public domain. This is why she burned the photograph after her pilgrimage; but fortunately, as her granddaughter Muzna Ahmed told me, the negative was saved. It was enlarged in the Bakor Studio, and her descendants are happy to be able to remember her in the photograph. Photographs originally produced within the colonial relationship could thus assume new purposes and meanings representing highly treasured ancestors who provided a connection between the past and the present.[49]

In these narratives, the highly ambivalent attitude toward photographic portraits produced by the state is displayed. Whereas descendants may cherish the reworked photographs of their ancestors in new framings, they nevertheless stress in their narratives that the preservation of the pictures was not intended by the persons photographed but happened more or less accidentally. Obviously, because the colonial and postcolonial government's visual politics was bent on unveiling Islamic women through photographs, it actualized and reinforced what now is seen as an essential part of local tradition, culture, and religion—the veil, *purdah,* and the "interdiction of figurative images." When Muslim women today critically associate photography and unveiling, they refer to their experiences of forceful unveiling in front of a photographer working for the postcolonial administration and a state that insists on a visual regime of transparency.

Studio Photography and Weddings

Whereas identification photographs fix the individual in the form of a depersonalized, atemporal, and singular index, photographing family rituals generates an iconic mapping of ritual processes, celebrating, enhancing, and extending ritual's formal conventionality and replicability.[50] Against the constraint of state photography, it was the institution of the photo studio that provided a space of playfulness and experimentation and allowed people to escape fixed identities. As Liam Buckley has suggested, it is, however, impossible to clearly separate administrative photography from studio photography as some sort of vernacular photography.[51] Yet, although (colonial) hegemonic powers have shaped the studio, we can also observe conscious moments of opposition and subversion to state photography, its formats and its aesthetics. Thus, despite the shock and initial rejection that accompanied the new technology, studio photographers since the 1940s provided services that were largely inserted into everyday life of Muslims and their rites of passage, in particular, weddings. Like other imported luxury commodities, photography—as act and object—entered the wedding rituals and became part of expenditure and the conspicuous display of wealth, prestige, and battles of status.[52] In addition, in the 1960s and 1970s, photographic portraits—produced in studios—became part of a "technique of the self," a new form of self-creation that offered a new way of relating to the self as well as to others. Photographic portraits formed part of a continuous process of feedback and adjustment that Foucault called "a network of permanent observation."[53]

Yet, since the 1980s, as mentioned before, pious Muslims have increasingly drawn attention to the complementary effects of unveiling and women's exposure in photographs and videos, both violating *purdah* and the "Islamic interdiction of figurative representation." This is why photographs of Muslim women have disappeared completely from the public show cases of studios in Mombasa's Old Town and Lamu. In addition, in the private domain of many homes, photographs of (male and female) relatives or friends have been removed from the sitting room and either put up in the intimate domain of the bedroom or stored in albums or boxes. However, I heard of only one case in which a pious woman destroyed all her photographs in order to comply with Islam's aniconism. The other women I talked to kept their photographs—more or less hidden—in albums or boxes in order to control access to them.

Whereas photographs before the 1980s were "a must" and "everything and everybody was photographed" during weddings, nowadays, many Muslim women prefer regulations that allow them to control picture taking. In fact, in such a context, not photographing becomes as much of a statement as photographing.[54] During Muslim weddings in Mombasa and Lamu, announcements nowadays are often made asking the guests to keep their camera phones closed and to leave the picture taking to the official photographers and video makers. And indeed, during most of the weddings I attended in 2011, women guests made no use of their individual camera phones, and the image recording was done by (female) professional photographers and video makers.

Whereas the audience before the 1980s also was photographed, nowadays a special decorated stage is reserved for taking pictures. Only those who want to be photographed (together with the bride) climb the stage while the others remain seated in a space where taking pictures is not allowed. At some weddings, women would use their veils even inside the room to protect their faces from being photographed. Furthermore, at a few weddings, no videos were taken. I was informed that some pious families preferred not to record weddings anymore.

Photographs as Gifts

During weddings in the 1960s and 1970s, photographs also served as gifts to be distributed among relatives and guests. They entered a process of transnational communication and circulation safeguarding against the individual's propensity to "keep to oneself" (Marcel Mauss). As at a potlatch, during weddings photographs formed part of the exchange of gifts and countergifts, and the quantity and quality of photographs distributed affirmed and added to the host's social standing. "People are crazy," one Indian photographer remarked, "they want 400 to 600 pictures for one wedding." Photographers were invited to take pictures of each and every action, he said. Sometimes the host spent so much money that he could not pay for the developing and printing and thus ruined himself and his family.

Photographs (and videos) were distributed as gifts not only to guests but also to relatives and friends living abroad in the diaspora who had not been able to attend the feast. Thanks to the new technology, people separated in space were able to maintain relations, share the experience of festivities and rituals, and form one transnational community.[55] In fact, photographs (and videos) constitute new spaces of connection and interaction. They allow one to animate, replicate, and extend the experience and sensations in the diaspora, as well as at home when reviewing the pictures. Information, sensation, and experience can be mobilized through photographic inscriptions across time and space; they stay immutable though they are displaced.[56] At home or in the diaspora, family members and friends would meet together with neighbors in front of a TV set to view the videos and photographic images of a wedding, sometimes actually repeating the feast and participating in the status struggles technical media not only record but have become part of.

While some Muslim families continued to send "modest" photographs and videos to relatives, others have stopped doing so. Whereas in the 1960s, 1970s, and early 1980s hundreds of photographs were produced as part of the ostentatious display of wealth and status and given as gifts to the guests, nowadays, at least in reformed families, only a few photographs are printed for the wedding album of the bride. And this wedding album does not circulate among friends and relatives any more but stays at home. Thus, the exchange and circulation of photographs (of women) as a gift and countergift and as a kind of "family currency" has been greatly restricted, sometimes even halted. Pious families dispensed with one of the most important qualities of photography, namely, its capacity to celebrate the extended family as a unit and, at the same time, as an instrument and tool to effect that unity.[57] They have also dispensed with the specific qualities of photographs as gifts, as a possibility of giving oneself to another by offering oneself in a picture. To assure *purdah,* they renounced the "binding" and "relational quality" of photographs and videos and the chance to share the "special moments" of heightened social density a wedding provides when reviewing the wedding video or the wedding photographs. In a way, this withdrawal of photographs mirrors and reproduces Muslims' marginalization in Kenya in an ambiguous manner.

As mentioned before, the role of new media is not only to expand transnational Muslim networks and to increase visibilities—as has been assumed in a rather general way by scholars such as Eickelman and Anderson. Rather, there are also counterattempts to withdraw from visibility, to interrupt the flow of images, in particular the images of women, and to create new opacities.[58] As a negative reaction to globalization processes, some pious Muslim women and men have increasingly started to cut their transnational networks and keep their photographs (as extensions of themselves) at home, sometimes even hidden in a box.

Although seemingly contradicting the logic of mass media, the withdrawal from visibility should, however, not be understood only as a loss, but also as an act of empowerment. Defacement and other strategies to withdraw from visibility are not destroying value but instead exert a curious property of magnifying.[59]

It is not only pious Muslims who have challenged the hegemony of vision. Walter Benjamin saw the interdiction of figurative images as going far beyond the warding off of idolatry, so much feared by monotheistic religions. In its deepest sense, he suggested, the refusal of images attempts to take precautions against the error that man as a moral being could be represented.[60] And it was the Hebrew iconoclastic attitude—and not the Islamic "interdiction of images"—that served as a countermodel for Emmanuel Levinas to construct a feminine mode of being that consisted in slipping away from the light, allowing mothers, wives, and daughters a secret presence, a hiding in modesty, depicting the dimensions of interiority itself and making the world habitable.[61] There is thus some convergence between a few Western intellectuals who in their critique of Western ocularcentrism take recourse to religious iconoclasm and constructions of femininity in the Old Testament and the critique of images as formulated by Islamic scholars along the East African coast. Both understand visuality as a potential trap, and to escape it, (gendered) veils, obstacles, opacities, and domains of unsurveyability are (re)created.

Notes

1. See Heike Behrend and Tobias Wendl, eds., *9/11 and Its Remediations in Africa* (Berlin: Lit Verlag, 2015); Heike Behrend, *Contesting Visibility: Photographic Practices on the East African Coast* (Bielefeld: Transcript, 2013); Rüediger Seesemann, "Kenyan Muslims, the Aftermath of 9/11, and the 'War on Terror'," in *Islam and Muslim Politics in Africa,* ed. Benjamin F. Soares and René Otoyek (New York: Palgrave, 2007), 157–76.

2. As exceptions, see Siegel 2009; Patricia Spyer, "In and Out of the Picture: Photography, Ritual, and Modernity in Aru, Indonesia," in *Photographies East,* ed. Rosalind Morris (Durham, NC: Duke University Press, 2001); Spyer 2009; and De Witte 2010.

3. For a more detailed description of the circumstances and predicaments of my fieldwork approach, see chapter 3 in Behrend, *Contesting Visibility.*

4. See Behrend, *Contesting Visibility,* chapters 5, 6, and 7.

5. Spyer, "In and Out of the Picture."

6. Diane Waggoner, "Photographic Amusement, 1888–1919," in *The Art of the American Snapshot, 1888–1978: The Collection of Robert E. Jackson* (Washington, DC: National Gallery of Art, 2007).

7. Jack Goody, *Representations and Contradictions: Ambivalence towards Images, Theatre, Fictions, Relics and Sexuality* (Oxford: Blackwell, 1997), 35.

8. Fritz Kramer, "Praktiken der Imagination," in *Die Unvermeidlichkeit der Bilder,* ed. Gerhard von Graevenitz, Stefan Rieger, and Felix Thuerlemann (Tübingen: Gunther Narr Verlag, 2001).

9. Goody, *Representations,* 56.

10. Ludwig Krapf, *Travels, Researches and Missionary Labours* (London: Truebner, 1968), 202.

11. H. W. Brown, "Coins of East Africa: An Introductory Survey," *Yarmouk Numismatics* 5 (1993): 9–16.

12. Kramer, "Praktiken der Imagination."

13. John Middleton, *The World of the Swahili: An African Mercantile Civilization* (New Haven: Yale University Press, 1992), 150.

14. David Parkin, "Latticed Knowledge: Eradication and Dispersal of the Unpalatable in Islam, Medicine and Anthropological Theory," in *Counterworks: Managing the Diversity of Knowledge,* ed. Richard Fardon (London: Routledge, 1995), 212.

15. Sandra Dudley, "Material Visions: Dress and Textiles," in *Made to Be Seen: Perspectives on the History of Visual Anthropology,* ed. Marcus Banks and Jay Ruby (Chicago: University of Chicago Press, 2011).

16. Michael Taussig, *Defacement: Public Secrecy and the Labor of the Negative* (Stanford: Stanford University Press, 1999).

17. Laura Fair, "Dressing Up: Clothing, Class and Gender in Post-Abolition Zanzibar," *Journal of African History* (1998): 93.

18. Ibid, 82.

19. Cf. Leila Ahmed, *Women and Gender in Islam: Historical Roots of a Modern Debate* (New Haven: Yale University Press, 2011), 87.

20. Alain Besançon, *L'image interdite: Une histoire intellectuelle de l'iconoclasme* (Paris: Fayard, 1994), 151.

21. Dorna Safaian, "After the Machine: The Economy of Innovation and the Iconotechnics of Islam," in *Medium Religion: Faith, Geopolitics, Art,* ed. Boris Groys and Peter Weibel (Cologne: Walther Koenig, 2009), 69.

22. Annemarie Schimmel, *Deciphering the Signs of God* (Edinburgh: Edinburgh University Press, 1994), 57.

23. Rudi Paret, "Textbelege zum islamischen Bilderverbot," in *Das Werk des Künstlers,* ed. Hans Fegers (Stuttgart: Kohlhammer, 1960), 36.

24. Silvia Naef, *Y a-t-il une "question de l'image" en Islam?* (Geneva: Tetraede, 2004), 17.

25. Ibric Almir, *Das Bilderverbot im Islam* (Marburg: Tectum Verlag, 2004), 60.

26. Paret, "Textbelege," 45; Naef, *Question de l'image,* 18.

27. Naef, *Question de l'image,* 21.

28. Paret, "Textbelege," 46.

29. Almir, *Bildverbot,* 95.

30. ibid.

31. Hans Belting, *Das echte Bild: Bildfragen als Glaubensfragen* (Munich: C H Beck, 2005).

32. Oleg Grabar, "The Story of Portraits of the Prophet Muhammad," *Studia Islamica* 96 (2003).

33. Ibid, 35.

34. Ibid, 26.

35. Naef, *Question de l'image,* 26.

36. Johan Christoph Bürgel, *The Feather of Simurgh: The "Licit Magic" of the Arts in Medieval Islam* (New York: NYU Press, 1988).

37. Naef, *Question de l'image,* 31; Oleg Grabar, *Die Entstehung der Islamischen Kunst* (Cologne: Boehlau, 1977), 101.

38. Schimmel, *Signs of God,* 34.

39. Naef, *Question de l'image,* 51, 58.

40. Ibid, 28.

41. Grabar, *Islamische Kunst,* 104.

42. Wahhabism is named after the eighteenth-century preacher and scholar Muhammad ibn Abd Al-Wahhab (1703–92), who started a revivalist movement of Sunni Islam that later succeeded in forming an alliance with the Kingdom of Saudi Arabia. The movement stands for a literalist interpretation of Islam, including a strong prohibition of images.

43. Janet McIntosh, *The Edge of Islam: Power, Personhood and Ethnoreligious Boundaries on the Kenyan Coast* (Durham: Duke University Press, 2009), 127.

44. Ibid, 135.

45. See Allan F. Roberts and Mary Nooter Roberts, *A Saint in the City: Sufi Arts of Urban Senegal* (Los Angeles: University of California Fowler Museum of Cultural History, 2003), 8.

46. Isolde Anna Brielmaier, "'Picture Taking' and the Production of Urban Identities on the Kenyan Coast" (PhD diss., Columbia University, New York, 2003), 131.

47. Jean-François Werner, "Photography and Individualization in Contemporary Africa: An Ivorian Case-Study," in "Photographies and Modernities in Africa," ed. Heike Behrend and Jean-François Werner, special issue, *Visual Anthropology* 14, no. 3 (2001).

48. Justin Willis, *Mombasa, the Swahili and the Making of the Mijikenda* (Oxford: Blackwell, 1993).

49. Jane Lydon, *Eye Contact: Photographing Indigenous Australians* (Durham, NC: Duke University Press, 2005), 225, 237.

50. See Karen Strassler, *Refracted Visions: Popular Photography and National Modernity in Java* (Durham, NC: Duke University Press, 2010), 21.

51. Liam Buckley, "Cine-Film, Film-Strips and the Devolution of Colonial Photography in the Gambia," in "Photography in Africa," ed. Sylvester Okwunodu Ogbechie and John Pfeffer, special issue, *History of Photography* 34, no. 2 (2010): 147–57.

52. Heike Behrend, "'The Terror of the Feast': Photography, Textiles and Memory in Weddings along the East African Coast," in *Photography in Africa: Ethnographic Perspectives,* ed. Richard Vokes (Oxford: James Currey, 2012).

53. Michel Foucault, cited after Jonathan Crary, *Suspension of Perception: Attention, Spectacle and Modern Culture* (Cambridge, MA: Harvard University Press, 1999), 76.

54. Cf. Eric Michaels, "A Primer of Restrictions on Picture-Taking in Traditional Areas of Aboriginal Australia," *Visual Anthropology* 4 (1991): 270.

55. James Clifford, *Routes: Travel and Translation in the Late Twentieth Century* (Cambridge, MA: Harvard University Press, 1997); Crary, *Suspension of Perception,* 246.

56. Photographs are what Bruno Latour has called "immutable mobiles": they allow the transfer and translation of an object without modifying its internal properties. They create "optical consistency," a translation without corruption that invites mobilization, travel, and displacement. See Bruno Latour, "Visualisation and Cognition: Drawing Things Together," *Knowledge and Society* 6 (1986): 7, 8, 14.

57. Pierre Bourdieu, ed., *Eine illegitime Kunst: Die sozialen Gebrauchsweisen der Fotographie* (Frankfurt: Suhrkamp 1981).

58. Dale F. Eickelman and Jon W. Anderson, eds., *New Media in the Muslim World* (Bloomington: Indiana University Press, 1999), xiv.

59. Taussig, *Defacement,* 54.

60. Walter Benjamin, "Ursprung des deutschen Trauerspiels," in *Gesammelte Schriften,* ed. Rolf Tiedemann and Hermann Schweppenhäuser (Frankfurt: Suhrkamp, 1974), 1: 924.

61. Martin Jay, *Downcast Eyes: The Denigration of Vision in Twentieth-Century French Thought* (Berkeley: University of California Press, 1994), 559.

FIVE

Vernacular Media, Muslim Ethics, and "Conservative" Critiques of Power in the Niger Bend, Mali

BRUCE S. HALL

PRIVATE RADIO STATIONS, BROADCASTING IN VERNACULAR LANGUAGES, are almost certainly the most influential and widely consumed form of media in Mali today. After the fall of the authoritarian regime of Moussa Traoré in 1991, dozens of privately owned radio stations were established throughout the country. The programming on these stations—and in mass media more broadly—has clearly been important in reshaping many aspects of public life in Mali, not least on questions of politics, gender roles, social hierarchy, and religious belonging.[1] As Dorothea Schulz has shown, new forms of media have changed the conditions by which religious authority is configured and contested, in large part by its ability to engage new interpretive publics.[2] Indeed, the literature on mass media in broader Muslim contexts—including audio and video cassettes, radio, and television—has long focused on the transformations of religious practice produced by encounters with new forms of media.[3] But as important as new kinds of media have been in reshaping Muslim religious sensibilities in ways that have deepened support for the Islamic revival in Mali in general, and for individual reformist leaders and groups in particular, there are many other ways that mass mediation has effected Malian publics. In this chapter I explore a genre of vernacular storytelling that has become more widely accessible as a result of the production and distribution of cassettes and their broadcast on private radio stations. This form of mass media is self-consciously folkloric, celebrating "traditional" ideas about ethics and morality that draw on the older religious and social sensibilities of many Malians.[4] It is "conservative," not in the sense of political ideology necessarily, but in terms of the invocation of values associated with "traditional"—or perhaps more accurately "historical"—forms of social hierarchy, gender roles, and styles of comportment. By focusing on mass-mediated vernacular oral arts, the chapter demonstrates how issues of slavery and nobility, legitimate authority and corruption, continue to be invoked as constitutive features of Muslim modernities in Mali and elsewhere in the West African region.

My claims in this chapter are necessarily limited by the fact that I examine only a single oral performance broadcast on local radio in a minority language called Western Songhay (*koyra chiini*), which is spoken predominantly in northern Mali along the western half of the Niger Bend, from Djenné in the southwest to Timbuktu in the northeast. The performer is named Muhamane Tindirma, and he is easily the best-known storyteller among speakers of Western Songhay today. He recorded perhaps a hundred performances on cassette, and these have been broadcast repeatedly by local FM radio stations in northern Mali for the last two decades.[5] The story that I focus on here is known as "Jibo" and recounts the trials of a man named Hamidu Hamma Kula Musa, the rightful heir to the chieftaincy of Jibo (or Djibo), an ethnically Fulbe town located in the far north of modern Burkina Faso. This was historically the center of the province of Jeligoji, part of the wider Masina Empire of Hamdullahi during the nineteenth century.[6] The story takes place in a somewhat uncertain time, although probably in the early twentieth century. It centers on a chieftaincy dispute and culminates in a disaster for the people of Jibo at the hands of enemy Mossi warriors, because Jibo had chosen to deny the office of chief to its rightful heir. Although it is but a single story, it is not unlike many other stories from Mali and the wider Sahelian region that are about corruption and the betrayal of legitimate political authority.[7] As such, I read this story as an instance of a larger motif in Malian literature and as a parable, meant to point to the moral and political failings of contemporary Malian societies.

The "Jibo" story that I will discuss in this chapter lasts sixty minutes and adds up to 10,816 words in my Songhay transcription, and 13,070 words in the English translation. I highlight three themes that emerge from the story—mass mediation in vernacular storytelling, Islam, and the defense of social hierarchy.

The story of "Jibo," and the manner in which it was performed and broadcast, suggests a number of possible lines of analysis. Within the existing academic frameworks that have dominated African studies, one would expect to perhaps highlight the deep vernacularity of this performance. As such, we could think of it as folkloric, recounting an oral epic tradition, which is a genre of specialized performance well-known in West Africa as the work of praise singers and oral poets, often credited with having memorized histories of important kings, kingdoms, and the like. These people are often referred to by the French term griots, or in Mali, by the Bamana term *jeliw*. (In Western Songhay they are called *maabe-yo*.) African history as a discipline was virtually built on the development of methodologies that could take such oral traditions and use them to reconstruct deep historical periods for which there were no written records.[8] But we now know that there is much interplay between written and oral sources,[9] and in a country like Mali, where locally composed written records date back to the fifteenth century, we should not assume that orality is necessarily primary. The central motif of the story that I discuss in this chapter, about the betrayal and corruption of legitimate political and moral authority, can be found in written texts about fourteenth- and fifteenth-century kings of the Mali and Songhay Empires. As Ralph Austen and Jan Jansen have argued in the case of the Sundiata epic, it is highly likely that the oral versions of the history of the Mali Empire are the product of consultations with written texts, and are not therefore more authentic accounts of this history.[10]

Muhamane Tindirma's "Jibo" is situated in the less-distant past, and it includes an important plot element of a colonial official confirming the usurper in his office of chieftain. The role of the colonial state—or more commonly of individual colonial officials—in confirming illegitimate candidates in positions of power is a major leitmotif of twentieth-century literature in Mali, both oral and written. Amadou Hampâté Bâ's novel *The Fortunes of Wangrin* is the best-known example, but it is one of many versions of a similar idea.[11] Typically, a colonial official makes the wrong choices and fails to understand or respect the ways that power has been recognized historically. Very often, those illegitimate office-holders elevated by colonial ignorance or perfidy should have been ineligible to rule because of low social status but benefit from a colonial inversion of social hierarchy. So the mass-mediated form of the story as an oral performance is part of a larger interplay between written texts in Arabic and French and oral performances in vernacular languages.

Another line of analysis of Muhamane Tindirma's story is to understand it as a defense of "traditional" and "vernacular" West African Muslim practice. Much of the literature on the role of new media in transforming the public sphere in Muslim areas of sub-Saharan Africa focuses on broadly Salafist or Muslim modernist efforts and effects in shaping public discourse about Islam in ways familiar in other Muslim-majority countries outside of sub-Saharan Africa. These are the cosmopolitan trends, drawing on currents from across the Muslim world.[12] But the focus on more cosmopolitan currents of Muslim reform and critique of the often Sufi-inflected practices that tend to be identified with vernacular or traditional cultural forms—by both Muslim reformers and academics alike—can sometimes miss the ways in which other kinds of ethics, grounded in Islam but expressed in highly vernacular forms, continue to be very important in shaping what we might call the "social imaginary" in this region. In other words, the popularity of broadcasts of performers like Muhamane Tindirma, and the ways in which their stories celebrate a certain kind of Muslim ethics, suggests that we need to complicate cosmopolitan-vernacular dichotomies.[13] Muhamane Tindirma's story is a commentary on the postcolonial predicament that Malians find themselves in. I will argue that we should understand this story—and Muhamane Tindirma's wider body of work—as providing important figures to think with in the present. As Jean-François Bayart says, these figures are necessarily fragmentary and polysemous.[14] I think they are also productive of different kinds of Muslim modernities that can be deeply vernacular without being backward in time.

A central theme in Muhamane Tindirma's "Jibo," and in other stories, is a defense of the naturalness of social status positions. Authority is both inherited through noble genealogies and earned through strict adherence to codes of behavior that mark off noble, Muslim men from others. Slave status is also heritable, as one would expect, but also a consequence of ignoble behavior by people born to higher social status positions. Muhamane Tindirma does not defend slavery per se, but he assumes it as a natural category in the ideal world that he describes. Since the people of Jibo have failed to respect the natural order of authority, they are condemned in the end to enslavement at the hands of their enemies, the Mossi. This idea of the naturalness and legitimacy of slavery is of course widespread in many African countries where slavery was important historically. Mali should be understood as a postemancipation society, with the kinds of struggles over the meanings attributed to freedom and citizenship after slavery found in other postslavery contexts.[15] Muhamane Tindirma's storytelling is emblematic of a widely held view, which I characterize as "conservative," that connects the changes in social identity and economic position of former slaves and their descendants with the corruption of the older, precolonial, social order.

The rise of people of slave descent to positions of authority in the colonial and postcolonial period—even if this is more imagined than real—represents an ethical challenge to models of noble behavior that justified slave and noble status positions in religious terms. As we will see in Muhamane Tindirma's story, nobility is defined by particular behavior and knowledge of Islam. It should not be surprising therefore that the descendants of slaves in Mali and other majority Muslim parts of Africa often focus their grievances about slave pasts on the ways that masters prevented them from gaining knowledge about Islam. By failing to fulfill their religiously obligated role in educating slaves about Islam, masters are often accused of denying slaves access to knowledge that would permit them to achieve full Muslim citizenship.[16] In this sense, full personhood is defined in religious terms, and slavery is condemned not so much as an oppressive institution in and of itself, but according to the failure of masters to behave in Islamically prescribed ways in order to bring enslaved people to Islam.[17] In Muhamane Tindirma's story, which ends with the enslavement of the entire population of Jibo, slavery functions as a symbolic marker of corruption and of the failure to follow prescribed norms of behavior in both the interpersonal and political sphere.

So far, I have focused my analysis on the content of Muhamane Tindirma's stories as constituting a field of mass-mediated discourse in Mali distinct from that associated with the Islamic Revival. But there is clearly an affective quality to the broadcasts of his performances that work on less obviously discursive levels. What of the nondiscursive "acoustic architecture," to borrow Charles Hirschkind's phrase, that supports distinct ethical sensibilities?[18] Muhamane Tindirma's performative style is attractive for reasons far beyond the content of his stories and commentaries. His performances are highly stylized streams of speech, accompanied by a traditional musician playing the *njarka*, a local string instrument. The narrative is often broken so that Muhamane Tindirma can add bits of wisdom, proverbs, jokes, and other references that help the audience understand the wider meaning of the story being recounted. This kind of oral performance is spellbinding and very well known amongst Western Songhay speakers. In the time that I spent in Timbuktu on different stays between 1999 and 2009 (a total of three years altogether), Muhamane Tindirma was a central feature of the auditory experience of life there. A private FM radio station in Timbuktu called Radio Bouctou broadcast Muhamane Tindirma's cassettes every evening after maghrib prayers. His bits of wisdom or wit were easily the most quoted things that I heard from people in conversations. I spent a lot of time with people of slave descent in Timbuktu, and these people seemed not to be bothered at all by his evidently "conservative" point of view on social hierarchy. Part of this must be attributed to the entertainment value of Muhamane Tindirma's performances, and perhaps another part to the pride that many people, of both slave and free descent, take in local cultural forms. Although it is impossible for me to give more than broad impressions of audience responses to Muhamane Tindirma's broadcasts, I think the fact that it is both "traditional" in content and in vernacular performance style, yet also highly entertaining, suggests that it engages people at different levels of emotional and cognitive experience.

Muhamane Tindirma's narrative itself is about the trials and tribulations of a man named Hamidu Hamma Kula Musa, who is denied the office of chief of Jibo, first because he is too young to rule at the death of his father, who had been chief for twenty-eight years, and then because the people of Jibo choose to reject his legitimate claims to the office in favor of his cousin Mamadu when the next succession takes place. Mamadu becomes chief at the death of his father—Hamidu's uncle—who was chief of Jibo after the death of Hamidu's father. In response to his rejection, Hamidu turns to no avail to the French colonial administration and then retreats from Jibo into obscurity. However, when the neighboring Mossi kingdom learn of the problems in Jibo because of the betrayal of the rightful chief, they launch an attack which destroys the town. Hamidu uses this occasion to demonstrate his power and to take his revenge on Jibo.

The Jibo story places a high value on the symbolic power of Islam. Muslim authority is bound up with access to secret knowledge and transmitted exclusively by lineal means. Hamidu's father went to great lengths to ensure that his son would inherit his office as chief, insisting that the people of Jibo bear witness to the fact that he intended that his son become chief once his uncle, the new chief, had died. This was written in a document to guarantee that it was not forgotten. All of this suggests a deep presence of Arabic literacy and use of Muslim forms of witnessing. As Hamidu grew up, he came to embody the qualities of an ethnically Fulbe and noble Muslim man whose chief occupation was raising cattle in the countryside. He became wealthy, owned a slave, married, acquired a uniquely powerful horse named Koowel, which he learned to ride with great skill, and attracted followers. All these are signs of his natural authority. In describing this, Muhamane Tindirma comments on the nature of social hierarchy in Mali. "Hamidu was a good young man. Hamidu found wealth. Hamidu was brave. Ahah! The sons of the poor are not often audacious, indeed, the sons of the poor are not often audacious. If the sons of the poor are audacious, their life will be short. They will kill them for nothing. It is the son of the rich man who must be audacious." When Hamidu is denied his rightful place as chief of Jibo, he says to the people of the town, "Jibo, you have betrayed me. . . . I beg God that he may show you the price of this betrayal." Addressing his cousin and rival Hamidu, he also appeals to his Muslim ethics, saying "Mamadu, my younger brother. . . . Our chieftaincy, Jibo will come between us. I implore you in the name of God. We must put our chieftaincy in the same way that we found it . . . If it is not thus, Jibo will cause us to fight against each other." But Mamadu responds saying that he would not swear by God or make any oath that would relinquish his position as chief. Muhamane Tindirma tells us that "Mamadu was so ugly that when he prayed, he moaned. Just ugliness!" Mamadu's behavior is the antithesis of that of a good Muslim.

Hamidu then appeals to the French colonial administration at Douentza across the border in present-day Mali (although at the time both Jibo and Douentza were part of the same administrative territory of Soudan français). The French function as the final arbiter on the questions of whether Hamidu or Mamadu should be the rightful chief of Jibo, but because the people of Jibo lie to the colonial officer, Mamadu is confirmed as chief. In his performance, Muhamane Tindirma builds the drama of the meeting with the colonial official. He describes

Hamidu's preparation for the meeting, beginning with a dialogue between Hamidu and his mother (Ine).

> "Ine, if I should not die where I lie down for the night, then tomorrow I will go at dawn to Douentza. I will go and look for my chieftaincy. If I get it, I will get it in a judicial way (*kubey*) and be appointed to it (*jeŋey*). Or, I will be stripped of it in a judicial way." The mother said: "May God protect you and us." Hamidu went to bed. In the morning he would go. Hamidu had a slave named Beydi who watched over the young cows and milked them. He brought milk. They ate breakfast until their stomach muscles were stretched with tightness. Hamidu washed himself. He put on his pants (*sere siibi*). He put on his best clothes (*wolfo-wolfo*), He put on his grand boubou (*dolonche*) and took his rifle. . . . He put on his leather slippers (*timbaku*), which are called *albalga-diyo* [in Songhay]. . . . Hamidu attached the martindale and the breastplate cords, and he mounted the dressing blanket and the saddle, then he stepped into the left stirrup and the right stirrup, and he pulled on [the bit] in the mouth. He pulled [the reins] until it became a handful (*looma*). He pulled it until it became tight.

Muhamane Tindirma then interrupts this story of this regal man preparing for a formal meeting with the colonial authorities to remind his listeners of the credit Hamidu brings on all people with the family name Cissé. "Thank you to the Cissés because Samba [the man recording his performance], you know him, your intimate friend himself, everything that you find to be good (*boori-ndi*) in the world, Samba, your namesake, did it."These stories are not only about the past; they carry didactic value in the present.

The scene in Douentza is long and dramatic. Hamidu rides on his magisterial horse Koowel in his finest attire to make his claim to the French official. In response, the colonial officer summons the people of Jibo to come and decide the matter. Before arriving at the colonial office, a praise singer (*maabe*) among the people of Jibo speaks frankly to the usurper Mamadu about the true nature of his power and who is responsible for his position.

> There was a praise singer (*maabe*) among them who said: "Mamadu Amiru, you have brought us into this conflict. We must say to you that unless you look for the proposal that you are going to bring to

> the office, you will no longer have the chieftaincy. Hamidu Hamma Kulla Musa, Hamidu is a good youth (*kosow*); Hamidu is courageous (*assaja*). He has a good horse; he has a good set of clothes; he has reasonable proposals. If you go to meet with him you will speak like a deaf person to the district officer. If you do, you will not get the chieftaincy. Everything that has happened between you and Hamidu is on account of us."

Here, Muhamane Tindirma attributes the success of Mamadu in claiming the office of chief to the machinations of the so-called griots. Mamadu does not rule because he is endowed with the qualities necessary to rule justly; he holds his office because of the corruption and tricks of the griots who have fooled the people of Jibo with their dark arts. The results will be calamitous for everyone.

Mamadu begins the scene by asking the nobles of Jibo assembled at Douentza to lie about Hamidou.

> All of the inhabitants of Douentza, including the notables, who learned about the summons of Hamidu Hamma Kulla Musa and Mamadu Amiru, came to the meeting. Each one put on their good clothes. They came and sat down to see how those two brothers would lie about each other, and who would put the rope on the neck of the other here in Douentza. Such was the power of blood relationships in this era. . . . They gave Hamidu a chair. They gave Mamadu a chair. The European was intelligent. He looked at Hamidu. He looked at Mamadu. He knew that these two people were from the exact same house. He said, "Hamidu." He said "Yes." He said, "Mamadu." He said: "Yes." He said, "You two people should discuss amongst yourselves. You should agree. You should allow the chieftaincy to go to one person. The person about whom you agree among yourselves, come and say it to me. I will accept the proposal. The whole country must agree to it." Mamadu was scared. He said, "I swear that we cannot meet together, District Officer. Hamidu summoned us here. We do not know Hamidu's father. We do not know Hamidu's mother. Hamidu arrived on foot one day in Jibo unknown to us. Jibo was sweet for him. He looked for a way to rule us but we did not agree. For this he summoned us here." Hamidu did not do it on purpose but he took Mamadu's shoulder and said, "Really, Mamadu, my younger brother. Because of the chieftaincy you will say that you do not know my father and

> that you do not know my mother. You have denigrated me in front of the people of Douentza and Jibo together." He said, "By God, I swear that I said that." He said, "Off. Mamadu my younger brother, if I knew the chieftaincy would affect you to this extent that you would say right now what you have said, by God, we would not dispute this chieftaincy. So take the chieftaincy. I leave it for you. I put the chieftaincy in the same place that the Prophet put millet beer (*doro*).[19] I will not rule. I will not sire a child who will rule in this world." Hamidu wanted to attack him. The district officer said to him, "Sit down Hamidu. Jibo, I asked you by God, about that which Mamadu Amiru said about Hamidu. Is it true or a lie?" They said swearing to God that they did not know his father and that they did not know his mother. He came to Jibo on foot as a stranger. Jibo was good to him. He looked for the chieftaincy over them but they did not agree. Then Hamidu stood up. Hamidu's tears welled up in his eyes and then streamed down his face. Hamidu said that he beseeched God to allow him to live up to his name Hamidu, and not take his life or the lives of the people of Jibo until the day that will bring them all together again in a more dangerous situation than that in which they have been brought together now in order to denigrate Hamidu Hamma Kulla Jibo.

The language of lineage and rightful authority are even recognized by the colonial officer, who is credited with being intelligent and seeing clearly that the two claimants are from the same family. But because Mamadu lies, claiming that Hamidu is not from the rightful line of rulers of Jibo, misfortune will befall Jibo.

Hamidu's response is to swear that he will not sleep again in Jibo. Muhamane Tindirma then interrupts the story to explain to his listeners that his story is a panegyric for Hamidu that he himself never had the chance to hear. In passages like this, we hear the formal performance interrupted in order to directly address the audience in a very self-conscious manner about the form of media being used to record the story.

> Wait . . . [for the musicians] Samba Afoo Mohamane, Bureyma Mohamane, Samba Mohamane Gallo Sisse, Samba, are your eyes open? This cassette belongs only to Hamidu. That which is laid out, we have laid it out ourselves! Hamidu did not hear the praise song. Hamidu did not hear the praise song for even one morning

> until his death. It was only after Hamidu's death that they played that praise song. They made the praise song for Hamidu like his father. They sang Hamudu Hamma Kulla Musa Jibo. The song is "*ñaaka ñaaka aduley batu baawo aduley suwadu Jibo*,"[20] Because the Bambara say [he says this in Bamana][21] "If you pound iron until it becomes cream, some drink the liquid and others cannot chew it. Some can chew it but not drink the liquid." The person who chews cannot drink; he who drinks water does not chew. The people of the crowd always provoke war, those who provoke war do not remain in the fight. But those who fight in wars are not those who provoke them.

This is an appeal to folk wisdom and a critique of those in power. It is here and in similar interruptions in the story that we can perhaps better understand the appeal of Muhamane Tindirma to his audience. Even if he supports a "conservative" point of view on social hierarchy, he also appeals to his audience as an observer of the drama of powerful men.

At this betrayal, Hamidu moves his family into the bush far from Jibo, into land in which people are in great danger of being captured as slaves. But because of Hamidu's powers, he is able to live in this dangerous land. What is interesting in the description of this time is the extent to which the bush is represented as wilderness (*badiya*) and, by contrast, how closely the imaginary of Muhamane Tindirma is tied to settled life in towns.[22]

> Hamidu headed into the bush. Hamidu continued to march until he reached a dune with a small pond beside it. At that point Hamidu Hamma Kulla Musa got down. He gave the slave an ax. He took the ax. He continued to chop until he had succeeded in clearing [the land]. They gathered up the thorns and they made an enclosure (*kali*) out of them. He made a smaller enclosure inside it [to keep the animals]. He tied up Koowel in it. He set up two houses. He planted their spear [in the ground]. He came to sit down in the shade in the late afternoon. He said, "Beydu." He said, "Yes." He said, "We have become people without any relations (*badiya*)." He said, "What are badiya?" He said, "Those who earn something will savor it. Those who earn [something bad] will also savor it. This is badiya. Everything that those who are badiya earn must be savored. If a cow dies, he must remove the skin alone. One must cook it alone. But if he has a stomach ache, he will suffer it

> alone. Those who have stomach aches will suffer it alone waiting for someone to help. . . ." Hamidu Hamma Kulla Musa in this way became an orphan in the bush. If it had been someone other than Hamidu who found himself in this situation, he would never have gone into the bush because that is where the Futanke would capture him [as a slave]. They would hit him until he was abandoned as a bloody mess. They would pour water over his head. They would shave it. They would scarify him. They would leave a tuft [of hair] on either side of the head or below the nape of the neck, or a strip on the forehead (*sosengu*). They would make his name Salmana, or Beydari or Mbergaji or Bilali or Biloribajimba, which are the real names of slaves. Only Hamidu or someone similar to Hamidu could stay there [without being enslaved like this].

So Hamidu's natural authority prevents him from being enslaved. This is fairly close to saying that social status is natural, and that slaves and rulers, even betrayed rulers, are inexorably different. It also highlights the absolute importance of membership in a community, for reasons of protection and self-worth. Hamidu is forced to live outside of society by the betrayal of the people of Jibo.

However, on Fridays, Hamidu made his one exception to his social isolation, mounting his horse Koowel and going to spend the day in Jibo. This is a reference to his explicitly Muslim piety; he could not join in congregational Friday prayers in an isolated place in the bush. The requirement of a Muslim community in order to perform congregational prayers made it necessary that Hamidu go to Jibo on Fridays. The same insistence on Hamidu's correct Muslim comportment arises in the way he carries himself while in Jibo.

> When he arrived at the public spaces of Jibo, he said, "Jibo, salaam alaykum." Jibo did not respond. He said, "Mamadu my younger brother, salaam alaykum." He did not respond. . . . The people of Jibo passed the day discussing things. They swore invoking the name of God. . . . They made rope. They played *wali*. They got up two by two. They went to eat lunch. Nobody called Hamidu to eat with them. If Hamidu spoke to someone, the person would not consider his words. In Jibo, they treated Hamidu as they would any outsider (*chee ka kaa*). Misfortune is not an attractive thing. For everyone whose house he went to, if his wife said to him, "We hear that Hamidu came to spend the day here. Hamidu and

> you are direct cousins. Why did you not invite him to come for lunch?" Some broke their wives water jar (*hoobu*), some hit their wives, some made [their wives] leave. [For] those who once knew Hamidu, [they said] "you must be his former lover." They said, "He will not rule over us." None of the women in Jibo accepted the fact that Hamidu had not become the chief. Some of them divorced because of that. Why did you not invite him to eat lunch?

After mid-afternoon prayers, Hamidu would leave Jibo and return to the bush.

In the narrative of Muhamane Tindirma, the time spent in Jibo, and the poor way that Hamidu is treated while in the town, leads to the cataclysm that is to come. In one passage, Hamidu's mother asks him how his day in Jibo was.

> When he arrived, he said, "Ine, I passed the day in peace in Jibo." She said, "Hamidu, come, this is the first time that you have lied to me. Someone who has sent another person away does not greet him subsequently. Chieftaincy is like the drum. If you beat the drum, you will hear. Someone who is far away from you will hear it. [The knowledge of your] chieftaincy will spread until it reaches the chief of the Mossi. They have an old quarrel with Jibo. The war is written about in the historical chronicles that are stored away. They asked all around the country until they heard that Hamidu did not rule. Hamidu's father died and his younger brother ruled. Mamadu rules [now]. They began to prepare for war. Every Friday, Hamidu spends the day in Jibo."

So the danger is from the neighboring Mossi, who intend to take advantage of the betrayal of Hamidu in order to destroy Jibo.

> This is what happened there. No one called him. No one spoke with him. If he spoke to someone, no one would respond to him. Before the year was done, Hamidu went to spend the day in Jibo. Hamidu sat under the shelter of Jibo. Four Mossi came, wearing ammunition belts (*lasasi*) with bullets in them. They placed the rifles on their right shoulders. [The rifles had] two barrels per rifle. They also carried arrows held in a horn. They held the bows attached to the saddles. Four horses stood in Jibo in front of the shelter. They gave the people of Jibo a powerful greeting. Jibo responded. They said, "Chief of Jibo." They said, "Mamadu do you hear." [Mamadu

> responded] "May peace be upon you." They said, "The chief of Mossi sent us to you with a message. We carry this message. We do not want to spend the day here. We do not want water [to drink]. We do not want a mat [to lie on]. We do not want anything from you. We only want to transmit this message. The chief of Mossi said, 'There was a quarrel between your grandfather and his grandfather. If you leave the quarrel alone, he will provoke it again. If you provoke the quarrel, he will also provoke it. Next Friday, which is not this day, they will encircle you. If there are four contingents of warriors, each one will consist of 4,000 warriors. If you want, you can flee and leave your town. These [four Mossi] have not left [anyone in their country] who could beat them and there is no one here [in Jibo] who could do it either.'" Like that they left.

At this menace, Hamidu became happy for the first time in the story. "Hamidu was sitting on his behind. He said, 'Praise be to God, Lord of the two worlds.' He thanked Almighty God. He beseeched God, who had given His name to Hamidu, that he should not be killed [before the Mossi attack]. 'This speech which has been made in front of you today, you will see it when it is brought to a conclusion. That is what will happen next Friday.' When he returned home, he said, 'Ine, I have brought something sweet.'" Here, the first side of the cassette ends with the tension raised. As the second side of the cassette continues, the story begins to grow to its climax. Mamadu is an ineffective chief and Jibo is greatly imperiled by the Mossi. But Hamidu will not come to the rescue. "So, Ine, help me by begging God Almighty, if my allotted lifetime (*lumur*) is not reached before this coming Friday. May God permit me to reach Friday, so that I may have my revenge on Jibo and so that I may go to eat breakfast on the Day of Judgment."

On the eve of the big day,

> Hamidu, his wife, his slave, and his mother, all ate from the same bowl. The slave milked the cows and he brought the milk. He brought supper. He brought water. Then, they sat in front of the Thursday evening meal. Friday was also awaited by the Mossi and Jibo because of the deadline. Ah! Trouble has long been found in Burkina. Trouble has long been found in Burkina. I swear that trouble has long been found in Burkina. They are accustomed to it. When they were sitting down for dinner, Hamidu took two handfuls of food.[23] Hamidu laughed. He said, "Ine." The mother

> said, "Yes." He said, "Ine, forgive me for God's sake for laughing in front of you. Since my father died, you and I have eaten together and I have never laughed. But I laughed this evening because I am so happy that Friday has come." She said, "Hamidu, for me this is a miracle. I have never been able to meet your eyes until I met them this evening because you are laughing." [The mother said] "I remember now that this is the eve of Friday, Hamidu. Everything that God makes you want to say in this world this evening, sit beside your wife and say it. I will forgive you for it. I am your mother."

So Hamidu spoke to his wife.

> This child which is in your belly, if it is a girl, she will inherit your spinning tools and cotton and ladles. If it's a boy, he will inherit the spear that is hanging in my house and the talisman to tie around his waist, and Beydi who is sitting beside you. He will inherit the cows, and everything that remains there where I will sleep tonight. If I don't die in the place that I sleep, I will go and fight the Mossi tomorrow morning. If breakfast time arrives, I will want to eat breakfast in the other world. I, Hamidu Hamma Kuulla Musa, Haa! Play! (*kari*!) "It's me, Hamiduu Hamma Kulla Musa Jibo." There in that place keep playing that scale [*kanje*].[24]

On Friday morning, Hamidu got dressed in his elegant clothes and wore his powerful amulets, which would make him invisible to the Mossi warriors. And as he had promised, he ate no breakfast because he wanted to eat his breakfast in the next world. The milking cow then tries to tempt Hamidu by telling him that by drinking her milk, he will become invincible in the battle. But Hamidu wants to die and so he goes into battle without the milk's protection.

> He went to his horse. He mounted it. Hamidu possessed amulets (*yerkoy ŋaare yo*) so that when Hamidu went into battle, no one would see him. Hamidu would be able to see the others, but he would look like smoke (*siisi*) to people's eyes. Hamidu mounted Koowel. Hamidu left. He found the Mossi encircling Jibo, [making] four layers of blockade so tight that it was like a finger and a ring. No one could enter. No one could leave. The amir of Jibo announced to all the men in Jibo that they should assemble in the doorway of his house. If Hamidu comes at that time, perhaps it will be good. If Hamidu does not come, their mother's house

> [hometown] will be destroyed. [The chief] did not know the way of the Mossi. He had never lived in the land of the Mossi. Hamidu cut across [all of the] Mossi because they could not see him. Nine groups of cheerleading women stood in Jibo. These women were not used to going out in the sun, but they stood there in the sun. They applauded and shook their bodies like clothes made from silk [lilo derbe]. They said, "Hamidu Hamma Kulla Musa Jibo, *hammadi ñaaka aduley suwadu ñaaka aduley suwadu batu na aduley suwadu. wallahi nda hammadi na sawa-nda hõõ.*"[25] [If Hamidu does not come] they will be made to go and carry the children of the Mossi on their backs [as slaves]. The thing that the group of women said was repeated in the answers by others. The women cried until their tears made the sand wet. The men ran right and left from their houses. They rushed to the house of the chief of Jibo. They were so afraid that some of them did not put their pants on their legs. . . . They shit their pants until their shoes got wet.

But when Hamidu arrives on the scene, he shows no intention of saving the town with his powers. Instead he chastises Mamadu for his lies in stealing the chieftaincy from him.

> "Have you forgotten what you said at the office of the district officer of Douentza? That which I have asked from God, He has brought it for me." They said, "It has come." He said, "Those who say that they are men in Jibo, all of them today have attached a length of cloth.[26] Everyone who left here to go to Douentza on horseback, wearing their best clothes. Today, all of you are sitting in shit. I alone am wearing my best clothes. I am up here sitting on Koowel. I, Hamidu Hamma Kulla Musa. I am alone (mi wane)."

Then, Hamidu engages in battle with the Mossi, killing many. But the Mossi are known as fierce warriors who are not afraid of death. This attitude seems to inform Hamidu's intentions on this day because at a certain point he removes his talismans, which had made him invisible, and he was then shot by a Mossi arrow and killed. At this point, the narrative takes an unexpected turn because Hamidu's pregnant widow is presented with Hamidu's talismans by his slave Beydi, who has accompanied him in battle.

> Dado [Hamidu's widow] said, "Hamidu has died." She said," Really." [Beydi] said, "I swear to it." She said, "God is great! Oh God!"

> The slave opened the talismans. He gave them to the woman. She put them on her own body. He flipped over the mortar. He helped her until she sat on the horse. When she sat on the horse, she pulled hard [on the reins] until it reached the door of the mother's house. She said, "Ine, may you forgive me. The way that you have seen me just now will be the last time that you will ever see me. God will not cause this child to be born in this world let alone have his slave take him in his hand, or that his grandmother take him in her hands, or that someone who loves him would see him, or that his enemies see him, whether [the child becomes] a man or a woman, you will never know Ine." . . . Then the woman pulled [on the reins] of the horse until she spotted the Mossi. She saw Hamidu lying amongst the dead bodies, an arrow sticking through his neck. When she saw Hamidu, she was so choked up that she unintentionally spurred the horse. Then the horse stood on its hind legs, until he came down on the Mossi. Everyone who was found living, each of them thought that Hamidu had stood up, so much so that even today, the Mossi say that "if you kill a Fulbe and you do not cut off his head, he will rise again. If you leave the head on the body, he will rise again." When reason returned to the woman, there remained only one contingent of warriors. She said if she could put an end to those Mossi, she would have a husband or a lover from Jibo. That could never be allowed to happen [because] of what had happened between her and Hamidu in the world. Then she took off the talismans. She put them in the saddle. Then one Mossi threw a spear at the woman. He stuck the spear in the side of her belly. The spear slid into the belly. It slid into the fetus. It came out on the other side of the belly. They began to fall together in the sand. The spear was implanted until it reached the sand. The horse left. The Mossi bent over the spear and they pushed on it some more. The woman called out until some *cram-cram* [*ndani*—a kind of burr] covered her. Before her soul had left her, they ripped open the stomach. They removed the dead fetus and put in on the ground.

So with this, the only heir to Hamidu is killed, thus extinguishing his line. Hamidu's mother then went to Jibo using the talismans and magical horse Koowel, and when she removed them, she too was killed by the Mossi.

Then,

> The four Mossi stood up. They shared between them Hamidu's talismans. They took Hamidu's horse. They looked for three horses until they found them. Then, they went to meet Jibo. They stopped at the door of the house of the chief of Jibo. Before they said "salaam alaykum," they threw spears at the chief of Jibo until his neck could be played like a *njarka*. They assembled the women and men of Jibo, the young and the old, the healthy, but not the blind and the crippled. They were all assembled and the four Mossi went with them. They destroyed Jibo. They went with them to Morenaba [the chief of the Mossi]. Two people stood in the middle. Each one looked out for themselves. They loaded the horses [with booty]. They loaded the cows [with booty]. They loaded the donkeys [with booty]. People carried things on their head. Mothers wept for their children. Children wept for their mothers. Brothers wept for their sisters. Sisters wept for their brothers. No one took strength from his friend on that day in Jibo. No one existed who could take strength from their friend. Husbands wept. Wives wept. Husbands were beaten in front of their wives. Wives were beaten in front of their husbands. Sisters were beaten in front of their brother. This heart of troubles passed the day, Cissé.

And the story ends with colonial forces attempting to restore order.

The symbolic authority of Hamidu in the Jibo story is an Islamic authority, manifest in the power of the talismans that Hamidu possesses, and in his noble Fulbe lineage. His right to rule is not drawn from the people ruled but from the qualities of the ruler. And the ruler draws his authority, Muslim and otherwise, from his lineage. Nobility is an old language of power across the Sahel region, and it is more or less naturalized and even racialized in many Sahelian stories. Here, Hamidu's authority as rightful chief is bound up in his noble lineage, fortified by his Muslim ethics. Because this is a story about betrayal and corruption, there are clear echoes of broader Malian critiques of the present, in which corruption and materialism are central themes.[27]

The story analyzed in this chapter is just one story, known to (perhaps) many speakers of Western Songhay, which is, however, only a small minority of Malians. I cannot draw sweeping conclusions on this basis alone. But in offering this detailed engagement with this story, I have suggested that it is an example of a wider phenomenon created by new forms of mass mediation in Mali in which apparently "traditional" oral arts can be turned into vehicles for transmitting ideas deeply entwined in local imaginaries of gendered ethics, social hierarchy, Islam, and power. Muhamane Tindirma's story therefore helps constitute a wider field of moral critique that mass media has amplified over the last decades in Mali. Too often, "traditional" vernacular cultural forms, and Muslim ethics, are assumed to be on the defensive in the face of modernizing and cosmopolitan critiques of local backwardness; what I have argued here is that we should understand the broader range of cultural production that different forms of mass mediation make possible in a broader spectrum. Social marginality can just as easily be naturalized as challenged in new media forms. Muslim ethics can be just as successfully used to support social hierarchy as to undermine it. Vernacular media can be as creative and critical as more cosmopolitan voices.

Notes

I would like to acknowledge my debt in this project to the late Aldiouma Ahmadou dit Diadié Cissé and to Stella Dee.

1. Dorothea Schulz, "A Fractured Soundscape of the Divine: Female 'Preachers,' Radio Sermons and Religious Place-making in Urban Mali," in *Prayer in the City. The Making of Muslim Sacred Places and Urban Life,* ed. Patrick Desplat and Dorothea Schulz (Bielefeld: Verlag, 2012), 239–64.

2. Dorothea Schulz, *Muslims and New Media in West Africa: Pathways to God.* (Bloomington: Indiana University Press, 2012), 194.

3. Dale F. Eickelman and Jon W. Anderson, "Redefining Muslim Publics," in *New Media in the Muslim World: The Emerging Public Sphere,* ed. Dale F. Eickelman and Jon W. Anderson (Bloomington: Indiana University Press, 2003), 1–18; Charles Hirschkind, *The Ethical Soundscape: Cassette Sermons and Islamic Counterpublics* (New York: Columbia University Press, 2006).

4. The proliferation of private radio stations has permitted the emergence of niche stations that broadcast in local vernacular languages across Mali. Cécile Leguy has written about one such station called Radio Parana in the town of San, which broadcasts in a small minority local language called Boomu and is especially focused on collecting and broadcasting local folk stories and oral histories as part of its mission to validate the local culture and heritage of Booma speakers. Cécile Leguy, "Revitalizing the Oral Tradition: Stories Broadcast by Radio Parana (San, Mali)," *Research in African Literatures* 38, no. 3 (2007): 137.

5. Some of these stories have been published either in French translations or in Western Songhay. See Yuusuf Mohamed Haydara, Ibirahima Sango, and Mahamman Tindirma, *Farang maka boote* (Bamako: EDIS, 2007); Yuusuf

Mohamed Haydara, Ibirahima Sango, and Mahamman Tindirma, *Tooya farru* (Bamako: EDIS, 2010); Albakaye Ousmane Kounta, *Contes de Tombouctou et Macina,* 2 vols. (Paris: L'Harmattan, 2000).

6. On Jelgoji, see Paul Reisman, *Société et liberté chez les Peul djelgôbé de Haute-Volta: Essai d'anthropologie introspective* (Paris: Mouton, 1994); Michel Izard, *Gens du Pouvoir, Gens de la Terre. Les institutions politiques de l'ancien royaume du Yatenga (Bassin de la Volta Blanche)* (Paris: Editions de la Maison des sciences de l'homme, 1985); David Robinson, *The Holy War of Umar Tal: The Western Sudan in the Mid-Nineteenth Century* (New York: Oxford University Press, 1985).

7. For a written textual example, see Bruce Hall, "An Early Tuareg Anti-Colonial Manifesto? A Local Critique of the French Occupation of the Niger Bend," in *Le temps des Oulèmas: Les manuscrits africains comme sources historiques,* ed. Seyni Moumouni and Viera Pawlikova-Vilhanova (Niamey: Etudes Nigériennes, 2009), 107–48.

8. Jan Jansen, "The Sunjata Epic: The Ultimate Version," *Research in African Literatures* 32, no. 1 (2000): 14–46.

9. Jack Goody, *The Interface between the Written and the Oral* (Cambridge: Cambridge University Press, 1987).

10. Ralph Austen and Jan Jansen, "History, Oral Transmission and Structure in Ibn Khaldun's Chronology of Mali Rulers," *History in Africa* 23 (1996): 17–28.

11. Amadou Hampâté Bâ, *The Fortunes of Wangrin,* trans. Aina Pavolini Taylor (Bloomington: Indiana University Press, 1999). I have analyzed a similar text of betrayal and colonial perfidy produced by a Tuareg group in the Niger Bend called the Iglad. See Bruce Hall, *A History of Race in Muslim West Africa, 1600–1960* (New York: Cambridge University Press, 2011), 195–206.

12. Benjamin Soares, "Islam in Mali in the Neoliberal Era," *African Affaires* 105/418 (2005): 77–95.

13. On this broader question in a different context, see Sheldon Pollock, "Cosmopolitan and Vernacular in History," *Public Culture* 12, no. 3 (2000): 591–625. Mass media have sometimes been deployed to defend "traditional" forms of religion in Africa. For the example of "Afrikan Traditional Religion" in Ghana, see Samuel Gyanfosu, "A Traditional Religion Reformed: Vincent Kwabena Damuah and the Afrikania Movement, 1982–2000," in *Christianity and the African Imagination: Essays in Honor of Adrian Hastings,* ed. David Maxwell and Ingrid Lawrie (Leiden: Brill, 2013), 271–94. Marleen de Witte, "Media Afrikania: Styles and Strategies of Representing 'Afrikan Traditional Religion' in Ghana," in *New Media and Religious Transformations in Africa,* ed. Rosalind Hackett and Benjamin Soares (Bloomington: Indiana University Press, 2015), 207–26.

14. Jean-François Bayart, *The Illusion of Cultural Identity,* trans. Steven Rendell, Janet Roitman, and Jonathon Derrick (London: C. Hurst, 2005), 227–28.

15. Frederick Cooper, Thomas C. Holt, and Rebecca J. Scott, *Beyond Slavery: Explorations of Race, Labor, and Citizenship in Postemancipation Societies* (Chapel Hill: University of North Carolina Press, 2000).

16. In his work on slave culture in nineteenth-century East Africa, Jonathon Glassman termed efforts by slaves and people of slave descent to be recognized as full members of Muslims communities "struggles for Swahili citizenship." Jonathon Glassman, *Feasts and Riot: Revelry, Rebellion, and Popular Consciousness on the Swahili Coast, 1856–1888* (Portsmouth, NH: Heinemann, 1995), 23.

17. Ousmane Kamara, "Les divisions statutaires des descendants d'esclaves au Fuuta Tooto mauritanien," *Journal des Africanistes*, 70, no. 1–2 (2000): 284–85; Roger Botte, "Pouvoir du Livre, pouvoir des hommes: La religion comme critère de distinction," *Journal des Africanistes* 60, no. 2 (1990): 48–49.

18. Hirschkind, *Ethical Soundscape*, 8.

19. This refers to the banning of alcohol.

20. This is a Fulfulde praise song that I have been unable to translate directly. But see the analogous expression cited in Bamana, the most widely understood language in Mali, followed by a Songhay explanation.

21. "Nege ni ya susu ka kee dege a sege doo, doo ba jiimi doo ti se ka ñimi, do baa ñimi u ti se ka jiimi."

22. See Judith Scheele, *Smugglers and Saints of the Sahara: Regional Connectivity in the Twentieth Century* (New York: Cambridge University Press, 2012).

23. He was so happy that he didn't eat the first handful of food that he took.

24. Muhamane Tindirma is referring to the musicians accompanying his performance.

25. This is another Fulfulde verse of praise like the earlier one that I have been unable to translate.

26. Only women wrap themselves in cloth—so he says that the men of Jibo have been reduced to the level of women today.

27. Schulz, *Muslims*, 105.

SIX

"The Angel of the Sabbath Is the Greatest Angel of All"

Media and the Struggle for Power and Purity in the Shembe Church, 2006–12

LIZ GUNNER

THIS CHAPTER DEALS WITH HOW THE LEADERSHIP STRUGGLE IN THE Shembe Church (officially called the Nazareth Baptist Church) was covered by the *Sowetan*, the South African national daily newspaper, between 2006 and 2012. African Independent Churches (AICs) are still by far the biggest Christian group in South Africa, and the Shembe Church is the second largest in that group after the Zion Christian Church. Joel Cabrita's recent authoritative study of the church puts its membership at between four and six million members, although she also mentions a figure as high as twelve million if one estimates members of the church from the southern African region rather than from South Africa alone.[1] To understand more fully the church itself, the postapartheid nation in this period, and the interplay of the media and religion in this slice of postcolonial time in southern Africa and South Africa in particular, one needs to know what the *Sowetan* reported about the country's second-largest black church at a time of crisis, why the newspaper took the line it did, and how it shifted its lens at certain moments.

In brief,[2] the Nazareth Baptist Church was founded in 1910 at Inanda outside Durban by the prophet Isaiah Shembe, who came to the port city from the small border town of Harrismith in the Orange Free State. Shembe created the church's theology by drawing from both mission and Pentecostal sources, rooting it in beliefs about direct revelation from God, hierarchy, healing, and the figure of the leader as sent from God—the Black Christ. Alongside this theology was a body of hymns composed by the founder through divine inspiration and set in print form by his son and successor, Johannes Galilee Shembe, after Shembe's death.[3] After the early decades of the church came the adoption of older cultural forms—largely Zulu—and the building of a distinctive body of sacred dances and hymns.

Also significant in the built life of the church was its collection of texts, which included testimonies, autobiographies, and histories of revelations and miracles. Unlike the vibrant body of autobiographies, testimonies, and what Derek Peterson calls "ornamentalisms" of patriotic histories that marked the later revivalist period in east Africa,[4] the collection of texts in the Shembe Church have come to be seen as part of its "national weight" linked to its presence in a national history, rather than challenges to such bounded identities. The Shembe Church established from its early years a discursive and political presence in black life. It was a church that, through its emphasis on memory and a semiotic ideology,[5] rescripted a particular form of black religious practice. The emphasis of the Shembe Church on memory, place, and a sense of the past—articulated in its hymns with at times an evocation of Zulu history standing in for a wider lost African dignity—are the factors that have led to its being considered in some ways "national" well before the advent of the democratic postapartheid government.[6]

As I show below, the church's identification with the nation can be a hugely limiting factor for believers. It can bind too closely perceptions of church and nation and can hide the essential "purity" of the church itself—its "Angel of the Sabbath." Such a "binding" is in contrast to the looser, freer position of the growing Pentecostal churches in South Africa, which have a far freer interaction with the state, with memory, and with nation.[7] Of huge and growing importance in the southern African region, the Pentecostal churches, in Zimbabwe for instance, have often contributed to social cohesion and the making of modern subjects in an era of turbulence and political instability.[8] However, they have not had the same close association with "nation" in the way that the Nazareth Baptist, or Shembe, Church has in South Africa. As Jewsiewicki points out, Pentecostal presentism can be a negative factor in the modern postcolonial state. "The presentist concept of time has become widespread today [in Africa] through the practice of Christianity in

African Pentecostal inspired churches. This practice upholds the subject's individualism face to face with God, devalues cumulative time and abolishes the privilege of anteriority, exchanging conversions for elections."[9] Nevertheless, we can also see Pentecostals as being open to innovation and freedom from the restraints of a narrow state ideology of bordered nations and a past full of the constraints of tradition. This is a point well made by Peterson in comparing the cross-border mentality of present-day Pentecostal movements in eastern Africa with the revivalist movements of the 1930s to the early 1970s.[10]

Religion, particularly in the guise of Christianity and spiritual matters in general, has always had a far wider coverage in the South African black press—by which in the broadest terms I mean papers produced primarily for consumption by African readers—than in papers aimed primarily at white European readership. A quick glance through the archives of *Umteteli waBantu, Imvo, Ilanga,* or *Bantu World* would corroborate this.[11] The recent history and anthology of *Abantu Batho,* edited by Peter Limb, also illustrates this point.[12] This suggests that for the black public the sphere of "religion" has never been "the other" of modern media practice as suggested by Stolow.[13] The mediation of religious matters in South Africa has not to date seen the creation of an alternative public sphere through a convergence of Pentecostalism and popular culture of the kind Birgit Meyer depicts in the case of Ghana. Instead, religious affairs have coexisted in the black press as a strand within the narrative of an assertive black identity, of performativity, and of a wider national identity seeking a place within a public sphere that—pre-1990—sought to erase such a presence or ignore its existence. The African press can thus be seen as part of an alternative or counter public culture persisting into the present moment.[14]

The Shembe Church leadership dispute was of intense interest to the *Sowetan* because of its historic position as an African Independent Church that through the decades of black erasure in the public sphere, in terms of heritage or historical inclusion, simply continued as a public presence. It did this by asserting a cyclical public ritual of memorial enactment as a primarily black African church. This public ritual was the annual January pilgrimage to the mountain of Nhlangakazi north of Durban. Coverage of the pilgrimage in both the European and African presses in fact constituted an acknowledgement of the public nature of this event as religion and a memorial action of black worship. It was thus forcing itself into a public sphere marked symbolically by monuments, public holidays, and impressive buildings[15] from which black memory and the African majority was excluded. The Shembe Church thus created its own social and religious rituals of remembering[16] against the grain of the times and in the face of successive regimes of white power.

In the post-1994 postapartheid dispensation in South Africa it may not be true to see the Shembe Church as part of what Meyer—in the situation of Ghana under Rawlings—has called a "state driven politics of identity."[17] Nevertheless, it is not entirely outside such a process, and Joel Cabrita argues that the embrace of church and the state in the form of the ruling ANC has become increasingly public and very close. Yet at the same time if we see "religion as a particular practice of mediation,"[18] and the Shembe Church within that, then it has its own practices of mediation that are not dependent only on the identity lens of the state. It is thus in the unstable in-between space of "the state" and outside the state: a powerful signifier of religious and black identity and of modernity that eludes easy capture. It is in this volatile "in-between" space that the Shembe leadership dispute and its press coverage in the *Sowetan* between 2006 and 2012 should be seen.

In focusing on the *Sowetan's* mediation of the long (and only recently resolved)[19] leadership tussle in the church as it played out from 2006 to early 2012, I argue that we see in operation the state's desire to "own" the church, or at least to mark it as a significant ally. We see too the church's own attempts to occupy a share of the public space and so be tied into a national discourse, but perhaps not a nationalist one. There is, however, vacillation. The desire to claim public space leads at moments to church leaders asserting the need to be seen within a national narrative. At other moments, we see the desire of a leader to assert an authority of the spiritual that is outside and beyond the domain of the state. At yet other moments the church and political power seem locked in a mutual self-regarding gaze, each caught in the image of the other. In a final scenario, church members through the *Sowetan* gaze seem to assert the church's right to a space within the public sphere, but one marked as holy and outside the manipulations of political and state power. Over all this is the question made important by Meyer's work about how the media reshapes the religious space and the public sphere.

What my discussion below shows in particular is the unstable gaze of the media—in this case the press in the form of the *Sowetan* newspaper. At moments, the *Sowetan's* agenda of celebrity reporting dominates its handling of church affairs. At other moments, the strong, historical link of the church with the poor and the marginal asserts itself. As Thabo Mbeki's second term in office runs into problems, anxieties over national instabilities and the diminishing confidence in an optimistic postapartheid national narrative seem to affect reporting on the Shembe Church. A longing for a strong African church and nervousness at the fracturing of the Shembe Church comes to the fore. As the reporting continues and a general public disillusionment with politics and corrupt leadership asserts itself, so the sharp media focus on the church shifts to questions of financial assets in the church itself, perhaps a response to national political preoccupations. Pertinent to the leadership struggle and its mediation in the *Sowetan* from 2006 to the early months of 2012 is the larger question posed by Joel Cabrita, who asks, can this "great church" survive as a single unit, bound together by a coherence of textuality established first by the founder Isaiah and continued later by his successor and son Johannes Galillee, or will it rather return to its early Pentecostal roots and split and split again following the drives of the Spirit and charismatic authority?[20]

The national tabloid daily, the *Sowetan,* was estimated in 2013 to have a readership of close to 1.7 million with a circulation a little below one hundred thousand.[21] A major player in the black print media public,[22] with a history that takes it back to the apartheid era of the 1980s, the *Sowetan* is now viewed as the main competitor to the newer *Daily Sun* tabloid. This, with its largely black readership of 5.6 million, focuses with great success on gossip and the sensational ordinary in people's lives, the "politics of the everyday."[23] The *Sowetan,* established in 1980 by the Argus Printing Company, was a successor to the *Post* and the *World* (previously the *Bantu World*), two "black-readership newspapers that were closed down by the South African state for their opposition to apartheid."[24] With a long history of association with Black Consciousness organizations rather than the Congress movement, the *Sowetan* under the dynamic Aggrey Klaaste, its editor from 1988 to 2002, focused on "nation-building" rather than pure oppositional politics. It was a phrase coined by Klaaste and drew on a core of Black Consciousness ideas linked to "*ubuntu,*" community-building and the "arguments that empowerment came from freeing the mind . . . from the oppressor in order to take back what had been lost."[25] The paper was hugely successful in creating "an alternative public"[26] built around the black urban classes that were to constitute the post-1994 citizens of the new democratic state. In 1996 it was the most widely read of all South African papers. But Cowling concludes that it declined in influence from 2004, with new ownership and a different editor.

The paper's close following of the leadership dispute within the Shembe Church shows it has maintained its historic interest in the building of community and nation without tamely following the narrow liberation struggle narrative of the postapartheid era constructed by the ruling African National Congress (ANC), in power since the first democratic elections of 1994. So the paper can be seen as reflecting a "counterpublic," one that overlaps with the publics convened by other sections of the press but that has its own core of constituted difference outside the elite reading publics of the largely "White" press, or the government-controlled *New Age*. The *Sowetan* with its Gauteng base but national gaze also has a readership marked off from other sections of the black press such as the influential Zulu language papers, *Ilanga* and *Isolezwe,* both of which have their main locus in KwaZulu-Natal.

Mediating Anxiety, Power, and Glamour

The split in the once unitary Shembe Church began in 1976 after the death of Johannes Galilee, son of the founder Isaiah. The old Ekuphakameni congregation continued under Johannes's son Londa. The new but far larger Ebuhleni congregation under the founder's younger brother Amos moved a few miles south and west onto "tribal" land under the control of the Ngcobo chiefs. Both centers are outside Durban and only a few miles apart, but they represent important sites of difference and uncertainty as to who ultimately leads this important South African church.

The *Sowetan* focus between 2006 and 2012, which I discuss here, was on the continuing leadership tensions between these two sites, with the presence of the "outsider" figure of Phakama based in Johannesburg also commanding early interest from the paper. Vimbeni Shembe of Ebuhleni, the "rogue" contestant Phakama Shembe from Johannesburg, and the volatile Ekuphakameni group led by Vukile Shembe, son of Londa, are the key figures covered here.[27]

Phakama Shembe—The "Outsider" from Gauteng

Most prominent in the *Sowetan* in 2006 was its reporting of the self-styled leader of the Gauteng "faction" (a term favored by the press), Phakama Shembe, who captured the paper's coverage of the Shembe

Church in the years 2006–7. Always given the title of *Inkosi* ("King"), "Prophet," or "Bishop," Phakama often featured in the *Sowetan* in striking visual images, clothed in the apparel used by modern African prophets and by some African heads of state. He favored flowing, sparkling blue, silver, or crimson robes usually topped with a deep frontal collar of leopard skin. The *Sowetan* presented him as an ambiguous figure: a celebrity, an African icon, a man of his church concerned with making his mark on the public and religious life of Gauteng.

Certainly at this point in the *Sowetan* reporting, the image of religious leader, celebrity, and the visionary politician mingled. Phakama mixed the visionary and the political and thus brought the domains of nationalist liberation struggle, the politics of equality, and prophetic vision into the same public sphere. The *Sowetan* reported the announcement of Phakama's visions of Joe Slovo, the late South African Communist Party leader (and a former government minister), which led to "prayer intercession at Slovo's graveside in Avalon Cemetery in Soweto, to pray for workers and peace."[28]

Phakama's pronouncements usually came through an appointed intermediary. He was thus adapting the convention of exalted figures such as Akan royalty who have an appointed "voice" speaking for them. The eloquent intermediary projects and enhances the charisma of the elevated person for whom they speak.[29] Such a practice both "distanced" the speaker but covered them in an aura of glamour. The pronouncements by Phakama's spokesperson, Pat Dooms, were often bizarre and glitzy, conferring a certain unearthly power on Phakama Shembe, the source of the utterance. Dooms was quoted as saying, "The divine prophet is to take responsibility to intercede on behalf of the working class," as part of "Shembe's mission and responsibility on this planet."[30]

At other moments, Phakama's actions spoke even more of excess and spectacle. Prancing on the table at a media conference in the classy suburb of Rosebank, Johannesburg, he stated, "I am the real Shembe . . . I am the King of Shembe."[31] The reports of 2006 continued to convey this contradictory sense of Phakama: his understanding of the initial vision of the church regarding the poor and outcast and its relevance in postapartheid neoliberal South Africa alongside his publicity pranks and his wealth. When his white Mercedes was hi-jacked in Orlando, Soweto, on Good Friday, he was reported to have said, "good Friday's bad."[32] His public presence as visionary prophet continued through the announcement of a "Holy Walk" set for April 15 through the streets of

Orlando, Soweto, and "aimed at ushering in a season of prayer, meditation and rededication to peace, life and good health."[33]

During the rest of 2006, the *Sowetan* continued to cover Phakama and his reaching out to the marginalized and neglected. The paper was thus projecting an image of a religious leader challenging the inequalities of South African postapartheid society in the new millennium. What was becoming increasingly obvious was that the years of "the Mandela miracle" were slipping away with gaps of wealth and poverty increasing in South African life.[34] Reports in June read "Shembe Church Goes to War." Phakama's spokesperson, Pat Dooms, announced that the Shembe Church "is planning a spiritual war against the spread of the HIV-AIDS pandemic, and sodomy in prisons." The report made it clear that this was not an act by the leader alone: "Congregants and leaders of the church will hold a prayer meeting next Sunday . . . in Johannesburg Prison popularly and cynically known as Sun City—the name of the famous luxury resort west of Johannesburg."[35] The following week featured the actual gathering by "Shembe members . . . to pray for HIV positive prisoners." Also mentioned was the church's desire to pray inside the prison once permission to do so had been granted.[36] What was emerging for *Sowetan* readers was a fractured yet fascinating image of the great Shembe Church: celebrity status, fidelity to the church's fundamental tenets of equality before God, and political flamboyance clashed, leaving readers confused and perhaps intrigued. This image of the church was certainly not of a significant religious body courting the state or tamely kowtowing to it. This was the sphere of the religious mediated outside the sphere of the ruling political power.

As 2006 drew to a close, the political tensions in the country reflected a divided leadership, wide popular disillusion with Thabo Mbeki, and sympathy for his "disgraced" deputy president Jacob Zuma, whose cited involvement in the Shabir Sheik financial scandal led to his dismissal by President Mbeki.[37] The *Sowetan* reporting on Phakama continued to highlight the mix of flashiness and political commitment to the poor that was a part of his "style" as a religious leader. Phakama—absolutely in sync with the widespread disillusion of the time—dropped his ANC membership, accusing the ruling party, the ANC, of "serving the elite and party leaders" and neglecting the poor and uneducated.[38]

Phakama's spiritual authority and his links with the poor—as reported by the *Sowetan* throughout 2006—were in marked contrast to the behavior of national politicians. And the paper may have been highlighting this contrast. Religious authority was overtly stating its claim in the public domain of the state—through the pages of the *Sowetan*. Phakama's last act of the year reported by the *Sowetan* was his visit to Soweto hostels—homes to migrant workers, many from KwaZulu-Natal—to deliver condoms. Run-down "memorials" to apartheid labor practices and ongoing migrant life,[39] the hostels often had Shembe temples next to them. Also, because of the AIDS denialism of President Mbeki, there was no national availability of antiretrovirals (ARVs) for those who were HIV positive or had developed full-blown AIDS. ARV roll-outs began only in 2008 when Jacob Zuma was president.

Throughout 2006, the contradictory figure of Phakama Shembe—prophetic leader, activist for the marginalized, and at the same time glamorous publicist—dominated *Sowetan* reporting of the Shembe Church. However, in 2007 there was a distinct shift of focus in terms of how the church was mediated by the *Sowetan*. The paper's reporting on the Shembe Church shifted to a broader, national, and less regional focus, and Phakama Shembe faded almost entirely from its pages.[40] National politics became increasingly focused on the struggle for leadership of the ruling ANC, with Thabo Mbeki facing a challenge from Jacob Zuma—his reinstated deputy president. Gillian Hart's account of the increasing uncertainty and the fractious nature of ANC politics at the level of leadership and policy captures very well the rudderless nature of national leadership in these years.[41] As anxiety about the fracturing ruling party and weak government became prevalent, so too reports of a search for an elusive Shembe Church unity dominated the *Sowetan* coverage. Was the *Sowetan* reportage conflating separate issues? Or did the two questions both in the public sphere begin to converge as in some ways a single point of interest for the paper and its reporters?

Mediating the Search for Unity

The deteriorating situation in 2007 between Thabo Mbeki and Jacob Zuma dominated national politics.[42] In the *Sowetan's* coverage of the church, its place as a "significant institution of the state," as Cabrita has called it,[43] and the dangers of its collapse dominated. Moreover, it became clear that at least one of the *Sowetan* reporters, Canaan Mdletshe and possibly also Mhlaba Memela, was extremely well versed in church affairs.[44] Both were in the main KwaZulu-Natal base in their time with the *Sowetan*, which would help explain their expert knowledge of

Shembe intricacies. The *Sowetan* focus shifted from Gauteng and the unpredictable Phakama Shembe back to the church's two main centers, the new(er) and old centers of Ebuhleni and Ekuphakameni, both to the north of Durban. Part of this spatial shift included coverage of the annual ritual church pilgrimage to the holy mountain of Nhlangakazi. It combined a report of the January pilgrimage by the smaller of the two groups with a call for unity from the leader, Vukile Shembe, as he and his followers ascended the mountain.[45]

At this early point in 2007, a wider church unity must have seemed imminent (in contrast to the fractious political scene and the predicament of the ruling ANC). Indeed, the *Sowetan* journalist Canaan Mdletshe titled his next story "30 Year Feud Finally Over."[46] With a picture showing the two leaders (Vukile and the older Vimbeni) laughing and shaking hands and captioned "Peace restored," the report claimed that the long-standing court case (over church leadership) was to be withdrawn.[47]

In February 2007, the *Sowetan* reporters' expertise in church affairs was evident together with a sense of why it considered the state of the church to matter to its public: it represented a matter of national interest that was beyond party politics. In his next *Sowetan* report, Canaan Mdletshe expanded on the movement for unity within the church and included a long and full account of the split "following the death of Bishop Johannes Shembe in 1976." He continued, "The church is one of the oldest and most powerful African independent groups in Southern Africa." Here what was being emphasized by the paper for modern readers was the role the African Independent Churches had played in African self-determination and the establishing of an "African Christianity" outside the control of European-dominated mission Christianity and its long disregard of African church leadership. In other words, the Shembe Church had its own historic and national credentials, regardless—as Canaan Mdletshe seemed to imply—of the waxing and waning of political parties. Mdletshe's use of the regional "Southern" was an implicit recognition that many members of the church who came regularly to attend the January holy mountain pilgrimage (and other ritual meetings such as the July and September gatherings) were from Zimbabwe, Mozambique, and Swaziland. It was thus a national "independent [church] group," but its networks of congregations went well beyond state boundaries. It was both "national" and transnational.

Late September 2007 saw the *Sowetan* carrying journalist Canaan Mdletshe's detailed account of the church's commemoration of the 1995 death of Amos Shembe (leader from 1976 to 1995 of the large Ebuhleni congregation and father of the incumbent leader, Vimbeni). At moments the *Sowetan* read like a play script, as if a drama of national proportion was being mediated for all its readers. Ceremonies of call and response between church leader and church members at Ebuhleni played themselves out in the text of the *Sowetan.* The press print became a performative script of remembered and reenacted strength and unity. It captured by allusion the performed texts of worship and prayer (from the Church hymnal and prayer book) in use since the early 1940s when Johannes Galilee standardized practices of worship.[48] The effect of a national script mediated through the lens of the paper was heightened by quotes of Bishop Vimbeni as he officiated the memorial event for his father, Amos Shembe. "May the spirit of Shembe bless you all" was followed by "the response of thousands of church members: '*Uyingcwele*' You are holy/He is holy."[49] The church's link with purity—of a way of life of the body and the spirit, and with flows of reciprocity between church leader and followers—filled the account.

As the report noted that members "from all walks of life" gave gifts "to pay tribute" to Shembe, the borders of the secular and the sacred blurred. Also recorded was the normal cycle of testimonies about the work and blessings of the late Amos Shembe, whose church praise name "*Inyanga yeZulu*" ("Moon of the heavens") was included in the *Sowetan* "script." The textuality of church life—with its constant recreation of multiple intersecting narratives of revelation, memory, and written text—was present in the *Sowetan.* The report was confident and knowledgeable of how memory worked as public enactment in the church. A day was devoted to the testimonies of women, Mdletshe noted, to be followed by the priests' testimonies.

Canaan Mdletshe, sure of his *Sowetan* audience's involvement in these rituals of holiness and institutional memory by the church, remarked that "the *Sowetan* will give you, our readers, a daily update of what is happening at Ebuhleni." What was being *enacted* textually in the *Sowetan* itself was the importance of the narrative of the church in a wider social and historical frame. It was also concerned with showing how narratives were constantly made in the church as part of the *longue durée* of the church and its history within a wider narrative of South African society. At this point, then, the mediation of events through the *Sowetan* becomes a strong call for an altered state of things in national life. For a moment, the church enactment of wholeness and memorial coherence can be seen as standing in for a struggling and fractured secular state with no coherent narrative.

Yet the *Sowetan* accounts of the enactment of memory and institutional solidity were themselves only part of the profoundly unsolid state of church affairs. Violence and danger marked the paper's brief (and agonized) report even on the following day, when a police protection and escorts were to be discussed for "Vimbeni Shembe . . . leader of the biggest and most followed church in the country."[50] From early in 2008, forces set against a unified church, and against Vimbeni Shembe, asserted themselves. The earlier emphasis on church unity was brutally disrupted. The quite public tussle over meaning, power, and wealth in the Shembe Church began in earnest.

The *Sowetan* continued its careful coverage, determined, it seemed, to assert its hopes for the church as a steady, unified presence in national life—a welcome contrast to increasingly chaotic political affairs. Shifting focus between Gauteng and KwaZulu-Natal, the *Sowetan* narrative centerd in the main on the dignified and "charismatic" figure of Bishop Vimbeni Shembe, who desired church unity. Yet parallel to the *Sowetan*'s projected image of Vimbeni's steadying power and charisma was its projection of the church beset by violence, guns, fire, "double agents," and charges of financial duplicity against Vimbeni Shembe himself.[51] However much the paper, and perhaps in particular those journalists expert in the affairs of the church, may have wished for a unitary narrative, it was not possible. It had to report Vimbeni Shembe's despair[52] and even a request by the Gauteng Phakama Shembe for Jacob Zuma (now president of the ANC) to intervene.[53] Zuma did not intervene but was one of a number of politicians who kept a constant Shembe presence as events unfolded. Certainly at this point, the public space of church and nation are intertwined, and the *Sowetan* shows this overlap. It mediates the turbulent church affairs while keeping its readers informed and reminding them of the church's stature.

At this point, possibly, the *Sowetan* was consciously attempting to contain the turbulence of the Shembe Church. A *Sowetan* editorial stated, "Let Peace Prevail: Christians are expected to seek divine intervention to give them strength to prevail over tensions." Clearly this was not happening at Ebuhleni, the writer stated tersely.[54] As the public battle in the church continued, the *Sowetan* stressed the proximity of the church to figures of the state. In this instance, it was with a focus on KwaZulu-Natal. The *Sowetan* stated that guests at the opening of the provincial government parliament in KwaZulu-Natal "included high commissions, consular corps, religious leaders *including the leadership of the Shembe Church* and organized business."[55] Also striking in its implication of interdependence between church and state was the short account of a Gauteng encounter some months later. In early November 2008, when the new state president Zuma "charmed" the Soweto crowd at the historic Jabulani Amphitheatre in Soweto, two distinctive groups were reported in the audience: one was "Shembe church members in white," and the other was the "ANC Women's League in green."[56] Both these groups were the mirror providing the reflection of the self that every politician needs; here it was the new South African president, Jacob Zuma, who could see his own face.

"This congregation is not yours, but God's congregation"—Vimbeni Shembe

As the *Sowetan*'s mediation of church events continued into 2009, it gave maximum coverage to the ritual January pilgrimage to the holy mountain where church and state engaged in conversations meant for a far wider audience. Church and state were together in the foothills of the holy mountain. Again, the reporting was in the hands of Canaan Mdletshe, who emphasized both the prophetic figure of authority (and proponent of unity), Vimbeni, and the speeches of senior politicians.[57] Under the heading "Shembe Calls for Peace in Church," Mdletshe punched home Vimbeni's plea for "peace, tolerance and reconciliation among [the church's] warring factions," "The armed conflict within the congregation is preventing the church's leaders from doing its work. . . . Here at Nazareth[58] there's no more love, but the bells of war are ringing. . . . There's a lot of hatred. I want this to stop. *This congregation is not yours, but God's congregation.*"[59] Significant in the report is the foregrounding of political presence and the words of politicians, alongside that of Vimbeni and his pleas. Politicians of the ruling party were there: KwaZulu-Natal premier Sbu Ndebele and the veteran leader of the Inkatha Freedom Party (IFP) Mangosuthu Buthelezi. The IFP, a Zulu nationalist party, was now little more than an empty shell, but its leader, with his close ties to the Zulu royal house and the church, still commanded great respect. Both Ndebele and Buthelezi were astute politicians; they chose to emphasize different things: Premier Ndebele recalled that the church was as much a national institution as the ANC itself. "This church will be celebrating one hundred years of its existence.

It is one of the oldest churches and was established at the same time as the ANC."[60] Each leader remarked on the "Zuluness" of the church, but Ndebele was careful to place this in a wider national context.[61]

The *Sowetan*'s coverage from the foothills of Nhlangakazi Mountain doubtless reminded the *Sowetan* readers of the entangled secular and spiritual space of the nation. The paper itself possibly also felt impelled to give equal weight to church and political figures. Prophet, mountain, and politicians were operating beyond the obvious domains of the modern—the city, the courts, parliament—but were intrinsically part of it. The African spirituality that was evoked by its coverage was thus putting forward a more complicating view of the plural spaces of the South African national imaginary and of the order of what the Comaroffs have called "the signs and practices" that shaped those spaces.[62]

Still intent on punting a line of the Shembe Church and its national status, the *Sowetan* carried in early 2010 a picture of KwaZulu-Natal premier Zweli Mkhize at Ebuhleni with "Inkosi Vimbeni Shembe" at the unveiling of a monument to mark the centenary of the church. The caption to the picture of premier and church leader highlighted the church's African roots, and by doing so it created for readers a script of a "national ontology" outside the quite problematic construction of the rainbow nation.[63] It read: "Despite much reference to the Old Testament and conventional Christian rituals, the Shembe's spiritual resonance is more African than Western. Every year followers make a pilgrimage to Mount Nhlangakazi."[64]

Linked to the vexed question of unity that the *Sowetan* appears to have seen as part of the symbolic capital of church and nation was a sense of its anxiety as to the inheritance of prophetic authority within the Shembe Church—and perhaps linked to that, the question of purity and fidelity to its founding roots and prophetic vision in 1910. Would the church unravel, and how could it survive its feuding over money and power?

The *Sowetan* attempts both to interpret and to mediate church events in all their scandal, uncertainty, and importance on a national scale can again be seen in its coverage of the death of Vimbeni Shembe, the leader who had attempted to reunite the Shembe Church and bring together the two main centers in Ebuhleni and the historic Ekuphakameni. On March 29, 2011, the *Sowetan* noted, "Shembe leader Vimbeni passes on after a long illness." It noted too, the church's assets of "over R100 million," that the church now had four factions, and that "throngs of worshippers and the general public of Inanda, north of Durban broke down and wept."[65] Vimbeni Shembe was buried on April 3, and the funeral was a dramatic event that brought its own resolution, but not church unity. The event in some respects had the air of a state funeral, made more so by the byline of the *Sowetan,* "Zuma pays his respects to late Bishop." Canaan Mdletshe again reported for the paper. He impressed on readers the significance of Vimbeni's passing. It was not a funeral to be taken lightly: when he arrived at Ebuhleni village at 4 a.m., "it was already full." Zuma called Bishop Vimbeni a "lighting torch in Africa." Mangosuthu Buthelezi of the IFP "poured his heart out," and even the leader of the breakaway NFP (National Freedom Party), Zanele Magwaza-Msibi, spoke, telling mourners that "these are trying times for the church."

The real drama of the funeral was still to come. Vimbeni's will clearly stated that his successor was to be his cousin Vela Shembe, who was to lead the larger Ebuhleni faction and so unite the divided church. But by the time the lawyer Buthelezi was given the space to read the will, Chief Ngcobo (on whose land Ebuhleni was placed)[66] had already announced that Mduduzi Shembe "would ascend the throne." It appeared that the legally signed will deposited with Vimbeni's long-standing lawyer had been overruled by chiefly authority, relatives, and "top church elders." Vimbeni's vision for unity and the prophetic legitimacy of the church—"This congregation is not yours, but God's congregation," as he had defiantly proclaimed in 2009—had been thwarted.

Certainly, viewing the reporting of the *Sowetan* at this point over the five years since its coverage of the "outsider" figure of Phakama Shembe, we can see a pattern of knowledgeable mediation of church events, particularly by the well-informed *Sowetan* journalists, Canaan Mdletshe and Mhlaba Memela. We see also the newspaper's desire for unity as the outcome of the church struggle and an interest in the church as a national body beyond the sphere of the ruling party. When the spheres of church and ruling political party overlap, the paper shows this to be so. Yet above all it provides a strong sense of the presence within national life of a church with its own narrative of African belonging, dignity, and weight. In a sense, the *Sowetan* mediation, perhaps particularly through the writing of Canaan Mdletshe and Memela, seems to have given weight to Vimbeni and his attempts at a new church unity. But this was not the outcome.

The paper's coverage of the church continued. With the late Vimbeni's supporters on the run,[67] the little-known Mduduzi Shembe—announced as leader by Chief Ngcobo, first born son of the late leader, born out of wedlock and with only a fourth-grade formal education—had been welcomed joyfully by the assembled mourners. A modest man who had never pushed himself forward to be leader, as it was claimed Vela Shembe had, Mduduzi represented for many ordinary congregants a purer solution.[68]

A Way Lost?

In 2011 the Shembe Church appeared to be in great disarray. The weight of the church in national life, and at times the closeness of church and ruling party, evident at moments in earlier *Sowetan* reporting, was not to be seen in the paper's coverage of the church. Perhaps the similarities of disarray in the ruling party, as the young firebrand politician Julius Malema (originally part of the Congress' Youth League) challenged the ANC and was then expelled from it, and the confusing claims of church "legality" as regards leadership were there to be seen. Were the great Shembe Church and the once-revered ruling party, the ANC, both in danger of becoming empty signs? The *Sowetan* did not make any such overt comparisons, either in its editorials or in its reports. The narratives of church and ruling party seemed to draw apart. Yet there were perhaps similarities uncommented on by the paper. With a will overturned, applications to freeze church accounts, and a single faction (the smaller Ekuphakameni one) claiming the right to the "Nazareth brand,"[69] what remained of the deeper nature and meaning of the one-hundred-year-old church? Was this the fate of the party in power as well? Had it bankrupted its rich legacy, reducing itself too to an empty sign?

Continuities

A newspaper does not stop its mediation of either church or national events simply because events have taken a surprising turn. *Sowetan* coverage of the church continued to point to elements of the life of the church suggesting its place in what I earlier called "the unstable in-between space" of the state and outside the state, perhaps best called the religious space in the public sphere. In this report of early February 2012, there are no politicians or any hint of a political space. The reporters this time are Karen Singh and the experienced Shembe reporter Mhlaba Memela. The *Sowetan* is once more on Gauteng territory, but there is no Phakama. We see through the lens of the *Sowetan* reporters the presence of the Shembe Church in the heart of the city of Johannesburg—the old, run down part far from any obvious glamour or power. The focus is on a new leader present at the church's "temple," its space of worship, which is adjacent to the train station of Doornfontein deep in the original city center. "The Sowetan team" has gone to the *Sandanezwe* ("We are all over the country") Temple in inner-city Doornfontein to cover the visit of Bishop Mduduzi Shembe, "son of the church's former prophet Vimbeni Shembe, leader of the Ebuhleni faction," and his welcome by a "large group of Nazareth Baptist devotees." This carefully worded and quite atmospheric short extract from a much longer account, full of specific visual details, gives readers a glimpse of the impression of sanctity conveyed by the Sowetan reporters and the particular aura of the power of a religious leader with his followers.

> The open-air temple is situated next to the Doornfontein train station and is partitioned from the public with plastic tape. Colourful balloons were tied around trees yesterday and all the members were seated on the ground.
>
> Barefoot men greeted the *Sowetan* team as we approached the entrance and requested that we remove our shoes before stepping onto the holy ground. Although we were wearing long pants [not the white gowns of members], we were granted special permission to enter. . . . There was a sense of urgency when Mduduzi stepped out of his car, with many followers rushing to kneel in front of him to receive blessings and healing.[70]

The report ends by rehearsing in brief the leadership disputes in the church and its wealth. It is in a sense inconclusive. Possibly it has to be because that is what the function of mediation is. It views, it interprets, it contains an element of uncertainty.

Conclusion

Press mediation of the Shembe Church through the lens of the *Sowetan* between 2006 and early 2012 does at moments show the closeness of church and ruling political party, but it also provides a strong sense of the Shembe Church as beyond the state yet nonetheless somehow situated in the public domain—old, venerable, with an uncertain future, and distant from the visionary purity of its founder,

Isaiah Shembe. Possibly the press at moments distorted the lens and saw the leadership dispute in the Shembe Church too much in terms of secular power politics. Yet accounts, particularly by Canaan Mdletshe and Mhlaba Memeela, undoubtedly communicate the elements of the Shembe Church's public presence during the leadership struggle that remain beyond secular political power and even beyond church power struggles. The details of Vimbeni's impassioned appeal from the foothills of Mount Nhlangakazi highlight this. More than that, the last account of February 2012 points to the numinous and the transcendental within the life of the church. These factors too were also fought over. It hinted at another battle—that over sacred meaning in the church and the source of its power and purity. Hence the title of this chapter, taken from an Ukhozi FM radio sermon in 2012 by the exiled minister Mthembeni Mpanza, who followed Vimbeni Shembe in his failed bid to unify the church, was forced to flee for his life, and then started a smaller breakaway Shembe church: "The Angel of the Sabbath is the greatest Angel of all."[71]

Notes

I am grateful to Skhumbuzo Ngubane, a member of the Ebuhleni congregation of the Shembe Church, for discussions on church matters over a long period of time but particularly in 2015; also to Faith Xaba for her local knowledge of the Shembe Church in Soweto and Johannesburg and on its preaching on the trains. My thanks to the Times Media Library, Rosebank, Johannesburg, and to the librarian Michelle Leon for her help in accessing the *Sowetan* digital records while I researched this chapter. My thanks too to Maria Frahm-Arp and Natasha Erlank for many helpful discussions; to Joel Cabrita for her helpful comments, insights, and patience; and also to the two anonymous reviewers of the initial version of this chapter.

1. Joel Cabrita, *Text and Authority in the South African Nazaretha Church* (Cambridge: Cambridge University Press, 2014), 252. Her source is given as the *Sowetan,* September 16, 2010.

2. Cabrita, *Text and Authority.* Cabrita covers Isaiah Shembe's early life and ministry very thoroughly. See in particular chapters 1 and 2.

3. Johannes Galilee Shembe, *Izihlabelelo zamaNazaretha* (Durban: W. H. Shepherd, 1940).

4. Derek R. Peterson, *Ethnic Patriotism and the East African Revival: A History of Dissent, c. 1935–1972* (Cambridge: Cambridge University Press, 2012).

5. Webb Keane, *Christian Moderns: Freedom and Fetish in the Mission Encounter* (Berkeley: University of California Press, 2007).

6. Elizabeth Gunner, *The Man of Heaven and the Beautiful Ones of God* (Leiden: Brill, 2002).

7. Maria Frahm-Arp, *Professional Women in Pentecostal Charismatic Churches in South Africa* (Leiden: Brill, 2010); Ilana van Wyk, *The Universal Church of the Kingdom of God in South Africa: A Church of Strangers* (Cambridge: Cambridge University Press, 2014).

8. See for instance David Maxwell, *African Gifts of the Spirit: Pentecostalism and the Rise of a Zimbabwean Transnational Religious Movement* (Athens: Ohio University Press, 2006); Matthew Engelke, *A Problem of Presence: Beyond Scripture in an African Church* (Berkeley: University of California Press, 2007).

9. Bogumil Jewsiewicki, "Historical Memory and Representations of New Nations in Africa," in *Historical Memory in Africa: Dealing with the Past, Reaching for the Future in an Intercultural Context,* ed. Mamadou Diawara, B. Lategan, and J. Rüsen (New York: Berghahn, 2010), 56.

10. Peterson, *Ethnic Patriotism,* 288–89.

11. Les Switzer, ed., *South Africa's Alternative Press: Voices of Protest and Resistance: 1880–1960* (Cambridge: Cambridge University Press, 1997; Natasha Erlank, "'Brought into Manhood': Christianity and Male Initiation in South Africa in the Early Twentieth-Century," *Journal of Southern African Studies* 43, no. 2 (2017): 251–65.

12. Peter Limb, ed., *The People's Paper: A Centenary History and Anthology of* Abantu Batho (Johannesburg: Wits University Press, 2013).

13. J. Stolow, "Religion and/as Media," *Culture and Society* 22, no. 4 (2005): 119–45.

14. See Birgit Meyer, "'Praise the Lord': Popular Cinema and Pentecostalite Style in Ghana's New Public Sphere," *American Ethnologist* 31, no. 1 (2004): 92–110; and Michael Warner, "Publics and Counterpublics," *Public Culture* 14, no. 1 (2002): 49–90.

15. Patrick Harries, "From Public History to Private Enterprise: The Politics of Memory in the New South Africa," in Diawara, Lategan, and Rüsen, *Historical Memory,* 121–23.

16. Paul Connerton, *How Societies Remember* (Cambridge: Cambridge University Press, 1989).

17. Meyer, "Pentecostalite Style." See also Meyer, *Sensational Movies: Video, Vision and Christianity in Ghana* (Berkely: University of California Press, 2015).

18. Meyer, "Pentecostalite Style," 92.

19. In October 2016, after a five-year battle, the court finally ruled that Vela Shembe was the rightful leader of the church.

20. Cabrita, *Text and Authority,* 252–64.

21. *SA Info Reporter,* September 12, 2013.

22. Lesley Cowling, "Building a Nation: *The Sowetan* and the Creation of a Black Reading Public," *Journal of Southern African Studies* 40, no. 2 (2014): 325–41.

23. Herman Wasserman, *Tabloid Journalism in South Africa: True Story!* (Bloomington: Indiana University Press, 2010), 10.

24. My reading of the *Sowetan*'s role is based largely on Cowling, "Building a Nation."

25. Ibid, 329.

26. Ibid, 341.

27. For a map of the genealogy of leaders and the splits, see Cabrita, *Text and Authority,* 6.

28. *Sowetan,* May 5, 2006.

29. Kwesi Yankah, "Power and the Circuit of Formal Talk," in *Power, Marginality and African Oral Literature,* ed. Graham Furniss and Liz Gunner (Cambridge: Cambridge University Press, 2008), 211–24.

30. *Sowetan,* May 5, 2006.

31. *Sowetan,* January 6, 2006.

32. *Sowetan,* April 24, 2006.

33. *Sowetan,* March 26, 2006.

34. Deborah James, "Money-Go-Round: Personal Economies of Aspiration and Indebtedness," *Africa* 82, no. 1 (2014): 20–40; James, *Money from Nothing: Indebtedness and Aspiration in South Africa* (Johannesburg: Wits University Press, 2014).

35. *Sowetan,* June 26, 2006.

36. *Sowetan,* July 3, 2006.

37. Elizabeth Gunner, "Jacob Zuma, the Social Body and the Unruly Power of Song," *African Affairs* 108, no. 430 (2009): 27–48.

38. *Sowetan,* October 25, 2006.

39. Peter Delius, Laura Phillips, and Fiona Rankin-Smith, eds., *A Long Way Home: Migrant Worker Worlds 1800–2014* (Johannesburg: Wits University Press, 2014).

40. Phakama Shembe was in March 2007 reported to be joining forces with suspended Roman Catholic priest Reverend Ngcobo to start a "Diocesan Black Catholics Movement." Later he made contact with Jewish religious leaders.

41. Gillian Hart, *Rethinking the South African Crisis: Nationalism, Populism, Hegemony* (Pietermaritzburg: University of KwaZulu-Natal Press, 2013), 66–75.

42. Hart, *Rethinking the South African Crisis.*

43. Cabrita, *Text and Authority,* 252.

44. When I enquired about these two reporters in 2016, I was told that neither still worked for the *Sowetan.* They may also have been members of the church, but I cannot confirm that. Mhlaba Memela now works for the *Natal Witness,* covering the Durban region for the paper, which is based in Pietermaritzburg. Canaan Mdletshe was harder to trace. It is possible that he is now the spokesman for the leader of the National Freedom Party, Zanele Magwaza-Msibi (a breakaway from the Inkatha Freedom Party). Her spokesman is Canaan Mdletshe, but whether it is "the *Sowetan* Canaan Mdletshe," I was unable to ascertain. I think it probably is.

45. *Sowetan,* January 3 2007.

46. *Sowetan,* February 2 2007.

47. For the details of the dispute see Cabrita, *Text and Authority.*

48. Cabrita *Text and Authority;* Gunner *Man of Heaven;* Shembe *Izihlabelelo*)

49. *Sowetan,* September 25, 2007.

50. *Sowetan,* September 26, 2007.

51. *Sowetan,* January 8, 2008; *Sowetan,* January 11, 2008.

52. *Sowetan,* January 30, 2008.

53. *Sowetan,* January 10, 2008.

54. *Sowetan,* January 31, 2008.

55. *Sowetan,* February 2, 2008. Italics added.

56. *Sowetan,* November 3, 2008.

57. *Sowetan,* January 19, 2009.

58. Bishop Vimbeni's shorthand for the formal name for his church, the Nazareth Baptist Church.

59. *Sowetan,* January 19, 2009. Italics added.

60. In fact, the Shembe Church was older than the ANC, which first began as the South African Native National Congress in 1912.

61. *Sowetan,* January 19, 2009.

62. Jean Comaroff and John L. Comaroff, *Of Revelation and Revolution: Christianity, Colonialism and Consciousness in South Africa,* Vol 1. (Chicago: Chicago University Press, 1991), 23; quoted in Peterson, *Ethnic Patriotisms,* 11.

63. Ari Sitas, *The Mandela Decade 1990–2000* (Pretoria: Unisa Press, 2010), 27; quoted in Hart, *Rethinking,* 168.

64. *Sowetan,* March 15, 2010.

65. The four "factions" referred to were Ebuhleni, Ekuphameni, Gauteng, and Ginyezinye, a small base in KwaZulu-Natal led by another descendant of Johannes Galilee Shembe.

66. Heather Hughes, *First President: A Life of John Dube, Founding President of the ANC* (Johannesburg: Jacana, 2011).

67. *Sowetan,* April 13, 2011.

68. This was the view of Skhumbuzo Ngubane, who claimed too that some senior members of the church had begun to "worship" Vela even before Bishop Vimbeni, *Uthingo lweNkosazana* (The Rainbow of the Princess), had passed away. Interview by the author, February 26, 2015.

69. *Sowetan,* May 26, 2011

70. *Sowetan,* February 16, 2012

71. Ukhozi FM has a Shembe service every Saturday morning, the church Sabbath at 7 a.m. Reverend Mthembeni Mpanza often has this slot, although it is shared out as well to speakers from the Ebuhleni and Ekuphkameni congregations.

SEVEN

Charisma as Spectacle

Photographs and the Construction of a Pentecostal Urban Piety in Nigeria

ASONZEH UKAH

NIGERIA, WITH A POPULATION CURRENTLY ESTIMATED BY THE United Nations to be 184 million, dominates the Pentecostal landscape in Africa.[1] With about 40 to 43 percent of its population being Christian and between 12 and 15 percent of the Christian population constituted by Pentecostal-Charismatic Christians, the precedents set by Nigerian Pentecostal Christians in their engagement with images and advertising become a norm of practice in other African countries. In two previous essays dealing with how Pentecostal Christians engage in the commercial practice of advertising in Lagos and its environ, I argued that for Pentecostal Christianity, seeing is more than believing; that is, there is more to perception than conviction.[2] The dense and diverse ways and forms that Pentecostalism constitutes its image economy partly accounts for its appeal in Africa. The production, circulation, and consumption of texts (broadly defined to include images, clothing, and computer graphic designs) are significant in the constitution of Pentecostal ethos. In this chapter, my argument is slightly different: to believe is to see; belief predisposes the believer to perceive, or see, divine power in her everyday existence. The reality of spiritual power, whether as a property of divinity or humans, is such that it must be materialized. Charisma must, therefore, be seen, be visible, and become a spectacle. With this understanding in mind, many Pentecostal leaders in Lagos have engaged in practices that stage and display their purported spiritual gifts and authority. Engaging in projects of grandiose and astonishing scale has become an important demonstration of spiritual power and its relevance to the society. To achieve this objective, photographs and other forms of images have been pivotal in this Nigerian Pentecostal program of spectacularizing charisma.

Photographs are about perception and power. In contemporary gadget-dominated society, religion is increasingly visual and materialized; photography is one important technology of materializing religious beliefs and dispositions. Much of religion, especially public religions, in contemporary society is about photographs, perceptions, and power. Pictures with a religious undertone have agency; they are actors, and as actors, they act "with and on the body."[3] They also act on the environment, context, or institution where they are displayed. People, as well as organizations, do many things with pictures—from selfies to family photographs to sunset landscapes and cityscapes. Photographs, however, do not tell single stories. The ambivalence of photographs is seen in their "dead form"[4]—after all, they are printed or painted materials often framed on paper, cloth, or wood—yet, they are animated and powerful in their own right. An important visualized and materialized religion is demonstrated in the pictures that accompany religious personalities and in those deployed to illustrate religious themes and ideas. There is a diversity of such pictures; some are what may be called religious or pious pictures, such as pictures of saints or religious themes. Others are pictures of religious leaders or personages. Pictures may represent, communicate, illustrate, or conceal important information or ideas about the world as it is or as it could be at some future time.[5] In advertising, for example, pictures are often used to build, generate, and sustain desire, hope, and expectation about a possible better future.

The pictures I wish to discuss in this essay constitute an assemblage that engages believers and visitors when they are at a prayer site in Lagos, Nigeria. The pictures, sourced from a wide repertoire, are important structures in the social construction of Pentecostal piety and the perception of the sacred. This is especially true of the Nigerian Redeemed Christian Church of God (RCCG), within whose ritual facility the pictures are displayed. The RCCG is an institution with an intensely iconophobic and purist past, which claimed in its *Fundamental Beliefs*—a booklet on its central doctrines—that "we do not do anything that is not in the Bible."[6] The history of the RCCG indicates that the organization vacillates from a strict, literalist-inclined organization to a more pragmatic one in terms of adapting to context and (pictorial) technology. From a strict holiness organization, the RCCG transformed and rebranded itself in the late 1980s as a "prosperity gospel" church and at the same time inserted itself into urban commercial culture, particularly in the financial and real estate industries. Rather than rejecting, critiquing, and avoiding the market, the RCCG embraced it, thereby transforming the church's practices of piety. In the course of nearly four decades since the death of its founder in 1980, RCCG's religious forms have become highly embodied, material, sensuous, physical. Faith (as preached and practiced by its present leadership and membership) is realized in the here and now, and in the material world.[7]

Although this is seen most obviously in the much commented-upon prosperity gospel teachings of the RCCG, this attention to the material is also seen in the proliferation of religious images and pictures in worship sites. On the one hand, the church vilifies images and their use in worship; on the other hand, it actively, almost promiscuously, adopts and utilizes images in framing, articulating, communicating, and performing belief, power, and spectacle. The present chapter focuses on how believers respond to and interpret photographs prominently displayed in an important RCCG site; these are known as "pictorial quotations" and consist of photographic illustrations of scriptural texts considered to be particularly inspiring or important for congregation members.

The pictures induce sacrality and divinity beyond the words of the leader of the church—who is believed by many to be an oracle of the divine. The pictures—through the interplay of image and text—speak a certain kind of language, which is understandable and intelligible to viewers. To discern what this language is and the mode of communication it relies on is an important aspect of researching religious images and the use of images in the context of religious activities. With respect to the photographs that saturate the RCCG auditorium, is there a way to unhinge them, unmoor them, or mobilize them into the social actors that they truly are in the construction of social piety within the Pentecostal community in Nigeria? That is the task of this essay.

As these photos are displayed principally in the context of Pentecostal worship, they constitute an integral part of performative religiosity within the RCCG. This is the first hint to their meaning and function: to "trigger an imaginative response in viewers."[8] The images may inhabit a lifeworld all their own, revealing what they intend to reveal of themselves, but also offering viewers an access into the intentions of their producers. The type of response producers of such images expect or anticipate is framed according to an evangelical imaginary—the imperative of a believer to imagine an otherworldly reward in a heaven according to Christian eschatology. More importantly, these images are framed along the line of creating a new order of sensibilities, a New Jerusalem against an old order of chaos, natural wildness, and urban dysfunction. A new visual order is integral in achieving this objective. To understand how the set of images lined up and hung around the site performs this task, a background history of the retreat camp of the RCCG on the outskirts of Lagos is required.

The Church and the Site

In the last three decades, there has been a proliferation of Pentecostal ritual facilities in Nigeria (but also in other West African countries generally) popularly called "prayer camps." Prayer camps are places of retreat; religious believers conceive of them as "miracle cities," sites with a high concentration of divine presence where prayers and supplications are answered in a spectacular fashion. The miracle city is a prayer place dedicated to the production and distribution of miracles according to the visions and missions of a particular charismatic figure. In Nigeria, there are close to fifty such sites between Lagos, the former capital and commercial port city, and Ibadan, the Yoruba hinterland some 110 kilometers away.[9] The names of these retreat sites indicate the significance with which their owners want the Christian public to regard them: Success Camp, Miracle Camp, Camp City, Prayer City, Anointed Miracle Camp. The concentration of religious sites along this highway has earned it many monikers, such as "heaven's gate"[10] and a "spiritual highway."[11] By far the most important and popular of these retreat centers, which eminently exemplifies a "miracle city," is Redemption Camp, situated on 1,540 hectares of land 42 kilometers outside of the city of Lagos. Originally established in 1983 as a retreat location for church members, Redemption Camp is owned and operated by the RCCG, arguably the largest and fastest growing Pentecostal church in Nigeria.

Established in 1952 by semi-illiterate prophet Josiah Olufemi Akindayomi (b. July 5, 1909; d. November 20, 1980), the RCCG was characterized as a "tribal" church made up of those who could hardly read or write in the backwaters of Ebutte-Metta, next to the Lagos lagoon. Born into a family of Ogun worshippers—the Yoruba deity of war and iron—Josiah's parents were farmers. He grew up to become a farmer and a proficient traditional medicine man and healer. In the process of acquiring a Western-type education and also satisfying his spiritual quest, he converted to the Anglican Church Missionary Society at the age of eighteen. About 1931, Josiah left the Anglican Church and joined the newly formed Cherubim and Seraphim Movement (C&S), one of the earliest Aladura groups in Yorubaland.[12] He climbed up the leadership rungs of the C&S and soon became a prophet, the second most important spiritual position in the church. Because of disagreement with the church leadership over control of a prayer group that he organized, Josiah was excommunicated by the C&S in 1952. He subsequently organized his prayer group into an independent church along the lines of the C&S.[13]

Under Josiah, the RCCG developed as a strict, holiness-centered, world-rejecting organization that discountenanced the consumption of alcohol or tobacco and employment in the armed forces or law enforcement. It also forbade women to wear trousers or any clothing defined as male attire. The church attracted mainly poor and less educated people and mainly from the Yoruba ethnic group. Throughout the same period, however, the RCCG was gradually becoming a more "Pentecostal" church through progressive appropriation of Pentecostal doctrines and practices and affiliation with the Apostolic Faith Mission (of South Africa) from 1955 to 1960. Josiah died in 1980, and after a series of internal leadership struggles, a new leader, Enoch Adejare Adeboye (b. March 2, 1942), emerged in 1981. Adeboye had left the Anglican Church to join the RCCG in 1973, following his wife's earlier conversion to the group. With a doctorate degree in mathematics from the University of Lagos (and lectureship experience at the Universities of Lagos and Ilorin), Adeboye became one of the most educated Pentecostal leaders in Nigeria in the 1980s, exemplifying the growing popularity of Pentecostalism among university graduates and the educated in Nigeria during this period. Following the introduction of a series of innovative rituals and administrative practices in 1981, the church experienced a massive influx of upwardly mobile and educated people, which in turn demanded an expansion of its worship site in downtown Ebutte-Metta, Lagos. As the surrounding environment had already been developed at this time, the church leadership decided to construct a site strictly dedicated to its monthly and annual events. This site was not initially designed to be a permanent habitation but only a temporary site for occasional worship and hostings of public events.[14]

Today, the RCCG hosts three principal religious activities at Redemption Camp (see figure 4 below). The main reason for acquiring the property in 1983 was to host an annual weeklong convention. At this event, the church's leadership interact with the membership in assessing the organization's performance and mapping out new programs. The second event is the Holy Ghost Service (HGS), an all-night vigil that is held on the first Friday of each month. The HGS was launched in March 1983 by the new leader Adeboye as a "miracle service," an occasion that draws on the power of God to solve human problems. The looming public anxiety during this time was the increasing economic difficulties that Nigeria as a nation was facing as a result of the slump in oil prices, a situation that inexorably affected the economic wellbeing of citizens. Religious institutions and leaders became increasingly drawn into responding to this-worldly concerns of believers. For many Pentecostal churches such as the RCCG, the production of miracles and deliverance services became an important concern in its self-understanding and repositioning in an increasingly competitive religious market. The third event is the annual Holy Ghost Congress, which also lasts for a week. All three events draw immense crowds of between 300,000 and 400,000 congregants. Also being transdenominational (not only RCCG members attend these meetings), these events bring people from different spiritual traditions together.[15] Redemption Camp is thus a hybrid space, a site inscribed with power, where large-scale religious exercises cutting across denominational affiliations are performed, economic transactions are executed, and political deals are negotiated.

In recent years, as the worldwide Nigerian diaspora has rapidly grown, the RCCG has expanded its congregations, particularly in Africa, Western Europe, and North America. In 2015, for example, there were more than 700 congregations in the United Kingdom, with a total membership of about 120,000,[16] while in continental Europe, there were more than 230 congregations of the RCCG.[17] Similarly, in 2011 there were more than 600 parishes in North America, a figure that would double by 2016.[18] Within Africa, the RCCG boasts of more than 2,500 congregations of varying sizes and strength. In Nigeria, the church is expanding enormously—claiming to have converted 840,272 persons and built 60,618 new congregations between 2012 and 2015. The church now claims to have set up branches and congregations in about 188 countries.[19]

The growth of the RCCG from the 1980s onward occurred in the context of great social and economic difficulties in Nigeria. The expansion of the education system in Nigeria during the oil-boom era of the 1970s and early 1980s produced a large pool of educated Nigerians who were well-integrated in a wider social and economic network of travels and connections with the outside work. The collapse of oil prices in the 1980s and the imposition of austerity measures designed by the World Bank and International Monetary Fund from 1986 caused much dislocation in Nigeria. The national currency was devalued and social infrastructure was downsized, causing (graduate) unemployment and increased poverty. In this context, Pentecostal Christianity became very important for precisely this educated class as a means for the provision and fulfillment of the promises and functions of the postcolonial state. The RCCG was especially able to appeal to educated members by redefining its doctrines to meet their social, economic, and spiritual expectations.

Leaders, such as Adeboye, who emerged from this crucible were both religious and economic "visionaries who creatively responded to the demands of their immediate environment."[20] In particular, the RCCG's emphasis on the salvation and success of the believer and the potential of the new-found faith to generate a new self and subject was among its attractive features for contemporary Nigerians. Prosperity doctrines and entrepreneurial practices entered the RCCG in the mideighties through the interaction of Adeboye with the charismatic Kenneth Hagin Youth Camp in Tulsa, Oklahoma, in the United States. Like Hagin, Adeboye today preaches that a true believer who "sows" (gives) unconditionally to God is legally entitled to wealth and health. Giving to God in order to receive material blessings is a strong pillar of RCCG prosperity doctrines. Adeboye advises followers thus: "Do yourself a favour by using [giving] the biggest denominations [of foreign currency] so to get the greatest harvest."[21]

The RCCG is a complex organization, straddling the production and distribution of spiritual, economic, and political goods. It functions as "a state within a state" and has a range of ministries, portfolios, institutions (schools, orphanages, maternities, clinics, and hospitals), municipal infrastructure (electricity-generating plants, surface dam for water supply), and commercial enterprises (banks, real estate, business schools, insurance firms, and mortgage and financial companies) that try to replicate the way the political state and economy functions. The RCCG world, which includes ritual, economic, and political activities and institutions, extends to the church's global outreaches in Europe, North America, and elsewhere outside Nigeria.

Redemption Camp is the centerpiece of the church's activities and a physical demonstration of its spiritual and material power and success.[22] Of the 2,335 individual buildings or structures constructed in this camp, the single most impressive and most important structure is what the church calls its "auditorium." Built on an area of the camp originally called "the Congress Arena,"[23] the facility is where audiences sit, listen to, and participate in ritual performances. This facility is the third the church has built at the camp since the acquisition of the land; the previous two were at different times considered too small to accommodate the expanding members of the church and miracle seekers, who monthly throng to the site in worship and search for spiritual and material succor. According to Adeboye, the powerful patriarch of the RCCG, the camp is a precursor of a new City of God, which will be instrumental in the spiritual fulfilment of the destiny of the country of Nigeria. According to him, Nigeria will be great only insofar as the nation and its citizens work to restore the rule of God in the world. The ritual facility, therefore, is a structure in the evangelization of the country and in the distribution of miracles, God's special intervention in the affairs of people.

The Three Orders of Disorder

Despite this triumphalist rhetoric, the acquisition of such a dizzying expanse of land has presented challenges for the RCCG and its principal officers. Camp managers have variously described the site as a "no-man's-land," a hiding place for armed robbers and dangerous criminals, a leftover of ritual places for the worship of idols or evil spirits of Yoruba Orisha religion, and as the habitats of dangerous animals and reptiles. To the RCCG, the land on which it now holds sway was disorderly, chaotic, and dangerous. The presence and activities of the church are thus also understood as civilizing the (dis)order of nature. In the origin myth of Redemption Camp, three orders of chaos are identified with the land on which the camp is now built. The camp director, Dapo Adesina, who has been in charge of the development of the structures of the facility since 1983, claimed that these elements, rather than the local people, were its true owners before the RCCG acquired it. Two of these elements were the forces of nature (represented by the presence of reptiles and dangerous animals) and the old indigenous religion of the local Yoruba people (who are deemed—in typically Pentecostal fashion—to worship "the devil and evil spirits"). And according to Adesina, the third "force" was the apocalyptic city of Lagos itself, which was responsible for the production of hoodlums and criminals who used the forest as their hiding place and which was typically portrayed by both residents and outside commentators as a site of extreme urban disorder.[24] This perception of Lagos as a site of disorder is what the RCCG's Redemption Camp is sometimes portrayed, particularly in official church sources, as ameliorating.

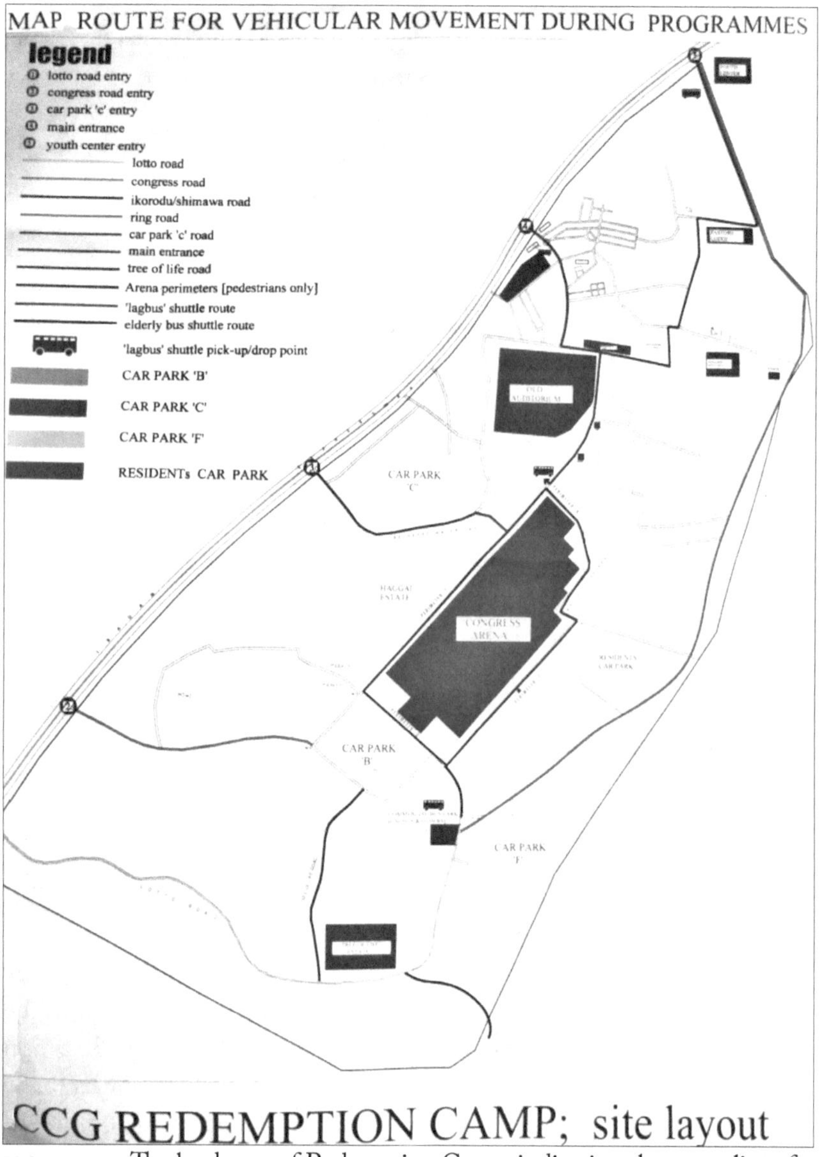

FIGURE 4. The landmass of Redemption Camp, indicating the centrality of the auditorium, "Congress Arena" (Photo: Author, 2012).

Collectively, these elements were cast as antithetical to the vision and mission of the church. By contrast, the RCCG's presence on this site restores order, form, and godliness. More importantly, the restoration of order is a necessary condition for the construction of the New Jerusalem, a place where the weak and the persecuted and all true believers will find refuge, safety, and wellbeing in the redeemed state of Nigeria. The construction of what it now calls the largest ritual facility in Africa is a clear demonstration of godliness and miraculous intervention. Although the entire landmass of Redemption Camp is sometimes construed as "a church," the holy of holies that enshrines the presence of the divine is the auditorium. "Congress Arena"—on which sits the auditorium—is bordered on one side by a range of banks, and on another side by real-estate houses.

Warehousing Miracles: The Auditorium

Built between 2007 and 2008, Congress Arena is the largest single structure on the camp. Of the 2,335 buildings housed at the camp at the end of 2012, 15 are dedicated religious buildings, 1,854 were residential, and the rest were put aside for offices or for academic or commercial uses. Built for sixty million dollars by a Chinese firm,[25] the auditorium is monstrous in dimension. According to the church's narrative, "God led us to China" after it failed to get local and African construction engineers to agree to its massive proportions.

Measuring 1,240 meters by 520 meters, Congress Arena is an unusually gigantic structure in many respects; it has no walls on all sides but one; it is constructed out of massive steel pillars, beams, and rafters and then long tile roofing (see figure 5). The seating arrangement of the arena is divided into 379 cells (with steel pillars supporting the roof), each measuring thirty-six square meters, and can comfortably seat between eight hundred and one thousand worshippers. The altar (stage) side of the arena is the only side that is walled. What forms the wall is a two-story office complex for the general overseer of the church and other senior church officials. The flooring of Congress Arena is partly covered with ceramic tiles and interlocking blocks that stretch from the altar and stage area toward the rear of the auditorium. A small section of the auditorium floor toward the rear is still unfinished and is made of bare earth and grass. The auditorium as a whole is partly unfinished and unfurnished. If form determines function, the form of Congress Arena is that of an industrial warehouse.[26] It has no resemblance to a

FIGURE 5. A side-shot of the auditorium with pictorial quotation (Photo: Author, 2012).

purpose-designed religious building. As the construction site is believed to have been identified and chosen by God, it is necessary for the church to indicate divine purpose and intention in the very structure and function of the arena itself. This is where the infusion of what a church official calls "pictorial quotations"[27] comes in.

Pictorial Quotations

There are more than 434 intersecting steel beams and pillars supporting the roof rafters. On more than 400 of these intersections hang one or two signboards containing a biblical verse and a picture. The church calls these special materials "pictorial quotations." Made from flat metal sheets and fastened with metal screws to the steel pillars, these materials are ubiquitous within and by the side of Congress Arena. Because of poor workmanship, or perhaps lack of maintenance, some of the signboards have fallen off their hinges and are resting at the bases of the steel pillars, deftly positioned to face the main road separating Congress Arena from the residential real estate opposite. The boards are not all of equal sizes; some are about one meter by two meters, and others are wider and narrower than the standard size. Furthermore, while most of the signs hang about five to six meters up from the floor, a few are hung at a height of less than two meters. These discrepancies indicate that they were hung at different intervals and by different sets of workers, which points to a haphazard, experimental approach to their installation. In addition to the pictorial quotations, there is a small group of what could be called mini-billboards, which advertise events at Congress Arena or elsewhere in the RCCG world. The church periodically replaces old pictorial quotations with new ones. In July 2016, and in preparation for the church's annual convention for the following month, a new set of signboards were installed to replace all those facing the road; it was not just replacement of old texts but also an addition of completely new ones. The signboards installed deep in the middle of the auditorium were left unchanged.

There are three different types of image on the pictorial quotations. The first, most prevalent type is of a photograph of human faces or body parts and is accompanied by a verse of the Bible. The second type is made of artistic paintings of human faces or body parts (such as the legs, hands, or lips), also with accompanying Bible verses. The third type contains computer-generated pictures or icons with accompanying biblical verses.

Pictorial (Loud)Speakers

Most of the pictorial quotations are fixed next to a set of public address systems, underscoring that these pictures are somehow an integral feature of the broadcasting system within Congress Arena. Indeed, for the designers who thought about how best to redefine a warehouse structure for the amplification of the divine presence, the pictorial verses are a visual loudspeaker system calling out to worshippers and visitors the

FIGURE 6. "Pictorial (Loud)Speakers" (Photo: Author, 2012).

presence of God.[28] This is so because the images on the boards primarily focus on expressing human emotions. As the work of Birgit Meyer and David Morgan testifies, restructuring human emotions, amplifying them through the generation of sensational forms, is a major type and purpose of religious expression.[29] The human face and body portrayed on these boards are types of religious loudspeakers that speak out about the need to address believers' bodily and existential concerns.

There appear to be no specific themes running through all the verses on display in Congress Arena. There are verses from both the Old and the New Testaments of the Judeo-Christian scriptures. In a random sample of fifty-two of the pictorial quotations, thirty were drawn from the Old Testament and twenty-two came from the New Testament. This is reflective of the deep attraction and power of texts of the Jewish scriptures for Nigerian Pentecostal Christians. It is remarkable that, of the thirty Old Testament power verses,[30] twenty come from what biblical scholars recognize as "wisdom literature," in this case, the Psalms (seven), Proverbs (eight), and Ecclesiastes (five) (figure 8).

Wisdom literatures deal with deploying divine knowledge in negotiating worldly or existential anxieties and concerns. It is not surprising that, in the context of ongoing social and economic crises and complications in Nigeria, the designers and producers of these visual texts

FIGURE 7. An example of a "power verse pictorial quotation" (Photo: Author, 2012).

FIGURE 8. "Pictorial advice" from the wisdom literatures (Photo: Author, 2012).

predominantly selected from wisdom literature to adorn Congress Arena and to admonish the believer on how to conduct their Christian life in the context of increasing social uncertainty. Nigerian Pentecostalism is a success-oriented religiosity that relentlessly searches for "power instruments" such as specific biblical verses with which to mobilize or empower believers. And according to these Old Testament scriptures, "wisdom" is both dependent on good education and a necessary ingredient for a successful and happy life. Furthermore, the destiny of the individual is at the heart of wisdom literature, another aspect that resonates with RCCG members. Character building is an important traditional social and public function of religion; it is clear from the concentration of texts drawn from the wisdom literature of the Old Testament that the RCCG positions itself as a major initiator of public religion in Nigeria. In ancient Israel, wisdom flourished in the courts of kings. Congress Arena, which houses the pictorial quotations, is likened by church members to a Nigerian "court of Yahweh," or more specifically, to the "court of Adeboye"; the arena, overseen by the RCCG patriarch, is where God's wisdom guides the believer in solving complex modern problems.

Of the twenty-two pictorial quotation verses from the New Testament, four come from the Gospel of John, four from the Letter to the Ephesians, four from 2 Corinthians, three from the Gospel of Matthew, two from Colossians, another two verses from Paul's First Letter to Timothy, two from Hebrews, and one from the Book of Revelation. The important themes running throughout these New Testament verses are God's strength and the promises God makes to the repentant and believing Christian. Again, it does appear that these verses are selected by RCCG officials to admonish the Christian to develop and cultivate the appropriate piety for the cultivation of material and financial success in their lives, in keeping with the prosperity-gospel ethos of the RCCG. Like the public-address systems mounted above many of these visual materials, these texts are designed to speak to contemporary Christians who visit the camp for religious miracles and succor. The claim of the church is that the proper worship of God is economically and socially profitable for those who subscribe to it.

In these pictorial quotations, images frame scripture. Writing commentaries on different aspects of the Judeo-Christian scriptures is an ancient practice. In the contemporary RCCG, however, pictures are today performing a similar function by drawing the scriptural texts into dialogue with contemporary issues. Such combinations of images and written texts—whether scriptural or not—constitute what the art historian David Morgan aptly describes as "imagetexts": "representations that are neither image not text alone, but a synthesis that needs to be classified separately because it is experienced neither as merely text nor as merely image."[31] Thus for the RCCG, alongside this focus on images, textual reading is nonetheless central to the formation of a good and believing Christian. The founder of the church, Josiah Akindayomi, although uneducated, was said nevertheless to read and understand the Yoruba Bible and to have received visions through inscribed writings on chalkboards. The visionary power of written text is at the core of the church's institutional identity. And in the pictorial quotations under discussion, it may seem as if the image is subordinated or subservient to the text, but this is not always the case, especially as many believers may be unable to read written texts and so depend on the image as the primary communicative channel for meaning making. Consequently, Pentecostal piety is not only enunciated in print but also performed as a visual spectacle.

The argument that the RCCG makes with these visual texts is complex and multilayered. As we have seen, the RCCG is a prosperity church that emphasizes stupendous wealth as a sign of God's blessing in this world. And yet, surprisingly, one of the scripture verses on display is "For the love of money is the root of all evil" (figure 9).[32] The tension in these images—in living a pious, holy life and being worldly wise and rich—cannot be more palpable. There is no attempt to resolve this other than to argue that it is not money that is the root of all evil, but the love of it.[33]

Through these pictorial panels, it is also possible to decipher a variant of Pentecostal spiritual inwardness or interiority. Pictures are produced

FIGURE 9. "Love of money," not money, "is the root of all evil."

to be perceived by viewers; they, therefore, mediate between the (perceiving) self and a sociocultural world. As religious texts and reading cultivate a certain kind of evangelical consciousness—as the Comaroffs argue in the context of southern Africa[34]—so also religious pictures are used in the construction of a certain type of subjectivity or self-making, an objective that is at the heart of Pentecostal material practices.[35] Gavin's argument that "the act of reading is at the heart of religion"[36] is consistent with the performance of scriptural text through pictorial quotations that the RCCG has displayed at Congress Arena. The pictures accompanying the quotations reawaken, reappropriate, and revoice the ancient text, accentuating its relevance and value and reinterpreting it in the context of believers' existential concerns and aspirations.

The RCCG has consistently argued—in line with the tradition of Evangelical Christianity—that being a Pentecostal Christian is the greatest achievement of any person. It is an achievement that comes with material success and contentment in this world, as well as the spiritual salvation of the believer. Many of the pictorial quotations in the auditorium convey this idea, as complex and difficult as it is, in simple imagetexts. Figure 11, for example, makes a visual argument that associates serenity and calm disposition with the life of a believing Christian. The image translates the verse "spiritual blessings in heavenly places in Christ" as being well-dressed and almost unperturbed by worldly concerns and detached from material worries. Adeboye has consistently taught his followers that sickness, poverty, and material lack are the consequences of unbelief or the work of the devil. Because the RCCG encapsulates the proper belief and truth about Christ and Christianity, many of his followers argue, Adeboye is God's special oracle, "God . . . hath blessed us." "Us" may not mean any Christian, but specifically members of the RCCG and followers of Adeboye. Associating with the church means that the believer/viewer will equally be blessed and receive "all spiritual blessings in heavenly places in Christ." More importantly, the believer will be seen by others to be wealthy, as being perceived to be wealthy is an important function of wealth. The piety that the RCCG constructs is devoid of any redemptive value to pain and suffering or persecution or even poverty. Suffering, pain, persecution, and poverty are not Christian virtues because they are the products of the devil, unbelief, and curses. "God does not make people poor."[37]

These materials, although chosen randomly during fieldwork, construct a public piety in which the search for practical solutions to human

FIGURE 10. Material wellbeing comes from "spiritual blessings"

FIGURE 11. Wisdom in decorating unsightliness (Photo: Author, 2012).

problems predominates. They frame and bring to life the past, the sacred revelation of which was encoded in textual form, and situate this past in a present where believers appropriate them afresh in search of answers to concrete human problems and meaning. The management of the present and the production of a meaningful future, whether framed as successful, healthy, or prosperous, is an important objective of the pictorial quotations. More importantly, these materials may be interpreted as giving shape to RCCG's ideas about what is important for contemporary Christians. In fact, as we have seen with the example of the ambivalent attitude toward wealth, it is simplistic to argue these materials embody a single idea; they are a complex of arguments about the present world and its future direction according to RCCG's ideology of inwardness and exteriority, that is, the believer's relation to the social world.

Reading Pictorial Quotations

The production of hundreds of "imagetexts" such as pictorial quotations presupposes that a large percentage of RCCG membership is literate and capable of reading and understanding English. It is surprising that none of the pictorial quotations are (re)produced in Yoruba—the majority of church membership is Yoruba—or any Nigerian language.[38] That all the texts are written in English and from the King James version of the Bible is indicative of the RCCG's immersion in global modernity, where the English language is a powerful tool of communication and engagement. Since the early 1980s, when Adeboye became the general overseer, the RCCG has invested enormous efforts in educating its members and clergy, building or running educational institutions, including Bible colleges; nursery, primary, and secondary schools; missionary institutes; a university; and vocational and business schools. The church created a directorate of Christian education in 1992 to boost the training and education of its lay members and clergy.[39] It is a safe assumption, therefore, that the majority of those who visit the camp as members or clients are literate and can recognize, read, and understand written texts. For those with difficulties, the pictures accompanying the text are useful in providing visual aid or interpretations of the written text.

Each day, hundreds of visitors and church members are exposed to many of the pictorial quotations on display at Congress Arena. The greatest exposure takes place during the first weekend of each month, when the Holy Ghost Service is held at the site. The HGS attracts close to half a million people to the facility. Because of the near-ubiquity of the pictorial quotations, their presence is inescapable. However, whereas nearly everyone on site recognizes them, it is hard to find out who reads them at all, or what readers of the texts make of them. First, because such interrogations would be possible only during religious events and many worshippers would not countenance such "disruptions." Second, the noise—boisterous shouting, hand clapping, whistling, and clanking sounds from tambourines or other locally made musical instruments (such as *shekere*[40])—and the crowded atmosphere of the facility during transdenominational events make such investigation less likely to yield any helpful outcome. It is, therefore, more meaningful to interrogate worshipers before or after events since there are usually many persons who linger and loiter within the auditorium for days after important ritual events. Esther is one such individual.

Esther is a thirty-three-year-old single lady who lives and works in Lagos but makes a once-monthly trip to the camp "to seek the face of God and have an encounter with him."[41] Asked if she notices the pictorial quotations and, if yes, what she makes of them, Esther narrates why she usually comes several hours ahead of the starting time of any event.

> It is hectic making it to the camp an hour before any event because of traffic holdup along the major roads. So, I come really half a day early if possible because I want a calm and quiet place for personal prayers before the actual events. Whenever I come to the camp, I come with a specific issue in mind, not necessarily a problem but something important I would want God to do for me. Wherever I sit within the arena, I usually have three or four of the scriptural verses in my line of vision. I begin my meditation by reading them one after the other until I am unable to see clearly the prints of those far afield. Often, one of the verses will strike me as an answer to my worry and then I will take my Bible and read more from that portion of the Scripture. I do not pay much attention to the images, but I usually remember the text when I remember the dramatic face or figure next to it.

For Esther, the biblical verses in her immediate sitting position prepare, even direct, her meditation and scripture reading. The boards are her first "point of contact" that first connect to a spiritual realm and predispose her for an "encounter" with the divine. The accompanying image, whether a photograph or a computer-generated picture, first attracts her attention and illustrates—or illuminates, in the sense of shading light, no matter how dimly—only an aspect of the message. The image embellishes the message, giving it a visual force and quality that it would otherwise not have. The fuller message, according to her, is in reading the Bible and allowing the Spirit of God to bring about conviction and knowledge, both of which resolve whatever worries or "important issue" she brings to the camp. The camp is a solution center; the first step to finding this solution is proposed by the pictorial quotations that advertise the words of God to passers-by as well as burdened seekers of God. Esther's explanation and method of experiencing the pictorial quotations is consistent with the description of the purpose of the camp given by a senior church official, who defines the site as "a place that has been earmarked to have . . . solemn relationship with God out[side] the hustling and bustling of the regular community."[42] For Esther, the first step of engaging in this relationship with God in the precincts of the camp is through the pictorial quotations.

Esther is not alone in using the biblical verses as a kind of divination board to discern divine intention. Baba Kunu, an elderly man in his early sixties and a staunch member of the RCCG, previously worked in a construction company in northern Nigeria but fled the crisis there and relocated to the southwest to begin life afresh. He uses the pictorial quotations as signs for interpreting God's intention toward him.

> Many times I have come to the camp crying because of numerous problems, but even before I meet any pastor to tell my story, the verses I encounter here as I come to prepare myself point me to the right direction for any answer. These verses are powerful; as there are many of them so also there are many people with different problems, each looking for answers. The verses speak to different people in different ways. I can tell you so because they have spoken to me in my situation many times. In fact, one verse can speak in different voices to different people because of their different backgrounds.[43]

Baba Kunu's business office is across the road from the auditorium. He encounters the pictorial quotations each day as he comes to work at his cottage beverage factory, which depends on the crowd of worshippers coming to the auditorium to stay afloat. From inside his office, he gazes across the road to three of these imagetexts as they stare back at him, reminding him, he says, of the day, soon after he relocated from northern Nigeria to the south, when he was anxious and worried but found consolation and solace in them. He says the texts symbolically hedge in the auditorium in a protective fashion demonstrating that the entire camp stands on the word of God as revealed in the Bible and preached by "our daddy GO" (as Adeboye is fondly called by his followers). Reading them also provides such textual protection,[44] inspiration, direction, and focus on the word of God for many believers, he argues.

Church leaders constantly repeat the argument that the ubiquity of billboards, colorful banners, and pictorial quotations, the Christian-themed names of streets and buildings, as well as the voice of the leader that booms from horn-speakers mounted at road intersections, feed the consciousness of believers and visitors with spiritual awe and godly focus.[45] They are not just reminders of God's word or wonder but the actual production of sacrality and divinity in a specific geography.

Although some of those who fervently read and internalize the scriptural verses on display take them to mean that the site is holy and is built on God's word, the practice of saturating the environment with biblical verses is a tangible form of constructing, sustaining, and maintaining (a leader's) charisma. The existence of the camp, the construction of the auditorium, and everything else that goes on at Redemption Camp center and revolve around the charismata of Adeboye, the general overseer of the RCCG.

Seeing as Knowing

Regardless of the fact that faith in the Christian tradition is usually described as a belief in things unseen, contemporary Nigerian Pentecostal Christians—in common with many Pentecostal-Charismatic Christians the world over—have a different orientation; seeing is more than believing, in the sense that seeing instantiates faith and belief. Seeing structures knowledge and articulates and communicates belief. As words are powerful and carry mystical force—for example, in cursing a person or even invoking spiritual energy in realizing an action—so also seeing informs and constructs the imagination.[46] The Nigerian Pentecostal theologian, Nimi Wariboko, succinctly articulates this point when he writes that "in Nigerian Pentecostalism, knowledge is often understood as a kind of vision; seeing and knowing are connected; knowledge is couched in the vocabulary of seeing . . . [and] believing is seeing."[47] To believe in the power of the invisible realm is to see the manifestation of that power in anything and everything around the believer. Seeing is deeply rooted knowledge about the unseen realm, the world of power. Invisible power must be seen to be known, to be encountered, to be useable, useful, and helpful. To be a Pentecostal believer, it is not enough just to read a sacred text such as the Bible; it is equally important to hear God—faith comes by hearing—and to see God. Seeing, therefore, is a privileged access to the supraempirical realm for believers. Seeing is knowing; hence, the urge to spectacularize spiritual power; wondrous acts, such as miracles, receive a high degree of attention among Nigerian Pentecostal Christians.

The obsession with miracles is the keen interest believers take in strenuously trying to make the invisible (energy, power) visible through material forms. However, invisible entities may also be powerfully dangerous, and hence one sees the relentless practice of exorcism, spiritual healing, and deliverances among Nigerian Pentecostal Christians.

(Non-miracle-performing pastors are generally left with little following, unlike those who claim and advertise their abilities to produce miracles and spectacles.) To know the wisdom of God as encoded in the scripture is to see it materialized. In the current case of pictorial quotations, Redemption Camp as a whole within which the quotations are produced and housed is the spectacular stage where the power of God is on display in the confirmation of the charisma of Adeboye. Congress Arena is the court of Adeboye, where the wisdom of God directs the gaze and faculties of the believer in search for practical answers to her epistemological and existential quests. The assemblage of a range of pictures and the selection of Bible verses create a version or an interpretation of the RCCG's model of public piety according to the leadership's understanding of its role in the society. The pictures and verses on display have multiple possibilities and interpretations; they perform any number of possible functions rather than a specific function assigned to them by their creator or producer. This possibility is part of the nature of pictures; they do many things at the same time, no matter where they are displayed. In the Pentecostal scheme of things, pictures are necessary as a special access to knowledge; and knowledge is power, which is even truer if the knowledge is spiritual. Pictures generate dialogue between the believer or viewer and the material; such dialogue may be internal or among believers.

Conclusion

The pictorial quotation presents us with a glimpse into the RCCG's construction of public piety in present-day Nigeria, a process that emphasizes the power of seeing and focusing for the believer. The spectacle is important in the expansion and appeal of Pentecostalism. Through the intensive adoption of media technologies, Pentecostal organizations such the RCCG claim to empower its previously marginalized members and reposition them into the mainstream of society, where they are encouraged to restructure power and institutions according to a specific ethos and piety. Such repositioning creates a new group of marginalized people, for example, members of the indigenous religious practitioners who live close to RCCG's Redemption Camp. To detractors and competitors, the RCCG points at Redemption Camp, which is morphing and expanding into a veritable city, along with all the self-supporting facilities housed in it, as a structure of legitimacy of both the church and the charisma of its present leader, Adeboye. The mammoth size of Congress Arena and the hundreds of scriptural verses excerpted and lined up along the beams and columns of the structure constitute important structures in the complex visual argument the church makes that correct belief has material, even spectacular, benefits.[48] In the age of the selfie, the spectacle is even more important in the public construction of charisma, power, appeal, and marginality.

Notes

1. This work is based on research supported in part by the National Research Foundation of South Africa (Reference number [UID] 85397). A follow-up fieldwork in July and August 2016 was carried out under the Nagel Institute for the Study of World Christianity project on "Religious Innovation and Competition: The Impact in Contemporary Africa," subproject "Miracle Cities: The Economy of Prayer Camps and the Entrepreneurial Spirit of Religion in Africa" (ID: 2016-SS350), with funding from The John Templeton Foundation. The opinions, findings, and conclusions or recommendations expressed are that of the author, and the NRF or The John Templeton Foundation accepts no liability whatsoever in this regard.

2. Asonzeh Ukah, "Seeing Is More Than Believing: Posters and Proselytization in Nigeria," in *Proselytization Revisited: Rights Talk, Free Markets and Culture Wars,* ed. Rosalind I. J. Hackett (London: Equinox Publishing Limited, 2008), 167–98; Ukah, "Roadside Pentecostalism: Religious Advertising in Nigeria and the Marketing of Charisma," *Critical Interventions: Journal of African Art History and Visual Culture* 2 (2008): 125–41.

3. David Morgan, "The Ecology of the Image: Seeing and the Study of Religion," *Religion and Society: Advances in Research* 5 (2014): 83.

4. David Freedberg, *The Power of Images: Studies in the History and Theory of Response,* (Chicago: University of Chicago Press, 1989), 20.

5. Alan Radley, "What People Do with Pictures," *Visual Studies* 25, no. 3 (2010): 269–79.

6. *Our Fundamental Beliefs in the Bible* (Ebute-Meta, Lagos: RCCGHQ, June 1999), art. §1.

7. The author thanks Joel Cabrita for comments on an early draft of this paper and for pointing out some of these material implications in RCCG's transformation.

8. Morgan, "Ecology of the Image," 90.

9. The Yoruba in Nigeria—a smaller group is found in Benin Republic and northern Togo–constitute one of the three major ethnic nationalities in Nigeria (the other two being the Igbo in the east and the Hausa-Fulani in the north). Numbering well over forty million (or 29 percent of the total population of Nigeria), the Yoruba predominate in the southwestern parts of Nigeria, where they are almost evenly divided between Christianity and Islam, with a significant number adhering to the worship of the Orishas, the indigenous religious deities. J. D. Y. Peel, *Religious Encounter and the Making of the Yoruba*

(Bloomington: Indiana University Press, 2000); *Christianity, Islam, and Orisha Religion: Three Traditions in Comparison* (Oakland: University of California Press, 2016).

10. Gideon A. Oshitelu, "Religion and Poverty Alleviation in Nigeria" (paper delivered at the Annual Religious Studies Conference, Department of Religious Studies, University of Ibadan, May 8–11, 2001).

11. Marloes Janson and Akintunde Akinleye, "The Spiritual Highway: Religious World Making in Megacity Lagos (Nigeria)," *Material Religion: The Journal of Objects, Art and Belief* 11, no. 4 (2016): 549.

12. Aladura is Yoruba for "owners of prayer." As an independent, nationalist Christian movement, the Aladura Church Movement emerged within the Anglican Church from 1918 in Yorubaland and blossomed in the 1930s through to the 1960s. It was (and still is) a self-directed, African initiative in Christianity, which addressed the practical, quotidian concerns of believers arising from religious contact between Christianity and Yoruba culture and religion. Aladura leaders emphasized a vibrant worship style, the appropriation of cultural elements in the liturgy, spiritual healing, prophecy, and visionary guidance. See J. D. Y. Peel, *Aladura: A Religious Movement among the Yoruba* (London: International African Institute, 1968); Robert Cameron Mitchell, "Religious Change and Modernization: The Aladura Churches among the Yoruba in Southwestern Nigeria" (PhD diss., Northwestern University, Evanston, IL, 1970); Akinyele J. Omoyajowo, *Cherubim and Seraphim: The History of an African Independent Church* (New York: NOK Publishers International, 1982).

13. Asonzeh Ukah, *A New Paradigm of Pentecostal Power: A Study of the Redeemed Christian Church of God in Nigeria* (Trenton, NJ: Africa World Press, 2008), 15–48.

14. For details of the history of the RCCG, see Ukah, *New Paradigm,* 13–86; for insider or hagiographical perspectives on the church, see Rebecca Bible-Davids, *Enoch Adeboye: Father of Nations* (Charlotte, NC: Biblos Publishers, 2009); Josiah O. Akindayomi, *This Is My Story: An Authentic Posthumous Autobiography of Reverend Josiah O. Akindayomi* (Dallas, TX: One-Hour Books, 2010); Modupeolu Faseke, ed., *Enoch Adejare Adeboye@70: The Story behind the Glory* (Lagos: The CIBN Press, 2011).

15. The events have uniform formats: long hours of praise and worship songs; preaching that lasts many hours; prayers, deliverance, and miracle sessions; the collection of offerings, donations, and tithes; brief session of testimonies; and final closing prayers. Many Nigerian politicians frequent these events. Former president Olusegun Obasanjo participated in these programs while in office; former president Goodluck Jonathan participated in the HGC on two occasions. A range of corporate entities, such as Unilever Nigeria Plc, Nigerian Breweries Plc, and Guarantee Trust Bank, among others, jointly finance and sponsor these principal revivalist events. In exchange for providing funding, the companies market their products and services for the duration of these events.

16. Ruth Gledhill, "How Reverse Missionaries Built the UK's Fastest-Growing Church," *Christianity Today,* June 5, 2014, http://www.christiantoday

.com/article/how.reverse.missionaries.built.the.uks.fastest.growing.church /37894.htm.

17. Anna D. Quaas, *Transnationale Pfingstkirchen: Christ Apostolic Church und Redeemed Christian Church of God* (Frankfurt am Main: Verlag Otto Lembert, 2011).

18. http://www.rccgna.org/ (accessed July 5, 2017).

19. See: Femi Aribisala, "Nigeria: Pastor Adeboye—'The Richest Man in the World,'" *Premium Times* (Lagos), August 15, 2015, http://allafrica.com /stories/201508170066.html (accessed July 5, 2017).

20. Asonzeh Ukah, "'Those Who Trade with God Never Lose': The Economics of Pentecostal Activism in Nigeria," in *Christianity and Social Change in Africa: Essays in Honor of J. D. Y. Peel,* ed. Toyin Falola (Durham, NC: Carolina Academic Press, 2005), 253–54.

21. Enoch Adejare Adeboye, *Open Heavens: A Daily Guide to Closer Fellowship with God* (Lagos: Open Heavens Publications, 2012), s.v. November 20.

22. Modupeolu Faseke, "From Redemption Camp to Redemption City: Mission Accomplished for Pastor Enoch Adejare Adeboye?" in Faseke, *Enoch Adejare Adeboye,* 231–44.

23. Ukah, *New Paradigm,* 250.

24. On Lagos as a site of apocalyptic disorder, see Rem Koolhaas, Stefano Boeri, Sanford Kwinter, Nadine Tazi, and Hans Ulrich Obrist, "Lagos," in *Mutations: Harvard Project on the City* (Bordeaux: ACTAR, 2000), 652; Rem Koolhaas, "Fragments of a Lecture on Lagos," in *Under Siege: Four African Cities: Freetown, Johannesburg, Kinshasa, Lagos,* ed. Okwui Enwezor, Carlos Basualdo, Ute Meta Bauer, Susanne Ghez, Sarat Maharaj, Mark Nash, and Octavio Zaya (Kassel: Hatja Canz Publishers, 2002), 177; Matthew Gandy, "Planning, Anti-Planning and the Infrastructure Crisis Facing Metropolitan Lagos," *Urban Studies* 43, no. 2 (2006): 371.

25. Asonzeh Ukah, "Die Welt erobern, um das Himmelreich zu errichten: Pfingstkirchen, Prayer Camps und Stadtenwicklung in Lagos," in *Urban Prayers: Neue religiöse Bewegungen in der globalen Stadt,* ed. metroZone (Berlin: Assoziation A und metroZone, 2011), 118; for a different cost estimate for the project, see Adedamola Olusegun Osinulu, "City on Edge: Constructing Efficacious Pentecostal Sites in Lagos" (PhD diss., University of California, Los Angeles, 2011), 107.

26. Only very large or global industries are capable of owning such a massive structure. The structure closely resembles warehouses owned by the likes of Amazon.com or eBay or even Airbus or Boeing aircraft hangers.

27. Personal interview with Fola Sanusi, specialist city planner for the RCCG Camp, October 16, 2015.

28. Discussion with Fola Sanusi, October 2015.

29. Birgit Meyer, "Religious Sensations. Why Media, Aesthetics and Power Matter in the Study of Contemporary Religion," (inaugural lecture, Vrije University, Amsterdam, 2006); David Morgan, "Religion and Media: A Critical Review of Recent Developments," *Critical Research on Religion* 1, no. 3 (2013): 347–56.

30. Pentecostalism is a religion of power that appropriates scripture verses considered to give the believers power and control over their circumstances. Power verses are those verses of Scripture believers frequently recite or proclaim as a form of exercising dominion over their (adverse) material circumstances.

31. David Morgan, *The Sacred Gaze: Religious Visual Culture in Theory and Practice* (Berkeley: University of California Press, 2005), 65.

32. I Timothy 6:19

33. Ukah, *New Paradigm,* 189.

34. Jane Comaroff and John L. Comaroff, "The Colonization of Consciousness in South Africa," *Economy and Society* 18, no. 3 (1989): 282.

35. Ruth Marshall, *Political Spiritualities: The Pentecostal Revolution in Nigeria* (Chicago: University of Chicago Press, 2009).

36. Gavin Dennis Flood, "Dwelling on the Borders: Self, Text and World," in *Religion on the Borders: New Challenges in the Academic Study of Religion,* ed. David Thurfjell and Peter Jackson (Stockholm: Södertörn University, 2009), 31.

37. Enoch Adejare Adeboye, cited in Ukah, *New Paradigm,* 152.

38. In the auditorium, there is a section that is reserved for members who understand only Yoruba. This section is on the left-hand side of the stage/altar and is marked "Yoruba Church." Historically, the RCCG is a Yoruba church; its founder, Josiah Akindayomi, and early members were all Yoruba. Akindayomi preached and communicated with members primarily in Yoruba. In the late 1970s, some of his sermons were simultaneously translated into English by Adeboye after the latter joined the group in 1973. Adeboye, on becoming the leader of the church in January 1981, started preaching in English. All his major sermons are in English and simultaneously translated into Yoruba. In the auditorium, all major sermons, important announcements, or testimonies are made in English and translated into Yoruba. (There are parishes of the RCCG where Yoruba is the primary language; these are called the Classical Parishes. There are others where English is the primary language of service; these are called Model Parishes. There are yet others where Yoruba and English are conveniently mixed and used in worship and service; these are called Unity Parishes. On the history and ecology of parishes in the RCCG, see Ukah, *New Paradigm,* 110–18.)

39. Ukah, *New Paradigm,* 106.

40. *Shekere* is a popular percussion musical instrument made of a dried gourd with (sometimes) colorful beads or cowries woven into a net covering the gourd. Many worshippers bring smaller versions to religious events at the camp.

41. Esther is not the real name of this interlocutor. Interview by the author, RCCG Auditorium, Redemption Camp, August 5, 2016.

42. Personal interview with Olaitan Olubiyi, pastor-in-charge of Province of Prince 54 (Lagos), Redemption Magazine Office, Redemption Camp, July 19, 2016.

43. Interview with Baba Kunu (not real name), Redemption Camp, July 19, 2016.

44. There are circulating testimonies that carrying or reading textual materials or identity media from RCCG not only repels evil and malignant forces but also protects from physical harm such as traffic accident or robbery attacks.

45. During fieldwork at the camp in 2012 and 2016, the chief security officer of the camp, chief planning officer, and the camp manager frequently stressed the efforts of officials in creatively structuring the physical environment of the site to produce the sense of a sacred place among both camp residents, worshippers, and visitors.

46. One of the ubiquitous religious books found among Nigerian Pentecostal Christians and sold mainly in Pentecostal bookstores in Nigeria is Frederick K. C. Price's *Name It and Claim It!* (Benin City: Christian Bookshop, 2005). This book has been reprinted many times in Nigeria.

47. Nimi Wariboko, *Nigerian Pentecostalism* (Rochester: University of Rochester Press, 2014), 4, 12.

48. RCCG is building a new auditorium just four kilometers away from the present one. Measuring approximately three square kilometers, the size of the new structure significantly dwarfs Congress Arena. As the construction has reached an advanced stage, in August 2016 the church held parts of the annual convention events at the new site, unveiling to the public its new spectacle and reinforcing its claim to define Nigeria's new Pentecostal paradigm of orthodoxy and practice.

EIGHT

Nzete Ekauka versus the Catholic Church

Religious Competition, Media Ban, and the Virgin Mary in Contemporary Kinshasa

KATRIEN PYPE

AFTER LEAVING THE MAIN BOULEVARD LUMUMBA, KINSHASA'S AORTA of commerce and human mobility, and upon entering the town of Kimbanseke (one of the twenty-four municipalities of Kinshasa), the attentive pedestrian or traveler suddenly observes a rusty sign planted in concrete and leaning against the corner of a bar. It is impossible to decipher the entire message on the signpost, but one can read the following (translated by the author):

STOP NZETE EKAUKA OF THE
IMMACULATE VIRGIN MARY
'MOTHER OF DISARMAMENT'
PATRON OF THE DRC
AND MOTHER OF AFRICA
COME FOR
MULTIPLE APPARITIONS
AV KIKWIT—KINSHASA-KINGASANI /DRC

The signpost faces the cement road and invites its reader to enter into a sandy driveway. About one hundred meters further down, two, sometimes three policemen in uniform are guarding the gate of a compound that does not seem like anything special from the outside. Upon entering this compound, however, one is sucked into a sacred territory, continuously under reconstruction. This is the homestead where Brother Raphael Minga Kwete grew up and has been receiving divine messages from the Virgin Mary, Jesus, the saints, as well as Catholic leaders such as Padre Pio and Francis of Assisi since 1986.

The property is subdivided into small parts, each harboring shrines and statues of Jesus and the Virgin; each small pavilion also houses altars, all differently decorated. Three other signposts in the compound urge visitors to honor Jesus and the Virgin Mary if they want peace in the country, on the continent, and in the world at large. The main, albeit modest, building in the compound is the house in which Brother Raphael, his siblings, and their parents lived. In recent years it has been transformed into a shrine for his late mother, who died a month before the first democratic elections in the DRC (in July 2006). Brother Raphael himself has retreated to a smaller annex at the back of the same compound.

The centerpiece of the sanctuary is perhaps a cave in the shape of a map of Africa, in which the DRC's borders have been carved out, and which houses a statue of the Virgin Mary. Underneath the statue a locked padlock suggests that the country is "stuck" (*ekangami; bloqué*). Its position beneath the Virgin Mary suggests that Mary is in control and that spectators should understand that they must pray to the Virgin in order to "unlock" (*kofungola*) the country.

In addition to viewing this huge cave, the visitor should also request to see a piece of the roots of a *badamier* tree (*terminalia catappa*) hidden in a tiny concrete structure planted in the middle of the compound. These roots are what is left of the tree where the Virgin Mary appeared to Raphael for the first time in 1986. But, as Brother Raphael recounts, as a consequence of Congolese disobedience to her wishes, the tree has now dried up. Hence the name of the compound: *Nzete Ekauka,* Lingala for "the desiccated tree." Where the tree used to stand, a well has now appeared. From time to time, Brother Raphael or his followers read messages from the stars appearing in the water of this well. In the past, the water turned red on two occasions. A few bottles of orange-looking water, placed next to another, hidden and difficult to reach statue of Mary, testify to these extraordinary events.

During the 1990s, this compound was the arena of fervent prayer gatherings where Catholic clergy, intellectuals, politicians, and even figures of the local music scene could be seen praying. Nowadays, the compound is nearly empty. The exodus started in the early 2000s, and today only a few dozen people (mainly women) continue to attend daily prayers, donate money, and spread the Virgin's messages more widely.

I had learned about the prophet in 2005 when I interviewed born-again Christians in Kinshasa. A common thread in these interviews was that the apparition of Mary in Brother Raphael's compound always predicted a new rumor of war in the country. One of my closest informants even argued that one should pray that the Virgin Mary would *not* appear in the Congo, so dire was the forecast were she to do so.[1]

As a student of Kinshasa's religious scene, I am interested in the dynamics that led to the gradual decline of the movement centered around the prophet Brother Raphael. As mentioned, since the early 2000s, the popularity of the Nzete Ekauka declined radically. People turned away from Brother Raphael. The interesting question is this: Why did Kinois (inhabitants of Kinshasa) turn their backs on a prophet who could enchant even the leading political elite? How did Brother Raphael move so dramatically from the center of spiritual activity in Kinshasa to its margins?

Media have played a significant role in the decline of Brother Raphael's popularity because Catholic Church authorities in Kinshasa issued an informal media ban on the prophet. With the 2002 ban, which appeared to have been honored by all mainstream audiovisual media outlets until early 2014, the prophet was suddenly denied all access to radio and television. Because of its disappearance from mass media, the Nzete Ekauka case offers fascinating material with which to examine interactions between media and religion in African societies and, more generally, to study the public dynamics of Christianity in African cities.[2]

An analysis of religious competition *within* Kinshasa's Christian landscape is important because current studies of African Christianity have emphasized Pentecostal-Charismatic Christianity and marginalized the Catholic Church. However, the Catholic Church has remained an important political and economic force in many African countries.[3] In the DRC, the Catholic Church still occupies important political positions (e.g., in 2006, when the DRC was having its first "democratic" elections, the head of the electoral commission was a bishop), apart from its domination of the educational system and health services. The archdiocese continues to speak out about domestic politics, denouncing, for instance, corruption and illegal extraction, and attacking undemocratic revisions of the constitution. While born-again Christianity might be the most popular form of Christianity in African cities, this case study will show that the center of political power on Kinshasa's Christian scene remains very much in the hands of the Catholic archdiocese. This case study will discuss contests, disputes, and struggles within Catholicism. As such, Catholic identity and the Catholic community are not approached as belonging to a single homogenous bloc, but rather as a fractured community.

Hackett and Meyer have drawn our attention to the role of audiovisual media in the proselytizing agendas of Pentecostal-Charismatic leaders.[4] Initially, media were studied as tools used by religious groups to expand. In a subsequent phase, scholars studied how Christian media also brought about the emergence of new genres in religious popular culture, new forms of Christian subjectivities, and new ways of transferring religious knowledge and mediating spiritual powers.[5]

Hackett points to a void in the study of religious media: "insufficient attention has been paid to the ways in which media institutions and representations may constitute an important site of conflict between religions and the state, and between religious groups."[6] Similarly, Meyer and Moors emphasize that contestations within the religious media field "are not only taken up with respect to the secular versus the religious but also refer to a great variety of positions within an emerging religious public."[7] These contestations are embedded within hierarchies, between those in power and those at the margins. However, thus far, the use of mass media in disputes within the Catholic world, and in particular regarding the question of access to media, has not received enough scholarly attention. The Nzete case study will situate media presence, production, and aesthetics within a larger field of competition between orthodox Catholicism and more popular forms of engagement with Catholic spirits. In addition, the idea of the Virgin Mary as a spirit who addresses the Congolese through the prophet draws our attention to the transformations urban religiosity has undergone in the late postcolonial era and to the enduring role of Catholic clergy in urban Africa.

The data for this chapter draw on a series of interviews with Brother Raphael (February, March, and April 2012, September 2013, August 2014) and conversations with Congolese Christians. In 2013 and 2014, I visited Brother Raphael on my own, while interviews in 2012, for a previous research project on old age, were co-conducted with my colleague Peter Lambertz and one of my key-informants. My key informant is a sixty-six-year-old woman, a divorced nurse who spends her free time (Thursdays and Saturdays) in Brother Raphael's compound. Her living room is decorated with Brother Raphael's photographs and prayer leaflets. She introduced my colleague and me to Brother Raphael and sat in on most of our conversations with the prophet. I also spoke to local intellectuals and media professionals. I attempted to obtain information from Catholic leaders but found them reluctant to discuss the conflict.

From the Center to the Margins

Raphael Minga Kwete is a single man in his early forties who uses epithets like "the hope of the cross," "Congolese patriot" and "living martyr of truth" to describe himself and his vocation. The most prestigious spiritual agent to visit him is the Virgin Mary. Through this spirit, Brother Raphael feels connected to the Holy Spirit, and claims the power to heal afflictions. Most contemporary followers, therefore, visit Brother Raphael with requests for healing. Brother Raphael's messages, however, do not thematize individuals' distress, but relate instead to broader political issues. From her first apparition in 1986, the Virgin identified herself as the "mother of disarmament" and has communicated messages of peace and war to the larger Zairian/Congolese nation (in 1986, the country was called Zaire) through Brother Raphael. Since 1986, the Virgin Mary has continued to appear to Brother Raphael, reiterating the following requests: Catholic masses must be said for Jesus, and a cathedral is to be constructed in the sacred compound; she wishes to be recognized, moreover, as the national spiritual patron of the DRC.[8] These instructions also come with a warning: as long as the Virgin's wishes are not fulfilled, the DRC will be constantly at war. In Brother Raphael's narrative, the Marial apparitions are related to Gorbachev's perestroika, the fall of the Berlin wall, and nuclear competition between Iran and the United States. Thus, despite his emphasis on domestic political instability, the prophet's predications also situate the socioeconomic conditions of the Congolese within a larger spiritual framework connected to global events, which are outside his followers' control. As such, he continuously cultivates fear among his followers. Prayer is the only means of averting the demonic actions that have led to such global instability. The Congolese are thereby afforded a strong sense of responsibility for political outcomes: if they do not pray and venerate the Virgin Mary as the Mother of Disarmament, more political disasters will ensue, both in the Congo and in the world at large.

According to Brother Raphael, various signs attest to the veracity of Mary's message. Among them was the peaceful defeat of Mobutu's army on May 17, 1997, when Laurent Kabila entered Kinshasa.[9] Moreover, Jesus-like stigmata on Raphael's body (dated October 29, 2006) and ongoing mystical pains in his neck prove that Brother Raphael is a privileged medium and confirm the Virgin's concerns for the Congolese. The desiccated tree (in Lingala, *Nzete Ekauka*), in which Mary appeared to him in 1986, is considered another important sign. The tree's drying out, beginning around the midnineties, is interpreted by him and his followers as a sign of anger from the Virgin because the Congolese do not heed her requests.

The Nzete Ekauka phenomenon drew academic attention from Congolese historian Isidore Ndaywel E Ziem and his Belgian colleague Jean-Luc Vellut, both of whom have written several academic articles on the movement.[10] As historians, they are mainly interested in the local and global genealogies of Marial apparitions, and the intertwinement of politics and religion in the Congo from the precolonial era onwards. Towards the end of their analyses both scholars offer explanations for the popularity of the Nzete Ekauka phenomenon in the 1990s. Ndaywel E Ziem situates the movement within the larger "cult for Mary,"[11] which intensified in the 1990s, and which manifested, in that period, in the rise of new textiles (*pagne*) dedicated to Mary, increasing numbers of people carrying rosaries around their wrists, new prayers addressed to the Virgin, and numerous prayer events dedicated to Mary.

Vellut also links the Nzete Ekauka phenomenon to a resurgence of devotion to Mary, which he connects to the influence of the Mamans Catholiques (Catholic women) association, and to the creation of "prayer schools" (*Ecoles de Prière*) by the Congolese abbot Kibwila Alphonse-Marie de la Croix.[12] The Mamans Catholiques is an association of all Catholic women—whether married, single, divorced, or widowed—pertaining to various strands of Catholic Christianity (for example, the Legion of Mary and the Jamaa movement, a local charismatic movement created by the Flemish Franciscan priest Placide Tempels in 1959). Cardinal Joseph-Albert Malula, who became the first Congolese cardinal in 1969, started the Mamans Catholiques association in Lemba's (Kinshasa) St. Augustinus Church on July 13, 1986, and gradually expanded it to the country's largest cities. The movement very quickly became important for the daily activities of women in Kinshasa, as, among others, the Catholic women gathered (and still continue to do so) every last Wednesday of the month, carrying out various forms of social work (visiting the elderly, the sick, and the needy) and engaging in collective economic activities (cultivating gardens, setting up small commercial enterprises such as sewing workshops, food stalls, etc.). According to Mutombo,[13] the Mamans Catholiques movement initially tried to make political claims by addressing political grievances to Congolese state officials, although it never really became influential on a political level.

The prayer schools initiated by Abbot Kibwila are prayer groups in which young and old receive spiritual training and supervision for a "real Christian" life. It belongs to a charismatic strand of Catholic Christianity whose main activities include healing prayers and stressing the miraculous gifts of the Spirit.[14] The emergence of these charismatic prayer schools, which have enjoyed the official approval of Kinshasa's Roman Catholic archdiocese (the highest power of the Catholic Church in Congo), is part of a broader strategy aimed at retaining Christians within the Catholic Church, in a climate of increasing Pentecostalization in the city.[15]

Vellut's and Ndaywel E Ziem's explanations for the Nzete phenomenon's rise in popularity are only partially valid. For example, their explanations do not account for the sudden decrease of followers in Brother Raphael's compound. In particular, given the fact that the war in the eastern part of the country has only recently ended (2013) and that political instability endured at least until 2006, one might expect that Brother Raphael's narrative, with its emphasis on the necessity of prayer to bring the war to an end, would continue to make sense. Also, given the fact that the Mamans Catholiques continue to meet today, attempting to pressurize civil society and be influential in the lifeworlds of Catholic women, one would expect that movements with similar political claims—such as the Nzete Ekauku—would have remained active as well.

And although published in 1999, Ndaywel E Ziem and Vellut's analyses do not take into account the conflict between Brother Raphael as a popular religious leader and the official hierarchy of the Catholic Church in Kinshasa. Relevant here are investigations, carried out by the Catholic Church board starting in 1997, into claims made by Brother Raphael, the results of which were communicated to Catholic followers during masses.[16] In 1998, then-cardinal Frédéric Etsou-Nzabi-Bamungwabi (Malula's successor) wrote a letter that was read out in all of Kinshasa's Catholic churches. The pastoral letter expressed official worries about the risk of heterodox deviations from correct Marial devotion in Nzete Ekauka practices. The cardinal appointed three chaplains who were responsible for overseeing the development of a "correct" Marial devotion and a "real" Christian piety at Nzete.[17]

While the letter closed with a call for Catholics to collaborate with the people at Nzete, another letter dating from 1999 took the step of rejecting the Nzete Ekauka movement outright: "To all my diocesans, concerning the events in Kisangani I; a rupture will henceforth be in effect between the official Church and the popular devotion movement started and practiced by Raphael Minga on the site of Nzete."[18] The cardinal informed Catholics that the bishop did not authorize the activities at the Nzete Ekauka compound, and in so doing, situated these practices outside of the remit and approval of the Catholic Church. In particular, the cardinal communicated the following reasons to Kinois Catholics for this official rejection of the Nzete Ekauka movement: Brother Raphael's disobedience and deliberate opposition to proper ecclesiastical authorities (including the refusal to have the cardinal's letters publicly read out in the Nzete Ekauka compound); a determination to transform the compound space into a private arena that allowed the followers of the Nzete Ekauka movement to exploit God's things, and in particular the Virgin, financially; the development of a blind fanaticism that does not accept true spiritual discernment; and alarming predictions potentially leading to widespread panics regarding imminent catastrophes about to befall the nation and the world (if the two masses supposedly required by the Virgin were not celebrated), thereby leading the Congolese to see the church as indifferent to the fate of the ordinary populace.[19]

The cardinal's criticisms of the movement are also echoed in contemporary popular discourse surrounding Brother Raphael. For many Kinois with whom I spoke about Nzete Ekauka, Brother Raphael is nothing more than a false prophet who has manipulated his followers and attempts to earn a living through fabricated narratives that cannot be verified.[20] Although during my fieldwork—taking place more than fifteen years after these condemnatory letters had been read out in Kinshasa's Catholic parishes—none of my informants referred to these pejorative texts, Brother Raphael is now nonetheless commonly perceived as a religious fraud. No doubt, the letters, which had been read out all over the city during Sunday masses, had a serious impact on mainstream Catholics' perceptions of his activities.

Relevant to this discussion is the fact that scholars researching Marial apparitions elsewhere in central Africa also document extensive conflicts between Marial devotees and local cardinals in which letters play a crucial role. So, this type of conflict between church and a prophet is not restricted to the Congo. Similar spiritual healing cults centered on the Virgin Mary have been observed in Tanzania, Kenya, Uganda, and Rwanda during the 1980s and 1990s.[21] Catholic Church boards in these African countries have actively tried to suppress charismatic cults originating outside the scope of the official Catholic Church, largely by mobilizing its distinctive spirit, the Virgin Mary, for their own purposes. These regional examples also draw our attention to the continuous conflicts taking place across sub-Saharan Africa's Catholic landscape more broadly.

Hierarchies are constantly contested and negotiated; in all the above-mentioned Marial cults, written media forms were mobilized as means of controlling new destabilizing voices such as emergent prophets, mediums, and new leaders who claimed direct and privileged access to the Virgin Mary. Significantly, letters were used by both the clergy *and* the prophets. During fieldwork, Brother Raphael would constantly mention the letters he had sent to the Vatican, requesting immediate intervention from the Pope. I was asked to write similar letters to the Pope's administration. So, letters being read out in the church or letters directed to foreign centers (the Vatican) are important technologies in this kind of religious conflict. Classic media, such as written letters, allow dissident voices to bypass local institutions of religious leadership and address their complaints to physically and hierarchically more distant centers of power. For Brother Raphael, members of the local church board are no longer considered the rightful representatives of the Vatican. The prophet makes skillful use of the potentialities of written information and communication technologies, which allow more direct access to the highest authority. The local church board, which in a normal context is understood to act as mediator between Christians and the Vatican, now has become a competitor. Handwritten or typed letters and other forms of communication technologies can be used to formulate complaints against these local representatives. Sending letters directly to the Pope is a powerful performative act that strips the local church board of its authority and power.

An Informal Media Ban

Today, Brother Raphael's main obstacle is a media ban. According to the injunction against him, also observed by private audiovisual broadcasters, he is not allowed to appear on public radio and television. There is, however, no formal evidence that the archdiocese issued a broadcast ban against Brother Raphael's media appearances, and I was unable to get comments from Catholic clergy on this.[22] In the course of my interviews with journalists and media professionals working for Kinshasa's public broadcast system and its various private TV and radio stations, I was told that various Catholic leaders had approached the heads of TV stations warning them about the negative impact Brother Raphael's media presence would have on the population. They also informed me that the TV station directors had told them they should not give any further airtime to Brother Raphael. As my interlocutors stressed, this media ban was informal, as the archdiocese does not have any formal power regarding local media regulation.

This informal denial of access to mass media is significant in an era when various religions, among them Christianity, are mobilizing audiovisual media as a means of attracting followers and spreading their messages.[23] In Kinshasa, Pentecostal and Kimbanguist media consider television an important space for religious instruction and healing.[24] When a guest on a TV show or an actor in a TV series mentions a Bible verse, Kinois reach for their Bibles and look up the verse; spectators also copy the mystical drawings and templates that are shown onscreen and explained in TV shows. In Kinshasa's contemporary religious media world, leading Pentecostal pastors have established their own TV stations (twelve in 2016); the Kimbanguist Church owns two, while the Protestant and Catholic Church each own one respectively. Of the twelve radio stations owned by religious groups and currently active in Kinshasa, only one belongs to the Catholic Church (Radio Elikya).[25] The Kinois Muslim community contracts airtime on a handful of commercial TV stations, and these stations broadcast a few hours a week of Islamic exegesis. Leaders of various religions thus consider media presence an important tool with which to establish and sustain a viable religious community. The informal ban against Brother Raphael, which many people (Brother Raphael included) have claimed was issued by the Catholic clergy, should be interpreted as first and foremost an articulation of my interlocutors' beliefs in the influence of the archdiocese on local society. It also suggests that banning someone from media platforms is a powerful political strategy in a society where religious leadership depends heavily on media presence.

Brother Raphael's absence from Kinshasa's audio-visual radio and television stations furthermore testifies to the intimate ties between local media outlets and the Catholic clergy. Whereas Catholic leaders might be only marginally present in Kinshasa's audiovisual media landscape (since they own only one TV station and are thus in a minority position when compared to the influence of other religious broadcasters such as the Kimbanguists or the Pentecostal-Charismatics), they apparently possess power "behind the cameras" and can even influence the all-important issue of media access.

Banning Brother Raphael from local media, even if only informally, contrasts strikingly with the Catholic priests' calls during the Mobutu era for an open press where a plurality of opinions could be freely voiced.[26] In the late 1980s and early 1990s, influenced by the politically progressive liberation theology teachings brought over from Latin America by the White Fathers, Catholic clergy not only organized protest marches against the corrupt and violent government (e.g., the March of the Christians on February 16, 1992), but they also regularly called for freedom of speech in the media.[27] The present informal censorship enacted by the Catholic clergy operates within a very different strategy of silencing voices and disavowing messages that undermine the official church's authority.[28] The media ban fits within a larger strategy to move the Nzete Ekauka movement to the periphery of public Christianity. The Catholic clergy is thus attempting to safeguard orthodox notions of what a Catholic Christian should be, how communication with the Holy Spirit should occur, and who is allowed to speak on behalf of the Virgin Mary. The Catholic Church board not only attempts to maintain control over the boundaries between accepted Catholic practices of faith and devotion and those that are too far removed from what is perceived as "normal" Catholic spirituality; there is also an intense competition over authority at play in conflicts such as these. Brother Raphael is not a priest; he defines himself as a prophet and does not inscribe himself institutionally or practically within the hierarchy of the local Catholic clergy. He began undergraduate studies in theology at the Catholic University in Kinshasa (Facultés Catholiques du Congo) but has not expressed the desire to enroll in formal training courses for priests or to be ordained as a priest. And, as mentioned earlier, Brother Raphael has also refused to have the cardinal's official communiques (1998 and 1999) read publicly in the Nzete compound. The prophet thus explicitly sets himself in opposition to the authority of the local Catholic clergy while at the same time strategically appealing to the more-distant Vatican to undercut the legitimacy of local clerics.

Photographs, Pamphlets, and a Website

Although Brother Raphael is not allowed access to radio and television, this does not mean he has abandoned media production. Rather, Brother Raphael has invested in various kinds of so-called small media, such as leaflets, postcards, photographs, and a website.[29] Within political anthropology and media studies, small media have been studied as spaces of political resistance and as circuits of alternative, prohibited narratives and images.[30] This is no different for the religious media produced by Brother Raphael and his followers. The most significant small media he uses are leaflets containing a short biography of himself, as well as a few prayers the Virgin communicated to him over the years for use by devotees. Other small media frequently circulating within the movement are postcards and calendars. The front side of one postcard features a pencil drawing in color of Jesus on the cross. It shows a close-up of the suffering Jesus, bending his head to the right and looking down. As Brother Raphael explained during an interview, this postcard features a picture created by a local photographer in 2003. He photographed Brother Raphael, but instead of the expected image of Raphael emerging, the photograph miraculously showed a suffering and bleeding Jesus on the cross. This image immediately began to circulate within the movement as yet another element of proof showing Brother Raphael's privileged spiritual connection with the Holy Spirit. Finally, photographs, printed in A4 format and laminated, are an additional form of small media in which Brother Raphael invests. These small media are all printed in limited numbers in cybercafés in Kinshasa. Flyers, pamphlets, and calendars are printed in batches of two hundred and are responsive to continual demand.

Although most of these media forms are easily accessible and transportable, the A4 photographs remain within the compound or in Brother Raphael's hands. These large photographs are spread out in the compound, and Brother Raphael carries them around town when he is being interviewed. For example, he used them for display purposes during TV interviews before the media ban, but they were also regularly invoked and shown during interviews with me and my colleague; some of them are also featured on a website (see below). These large pictures all depict a glistening star in the vicinity of Brother Raphael: the shiny star is either emerging out of his mouth or is located hovering above his head. All these largely visual small media offer evidence of Brother Raphael's privileged powers, and, insofar as they communicate the Virgin's requests in written form, these media platforms are also means of distributing her requests.

Significantly, the visual aesthetics in which Brother Raphael invests are very similar to contemporary Pentecostal aesthetics displayed in local evangelizing TV serials.[31] No doubt Brother Raphael and the Pentecostal media producers are both similarly drawing on the technological possibilities of new media in order to convince their audiences, also perceived as potential followers, of their special roles and spiritual legitimacy. Importantly, these Pentecostal aesthetics are not "new" but rather are part of an established genealogy within Congolese Catholic media history. The photographs that Brother Raphael uses share many similarities with the colonial evangelizing films of two "marginal" Belgian missionaries of the Congregation of the Immaculate Heart of Mary (CIHM, also known as the "Scheut Fathers"), De Vloo and Versteegen. Unlike their colleagues in Léopoldville (as Kinshasa was known during the colonial era) and Elisabethville (nowadays Lubumbashi), De Vloo and Versteegen used special effects in their films to visualize the animistic powers ascribed to thunder and lightning, for instance, and evoke the illusion of magical and divine powers.[32] Both missionaries operated in eastern Congo, far away from the colony's main Catholic centers. Ramirez and Rolot suggest the Scheut Fathers' territorial marginalization allowed for a greater degree of freedom and experimentation in film aesthetics. De Vloo's and Versteegen's geographical remoteness also meant a closer relationship with the local Congolese population, as well as greater familiarity with regional beliefs, both of which influenced the editing of their footage. The insertion of special effects to visualize supernatural powers was a novelty that did not comply with orthodox Catholic visual aesthetics and led to controversy among the colonial Congolese Catholic leadership. The two Scheut Fathers also worked more readily with Congolese as actors and technicians during filming. As has been documented, their films left a greater impression with local populations than other propaganda films. We thus learn how distance from religious institutions allowed for greater creativity and the production of audiovisual aesthetics that held greater appeal for Congolese Christians. The similarities between "dissident" Catholic film aesthetics and contemporary Christian media forms are striking and should not be overlooked in the analysis of contemporary media cultures. It is clear that local Christian ways of visualizing the workings of transcendent powers and representing Christian themes and narratives already thrived during colonial times.

Since late 2013, the Nzete Ekauka movement has also started its own blog,[33] which included PDF copies of the above-mentioned photographs, PDFs of the pamphlets distributed around town, and new prayers that the Virgin has communicated to Brother Raphael. These media texts merit scientific scrutiny, especially as they are embedded within local religious competition. I shall now analyze these media documents as texts that speak to Kinshasa's complex religious landscape and the conflicts over followers therein.

The header of the blog, which appears every time one visits another page of the website, reads "I am the Mother of Disarmament. I am Mary, *Your* Mother, she who disarms all forces of evil through the Holy Spirit" (translated from the French; author's emphasis). The use of the second-person possessive pronoun is an important form of address to the visitor. On this site's other webpages, prayer requests can be filled out and emailed to the blog manager. The immediate address to the visitor and the possibility of interactivity through the website are in line with Pentecostal e-aesthetics, which emphasizes Christians' involvement in the spiritual battle through a mobilization of spectators' and users' engagement with the media content.[34]

In the bottom right corner, and under the header "In Mary's footsteps" (*Sur les Traces de Marie*), the visitor can read the words *Fatima, Medjugorje, Lourdes,* and *Kibeho* with hyperlinks leading to websites of similar sacred spaces where followers believe the Virgin Mary appeared. The Nzete Ekauka phenomenon is thus digitally connected to other places of Marial apparitions, some of which (Lourdes, Fatima) are officially recognized by the Vatican. These virtual linkages can be read as symbolic attempts to inscribe the Nzete Ekauka within the larger, "official" list of acknowledged sacred spaces centered around the Virgin, even if repudiated by local Catholic clergy.

Apart from inscribing the Nzete movement within a larger global network and establishing an intimate, personal dyadic with visitors to the site, the website's main objective is seemingly to create a platform for Brother Raphael's conflict with Congolese Catholic clergy. A recent blog post, titled "22 May—Message from Brother Raphael to the Very Holy Father," contains a letter and a prayer addressed to the Pope from Brother Raphael. This is then followed by a note from Congolese philosopher and theologian Crispin Bakashal Mulumba.[35] In the letter, Brother Raphael informs the Pope about the metaphysical connections between nuclear war, the disappearance of the Malaysian Boeing airplane (March 2014), the expulsion of Congolese migrants from Congo-Brazzaville, and the end of the Cold War between the United States and the Soviet Union. The letter closes with an attack on the Congolese clergy, accusing them of plotting to bring about Brother Raphael's death.

More clearly relating to Brother Raphael's conflict with Congolese Catholic leaders is the fourth blog post (dated October 14, 2013), entitled "Le Cardinal du Congo . . . Cardinal Monsengwo! regard sur les apparitions. . . ." ("The Cardinal of Congo . . . Cardinal Monsengwo! view on the apparitions. . . ," translated by the author).[36] This rather brief post presents a picture of Cardinal Laurent Monsengwo Pasinya (current cardinal and archbishop of Kinshasa) and provides a (dead) hyperlink to a journal article in which Cardinal Monsengwo talks about the apparitions of December 23 2008; immediately below is a full written prayer that Cardinal Monsengwo addressed to Marie Mother of Disarmament on October 7, 1998. The prayer is said to have been included in a commemorative book published in 2008.[37] The blog exposes Cardinal Monsengwo as someone who in the past took the Nzete Ekauka phenomenon seriously, and even worshipped the Mary of Disarmament, but who nowadays discards the Nzete movement as a figment of Brother Raphael's imagination. Exposure of Cardinal Monsengwo seems to be an important raison d'*être* for this website, as it is the only text to which three hyperlinks lead (the blogpost of Oct 14, 2013; the category "clergy" leads only to this post; and the subheading tab "ties with local clergy" [*Lien avec le clergé*] also leads to the same page).

While visual small media, like the photographs, could be taken as embedded within an aesthetics of revelation, the website appears to present a subtle aesthetics of exposure. The distinction is inspired by Meyer's elaboration on these two different forms of expression.[38] Whereas revelation means showing what is hidden without denying the power of the invisible, exposure is the act of bringing something in the open while immediately disrobing it of its value. Here, the cardinal is stripped of his anti–Nzete Ekauka stance.

The inclusion of blogs to express religious disputes finds precedent elsewhere in the world of Congolese religious media. Following a recent schism within the Kimbanguist Church, which led to the rise of two different, competing, groups venerating the deceased Simon Kimbangu, members of the two rival factions mobilized television, radio, and the

Internet in order to convince spectators and site visitors about the authenticity of their own particular strand.[39] Here too, in the digital conflict among the Kimbanguist churches, an aesthetics of exposure prevailed.

The Message of Small Media

It has been argued that small media such as pamphlets, photographs, websites, and mailing lists can generate revolutionary impact largely because of their capacity to mobilize masses in countering institutional authorities and claiming "justice," or to promote alternative leaders.[40] However, in my case study, Brother Raphael does not aim to overthrow the Catholic Church board with his polemical small media. Rather, he intends to construct a public of followers around him and increase his religious authority. In doing so, he implicitly challenges the exclusive authority of the Catholic Church. However, Brother Raphael and his followers do not in fact achieve their goal even though they are producing and distributing religious small media. Here, we are confronted with the limitations of media forms. The inefficacy of the photographs and digital and print texts aimed at convincing readers and spectators about Brother Raphael's chosen status reminds us that media in themselves do not possess revolutionary power. Rather, there need to be social and political vectors at work, all of which must be in place for small media to bring about change in times of social uncertainty.

Recently, Dorothea Schulz critiqued the "inherent" revolutionary potential of religious small media. Inspired by her research on Muslim media in Mali, Schulz argues that the "transformational or participatory potential" of the so-called small media have been overestimated and warns against the risk of technological determinism inherent in such approaches.[41] She further states, "we need to differentiate between different media and their effects, which depend on the ways that institutions of the state or commerce control their production, circulation and consumption."[42] Schulz's call to integrate politics and the market in the analysis of small media is certainly warranted in a situation where the censorship initiated by the archdiocese has proven effective. Brother Raphael can now express himself only through small media, which circulate in limited numbers (owing to a limited budget), resulting in fewer followers, fewer possibilities for printing, and thus a reduced potential for attracting outsiders.[43]

The influence of politics and the market is only one part of the explanation of why the impact of small media may be limited. The appeal of the disseminated message itself remains fundamental. Quite possibly, one of the reasons Kinois themselves do not actively contribute to the distribution of Brother Raphael's story resides here: his message does not sufficiently appeal to them. In particular, two trends in Kinshasa's contemporary popular religiosity are stronger than Brother Raphael's pronouncements, thus serving to work against the message he is endeavoring to propagate. First, Brother Raphael's message is disconnected from the personal worries and anxieties of individuals in society. Second, and just as important, the Virgin Mary has come to occupy an ambiguous spiritual position in contemporary postcolonial Kinshasa.

First, Brother Raphael's emphasis on "the nation" and his cultivation of public fear are not what Kinois search for when making choices about which religious leaders to follow; rather, most Kinois express a desire for personal transformation instead. When we visited Brother Raphael, we usually found him in consultations with followers, who were making requests for his spiritual healing powers and prayers. This is not how Brother Raphael markets himself; dispensing healing and miracles is not his primary characteristic of choice in discussing his ministry. His dominant narrative relates instead to national and global crises. Pentecostal-Charismatic Christian leaders by contrast raise hope among their followers and address their personal anxieties.[44]

Here, it is interesting to bring in Wilkens's analysis of Tanzania's Catholic Marian Faith Healing Ministry. This movement shares many similarities with Brother Raphael's Congolese movement with regard, in particular, to conflicts with Tanzania's Catholic Church board and to the emphasis on nationalism and Mary's role in keeping peace in the country. Yet, Wilkens highlights "a noticeable divide between the normative writings of Nkwera and the opinions of his followers. . . . He emphasizes the Apocalypse, and spreads millenarian warnings on what he calls 'the messages of Our Lady of Fatima." Tanzanian followers, on the other hand, "referred [in interviews] chiefly to the experience of the water service and the pastoral guidance" given to them by the prophet and people working closely with Nkwera. For the believers, the healing process was about themselves, "not about the general state of society or any specific idea of Catholic morality."[45] A similar devotion to Brother Raphael's healing practices was voiced by the Kinois nurse who introduced me to him. She did not warm to his musings regarding the political rift between the United States and Iran over nuclear energy, nor to his insertion of the DRC into patterns of global social upheaval. Rather, she was, and remains, impressed by his personal afflictions (as in the stigmata, his constant neck aches, and his imposed celibacy) and his reputed miraculous healings of the sick.

As long as the message continues to appeal to the public, small media can thrive and circulate widely in Kinshasa. This, however, is not the case with the small media that Brother Raphael produces. These remain within the small community of his ever-decreasing followers. Apparently, channeling Mary as she issues messages about an upcoming war is not what Kinois are looking for. In fact, one could argue that Brother Raphael's message about war was most powerful in the final years of the Mobutu regime, a time of utmost uncertainty and turmoil. Rumors circulated around town about the rebel Laurent Kabila gradually crossing the country and overthrowing the president. During the months preceding Kabila's arrival in Kinshasa, as communication with relatives and friends in the provinces confirmed the rebel leader's approach, Brother Raphael's message sounded highly plausible. My female interlocutor recalls that she even spent the night following Mobutu's overthrow praying at the Nzete compound, so frightened was she that Brother Raphael's prophecies were real. Followers of Brother Raphael, she added, contend that their prayers ensured a peaceful overthrow. In recent years, as Kinshasa has been spared from violent coups, and as the war in the east has quieted down, messages about upcoming wars have little resonance for most Kinois.

Mary versus Jesus

The conflict between Brother Raphael and the Catholic Church, which could be formulated as a silent dispute over issues of spiritual legitimacy and ownership of religious tropes, obscures a more fundamental issue for contemporary African urban societies: the gradual disappearance of the Virgin Mary from public spaces. Instead, it is the Holy Spirit and a host of demonic spirits that predominate, especially in urban contexts, public rituals, and public discourse.

In the precolonial history of Congolese religions, Marial apparitions have been documented as far back as 1703.[46] Kongo art dating to the colonial period imitated the Catholic Virgin Mother with child imaginary.[47] In addition, as Vellut describes, the material culture of the Kongo-Loango area combined biblical images of the serpent with local indigenous representations of water goddesses and sirens in their popular representations of motherhood.[48] In Sakata local healing cults, Bekaert observed that the Virgin Mary replaced ancestors in popular practice.[49]

In Kinshasa's contemporary religious landscape, Mary occupies a marginal and ambiguous position. This same marginalization of the Virgin can be found in academic writings about public Christianity elsewhere on the continent. Telling in this regard is that in Englund's edited volume, *Christianity and Public Culture in Africa,* the "Virgin Mary" appears in the index but has only one reference, describing the inspiration that Mary, as a human figure, provides to unmarried mothers.[50] The paucity of references to the Virgin suggests that, in the analysis of public Christianity in sub-Saharan Africa, Mary has become irrelevant. The degree to which this is a new phenomenon is questionable. In earlier academic literature on religion in Africa,[51] the Virgin Mary does not even appear as a category in the index, whereas Jesus Christ and the Holy Spirit do, as would be expected. One reason for this might be scholars' emphasis then on power structures, institutions, and the interactions between local healers and priests. Yet, given the protective role that Catholic missionaries attributed to the Virgin Mary during the colonial era in Congo and various other African countries,[52] this absence is striking. Although the absence of the Virgin Mary in these academic texts warrants more analysis in terms of a critique of the study of religion, I argue it is also a reflection of the fact that the Virgin Mary, as a spirit, has moved to the periphery of contemporary African Christianity.

The marginalization of the Virgin Mary in current religious discourse and practice in Kinshasa is the consequence of a reorganization in the spiritual landscape. In Pentecostal Kinshasa, the Virgin Mary has shifted from being a heavenly spirit to a mundane human being. Pentecostals, who describe Catholic devotion to Mary as superstitious and erroneous, do not adore the Virgin Mary as a spiritual agent. This might seem paradoxical because Pentecostal and Charismatic churches emphasize spiritual agency to a far greater degree than the Catholic Church. In Kinshasa, non-Pentecostals derogatorily call Pentecostal-Charismatic Christianity *churches of the small spirits* (*binzambe nzambe*). Yet, the Pentecostal partition of the spiritual universe into "good" and "bad" spirits is crucial to their religious vocabulary. In that spiritual pantheon, only one good spirit exists: the Holy Spirit. When Pentecostals talk about "spirits," in the plural, it is common knowledge that these can only be *demonic* entities. In this partition of the one good spirit versus the many bad spirits, there is no room for Mary as a good spirit.[53]

Whereas the influence of Pentecostal-Charismatic Christianity in other African regions has tended to demonize the Virgin Mary and to insert her within the iconography of the demonic Mami Wata figure,[54] such a thorough inscription of the Virgin as an agent of evil is not evident in contemporary Kinshasa. Furthermore, uncertainty concerning the Virgin Mary's spiritual qualities and morality in the overall Kinois religious field does not stop Catholic followers from continuing to venerate the Virgin. In Kinshasa, the Church of the Notre Dame is one of the city's most important churches. In the compounds of various Catholic churches (the Church of the Notre Dame being only one of these), one can pray in front of grottos and sanctuaries dedicated to the Virgin. In these spaces one can purchase cloth, rosaries, and other ritual objects depicting Mary's image. Mary remains the distinctive feature of Catholic devotion in Kinshasa. *Bana Marie,* "Mary's children," is the designation given to Catholics.

Brother Raphael, who inscribes himself within Catholic Christianity, identifies Mary as a powerful spirit, an active agent who conveys privileged knowledge about the world, who is able to heal, and who has the capacity to transform local and global conflicts and bring about peace. Brother Raphael's emphasis on Mary's spiritual presence is problematic in a city that claims to be governed by the Holy Spirit because of the dominant Pentecostal-Charismatic presence.[55] Whereas on the one hand, Kinois born-again Christians, Kimbanguist, and other Christians are familiar with the figure of Mary and her protective powers because of the country's Catholic history, there is also considerable uncertainty about the degree to which one "is allowed" to view Mary as a spiritual agent. The following anecdote is telling in revealing the lack of popular interest in the Virgin's spiritual agency. In December 2009, in the community of Lemba, a teenage girl, herself a born-again Christian, observed the imprint of the Virgin Mary on the ceiling of her bedroom. The imprint lasted a few days, and word spread quickly. Curious people were allowed to enter her room and take pictures of the imprint. Yet, after a week, as the imprint faded away, curiosity and interest also diminished. In the end, nothing of any spiritual significance resulted from the event. The room did not become a sacred space, and the girl who saw the imprint was never bestowed with the qualities of charisma or leadership. I interpret this as a symptom of the ambiguity surrounding the significance of the Virgin among Kinshasa's non-Catholic Christians. In my view, Brother Raphael suffers from contemporary public Christian cultures' uncertainties about the role of Mary. The Nzete Ekauka is not described as a demonic space, but neither is it recognized as a space inhabited by the Holy Spirit. The figure of the Virgin Mary as an active agent (thus not the historical character, but "the spirit") occupies an uneasy position in between the divine and the demonic, and so do the Nzete Ekauka compound and its prophet.

Conclusion: Regulating the Power of Media

In their analysis of the possibilities that audiovisual media offer religious leaders and practitioners for forming new communities, carving out new spaces and styles with which to discuss the common good, and offering new technologies for becoming religious subjects, Meyer and Moors conclude that "the outreach into the world, so advocated by different religious traditions, is certainly facilitated by modern mass media, and yet it implies new challenges, concerning, above all, the maintenance of religious authority."[56] The Nzete Ekauka case has illustrated that Catholic leadership in contemporary Kinshasa is well aware of the mobilizing possibilities of mass media for forming new leaders and new styles of devotion, as well as for jeopardizing the authority of established leaders. Whereas small media such as photographs, pamphlets, and websites are more difficult to control, the Catholic clergy has been most effective in mobilizing their own traditional means of communication (pastoral letters) and their political power to deny access to a leader who challenges the clergy. The Catholic Church in Kinshasa has undertaken no initiatives to curtail the small media texts published by Brother Raphael and his entourage.

One can assume that Brother Raphael's decline is a consequence of his deliberate insertion within Catholic Christianity. By emphasizing his subjection to Mary and the Vatican, Brother Raphael consciously, deliberately, and openly inserts himself within the sphere of influence controlled by the Catholic Church in Kinshasa. The signifier "Mary," however, remains the monopoly of the Catholic Church, even as Brother Raphael attempts to claim her as well.

Certainly, this case study requires more historical and theological analysis. We need to learn more about the symbolism of the altars in Brother Raphael's compound (as I describe in the introduction) in order to situate the movement more deeply within the Christian landscape.

And a study of the rhythms of the above-described conflict, relative to political transformations since 1986, would help us better understand changes in Brother Raphael's popularity. Moreover, Brother Raphael's former followers might illuminate, on a phenomenological plane, the significance of his teachings and positionality in the city.

This case study, with its explicit focus on an informal media ban, shows that media are firmly embedded within religious competition and that denial of media access and critical communication can lead to marginalization. It will be important to observe how the conflict continues to evolve and to see how Brother Raphael further communicates his messages.

However, I wish to emphasize that media visibility is not the only constitutive factor in the rise or decline of a religious leader's appeal. In fact, the degree to which Kinois would have been receptive to Brother Raphael's message, were he able to transmit it via mass media, is questionable. Emphasizing the institutional power and persuasive force of mass media risks neglecting the active participation of audiences in the construction of religious authority. If a public does not accept a message, then the messenger will not gain a large following. It is quite likely that Catholic Church leaders observed a similar waning of interest in Brother Raphael's messages among the population, and therefore decided not to act against the small media he was able to mobilize.

Postscript

By the time this volume went into production, the Catholic Church board had concluded its investigations into the Marial apparations, and decided in favor of Brother Raphael. On March 18, 2017, Archbishop Monsengwo issued a public statement that was quickly remediated in local audiovisual, written, and digital forums,[57] and on the Nzete website. The declaration stated that investigations had been carried out by two main commissions: a theological and doctrinal commission, examining various texts and forms of evidence deposed by the prophet and his followers; and a medical commission, looking into the prophet's physical and mental health. Based on their findings, combined with experiences described by other witnesses, various testimonies, the "dance of the sun" (meteorological phenomena such as solar eclipses) that all Congolese had been observing in 2016, and the context of enduring violence in the DRC, the cardinal concluded that the Catholic Church board deems it proven that God has called on the Congolese via the Virgin Mary in Kingasani in 1986. An explicit authorization for the Catholic clergy and lay people to visit the Nzete Ekauka compound and a call for prayers for sustainable peace concluded the statement.

Notes

First of all I wish to thank Maman Lostine, Brother Raphael, his entourage, the various journalists and media professionals who agreed to speak about this conflict, and Peter Lambertz. Each in his or her own way has helped me bring pieces of the puzzle together. The material of this chapter has been presented at the conference on "Religion, Media and Marginality in Africa since 1800" (School of Oriental and African Studies, London, March 2013), during the workshop "Religion, Media and Conflict" organized by the Africa Studies Center at the University of Leiden (June 2013) and at the conference "Actualités de l'Anthropologie Audiovisuelle" at Université Libre de Bruxelles (September 2014). I wish to thank all participants in these events for their constructive feedback. I am also indebted to the anonymous reviewers for their comments. Joel Cabrita has offered incisive suggestions to improve this chapter, and for these I am extremely grateful. Finally, I thank Isabelle de Rezende for her editorial assistance.

1. This equation of an apparition of Mary with danger and violence, and thus of bringing on anxiety, has also been documented elsewhere, e.g., in the Philippines. See D. de la Cruz, "Coincidence and Consequence: Marianism and the Mass Media in the Global Philippines," *Cultural Anthropology* 24, no. 3 (2009): 455–88.

2. Rosalind J. Hackett, "Charismatic/Pentecostal Appropriations of Media Technologies in Nigeria and Ghana," *Journal of Religion in Africa* 28, no. 3 (1998): 258–77; Birgit Meyer and Annelies Moors, eds., *Religion, Media and the Public Sphere* (Bloomington: Indiana University Press, 2006); Harri Englund, ed., *Christianity and Public Culture in Africa* (Athens: Ohio University Press, 2011).

3. David Maxwell, *African Gifts of the Spirit: Pentecostalism and the Rise of a Zimbabwean Transnational Religious Movement* (Athens: Ohio University Press, 2006), 2; Englund, *Christianity and Public Culture,* Introduction.

4. Hackett, "Charismatic/Pentecostal Appropriations"; Birgit Meyer, "'Praise the Lord': Popular Cinema and Pentecostalite Style in Ghana's New Public Sphere," *American Ethnologist* 31, no. 1 (2004): 92–110; Meyer, "Impossible Representations: Pentecostalism, Vision, and Video Technology in Ghana," in Meyer and Moors, *Religion, Media and the Public Sphere,* 290–312.

5. Katrien Pype, *The Making of the Pentecostal Melodrama: Religion, Media, and Gender in Kinshasa* (Oxford: Berghahn Books, 2012); Englund, *Christianity and Public Culture*; Meyer and Moors, *Religion, Media and the Public Sphere*; Marleen de Witte, "Altar Media's *Living Word*: Televised Charismatic Christianity in Ghana," *Journal of Religion in Africa* 33, no. 2 (2003): 172–202.

6. Rosalind J. Hackett, "Mediated Religion in South Africa: Balancing Air-Time and Rights Claims," in Meyer and Moors, *Religion, Media, and the Public Sphere,* 166.

7. Meyer and Moors, introduction to *Religion, Media, and the Public Sphere*, 12.

8. This is in fact a return to the introduction of Christianity in the Congo. In colonial times, the Congo was already placed under the Virgin Mary's patronage. In 1891, a large statue depicting "Our Lady of Congo" (*Notre Dame du Congo*) was planned. It never materialized, but multiple smaller statues of the Virgin spread around the colony. See J.-L. Vellut, "Quelle profondeur historique pour l'image de la Vierge Marie au Congo?," *Canadian Journal of African Studies* 33, nos. 2–3 (1999): 530–47.

9. In reality, the coup was not all that peaceful. Stories about "golden necklaces"—burning car tires thrown around individuals suspected to be Rwandese—dominate memories about Laurent Kabila's entry in the city.

10. Isidore Ndaywel è Nziem, "Du Zaïre au Congo: La Vierge du Désarmement et la guerre de libération," *Canadian Journal of African Studies* 33, nos. 2–3 (1999): 500–529; Vellut, "Marie au Congo?"

11. Ndaywel è Nziem, "Du Zaïre au Congo," 523.

12. Vellut, "Marie au Congo," 530.

13. M. Ngandu Mutombo, *Femmes dans les mouvements chrétiens africains: Récits de vie à Lubumbashi (R-D Congo)* (Paris: L'Harmattan, 1999), 40–41.

14. B. Kipanza Tumwaka, "Le ministère de guérison en Afrique: Chance et défi pour l'Église," *Nouvelle Revue Théologique* 122 (2000): 416–30.

15. Ibid., 423.

16. L. Sabuni Kitutu, "La notion de religion populaire appliquée au catholicisme en Afrique: Regard sur les conditions et les enjeux actuels de la piété populaire dans le champ religieux du continent africain" (PhD diss., University of Strasbourg, 2011), 95–96.

17. Ibid., 96.

18. Ibid., author's translation.

19. Ibid., 96–97.

20. Each time I told my Congolese host family that I was off to the Nzete Ekauka compound, they, as born-again Christians, would laugh at me and would even suggest I ask Brother Raphael questions that would expose him as a *charlatan.*

21. C. Comoro and J. Sivalon, "The Marian Faith Healing Ministry: An Expression of Popular Catholicism in Tanzania," in *East African Expressions of Christianity*, ed. T. Spear and I. N. Kimambo (Athens: Ohio University Press, 1999), 275–95; K. Wilkens, "Mary and the Demons: Marian Devotion and Ritual Healing in Tanzania," *Journal of Religion in Africa* 39, no. 3 (2009): 295–318; M. Kustenbauder, "Believing in the Black Messiah: The Legio Maria Church in an African Christian Landscape," *Nova Religio: Journal of Alternative and Emergent Religions* 13 (2009): 11–40; H. Behrend, *Resurrecting Cannibals: The Catholic Church, Witch-Hunts and the Production of Pagans in Western Uganda* (Oxford: James Currey, 2011); R. Vokes, *Ghosts of Kanungu: Fertility, Secrecy & Exchange in the Great Lakes of East Africa* (Woodbridge, UK: James Currey, 2009). On the same issues in a Rwandan context, see

Emilie Brébant, "La vierge, la guerre, la vérité: Approche anthropologique et transnationale des apparitions mariales rwandaises" (PhD diss., ULB [Free University Brussels], 2011).

22. It is very difficult to collect firm statements on these obscure political dealings. And much more research is needed to uncover the actual entanglements of the archdiocese with local media production.

23. Hackett, "Charismatic/Pentecostal Appropriations"; Hackett, "Mediated Religion"; Meyer and Moors, *Religion, Media and the Public Sphere;* De Witte, "Altar Media's *Living Word*"; Englund, *Christianity and Public Culture.*

24. Katrien Pype, "Media as Technologies of Enchantment. Initial Comparisons between Kimbanguist and Pentecostal Media Pedagogies," in *Simon Kimbangu. Le Prophète de la Libération de l'Homme Noir,* vol. 2, ed. E. Mbokolo and K. Sabakinu (Paris: L'Harmattan, 2014), 135–59.

25. J. P. Bodjoko-Lilembu, *Développement de la radio catholique en République Democratique du Congo* (Paris: L'Harmattan, 2011), 47.

26. W. Oyatambwe, *Église catholique et pouvoir politique au Congo-Zaïre* (Paris: L'Harmattan, 1997), 191.

27. Elsewhere in sub-Saharan Africa, Catholic clergy actively promote tolerance and openness in the media. Englund describes how in Malawi pastoral letters written by Catholic bishops have denounced radio programs containing hate speech (*Christianity and Public Culture,* 72). For a description of the continuous impact of the Catholic clergy in the public domain in postcolonial Zambia, see Marja Hinfelaar, "Debating the Secular in Zambia: The Response of the Catholic Church to Scientific Socialism and Christian Nation, 1976–2006," in Englund, *Christianity and Public Culture*, 50–66.

28. In local political media history, the Zairian/Congolese state has been known to regulate audiovisual media strongly. The censorship boards scarcely monitor popular culture or religious content. The Ministry of Culture has its own censorship board that controls the music video clips of local musicians, in particular with regard to immoral lyrics and footage that might incite sexual arousal among spectators. Hardly any religious leaders are ever attacked for their religious content. If a religious leader is silenced, it is as a consequence of political, antigovernment statements, not because of religious content.

29. It is unclear who runs the website and who posts the messages. Brother Raphael replied to my questions regarding the initiative behind this website or its management by saying that he "had no idea" and "had discovered this website by coincidence." I take this response as one of the various strategies Brother Raphael entertains to create a shroud of mystery around Nzete Ekauka, as well as to suggest that his movement is supported by individuals with the initiative and modern skills needed to set up a website and manage it. Various emails to the webmaster remained unanswered. Because all of the material is pro-Brother Raphael, one can easily imagine that he is closely involved in editorial decisions for web content.

30. Annabelle Sreberny-Mohammadi and Ali Mohammadi, *Small Media, Big Revolution: Communication, Culture, and the Iranian Revolution*

(Minneapolis: University of Minnesota Press, 1994); Debra Spitulnik, "Alternative Small Media and Communicative Spaces," in *Media and Democracy in Africa,* ed. Göran Hydén, Michael Leslie, and Folu F. Ogundimu (New Brunswick, NJ: Transaction Publishers, 2002), 177–205.

31. This is also described in Meyer, "Praise the Lord" and Meyer, "Impossible Representations."

32. Francis Ramirez and Christian Rolot, *Histoire du cinéma colonial au Zaïre, au Rwanda et au Burundi* (Tervuren: Musée Royal de l'Afrique Centrale, 1985), 407–10.

33. Nzete Ekauka's website is *Je suis la Mère du Désarmement* and can be found at http://meredudesarmement.over-blog.com/.

34. Katrien Pype, "The Liveliness of Pentecostal-Charismatic Christianity in Africa," in *Pentecostalism in Africa: Presence and Impact of Pneumatic Christianity in Postcolonial Societies,* ed. M. Lindhardt (Leiden: Brill Publishers, 2014), 345–78.

35. Nzete Ezauka, "22 mai—Message du voyant au Très Saint Père," *Je suis la Mère du Désarmement* (blog), May 27, 2014, http://meredudesarmement.over-blog.com/2014/05/22-mai-message-du-voyant-au-tres-saint-pere.html. The note by Mulumba is headed by the caption "Personal note by Crispin Bakashala Mulumba regarding the message of 22 May 2014" (translated from the French by the author). This page contains thoughts on a conversation between Crispin Bakashala Mulumba and Brother Raphael about a prayer addressed to the Pope. Mulumba confirms the urgency of the prayer.

36. "Le cardinal du Congo . . . Cardinal Monsengwo! regard sur les apparitions. . . ," *Je suis la Mère du Désarmement* (blog), October 14, 2013, http://meredudesarmement.over-blog.com/2013/10/le-cardinal-du-congo%E2%80%A6-monsengwo-et-les-apparitions.html.

37. The full reference below the prayer reads as follows: "*Monseigneur* Laurent MONSENGWO PASINYA Archbishop of Kisangani. Taken from the book written for the 25th anniversary of his episcopate in service by Gaïser R, Ndaywel I, '25 years of Episcopate in service of Truth, Justice and Peace (1980–2005),' Paris Ka[r]thala and Kinshasa mediaspaul, 2008 p. 295–6" (translated by the author).

38. Pype, "Liveliness"; Cabrita documents a similar embedment of media texts by members of the South African Church of Nazaretha to discipline unruly congregations or to compete with other strands within the church group. See Joel Cabrita, "Texts, Authority and Community in the South African Ibandla lamaNazaretha ('Church of the Nazaretha'), 1910–1976," *Journal of Religion in Africa* 40, no. 1 (2010): 60–95; and Cabrita, *Text and Authority in the South African Nazaretha Church* (Cambridge: Cambridge University Press, 2014).

39. Sreberny-Mohammadi and Mohammadi, *Small Media, Big Revolution*; Spitulnik, "Alternative Small Media."

41. Dorothea Schulz, *Muslims and New Media in West Africa: Pathways to God* (Bloomington: Indiana University Press, 2012), chapter 3.

42. Ibid.

43. It could even be argued that the lower prestige of small media also decreases respect and admiration.

44. See Pype, *Pentecostal Melodrama,* 225–27, for a discussion of the promises Kinshasa's Pentecostal pastors pronounce during public and private sessions.

45. All quotations taken from Wilkens, "Mary and the Demons," 307.

46. Vellut, "Marie au Congo?," 540.

47. Ibid., 541.

48. Ibid., 543.

49. Stefan Bekaert, *System and Repertoire in Sakata Medicine: Democratic Republic of Congo,* Uppsala Studies in Cultural Anthropology 31 (Uppsala: S. Academiae Ubsaliensis, 2000), 278.

50. Damaris Parsitau, "'Arise Oh Ye Daughters of Faith': Women, Pentecostalism, and Public Culture in Kenya," in Englund, *Christianity and Public Culture,* 131–48.

51. See, for example, Thomas D. Blakely, Walter E. A. van Beek, and Dennis L. Thomson, eds., *Religion in Africa: Experience & Expression* (Portsmouth, NH: Heinemann, 1994).

52. Vellut, "Marie au Congo?," 538.

53. Mary is absent also in the Kimbanguist tradition, another Christian tradition that has gained much influence since the 1990s, and according to which the Congolese prophet Simon Kimbangu replaced the figure of Jesus Christ. In Pentecostal-Charismatic Christianity, Mary is seen only as a human being who gave birth to Jesus, and Pentecostals describe Mary's veneration as idolatry, claiming that only Jesus should be worshipped.

54. Henry John Drewal, "Mami Wata: Arts for Water Spirits in Africa and Its Diasporas," *African Arts* 41, no. 2 (2008): 60–83.

55. To my knowledge, reliable statistical information on Kinois' religious belonging does not exist. Websites of embassies or Wikipedia speak about a majority of Catholicism all over the national territory and about group Pentecostal-Charismatic Christianity with the Protestant Christians.

56. Meyer and Moors, introduction to *Religion, Media, and the Public Sphere,* 19–20.

57. The full statement was also published here: http://7sur7.cd/new/2017/03/le-cardinal-monsengwo-autorise-les-catholiques-a-frequenter-de-nouveau-nzete-ekauka/.

NINE

Exploring Youth, Media Practices, and Religious Allegiances in Contemporary Mali through the Controversy over the *Zikiri*

ANDRÉ CHAPPATTE

EACH MORNING I MADE A STOP AT THE *SHEFAN.TIGIW*[1] (TEA/COFFEE and egg-sandwich shops) located along the main tarred roads crossing Bougouni. This provincial town in southwest Mali, where I undertook my PhD fieldwork between November 2008 and April 2010, was home to more than sixty thousand inhabitants. I started the day by drinking a strong Nescafé and chatting with traders and passersby while observing the big trucks, coaches, cars, and activities around me. People of various economic and social backgrounds were encountered in theses spaces of transit; listening to their conversations, I could gain an insight into debates shaping the public sphere in Mali. I once sat around a lively table at my favorite *shɛfantigi*. Customers were talking about many subjects: a serious accident that happened recently in Bougouni, the difficulty of finding *monnaiekun* (basic financing for starting a small trade) in Mali, and the controversial *zikiri* coming out of someone's mobile phone.

The *Bamanan* word *zikiri* comes from the Arab word *dhikr* (or *zikr*), which can be translated as a "remembrance" in the mind, or a "mentioning" and "relating" with the tongue.[2] In Islam, this prominent Sufi concept signifies "the remembrance or recollection of God—a recollection that can be performed either silently or aloud."[3] As a practice,[4] *dhikr* can simultaneously express a form of prayer, a devotional act, and a mystical performance and typically involves the repetition of the names of God, the supplications or formulas taken from Hadith texts, and verses of the Koran in order for the Muslim to come closer to God. Permitted at any time and at any place, such practice can be done either individually or in ritualized ceremonies performed in a group. In Mali, the *dhikr* is generally not accompanied by musical instruments because, according to most local Muslim scholars, music allegedly promotes heedlessness rather than devotional concentration.[5] As a chant accompanied with guitars and drums, this so-called *zikiri* was therefore controversial mostly because of its musicality.

In fact, the *zikiri* in Mali originated from the panegyric poetry of *maduhu* (in Arabic, *madh*), an ancient genre of Islamic praise the Arabic lyrics of which are performed a cappella.[6] Inspired by the *maduhu* culture of the towns at the edge of the Sahara (e.g., Djenné, Tombouctou), Racine Sall initiated the *zikiri* in the seventies by adapting the remembrance of God, the Prophet, and his descendants to contemporary popular music when he started chanting these Islamic praises in vernacular languages accompanied by local instruments.[7] The *zikiri*, as a religious music genre, came to the front in southern Mali only two decades later. Thanks to the democratic shifts of 1991, the country became characterized by an increasingly lively public sphere abetted by the new freedom of the press and association.[8] Helped by the multiplication of innovative media (e.g., TV, radio, audiocassette, mobile phone), such liberties have supported the visibility of Islam and the diversity and activism of Muslims in public.[9] The *zikiriw*, the musicality[10] of which typically appealed to the youth, hence became popular during the late nineties in Mali once Sufi reformist movements promoted them via aural media. In this regard, the anthropologist Pierre Prud'homme rightly invites us to consider the *zikiri* as the outcome of a "dialectic process between what is perceived as an Islamisation of the Malian culture and a Malian interpretation of Islam"[11] within the West African sphere of religious music.[12]

Tape-cassette recordings of *zikiri*, for instance, were abundantly found in the big market of Bougouni in 2010. Some of the "religious singers" (*zikiri.da.la*),[13] such as Nouhoum Dembélé, even rose to fame and became something like pop stars among young Muslims in Mali. Youth in Bougouni usually listened to *zikiri* through radio-cassette players and radios in *grins* (informal spots where men socialize);[14] housemaids turned on the radio and hummed them to themselves while doing household chores within courtyards. Bus drivers put *zikiri* cassettes into the radio-cassette player during the journey from Bougouni to Bamako,

Sikasso, and Yanfolila. Others loaded *zikiri* onto their mobile phones and stored them next to the songs of Tiken Jah Fakoly, Celine Dion, Nahawa Doumbia, and other African and Western musicians. *Zikiri* in Bougouni was listened to at any time and at any place in 2010.

This very morning in the above-mentioned *shɛfantigi,* a few young people were talking about *zikiri.* A teacher in a local *médersa* (Franco-Arab school) pointed out that many Muslim scholars blame the entertaining character of *zikiri* for inducing forgetfulness and therefore being disrespectful toward Islam, the Prophet, and God. However, he had nothing against *zikiri* as long as its lyrics were in agreement with Islamic sacred texts. Whereas secular popular music has often been classified as un-Islamic and identified with youth in Muslim West Africa,[15] *zikiri* is indeed labeled as "religious song" by its promoters owing to its Islamic lyrics. The owner of the mobile phone, a worker in a nearby gold mining site, liked *zikiri* because it mixes the pleasant (music) with the useful (knowledge of Islam). The shopkeeper added that the deceased local religious figure El-Hajj Ladji Blen (about 1900–1989)[16] used drums to call Muslims for the Friday communal prayer. He further stated that Christians accompany their prayer with music so as to ease the learning of the religious message. A student at the IFM (Institut de Formation des Maîtres) of Bougouni concluded the discussion by saying that "Haïdara agrees to the *zikiri.* The extremists disagree with them because they do not change with the society!" The French label *"les extrémistes"* here bluntly cast a wide emotional net over locals—among whom the elders and the so-called *Wahhabites* were often mentioned—who regularly criticized the modern lifestyles and ideas of Mali youth.

Because marriage, parenthood, and a decent job are the conventional gates to adulthood in this country, a youth in urban Mali can be defined largely as an unemployed single person without children.[17] However, age labels, such as "junior" (*dɔgɔ*) and "senior" (*kɔrɔ*), are used in conversation to denote youth and seniors as "social shifters" rather than to locate them in specific age groups or cohorts.[18] In social interactions, the meaning of the category "youth" is situational because it often draws attention to relations of power, rights, expectations, and hierarchy between people, and this especially when their age is similar.[19] In Bougouni, La Jeune Chambre Internationale, an association of young entrepreneurs, defined itself as an "association of young people between the ages of 18 and 40," a statement that demonstrates the flexible and extensible usage of this category in Mali.

When Malians speak about the epoch in which they grew up, however, the categories of "youth" and "elder" become more distinct because, as I will develop throughout this chapter, their generational discrepancy comes to the fore as an "idiom for ordering social and political relations and as a language of values and attitudes."[20] Against a backdrop of youths' traditional marginalization as "bad Muslims" by their elders owing to their alleged lack of maturity, my analysis explores what it means in contemporary Mali to be both male Muslim *and* young in generational terms. This chapter's focus on this growing category of actors across Africa further aims to reflect on the fact that they are potentially the most numerous recipients of competing religious discourses found in the local public sphere.[21] It attempts to do so by investigating "the political character" of the construction of male adult masculinities in this country through the prism of the ordinary.[22]

Most research on past and contemporary Islamic renewal in West Africa has focused on sharp religious affiliations, such as members of Sufi orders, reformist piety movements, and new Muslim associations and their religious leaders. This long-standing analytical tendency,[23] however, has set aside the study of the overwhelming majority of Muslims: the "ordinary Muslims," a category originally developed by Peletz in his study of Islamic resurgence in the Malay Peninsula.[24] Although the heterogeneity of such a broad category is problematic, Peletz wanted to understand how the vast majority of Malays perceive discourses of Malay Muslim reformers so as to "examine the production and consumption of contrasting discourses on Islam and Malay cultural identity in contemporary Malaysia."[25] Focusing on religious experience in Mali, Schulz coined as "observant Muslims" Muslims who are both unaffiliated and nonpracticing Muslims.[26] Marsden and Retsikas recently elaborated the category of "people of Muslim background," an all-embracing category that emphasizes Islam as a cultural trait.[27]

This analysis addresses the question of ordinary Muslims in relation to new media practices of *zikiriw,* which participate in the elaboration of a "local modernity" in Mali.[28] In this regard, I focus on the ramifications of the media promotion of religious authority via *zikiriw* into a wide audience in terms of bond. Based on an ethnography of youths' listening of *zikiri* in the provincial town of Bougouni, I explore the quality of the media-mediated allegiance that is forged between listeners of this recent religious music genre and its best-known promoter in Mali, Cherif Ousmane Madane Haïdara.[29] Whereas Dorothea Schulz studied Haïdara's creation of a "community of believers" through broadcast media,[30] I attempt to extend her analysis beyond his "devotees"[31] (e.g., members of his religious association *Ansar Dine*) by considering the growing emergence of a media-mediated religious actor in post-1991 Mali: the sympathizer.

I begin this chapter by outlining the categories of Muslims who disagree with the so-called *zikiri* (the reformists and the elders) in the light of Sufi-Reformist tensions[32] and changes in Islamic education, which have marked the field of religious allegiance in postcolonial Mali. Stressing the politics of generation that emerged during the coup d'état of 1991, I then analyze the category of the sympathizer as the result of an interplay between an increasing media-mediated sociology of Islamic knowledge and emancipatory forces. I do so through the exploration of the success of Haïdara among his most numerous sympathizers in Bougouni: young Muslims.[33] This chapter offers an insight into an increasing media-mediated realm of religious allegiance in a country in which the youths, supported by their demographic weight and their role in the events of 1991, have established themselves as powerful actors within local Muslim life. Beyond the case of Mali, this chapter reflects on the nature of the media-mediated ties between a contemporary religious entrepreneur and the broad group of listeners situated beyond the inner circle of his devotees.

"*Zikiri* Are Noise for Children!"

After World War II, Mali saw the emergence of reformist influences introduced by pilgrims and Islamic students returning from the Middle East. Helped by their knowledge of the Islamic sacred texts, these reformists have taken root in the country by speaking "forcefully about the need to combat *bid'a* ("innovation"), which means unlawful innovation in Islam."[34] They have vehemently criticized the imposition of local social structure on religious offices, the *maraboutage* practices, and the cult of saints. As a result, Islamic debates in Mali during the postcolonial period have been shaped by tensions between reformist movements and Sufi orders. Whereas the former decried the allegedly un-Islamic customs entangled in the local practices of Islam, the latter asserted the Islamic character of these practices, which are still widely adopted by most Muslims in Bougouni.[35] The heterogeneous group of reformist movements, who name themselves "Sunnis," have been labeled with the pejorative colonial-era term *"Wahhabites"* by those not affiliated to their doctrines.[36] Analyzing identity as "a process of . . . naming of others, naming *by* others,"[37] we see that the contemporary usage of the label "*Wahhabite*" by Malians expresses the fact that these Muslims are still considered a "threat." Whereas colonial administrators perceived Salafiyya ideas as subversive to colonial order, numerous Muslims in present-day Mali blame them for confounding Islam with Arabic culture, thereby neglecting (even betraying) their own culture. Although reformists represent only a small urban minority in Mali, they are highly noticeable in public because of what Malians mockingly call their "Arabic dress code," such as the men's white robes and trousers ending in the calf region (so as to avoid picking up soil that could invalidate the prayer) and women's black veils. Nonreformist Muslims also condemn reformists for socializing only among themselves; they reproach them for praying in mosques of reformist allegiance only, and more importantly, only attending the lifecycle rituals of the reformist community.[38] Numerous nonreformist Muslims in Bougouni think "the *Wahhabites* are undermining *adama.den.ya,*"[39] the fabric of local life that builds *ɲɔgɔndɛmɛ* (solidarity) and keeps *hɛɛrɛ* (harmony). However, both reformists and urban Muslim elders criticized *zikiri* as a kind of *bid'a,* the nature of which is not religious.

The Islamic traditions practiced by elders in Bougouni are historically rooted in the long-standing Qadiriyya and Tijaniyya presence in this part of West Africa,[40] the two Sufi orders that represented much institutional Islam during the colonial period in Mali.[41] Although the Muslim elders I met in Bougouni between 2008 and 2010 remembered their Sufi origins, the majority had never been affiliated to any Sufi leaders (*muqaddam*). By contrast with Senegal,[42] formal membership in a Sufi order was rather limited in most of West Africa.[43] The first Muslim families of southern Mali had little knowledge of Islam; its practice was often disparate and mixed with local religious traditions called *"Bamanaya."* Within the emerging context of an "Islamic sphere" promoted by colonial peace and the development of a road network,[44] foreign Muslim scholars settled in towns of southern Mali during the second half of the colonial period. As they preached in public and set up Islamic schools, Muslim identity came to be associated with standardized Islamic precepts, including the regular prayer, the ritual fasting, the Friday communal prayers in a mosque, and, if possible, the Hajj pilgrimage. By contrast to areas where reformist movements have set the terms for Islamic debate, thereby moving Sufi Islam into their grounds,[45] the local practices of Islam have mostly been preserved in postcolonial Mali. In response to increasing public expressions of piety observed among the followers of the Islamic movements developed in post-1991 Mali,[46] nonetheless, elders in Bougouni have also adopted the display of common outward signs of piety such as the white traditional robe or *boubou*, the rounded small white cap or *silamɛ fugulan* (Muslim hat), and the white slippers. Although these elders sometimes defined themselves as Muslim of Sufi obedience, they mostly received their religious education before 1991 from Muslims who, although not formally affiliated to any Sufi order, still regarded themselves as having a Sufi education.

In Bougouni, elders did not listen to *zikiri;* a few among them listened to cassettes of recitations of the Koran instead. In fact, most of them did not link *zikiri* to any Muslim-informed religiosity; its morality was even questioned during group interviews I carried out with those attending local mosques. As these meetings were held in the courtyards of mosques after prayer on days of the week other than Friday, my interlocutors were mostly Muslims who prayed diligently at the mosque, namely, the elders. Such regular religious observance has often been associated with old people in Mali,[47] those whom people call "old man" (*cɛkɔrɔba*) and "old woman" (*musokɔrɔba*). Their allegedly greater devotional practice, compared to younger generations, is motivated by acquiring social status and respectability in the local community and by accumulating "religious awards" (*baraji*) to prepare for death as the unavoidable gate to the Day of Judgment.[48] At that time, I was working with a young fieldwork assistant who was curious to know what elders and imams of the town thought about the *zikiri* he and his friends listened to. He took initiative in asking elders questions about *zikiri.* When this issue was raised, the elders often laughed mockingly. For them, *zikiri* was simply a "noise" (*mankan*) for "children" (*denmisɛnw*), the listening of which produces no "benefit" (*nafa*) at all. Ibrahim, a sixty-seven-year-old imam, stated that

> *zikiri* used to be performed with the tongue. Religious retreat used to be performed with the tongue. . . . In *zikiri* we utter the name of God many times so as to obtain religious rewards. If you utter the name of God many times, you will collect religious rewards. But to do it a bit on *balafon*[49] and things like that; this did not happen in our epoch! We did not do it. However, some people say it is done today and it does not spoil the religion. Others say it is shameful to do it like that.[50]

As these interviews were recorded, elderly Muslims, like Ibrahim, took care to moderate their view by stressing that "some people" tolerate the *zikiri*. I suspect they did not want to openly criticize Haïdara, the best-known promoter of *zikiri*, because they were aware of his popularity in town. But when the recording device was off, and I was about to go home, some often concluded by uttering that "*zikiri* are un-Islamic."[51] By saying "this did not happen in our epoch!" Ibrahim reveals the generational issue provoked by the advent of the *zikiri* genre in contemporary Mali.

"Generation Jakarta": The Youth in Post-1991 Mali

As Ibrahim hinted above, local elders used to differentiate between "[their] epoch" (*an tile*) and "today" (*bi*) in terms of the "spirit of times."[52] This compartmentalization of time often occurs as elders referred to their upbringing. For them, "the time when [they] were born" (*an tun bɛ bangin tuma min na*) corresponds to the period of their childhood and youth that they feel still shapes who they are decades after it ended. In contrast to the classic anthropological emphasis on the dynamics of the everyday in people's life, the elders' remembering of their upbringing illustrates the imprint of the earlier life stage of manhood formation in an adult's life. Most elders did not interpret the *zikiri* listened to by the younger generations in town as an "old thing" (*ko kɔrɔ*), thereby a legitimate *dhikr*. They rather perceived *zikiri* as a "*new* thing" (*ko kura*) that has nothing to do with the conventional Sufi *dhikr* practices of "getting closer to God" (*ka hakili jigin Ala la*) found in the Islamic education they received during their upbringing.[53] In the Mali of the early twenty-first century, people often segment the epochs of upbringing by distinguishing between those who grew up under the regime of Moussa Traoré[54] and those who grew up after 1991.

The military and dictatorial regime of Moussa Traoré was overthrown on March 26, 1991, by a coup d'état that paved the way to the first democratic and liberal era since Mali's independence in 1960. Officially cutting the link with a socialist conception of the state and its control of economic institutions, the Third Republic of Mali brought changes that still shape contemporary Mali, such as the civic liberties mentioned in the introduction. The expansion of a road network supported by the policy of *désenclavement* of the post-1991 governments (of this landlocked country), the massive arrival in early 2000s of affordable sophisticated goods made in China, and the popularization of mobile phones have in less than a decade transformed the mobility and the material and technological culture of urbanites.[55] In this regard, elders in town have labeled the youth *"Génération Jakarta"* in reference to the nickname of the Chinese-made motorbike in vogue among the urban youth.[56] These changes have prompted elders to think of the youth as a distinct generation shaped by a specific contemporaneity.

Elders in Bougouni did not reduce this contemporaneity to material symbols. They also related its nature to the youthful emancipation they have observed since 1991. The traditional gerontocracy still persisted within families in numerous ways. However, many elders pointed to youths' participation in the events of 1991 as a turning point in intergenerational relations in Mali.[57] Among other youth organizations,[58] L'AEEM (Association des élèves et des étudiants du Mali), a student trade union founded in 1990, illustrates the involvement of youth in the prodemocracy protests that triggered the coup d'état of March 26, 1991. Many young Malians were injured by the violent repression ordered by Moussa Traoré in response to the popular demonstrations of late January and March 22–26, 1991, in the capital and in regional towns.[59] In the aftermath of the coup d'état, Malian youth emerged not only as intimidating activists[60] but also as a democratic and responsible force in civil contestation, as demonstrated through the politics of l'AEEM in the 1990s.[61] The events of 1991 hence built a powerful generational cohort of youth who became increasingly self-conscious of their political weight in the Malian society. The arson attempt on the colonial and postcolonial archive deposits in the town of Bougouni,[62] which happened during the demonstrations of March 1991 in this provincial town, possibly marked a youthful desire to enact a rupture with the past.

On my way to the big market of Bougouni, I often stopped by Abdoulaye's workshop, which was located along a street leading to the house of my host family. When I encountered him in 2009, he worked as an electrician and was a married man about fifty years old. He was originally a farmer from the hinterland of Bougouni who settled in town in the early 1980s. Once when I met him, he was staring at a male teenager (*kamalen*) who was boldly smoking a cigarette in front of his workshop. He then pointed to the fact that the "respect" (*bonya*) traditionally associated with old age and the status of being the head of a family is regrettably being challenged by the youth.[63] Beyond the usual normative discourses around rebellious youth, older generations in Mali "openly long for some certainties" of the past, such as those found in the authoritative disposition of former regimes.[64] Abdoulaye welcomed the idea of democracy; nonetheless, he thought that this reform had not been properly understood by the majority of Malians and especially the youth: "Democracy arrived. But many people and the youth have only understood it as—you can do what you like."[65] Schulz already noted that "middle-aged and elderly farmers" of rural Mali equated *demokrasi* with "chaos" during the 1990s, mostly because they observed in post-1991 Mali "the absence of a central power and of the authority of the older over the younger generation."[66] Numerous elders I met in Bougouni indeed felt nostalgia for the respect for authoritative power they portray as characteristic of the pre-1991 period.

The advent of the Third Republic of Mali illustrates the linkages between regime change, nation building, and the transformation of masculinity that occur in contemporary Africa.[67] Under the government of Alpha Oumar Konaré (1992–2002), the first elected president of the Third Republic of Mali, the Malian state commemorated the sacrifice of the youth for the struggle for democracy and freedom in Mali by renaming public buildings and erecting monuments across the country (especially in Bamako). Arnoldi rightly argued that the Martyrs' Monument (depicting "a student protest march" above a "statue of a mother mourning the body of her dead son"[68]), the monument to the deceased student leader Abdoul Karim Camara, and the renaming of Le Pont de Badalabougou to Le Pont des Martyrs all "engage young people in remembering and supporting the political legitimacy of the Third Republic."[69] Whereas during the late 1980s the state power stressed the "youth peril," the Third Republic of Mali raised the youth to the rank of "martyr."[70] The Malian state also built monuments that celebrate the victory over colonialism in 1960. Read together these monuments "promote a shared postcolonial national identity in the public imagination by valorizing and linking the heroes of Mali's independence struggles with the student leaders of Mali's prodemocracy movement."[71] However, besides fostering an idea of shared struggle, I argue that these monuments simultaneously undermine the legitimacy of patriarchal gerontocracy in this part of West Africa by acknowledging the importance of male juniors as political actors in contemporary Mali.

Most political offices in the country are still in the hands of the elders. However, as power holders, the elders struggle to achieve national reputations unless they receive support from younger generations, such as illustrated in the power contest between the military junta led by

Captain Sanogo and The Economic Community of West African States (ECOWAS) after the coup d'état of March 22, 2012. ECOWAS had difficulty in establishing Dioncounda Traoré (the head of Mali's National Assembly) as interim president of the country, mostly because of the capital's youth, who regularly demonstrated on the streets of Bamako to show their support for Captain Sanogo and their opposition to foreign intrusion in Malian politics. It has often been noted in African postcolonial contexts that "men in power" harness "the vigor of young males" to advance their own cause;[72] such strategies may even be reinforced in a context of youth empowerment.

In numerous West African countries, the 1990s processes of media diffusion, political pluralism, and civil empowerment also transformed the youth into powerful social actors of the public sphere.[73] In this regard, being young in the Mali of 2010 meant living as an increasingly "enfranchised" actor in an epoch shaped by less close control of the state and parental authority owing to the new social dynamics fostered by civic liberties, democratic ideas, media technologies, and neoliberal forces.[74] Whereas some have argued that youth in post–Cold War Africa might be an economically "lost generation,"[75] an increasing number of young Muslims have undermined their traditional marginalization as "bad Muslims" by coming to the fore of public debate about Islam. Within the debate around conceptions of proper religious life, young Muslims are increasingly putting forward as an asset the youth's propensity to adapt to changes (by contrast to elders' rigidity).[76] This propensity is evident among the regular listeners of *zikiri* in Bougouni.

A New Religious Actor?

As illustrated with the *shɛfantigi*'s clients mentioned in the introduction, most young Muslims I encountered were affiliated neither to Sufi orders nor to reformist groups, an observation true to the whole sub-Saharan region.[77] The overwhelming majority of young Muslims in town merely told me "I am Muslim" (*nɛ yé silamɛ yé*). When I asked them whether they could define more precisely their Islamic affiliation, they stressed they were "*silamɛ dɔron*" (just Muslim). In Bougouni, the ground for such a broad religious affiliation was initially prepared through the postcolonial decrease in traditional Islamic education.

The master-disciple relationship characterizing formal Sufi education has mostly been a private and scholarly affair in Mali. In parallel to the progressive development of *médersas* (French-Arab schools) during the postcolonial period,[78] formal Sufi education became further marginalized since the process of mass Islamization hit the region in the early postcolonial period.[79] These French-Arab schools have also since supplied a modern alternative to the traditional Koranic schools (*duguma kalan*)[80] that, although in decline, still educate children and teenagers in Islamic teachings in southwest Mali through a rote learning of the Koran and an initiate-based form of transmission of Islamic knowledge based on a master-"student" (in Arabic, *talibe*; in Bamanan, *garibu*) relationship. Although less codified than in a Sufi order, this pedagogic bond also transmits values of "obedience, respect, submission, [and] sense of social hierarchy" to the student.[81] In Bougouni, furthermore, I observed that most young Muslims partially attended these Islamic schools so as to be familiar with basic Islamic practices such as the ablution, the prayer, and the blessing. Then they dropped out of or cut back on formal Islamic schooling in favor of an apprenticeship, a public school, or the informal sector because, as they often commented, such religious education hardly ever gives them skills to access local jobs. Nevertheless, they thereafter still cultivated and sometimes deepened their religious education by picking out guidance for their Muslim life in the numerous media-mediated Islamic discourses circulating in town.

Osella and Osella mention the existence of "just Muslims" in Kerala, India. These are Muslims who privately declare themselves not aligned with particular groups; however, in public they expressed a clearer religious affiliation owing to an overdetermination of identity by political events.[82] Such a situation of political pressure over the choice of a specific Muslim identity did not exist in Mali. "I am Muslim" and "just Muslim" are generic terms that rather refer to what Soares would call "the postcolonial way of being Muslim."[83] This is a process whereby the growth of secular education, the expansion of a public sphere, and new mediums of communication have resulted in a change in the "sociology of Islamic knowledge."[84] Muslims do not rely exclusively on spiritual leaders for Islamic education because of the increasing circulation in the public sphere of "small media,"[85] such as recorded sermons, radio programming, and pamphlets. As new forms of religious experiences and sociability are brought into being by media technologies, Islam has become more accessible to the illiterate, to women, and to the youth in Mali.[86] Therefore, ordinary Muslims in this country also belong to what Lambek calls "people on the path" because "everyone strives also, to one degree or another, to become and act as a well-informed [Muslim] citizen."[87]

In most of Mali's southern towns, such as Bougouni, I was further intrigued by the fact that a substantial part of the market of religious media and paraphernalia held the imprint of Haïdara and his association. In addition to his oratorical skills and outspokenness,[88] Haïdara has built a national reputation and become "a veritable media star" in Mali.[89] This is largely due to the promotion of his Islamic teachings in Mali's lingua franca through the media on a large scale since the early 1990s, such as is illustrated with the numerous audio recordings of his sermons found in local markets.[90] Ansar Dine,[91] the association he founded in 1983 in Bamako, has even become in less than thirty years one of the most powerful Muslim associations in contemporary Mali. In 2010, this religious association existed in twenty-four countries, mostly in the Bamanan-speaking communities of West Africa and their diasporas settled in the Western world.[92] The international success of Haïdara was regularly stressed by young Muslims in Bougouni as an important component of his legitimacy as a religious authority; in this increasingly global world, many of them proudly added "international" to his name.

In 2010, the *section*[93] of Ansar Dine in Bougouni was the most dynamic religious association in town; its committee was also supervising the opening of new *sous-sections* in the big villages of the surrounding hinterland. The association's members, called the "*Ansars*," were very active in town. They organized public "sermons" (*wajuli*) on a weekly basis. These events often ended with two public oaths of allegiance. The first certified someone's Muslim identity. According to Haïdara, the profession of the Islamic creed (*Shahada*)[94] does not completely certify adherence to Muslim faith. Someone adheres fully to Islam only through making the six Islamic promises (in Arabic, *baya*)[95] in public. The second public oath was a pledge of allegiance to Ansar Dine and its "spiritual guide"—Haïdara. By doing so, a certified Muslim became a member of the association; that is to say an *Ansar*, the genuine guardian of Islam. *Ansars* did not pray in specific mosques. Men did not wear recognizable symbols of allegiance. As for "*Anṣar* women," they wore partial *hijab*-style veils. This Islamic accessory made them easily recognizable within a crowd because ordinary Muslim women, when they covered their hair,[96] did not act in solely religious fashion. They rather wore colorfully aesthetic foulard in *bazin* called "*musɔrɔ*" (in French, *mouchoir*) that partially covered their hair, whereas older women loosely draped over their head and shoulder a scarf called "*kunna.biri*" (from elements meaning "the head as a body part" and "to cover"). Often used as a prayer shawl, this accessory traditionally indexes the respectable status associated with old age in Mali.[97] Although members of *Ansar Dine* were on the rise in Bougouni, they nonetheless represented only an active religious minority of the local Muslim community. On the other hand, Haïdara was an unmissable figure of the public sphere in town.

The figure of Haïdara was noticed through the circulation of his sermons on local radios, DVDs shown in *grins* and courtyards, and through the presence of his pictures on trucks, cars, and shops. The four radio stations of Bougouni broadcast eleven and a half hours of Islamic programing every week in 2010, among which I counted five and a half hours of Haïdara's sermons and one hour of *zikiri.* Haïdara and his religious singers accounted for 56.5 percent of all Islamic radio programs. Such wide media coverage promoted Haïdara's evocation in informal discussions between Muslims in town. Many among them quoted his teachings when debating religious issues, while some argued about them. At the very least nobody felt indifferent to Haïdara. In this media success, what struck me the most was Haïdara's popularity among the youth of the town in a country where they are in the majority. But the overwhelmed majority of these young people were not *Ansars:* how then can we qualify their bond to Haïdara? The bond between Haïdara and these young sympathizers—neither close disciples, nor members of Ansar Dine, nor certified Muslims—was mostly based on the media practices through which his name and teachings were regularly heard in daily social life in town. Among these media practices, the youth's listening to the numerous *zikiri* cassettes found in local markets played a considerable role in establishing this bond.

Being Young and Muslim: The Sympathizer of Haïdara

At the beginning of my stay in Bougouni, I regularly explored the town by bicycle and often let myself be guided by spontaneous invitations, street sounds, and the crowd. After having greeted the family of a local imam, I headed toward the sound of a loud voice; its clicking sound made me think that it was coming out of a nearby loudspeaker. I found a crowd of people bustling around the coach station at the town's exit toward Sikasso. They were preparing for an imminent stop of Haïdara, who was on his way back to Bamako from a trip to Sikasso. When the two four-wheel drives that conveyed Haïdara, his family, and close followers arrived, the religious fervor within the crowd heightened.

Surrounded by local *Ansar*s wearing uniforms, Haïdara stepped out of the vehicle, shook hands with leaders of the Ansar Dine *section* of Bougouni, and sat on a big sofa sheltered by a tent. He gave a series of blessings and then departed for Bamako. His stop lasted thirty minutes.

Despise the brevity of this event, there were several noteworthy elements. Street peddlers of religious paraphernalia were opportunistically circulating in the crowd. The spot itself was carefully decorated with various pictures and banners representing Haïdara, his family, and Ansar Dine. Observing the spatial organization of this event made it clear that one's position indicated the degree of allegiance to Haïdara. His close disciples were standing in a queue on his left up to his front. Behind them, local *Ansar* women sat on carpets on Haïdara's frontward left side. The leaders of the Ansar Dine *section* were on his right. Local *Ansar* men were on his frontward right side. Children sat in front of him. An *Ansar* cordon of people wearing uniforms was strategically positioned between the aforementioned *Ansar* arrangement and a large and disorganized crowd of sympathizers and onlookers. In this peripheral crowd, I met my friend Ali, a trader in his early thirties who, curious to see Haïdara, came here after being informed of his visit through a local radio broadcast.

Ali occasionally attended public sermons based on Haïdara's teachings organized by Ansar Dine in town. He sometimes listened to Haïdara's sermons in local radio programs when he was at work. He more regularly listened to *zikiri* on his mobile phone and in *grin* in late afternoon and evening. Haïdara is known to question the nature of Islamic faith by inviting Muslims to closely look at the *jogo* that they cultivate behind their everyday activities and religious practices. The term *jogo* is translated as "attitude" and "character";[98] in addition, Haïdara's followers often translated it into the French word *"intention"* because, according to Haïdara's teaching, there is no "correct attitude" without "correct intention" (*jogo ɲuman*).[99] In other words, the public conduct and the inward mind of someone are two sides of the same coin and shape one's true identity. How can a prayer be valid when a Muslim performs it while constantly thinking about un-Islamic matters, asked Haïdara? Such a portrayal of Islam as a form of moral guidance (rather than a normative dogma about practice) attracts many young Muslims because of its pragmatic and flexible approach.[100] It also helps them relativize breaches in the practice of a generic Islam. I once questioned Ali about the sensual nature of the musicality of *zikiri*. He replied that what matters is not "dance" (*dɔn*) and "music" (*donkili*) per se, but peoples' intentions as they engage in these activities.

In 2010, I attended an official *zikiri* performance during the most important yearly *Ansar Din*e gathering in Bamako for the celebration of the Maouloud, the birth of the Prophet. There I had the opportunities to converse with religious singers of Ansar Dine. For them, dance and music are more than accepted in Islam when practiced with pious intention; these activities call people to Islam by filling their "heart" (*dusu*) with the "love" (*kanu*) of God, the Prophet, and his descendants. Thirty-five-year-old religious singer Sidy Coulibaly Ba says,

> Uttering *zikiri* has existed from the creation of the Word until today. It is an ancient practice [*ko kɔrɔ*]. . . . Playing guitar on it is something new [*ko kura*], but it is not forbidden. Its usage is not forbidden. But if you do it wrongly, you are responsible for that. If you do it rightly, guitar and song are not forbidden. Music does not harm religion. What is important is the way you do it; nothing more. . . . Muslim women and Muslim men also dance; it does not matter. However, if this activity makes you forgetful, you should not do it.[101]

As hinted in Coulibaly's view of *zikiri*, many young Muslims put forward Haïdara's conception of a religiosity based on intention rather than, according to a young carpenter of Bougouni, a "straitjacket made of obligations." Such a religiosity also pleases the youth because it suggests the possibility of negotiating the moral implications of a given activity. For instance, the musicality of *zikiri* resonates with a local culture of entertainment; at the same time it draws on a dynamic of cultural transformation that updates tradition, such as *dhikr*, to the spirit of the current epoch. *Ko kɔrɔ* become aligned with *ko kura;* the listening of *zikiri* is still about "getting closer to God" through pious emotions and feelings.[102] Such sensual religiosity brings to mind the existence of a kind of "pious fun" in contemporary Mali.[103] The religious song of *zikiri* ultimately demonstrates "young people's capacity to mediate" the allegedly contradictory "socio-cultural frontiers" of tradition and modernity.[104]

Ali exemplified the numerous young Muslims who are sympathizers of Haïdara in contemporary Mali. Seizing the opportunity of Haïdara's short stop in Bougouni, he chose to see him in person because of his perceived status as a saint in West Africa. However, Ali did not attend the *Ansar Dine*'s celebration of the Maouloud in the capital. Although he appreciated Haïdara, he did not feel the need to follow his retinue to Bamako. He did not want to be an *Ansar* because he thought that to live a proper Muslim life, one is not required to be a member of a specific religious movement or to cultivate a firm allegiance to a religious leader. Ali also occasionally attended public sermons organized by followers of others religious leaders in Bougouni, such as Cheick Sufi Bilal.[105] Although he did not like reformist doctrines, Ali nevertheless agreed with the reformist criticism of the local custom of ostentatious marriages that burden families with debts. As with many "media fans" of Haïdara in Mali, Ali identified himself as "just Muslim." Avoiding the classic paternalistic approach and its related analysis of youth deviance, the case of Ali demonstrates how young Muslims are "simultaneously objects, victims, and agents of change" in Mali.[106] Besides illustrating that the religious singers of *zikiri* somehow "perform for [Haïdara] the 'traditional' [praise singers'] tasks of reputation management,"[107] these tape-cassette recordings of *zikiri* bring to light Haïdara's marketing of an Islam that addresses youth as religious actors who inform what is a proper Muslim life.

Media, Religious Allegiance, and Islamic Knowledge in Mali

The political power and dominant masculinity of elders has regularly been challenged in Africa, as is illustrated by "the new opportunities for slave emancipation, financial accumulation and wage labour, religious conversion, and education and literacy among young men and women."[108] Against this backdrop, this analysis of youth media practices invites the reader to question the resurgence of such generational politics in the light of the new civic liberties and expanding media technologies characterizing the public sphere of the Third Republic of Mali. My chapter explores the dynamics between youth culture, the listening of *zikiri* through media, and religious allegiance to a spiritual leader in contemporary Mali. This exploration of the youth's listening of *zikiri* in Bougouni offers new insights into the ways an increasingly mediated sociology of Islamic knowledge affects the audience of a spiritual leader, the quality of peoples' allegiance to him, and the control over the reception of his media transmission.

This chapter frames the allegiance to a spiritual leader in Islam as located along a spectrum, ranging from the very close master-disciple relationship characterizing formal Sufi education to the unaffiliated and self-reliant Muslim. Within this spectrum, how then shall we locate those sympathizers of Haïdara who, like Ali, claim to be "just Muslims"? First, the increasing media-mediated sociology of Islamic knowledge in Mali has transformed the audiences available to a spiritual leader. Thanks to his presence in the local media (e.g. radio, cassettes, pictures), Haïdara was a prominent figure of the public sphere of Bougouni. Haïdara's media promotion of *zikiri* in Mali has further helped build his renown (among the youth) as a modern spiritual leader who lives according to the "spirit of the times." In 2010, the unrivalled popularity of Haïdara in Mali conferred on him a powerful status that was respected and even feared among his opponents.[109] Thanks to these new media technologies, a spiritual leader can nowadays "channel youthful energy" on a national and international level,[110] thereby reaching an unprecedented popularity. However, this massive gain in audience is often achieved to the detriment of a faithful interpretation of Islamic knowledge given that, through new media, the pedagogical process "becomes dissociated from former personal chains of transmission of Islamic erudition."[111] With regard to the current debate about the individualization of religious engagement among young Muslims in West Africa,[112] the sympathizers of Haïdara illuminate the contemporary ordinary Muslim whose allegiance to a spiritual leader is neither exclusive, nor personal, nor codified in terms of rights and duties. Instead, it is an open, distant, and nonexclusive bond that is uniquely generated by new media practices. Numerous elders of Bougouni pointed to their juniors who were sympathizers of Haïdara as "immature" Muslims who inconsistently link themselves to Haïdara's teachings for merely fashionable purposes. These young Muslims, while being undoubtedly influenced by Haïdara, were all the same carefully selective among which of his teachings they felt resonated with their aspirations.

To conclude, I propose, based on the case of Haïdara in Mali, the existence of three levels of allegiance to a spiritual leader in contemporary "Muslim worlds."[113] In line with the formal Sufi education, a handful of close disciples (up to a few dozen), who at some point have shared Haïdara's daily life (lived next to him), devote their life to his teaching and his person. These are his most faithful devotees. Second, based on the membership to an associative structure, Haïdara's teaching is also followed by several thousands of *Ansars* via media and *Ansar* preachers;[114] from time to time they have the opportunity to personally meet Haïdara during religious celebrations (e.g., during Maouloud in

Bamako) and during his visits in the regional towns of Mali. In 2010, his close disciples and *Ansars* accounted for several thousands of people in Mali.[115] Finally, thanks to Haïdara's self-promotion through new media practices, tens of thousands of anonymous young sympathizers now feel connected to Haïdara. Better understanding of this loose and unaffiliated category of the sympathizer will open up new ways of studying the dynamics of activism that shape political Islam in this increasingly mediated world. We need to further explore spiritual leaders' loose and uneven influence on ordinary Muslims (and vice versa); these are affiliations that operate beyond the regulating frames of formal membership within a religious association as well as exceed the personal chain of transmission between a disciple and his spiritual leader.

Notes

1. Non-English words are written in italic. *Bamanan.kan,* the language of one of the largest ethnic groups of the Mande people (Bambara), is the lingua franca of Mali. Words in plural are written with a "*w*" at the end. The structure of compound words may be stressed by a period inserted between elements. Except for public figures, all names mentioned in this chapter are pseudonyms.

I am grateful to Marie Rodet, Joel Cabrita, and several anonymous reviewers for their critical readings of this essay.

2. See H. A. R. Gibb and J. H. Kramers, *Concise Encyclopedia of Islam* (Leiden: Brill Academic Publishers, 2001).

3. Annemarie Schimmel, *Mystical Dimensions of Islam* (Chapel Hill: University of North Carolina Press, 1976), 167.

4. Ibid., 167–78.

5. The bandiri-*dhikr* performed by branches of Qadiriyya in Northern Nigeria illustrates a *dhikr* that includes singing, music, and dance in West Africa. See Roman Loimeier, *Islamic Reform and Political Change in Northern Nigeria* (Evanston, IL: Northwestern University Press, 1997), 60–62.

6. See Emmanuelle Olivier, "Les louanges islamiques au Mali: Un art de la Filiation," in *Musiques au monde: La tradition au prisme de la création,* ed. E. Olivier (Paris: Sampzan Delatour, 2012), 93–116; Olivier, "Droits d'auteur vs usages locaux de l'autorité: Réflexion à partir d'une K7 de louanges," *Volume!* 10, no. 2 (2013): 151–72.

7. E. Djebbare and E. Olivier, "Des 'religions du terroir' à l'Islam et *vice versa:* Politiques culturelles et pratiques artistiques croisées," in *Le Mali contemporain,* ed. J. Brunet-Jailly, J. Charmes, and D. Konaté (Bamako: Editions Tombouctou, 2014), 349–50. At the beginning of my stay in Bougouni, my Bamanan skills were poor; I hence had difficulty in differentiating *zikiri* from other local musical genres because both sounded like contemporary Malian music to me.

8. Dorothea Schulz, *Muslims and New Media in West Africa: Pathways to God* (Bloomington: Indiana University Press, 2012), xii–xiii, 2.

9. See T. Perret, "Médias et démocratie au Mali," *Politique Africaine* 97 (2005): 18–32.

10. The "Bamanan sound" of *zikiri* leans mostly on *Cumba, Jazz Wassoulou, Takamba,* and *Bamana Foli.* See Djebbari and Olivier, "Religions du terroir," 356–58. For Pierre Prud'homme, the success of *zikiri* is based on three legitimate realms: Sufism, jeliya, and world music. See Prud'homme, "Les 'griots d'Allah,' ou l'émergence d'une musique religieuse populaire," in *Le Mali contemporain,* ed. J. Brunet-Jailly, J. Charmes, and D. Konaté (Bamako: Editions Tombouctou, 2014), 322–27.

11. My own translation.

12. Prud'homme, "Griots d'Allah," 327.

13. "Those who deliver the *zikiri*" (lit. "da" signifies "mouth" in this context).

14. For an analysis of *grin* as an important element of urban social life, see Dorothea Schulz, "The World Is Made by Talk: Female Fans, Popular Music, and New Forms of Public Sociality in Urban Mali," *Cahiers d'Etudes Africaines* 168 (2002): 811–12.

15. On similar views of *secular music* among Tuareg in Niger, see Susan J. Rasmussen, "Between Several Worlds: Images of Youth and Age in Tuareg Popular Performances," *Anthropological Quarterly* 73, no. 3 (2000): 133–44.

16. For a biography of El-Hajj Ladji Blen, see Mamadou Sissoko, *Odyssée héroïque, cinquante ans d'action de l'homme El Hadji Abdoulaye Koné Ladji-Blen: Belles lettres, connaissance mystique, morale politique; La palme du martyr, aventures, critiques sociales et religieuses: Une mission suicide* (Bamako: Editions Jamana, 2007).

17. "Marriage is essential in becoming a 'complete' woman (*muso dafalen*) and a 'real man' (*cɛ yɛrɛ*), that is in gaining full adult status" in Mali; see Schulz, *Muslims and New Media,* 56.

18. On social shifters, see Deborah Durham "Youth and the Social Imagination in Africa: Introduction to Parts 1 and 2," *Anthropological Quarterly* 73, no. 3 (2000): 113–20. In precolonial times age grades were regulated through associations of initiation and rites of passages; on Bamanan Institutions of initiation, see Jean-Pierre Colleyn, ed., *Bamana: The Art of Existence in Mali* (New York: Museum for African Art, 2001).

19. For an illustration of age as shifting/strategic criteria in men's circle at weddings and funerals in Botswana, see Deborah Durham, "Disappearing Youth: Youth as Social Shifter in Botswana," *American Ethnologist* 31, no. 4 (2004): 593–94.

20. Thomas Burgess and Andrew Burton, introduction to *Generation Past: Youth in East African History,* ed. Andrew Burton and H. Charton-Bigot (Athens: Ohio University Press, 2010), 5, 19.

21. On youth as a growing category of actors across Africa, see Mamadou Diouf, "Engaging Postcolonial Cultures: African Youth and Public Space," *African Studies Review* 46, no. 2 (2003): 1–12. Two-thirds of Mali's population

(66.46 percent) was under the age of twenty-five in 2016; see the Central Intelligence Agency's *World Fact Book,* https://www.cia.gov/library/publications/the-world-factbook/geos/ml.html.

22. See R. W. Connell, *Masculinities* (Cambridge: Polity Press, 1995).

23. See Benjamin Soares, "The Historiography of Islam in West Africa: An Anthropologist's View," *Journal of African History* 55, no. 1 (2014): 27–36.

24. See Michael G. Peletz, "'Ordinary Muslims' and Muslim Resurgents in Contemporary Malaysia: Notes on an Ambivalent Relationship," in *Islam in an Era of Nation-States: Politics and Religious Renewal in Muslim Southeast Asia,* ed. R. W. Hefner and P. Horvatich (Honolulu: University of Hawai'i Press, 1997), 231–74.

25. Ibid., 232.

26. On observant Muslims, see Schulz, *Muslims and New Media,* xiv, 6.

27. On people of Muslim background, see Magnus Marsden and Kostas Retsikas, introduction to *Articulating Islam: Anthropological Approaches to Muslim Worlds* (New York: Springer, 2013), 6–9.

28. On local modernity, see Emmanuel Olivier, "Musique et globalisation: 'Techno-logiques' de la création musicale," *Le Temps des Médias* 1, no. 22 (2014): 137.

29. For an analysis of *zikiri* in Mali promoted by the Communauté Musulmane des Soufis (CMS) led by Cheick Soufi Bilal, see ibid.

30. See Dorothea Schulz, "'Charisma and Brotherhood' Revisited: Mass-Mediated Forms of Spirituality in Urban Mali," *Journal of Religion in Africa* 33, no. 2 (2003): 146–71, and Schulz, "Promises of (Im)mediate Salvation: Islam, Broadcast Media, and the Remaking of Religious Experience in Mali," *American Ethnologist* 33, no. 2 (2006): 210–19.

31. That is, his followers or admirers.

32. Sufi-Reformist tensions has happened across Muslim West Africa, such as illustrated with the old religious rivalry between two powerful economic actors of the town of Bobo-Dioulasso in Burkina Faso. See B. Traoré, "Islam et politique à Bobo-Dioulasso de 1940 à 2002," in *L'Islam politique au sud du Sahara: Discours et enjeux,* ed. Muriel Gomez-Perez (Paris: Karthala, 2005), 417–47.

33. In the early 2000s, the strength of Haïdara's association in Bobo-Dioulaso was also based on his support among the youth. See ibid., 439–41.

34. See Benjamin Soares, *Islam and the Prayer Economy: History and Authority in a Malian Town* (London: Edinburgh University Press, 2005), 183. For an illustration of similar critics among reformists in Bamako, see Jean-Louis Triaud, "Bamako, la ville aux deux cents mosquées, ou la victoire du 'secteur informel' islamique," *Islam et sociétés au sud du Sahara* 2 (1988): 166–77.

35. On the politics of Sufi orders with regard to local practices of Islam in Mali, see Jean-Louis Amselle, "Le Wahabisme à Bamako (1945–1985)," *Canadian Journal of African Studies/Revue Canadienne des Études Africaines* 19, no. 2 (1985): 345–57.

36. On the Sunni and Wahhabite labels, see Soares, *Islam and the Prayer Economy,* 181–82; for a detailed definition of Wahhabis in Mali, see ibid., 180–209 and Louis Brenner, *Controlling Knowledge: Religion, Power and Schooling in a West African Muslim Society* (Bloomington: Indiana University Press, 2001).

37. See Louis Brenner, "Constructing Muslim Identities in Mali," in *Muslim Identity and Social Change in Sub-Saharan Africa,* ed. Louis Brenner (London: Hurst, 1993), 57–78.

38. In the aftermath of mass-Islamization in southern Mali, the Wahhabi identity became an important criterion of commercial reliability for those wishing to integrate into the established network of Wahhabi traders in the town of Sikasso. See Richard L. Warm, "Merchants, Muslims, and Wahhabiyya: The Elaboration of Islamic Identity in Sikasso, Mali," *Canadian Journal of African Studies* 26, no. 3 (1992): 485–507.

39. The term *adama.den.ya* is composed of two words: *adama* (Adam) and *den* (child), which together means "the son of Adam." The suffix "*ya*" stresses the condition of what is named; so *adamadenya* becomes "the human condition." The linguist Charles Bailleul translates it as "solidarity," "politeness," and "social relations." See his *Dictionnaire Bambara Français* (Bamako: Donniya, 1996). Altogether *adamadenya* indicates that in Mali social ethics is considered as a fundamental feature of the human condition, see Michael Lambek, introduction to *Ordinary Ethics: Anthropology, Language, and Action* (New York: Fordham University Press, 2010), 1–36.

40. For a criticism of studying Islam as a local phenomenon in West Africa, see Benjamin Soares, "Notes on the Anthropological Study of Islam and Muslim Societies in Africa," *Culture and Religion* 1, no. 2 (2000): 277–85.

41. For an overview of the importance of Sufi orders in the spread of Islam in West Africa, see Mervyn Hiskett, *The Course of Islam in Africa* (Edinburgh: Edinburgh University Press, 1994), chapter 4.

42. See D. B. Cruise O'Brien, *Symbolic Confrontations: Muslims Imagining the State in Africa* (London: Hurst, 2003); Leonardo A. Villalón, *Islamic Society and State Power in Senegal: Disciples and Citizens in Fatick* (Cambridge: Cambridge University Press, 1995).

43. For Mali, see Benjamin Soares, "Saint and Sufi in Contemporary Mali," in *Sufism and the "Modern" in Islam,* ed. Martin Van Bruinessen and Julia Day Howell (London: I. B. Tauris, 2007), 76–92.

44. On the Islamic sphere, see Benjamin Soares and R. Launay, "The Formation of an 'Islamic Sphere' in French Colonial West Africa," *Economy and Society* 28, no. 4 (1999): 497–519.

45. For Niger, see Adeline Masquelier, *Women and Islamic Revival in a West African Town* (Bloomington: Indiana University Press, 2009); for Nigeria, see Loimeier, *Islamic Reform.*

46. See Benjamin Soares, "Islam and Public Piety in Mali," in *Public Islam and the Common Good,* ed. Armando Salvatore and Dale F. Eickelman (Brill: Leiden, 2004), 205–27; Gilles Holder, "Un espace publique religieux: Pour une lecture contemporaine des enjeux politiques de l'Islam en Afrique, " in

L'Islam: Nouvel espace public en Afrique, ed. Gilles Holder (Paris: Karthala, 2009), 5–20.

47. See Gregory Mann, "Old Soldiers, Young Men: Masculinity, Islam, and Military Veterans in Late 1950s Soudan Français (Mali)," in *Men and Masculinities in Modern Africa,* ed. Lisa A. Lindsay and Stephan Miescher (Portsmouth, NH: Heinemann, 2003), 69–87.

48. For a similar relation between ageing and devotional Islamic practice among the Tuareg in Niger, see Rasmussen, "Between Several Worlds."

49. Traditional xylophone.

50. *Zikiri a tun bɛ da. Kaluwa tun bɛ da.... Zikiri, an bɛ Ala tɔgɔ fɔ ka caya pour an bɛ baraji sɔrɔ. Paseke ni ɛ yé Ala tɔgɔ fɔ ka caya, ɛ bɛ baraji sɔrɔ. Mais ka na a kɛ dɔɔni bala fɔ ni fɛn nin, ninnu kun tɛ an tile la de! An kɔni ma o kɛ. Mais bi a bɛ a kɛ ka o tɛ diinɛ cɛn. Dɔ wɛrɛ bɛ a fɔ ko a kɛ malo dɔɔni.*

51. *Zikiri nin tɛ silamɛ* yé.

52. On the spirit of the times, see Durham, "Disappearing Youth," 592.

53. For an illustration of similar intergenerational tensions over the legitimacy of "old ways" (*ko kɔrɔ*) that happened in southern rural Mali between 1940 and 1960, see Brian Peterson, *Islamization from Below: The Making of Muslim Communities in Rural French Sudan, 1880–1960* (New Haven: Yale University Press, 2011), 169–70. On the contemporary debate between *sila keebaa* ("old style") and *sila kutoo* ("new style") among Muslims in Gambia, see Marloes Janson, *Islam, Youth, and Modernity in the Gambia: The Tablighi Jama'at* (Cambridge: Cambridge University Press, 2014), 59–63.

54. For an illustration of the mention of "Modibo's *politiki* times" (1960–1968) in Mali, see Dorothea Schulz, "Praise without Enchantment: Griots, Broadcast Media, and the Politics of Tradition in Mali," *Africa Today* 44, no. 4 (1997): 454.

55. See André Chappatte, "Chinese Products, Social Mobility and Material Modernity in Bougouni, a Small but Fast-Growing Administrative Town of Southwest Mali," *African Studies* 73, no.1 (2014): 22–40.

56. The denomination "Jakarta" comes from the fact that this motorbike was previously imported from Indonesia.

57. The historian Ophélie Rillon argues in her dissertation that power in Mali between 1954 and 1993 was characterized by gerontocracy and patriarchy. See "Féminités et masculinités à l'épreuve de la contestation: Le genre des luttes sociales et politiques au Mali (1954–1993)" (PhD diss., Paris, Panthéon Sorbonne, 2013).

58. See Louis Brenner, "Youth as Political Actors in Mali," in *Transitions in Africa: Expanding Political Spaces,* ed. Pearl T. Robinson, Catharine Newbury, and Mamadou Diouf (unpublished, 2003), 7–8.

59. For an analysis of women's active participation but their media glossing over in these demonstrations, See Rillon, "Féminités et masculinitiés."

60. See Brenner, "Youth as Political Actors," 11–12.

61. On the politics of l'AEEM in the 1990s, see Zeric Kay Smith, "From Demons to Democrats: Mali's Student Mouvement 1991–1996," *Review of African Political Economy* 72 (1997): 249–63. In the aftermath of the events of 1991, the

urban youth managed to place four of their representatives among the fifteen civilians of the transitionary government of CTSP (Comité de Transition pour le Salut du Peuple). See Rillon, "Féminités et masculinitiés."

62. After Bamako and Kayes, Bougouni possessed one of the most important regional colonial archive fonds of Mali.

63. Such status is also challenged by women in Mali; see Schulz, *Muslims and New Media,* 53–58.

64. See Benjamin Soares, "'Rasta' Sufi and Muslim Youth Culture in Mali," in *Being Young and Muslim: New Cultural Politics in the Global South and North,* ed. Linda Herrera and Asef Bayat (Oxford: Oxford University Press, 2010), 241–57.

65. *Demokrasi nana. Nka mogow ani dɔgɔw caman yé o faamu dɔrɔn ko "min ka di* ɛ yé, *ɛ bɛ o dɛ kɛ."*

66. See Schulz, "Praise without Enchantment," 457–58.

67. See Cristophe Broqua and Anne Docquet, "Penser les masculinités en Afrique et au-delà," *Cahiers d'Études Africaines,* no. 209–10 (2013): 9–41.

68. See Mary Jo Arnoldi, "Bamako, Mali: Monuments and Modernity in the Urban Imagination," *Africa Today* 54, no. 2 (2007): 14.

69. Ibid., 11.

70. On youth peril, see Rillon, "Féminités et masculinitiés," 343.

71. On youth peril, see Arnoldi, "Monuments and Modernity," 12; on martyr, see Rillon, "Féminités et masculinitiés," 366.

72. See Burgess and Burton, introduction, 18.

73. See Marie-Nathalie Leblanc and Muriel Gomez-Perez, "Jeunes musulmans et citoyenneté culturelle: Retour sur des expériences de recherche en Afrique de l'Ouest francophone," *Sociologie et Sociétés* 39, no. 2 (2007): 39–59.

74. On youth as enfranchised actors, see Jean Comaroff and John Comaroff, "Reflections on Youth: From the Past to the Postcolony," in *Makers and Breakers: Children and Youth in Postcolonial Africa,* ed. Alcinda Honwana and Filip De Boeck (Oxford: James Currey, 2005), 22, 29.

75. On lost generation, see Fiona Klein Klouwenberg and Inge Butter, "African 'Youth' since Independence: Notes on a Bibliographic Overview, 1990–2005," *Africa Development* 36, no. 3–4 (2011): 59.

76. On the youth's propensity to adapt to changes, see Janson, *Islam, Youth, and Modernity,* chapter 1.

77. See René Otayek and Benjamin F. Soares, introduction to *Islam and Muslim Politics in Africa,* ed. Soares and Otayek (New York: Palgrave Macmillan, 2007), 1–24.

78. On the development of *médersas* in Mali, see Brenner, *Controlling Knowledge.*

79. On the process of mass-Islamization in southwest Mali, see André Chappatte, "Night Life in Southern Mali: Being a Muslim Maquisard in Bougouni," *Journal of the Royal Anthropological Institute* 20, no. 3 (2014): 527.

80. From the noun *dugu.ma* (soil) and the verb *ka kalan* (to study). Traditionally the students of such schools study the Koran while sitting directly on the ground.

81. See Stefania Gandolfi, "L'enseignement islamique en Afrique noire," *Cahiers d'Études Africaines* 43, no. 1–2 (2003): 265. For a novelistic illustration of the master-student bond, see Cheikh Hamidou Kane, *L'aventure ambiguë* (France: Julliard, 1961).

82. On "just Muslims" in Kerala, see Filippo Osella and Caroline Osella, "Islamism and Social Reform in Kerala, South India," *Modern Asian Studies* 42, no. 2–3 (2007): 317–46.

83. On the postcolonial way of being Muslim in Mali, see Soares, *Islam and the Prayer Economy*, 247.

84. See ibid., 222–38; Dale F. Eickelman and Jon W. Anderson, eds., *New Media in the Muslim World: The Emerging Public Sphere* (Bloomington: Indiana University Press, 2003).

85. On small media, see Annabelle Sreberny-Mohammadi and Ali Mohammadi, *Small Media, Big Revolution: Communication, Culture, and the Iranian Revolution* (Minneapolis: University of Minnesota Press, 1994).

86. See Schulz, *Muslims and New Media.*

87. See Michael Lambek, *Knowledge and Practice in Mayotte: Local Discourses of Islam, Sorcery and Spirit Possession* (Toronto: University of Toronto Press, 1993), 104.

88. On the oratorical skills and outspokenness of Haïdara, see Schulz, "Charisma and Brotherhood"; Schulz, "Promises of (Im)mediate Salvation," 210–19; and Schulz, "Morality, Community, Publicness: Shifting Terms of Public Debate in Mali," in *Religion, Media, and the Public Sphere,* ed. Birgit Meyer and Annelies Moors (Bloomington: Indiana University Press, 2005), 132–51. Muslim scholars often criticize Haïdara for his poor knowledge of Islam. Haïdara indeed did not receive extensive formal religious training and professes to be a "self-taught" Muslim scholar. See David Kimberley, "Preaching to the Converted: Charismatic Leaders, Performances and Electronic Media in Contemporary Islamic Communities" (master's thesis, Concordia University, 2002), 130–32. According to one of his followers, Haïdara attended two years of *dugumakalan* in the village of Tamani, six years of *médersa* in Segou, and four other years of Islamic learning in Fasongo; see Oumar Seydou Traoré, *Qui est Chérif Ousmane Madani Haïdara?* (Bamako: Oumar Seydou Traoré, 2007), 5.

89. See Soares, "Saint and Sufi," 80.

90. See Dorothea Schulz, "Evoking Moral Community, Fragmenting Muslim Discourses: Sermon Audio Recording and the Reconfiguration of Public Debate in Mali," *Journal for Islamic Studies* 27 (2007): 39–72.

91. *Ansar Dine* is an Arabo-Bamanan expression that means "the guardians /helpers/followers of religion."

92. See Gilles Holder, "Chérif Ousmane Madani Haïdara et l'Association Islamique Ançar Dine: Un réformisme malien populaire en quête d'autonomie," *Cahiers d'Études Africaines* 2, no. 206–7 (2012): 389–425.

93. Ansar Dine Mali is organized in a pyramidal structure: *bureau national, sections, sous-sections,* and *comités.* For further details on the association's internal structure and its history, see ibid.

94. The Muslim declaration of belief in the oneness of God and acceptance of Muhammad as his Prophet.

95. "I do not associate anything to God, I do not steal, I do not commit adultery, I do not kill my children, I do not slander, I do not disobey the Prophet" (Qur'an LX, 12).

96. Numerous Muslim women in Mali do not cover their hair.

97. For further information on the veiling practices of Muslim women in Mali, see Schulz, *Muslims and New Media,* 159–67.

98. See Bailleul, *Dictionnaire,* 167.

99. In contrast to having a "bad attitude/intention" (*jogo juguman*).

100. On the notion of "pragmatic Islam" among young Muslims in Niger, see Adeline Masquelier, "Negotiating Futures: Islam, Youth and the State in Niger," in *Islam and Muslim Politics in Africa,* ed. Benjamin F. Soares and René Otayek (New York: Palgrave Macmillan, 2007), 243–63.

101. *Zikiri da tɛ ko kura yé depuis kuma bɛ fɔ bi. Ko kɔrɔ de don. . . . Guitariw olu yé ko kura yé. Fɛn dɔ bɛ haramu tɛ. Haramu tɛ a kɔrɔ quoi. Mais ni ɛ yé ka a kɛ ka cɛn, ɛ de bɛ o kɛ ka cɛnba yé. Ni ɛ yé ka kɛ ka ɲie, haramu tɛ guitariw ani fɔli yé a kɔro. A tɛ diinɛ cɛn. Mais ɛ ka a ka cogo don. A bana. . . . Silamɛ muso and silamɛ kɛ, olu fɛnɛ bɛ dɔn kɛ. O tɛ baasi yé. Nka a ka a kɛ i ka damunu kono dɔrɔn ɛ kana dɔn son.*

102. For a parallel analysis of Islamic popular music in Senegal as the emergence of "new tradition," see Fiona McLaughlin, "Islam and Popular Music in Senegal: The Emergence of a 'New Tradition,'" *Journal of the International African Institute* 67, no. 4 (1997): 560–81.

103. See Samuli Schielke, "Pious Fun at Saints Festivals in Modern Egypt," *ISIM Newsletter* 7, no. 1 (2001): 23.

104. See Filip de Boeck and Alcinda Honwana, "Children and Youth in Africa: Agency, Identity & Place," in *Makers and Breakers: Children and Youth in Postcolonial Africa,* ed. Alcinda Honwana and Filip de Boeck (Oxford: James Currey, 2005), 10–11.

105. On Cheick Sufi Bilal, see Soares, "'Rasta' Sufi."

106. See Linda Herrera and Asef Bayat, "Conclusion: Knowing Muslim Youth," in *Being Young and Muslim: New Cultural Politics in the Global South and North,* ed. Linda Herrera and Asef Bayat (Oxford: University Press, 2010), 364.

107. See Schulz, "Praise without Enchantment," 451; "to praise someone" (*ka mɔgɔ tɔgɔ fɔ*).

108. See Stephan F. Miescher and Lisa A. Lindsay, "Introduction: Men and Masculinities in Modern African History," in *Men and Masculinities in Modern Africa,* ed. L. A. Lindsay and S. F. Miescher (Portsmouth, NH: Heinemann, 2003), 10.

109. In Bougouni I also met Muslims who thought that Haïdara was becoming a victim of his own success. They often blamed the *embourgeoisment* of Haïdara over the years (see G. Holder, "'Maouloud 2006,' de Bamako à Tombouctou: Entre réislamisation de la nation et laïcité de l'état: La construction d'un espace public religieux au Mali," in *L'Islam, nouvel espace public en Afrique,* ed. Gilles

Holder [Paris: Karthala, 2009], 237–89) and his closer followers' accumulation of wealth through Ansar Dine.

110. See Burgess and Burton, introduction, 16.

111. See Schulz, "'Charisma and Brotherhood' Revisited," 153.

112. See Leblanc and Gomez-Perez, "Jeunes musulmans et citoyenneté culturelle," 53–54.

113. On Muslim worlds, see Ulrike Freitag, "Researching 'Muslim Worlds': Regions and Disciplines," *ZMO Programmatic Text* 6 (2013).

114. *Ansar* preachers are preachers whose sermons have been certified by Ansar Dine; for this they must attend a series of workshop at the head of the association in Bamako. These workshops educate them to Haïdara's teachings and thereby control their preaching identity.

115. In 2010, I learned that Ansar Dine had roughly 30,000 members in Mali. According to an article on maliweb, Ansar Dine's members across the world reached 2,600,000 people in 2016; see http://www.maliweb.net/societe/cherif-ousmane-madani-haidara-a-louverture-du-2eme-congres-dansar-dine-nous-aurons-desormais-un-mot-a-dire-dans-la-gestion-de-notre-pays-147624.html (retrieved 11.04.2016). Given that statistics is about power, this information over the number of members of Ansar Dine should be treated cautiously. Haïdara's sympathizers are beyond membership, hence statistically uncountable. I would nonetheless assess them as reaching several millions across West Africa.

TEN

Pentecostal Charismatic Christianity and Social Media in South Africa

Mitigating Marginality, Prosperity Teachings, and the Emergence of a Black Middle Class

MARIA FRAHM-ARP

PENTECOSTAL CHRISTIANITY BEGAN IN THE 1900S IN PLACES AS diverse as Los Angeles, Wales, and India when groups of Christians began praying in tongues.[1] In the late 1970s a new wave of Pentecostalism known as Pentecostal Charismatic Christianity (PCC) emerged, which was strongly influenced by the Charismatic and Evangelical movements in America. One of the hallmarks of PCC in South Africa, in contrast to the country's African Independent Churches (AIC) and mainline churches, has been its use of cutting-edge media technologies. With huge TV screens inside their churches and a vast array of recorded sermons, books, videos,[2] and music for sale in their book stores, these churches have opened up new ways of presenting and performing Christianity.

This chapter examines the use of social media in three mega PCC churches in the greater Johannesburg area, all with a significant membership from the emerging black middle class: Rivers of Joy Church in Sandton (Rivers), His People Church (His People) in Rosebank, and Grace Bible Church in Soweto (GBC). The criteria used to determine what constitute the black middle class varies, but according to the UCT Unilever Institute of Strategic Marketing, in 2004 the population included in the black middle class was 1.7 million people, whereas in

2012 this had shot up to 4.2 million. The Institute for Race Relations calculates that one in every ten black people belongs to the middle class, but given South Africa's current economic crisis this figure may drop.[3] "While most analysts agree that a middle class is characterized by a relatively high level of income, specific occupations and specific levels of education, there is little agreement on precisely what it is about class that produces these effects," particularly in the South African context.[4] There is consensus that the end of the apartheid, economic and political policies that favored previously disadvantaged people, and improved levels of education have led to the emergence of a black middle class in South Africa. Mattes argues that the emerging black middle class in South Africa do have a few characteristics, including a growing skepticism about the ruling political party of the country, the African National Congress (ANC), that is nevertheless combined with an aversion to explicit political activism. Mattes states, "they are no more likely to hold democratic values than other Black South Africans, they are more likely to want the government to secure 'higher-order' rather than basic survival needs. They are less likely to identify with the governing African National Congress and to turn out to vote. They are also less likely to 'voice' their concerns by contacting officials or joining in conventional or unconventional forms of collective action."[5] This chapter will explore how this new South African demographic—forged in the two decades since the end of apartheid—uses the mediated resources of Pentecostal and Charismatic Christianity to critique the present government while at the same time showing little interest in building an alternative state, focusing instead on building lives of success and wellbeing focused around the family and the church community.

The three churches have been selected for several reasons: they were all founded in the 1980s and early 1990s before the end of apartheid; they have since grown into mega churches with branches throughout the country; they each have a head pastor of the church who resides in Johannesburg and who ministers at the main Johannesburg church; and finally, they all preach a similar type of prosperity theology that promises to move believers' from the margins of economic success and material prosperity to lives of triumphant attainment of all the goods of the world. In these churches—and unlike other Pentecostal-Charismatic churches—the healing of emotional, material, and physical needs through the miraculous gifts of the Spirit is not a primary focus of the ministry on a Sunday.[6]

The city of Johannesburg is the largest urban area in South Africa and is the hub of the domestic economy. As such, this city has the greatest cross-range of people from all ethnic, linguistic, and racial groups in South Africa. This diversity makes the churches situated there ideal for this type of study. All three of my selected churches have a mix of middle class, working class, and unemployed people, and in all three churches the emerging black middle class make up at least a third of the membership. These churches are located in different parts of Johannesburg. GBC is located in Soweto,[7] previously a black-only township, while His People and Rivers are located in previously middle class white areas that are now very popular with the emerging black middle class. Whereas His People and Rivers both have racially mixed congregations, GBC only has black members.

This study uses content analysis to analyze both the Facebook sites hosted by the three churches and the Twitter accounts of two of the head pastors, Pastor André Olivier (Rivers), and Bishop Mosa Sono (GBC). The study also analyzes the Facebook page of Pastor Roger Pearce (His People), who does not use Twitter because he likes to post longer messages, which Twitter does not allow. The study also includes visits I made to the different churches, where I observed and participated in their services, and three semi-structured interviews with purposively selected members of the marketing team at each church. By unpacking, categorizing, and then analyzing the conversations or discourses exchanged on the different social media sites, I show how these churches create particular views of the world that shape how people think about politics, family, success, and their faith. I begin with the premise that what it means to be a Christian or South African or a family unit are not a given, but something continually being constructed and reconstructed through discourse. Therefore, by looking at what is privileged in a text, what is omitted, and what concepts or words are repeated, we are able to see how knowledge in a community is created. In an online community, like any other community, power is held by those who control or steer the discourse, and thus the aim of this chapter is to unpack both the messages of leaders and the recipients' responses to these messages in order to identify contemporary trends shaping the South African PCC.

To do this, a particular qualitative methodology was followed. I downloaded all Sono's and Olivier's tweets and their comments and all the Facebook posts and comments to these for Pearce, His People, GBC, and Rivers from April 2015 to April 2016. This content was then coded and analyzed according to different themes, such as politics, family, religious experience, testimonies, devotions, and teaching on the Christian faith. A part of this analysis was to identify the ideas or concepts that were repeated often and those that seldom emerged, and also to determine where there was silence. I also traced trends that showed when posts were posted and how many responses different posts received, thus making it possible to determine which types of posts were posted most often and which sorts of posts received the most likes or shares.

The focus of this chapter is on the period from April 2015 until April 2016. In May 2014, South Africa held presidential elections. Jacob Zuma was voted into a second term of office, but a year into his second term (April 2015–April 2016), a number of significant sociopolitical and economic events took place. These events and the implications they have for the churches in this study will be discussed in the section on politics, social media, and PPC.

Although there is a growing body of work examining how churches develop and manage their online presence,[8] little work has been done on social media and PCC in South Africa.[9] Unlike other studies that argue that social media and websites are predominantly used by PCC churches to advertise upcoming events[10] and not to engage in dialogue with members,[11] this chapter shows how these churches use social media quite deliberately to shape the religious experience of believers, provide a space of testimonies, and offer new devotional material and channels for political engagement. In all this they use social media as a means to mitigate their members' experiences of social and economic marginality by promoting an ethos of success and upliftment.

Overview of the Churches in This Study and Their Use of Social Media

Grace Bible Church

GBC was established in 1983 in Soweto, a huge sprawling township created for black people during the apartheid era on the southwestern outskirts of Johannesburg. Mosa Sono, a young black man from Soweto who had been a student at the Rhema Bible College, began the church. Under his leadership it has become one of the largest mega PCC churches in South Africa, with twenty-three churches currently within the GBC family. Sono is referred to as the bishop of the twenty-three GBC family churches, which are all centered around his charismatic leadership.

The core of the churches' success is their message of purpose. Sono emphasizes over and over again that every person's life has a purpose—it might be to be a successful businessman, a stay-at-home-mom, an unpaid homebased caregiver to HIV patients, or a lawyer. Part of this message of purpose is that people should not allow themselves to be held back by poverty—they should pray and actively look for work, they should improve their education, and they should develop new skills. In his sermons, Sono continually gives people tips on how to succeed in the world of work and reminds them that Christians have the edge over nonbelievers because, through the Holy Spirit, Christians can vanquish the bad spirits of poverty, depression, hopelessness, and joblessness.[12] All the church members are black. The marketing team members I interviewed estimated that thirty-five percent are part of the emerging black middle class, whereas the rest are from the working and unemployed classes.

On an empty piece of land in Pimville, Soweto, bought by the church in 2002, GBC has built a large office-park style complex. This complex includes a church building that seats over four thousand people, computer labs, community and counseling rooms, a book store, church offices, a chapel, and a kitchen. Over fourteen thousand people stream to the church's various Sunday services from all over the larger Gauteng area. The interior and décor of the church is simple with sturdy plastic chairs, a few screens above the stage and no images, paintings, or statues on the walls. The only symbol or image is the word "dreams," written in large bold letters over the main church entrance. This word sums up one of the key mission statements of the church, which is to encourage people to realize their dreams through the power of the Holy Spirit. This go-getter ethos is echoed in the other two churches in this study and is a hallmark of many, but not all, PCC[13] churches in South Africa. In its buildings, sermons, conferences, and online presence, GBC thus presents itself as a body of churches succeeding in the modern urban world. It offers people the "keys" they need to unlock their own dreams of "success" in this world.

This chapter focuses on the main or "parent" GBC in Soweto, which maintains the church's website as well as its Facebook page. The website is irregularly updated, has little information about upcoming events, and mainly gives addresses and contact details of the twenty-three GBC communities. It is dominated by pictures of Bishop Sono and images from large church gatherings, mainly at sports stadiums that can accommodate members from various GBC churches at large church occasions. In a similar fashion, the church's Facebook page is neither innovative nor particularly exciting. The church posts regular updates about upcoming events, and members post comments reporting their experiences at a service, mostly saying how they were moved or inspired by the service. The Soweto church has about thirteen thousand members, and the Facebook page had 3,236 likes in April 2016.[14] As such, this pattern of posting echoes studies that found similar patterns in North American PCC churches where websites were dull and unengaging.[15] A far more lively site is Bishop Sono's personal Twitter account,[16] which is updated every day and has 28,400 followers, suggesting that he has people following him from many of the other GBC churches and not just from Soweto. On Sundays, Bishop Sono generally posts about thirty-two tweets, and there are on average sixty-seven tweets from church members. The vast majority of Sono's feeds are inspirational messages encouraging people to remain true to their faith, and to believe that through the power of the Holy Spirit they will become successful in their jobs and find meaning and purpose in their lives. The tweets from the church members are all in support of Sono's messages or testimonies of how a church service has touched their lives.

His People Church

Another church that was also begun in the mid-1980s was His People Church, started by a young white South African man named Paul Daniels. He was strongly influenced by the Pentecostal and Charismatic movements in South Africa at the time, and with his own charismatic personality and belief in the work of the Holy Spirit, he began establishing his own Christian community on the University of Cape Town's campus. He believed that if the next generation of the country's leaders were Christians, then South Africa would become a racially just and prosperous place for all its citizens. As black students started attending previously white-only universities, the membership of Daniel's student Christian group changed to include both black and white members. Over the next decade, branches of His People Church—as Daniel's new organization came to be known—were established on most university campuses in the country and very quickly became multiracial. During the 1990s, His People branches were established outside of university campuses, thereby attracting both university alumni and people in the wider communities. One of the first His People churches was in

Rosebank, a leafy, middle-class, northern suburb in Johannesburg.[17] The His People Rosebank church is a modern building that can accommodate just over two thousand people at any one time. In the church complex, there are several rooms used for meetings, bible studies, youth activities, administration, and the children's church on a Sunday. There is no book store, but the church recently opened up a coffee shop in the adjacent shopping center. From my two church visits, I observed that His People members are racially mixed, with just over 30 percent white members. In the student group, everyone is black. Sixty percent of the pastors are white, and the rest are black. The church attracts a large group of professionals but has a range of members from the working class, often people working as domestic workers in the area. According to the marketing team member I interviewed, the church has few unemployed people. The church has a total membership of just under three thousand people.

As with GBC, the main attraction of His People is its aspirational focus and the continual emphasis on offering people support to succeed in the workplace. In common with many PCC churches throughout the continent and beyond, much of this is done through business conferences, a monthly business support group, business and financial skills training, and projects to support entrepreneurship. But what is distinctive about His People is that its message of career success is also balanced by a strong message of work-life balance—being emotionally connected and available to one's family and being an active participant in the community are regarded as equally important. This church is additionally different from the other two churches in the study in that—because of its emphasis on community building—church leadership does not allow its branches to become larger than about three thousand members. After that number is reached, the branch is encouraged to split so that a sense of being known and being part of a community is maintained.

His People has a main website that proclaims its mission statement and is particularly focused on giving information about the various His People branches in South Africa. The site encourages people to connect with a particular church in their area. The His People Rosebank website gives information about all the upcoming events and some feedback on past events. Its Facebook page is lively with daily posts, functioning mainly as a way to advertise upcoming events and for people to post their comments about services and events. The Facebook page has

2,174 likes (therefore almost all the members are active on their church's social media site). Pearce is the head pastor of His People and has an even livelier Facebook page on which he posts messages related to helping believers live according to His People's particular understanding of Christianity, which focuses on strong nuclear family relationships, a hard work ethic, sober living, committed tithing, dedicated church attendance, and activity in church programs.

Rivers of Joy Church

Overcoming life's challenges and succeeding in the modern world is at the heart of the Rivers of Joy Church. Begun by Pastor André Olivier and his wife, Wilma, with a group of seventy mainly white people in 1992, Rivers is located in Sandton, an affluent area in Johannesburg.[18] The church has grown at a remarkable rate and currently has branches in most major cities in the country. Rivers churches in South Africa continue to attract large numbers of white middle class members, but according to the member of the marketing team that I interviewed, at least 60 percent of their members are black. A significant proportion of these are young and middle-aged black people who are part of the emerging black middle class and who now live in the previously white suburbs. The churches also attract some members from the working class and underemployed or unemployed black people who wish to find financial and career success. The church building in Sandton resembles a shopping mall, with a large spiral staircase leading to seating in the galleries. Throughout the complex, there are coffee shops and lounge areas where people can chat. There is also a food court, and according to Olivier, the church aims to help people become healthier by selling only fresh, organic, or otherwise healthy foods (arguably, cultivating fit physiques is part of the church's overall ethos of fostering successful, polished lives). The décor of the church invokes the current fashion for "industrial" interiors, featuring old copper pipes and factory appliances shipped to South Africa from the United States.[19] Given the high import duties charged by South Africa, this must all have been done at great cost. The décor makes a powerful and deliberate statement about the church's financial success as well as its connection to the United States.

The church has placed TV screens throughout the auditorium, the bathrooms, lobbies, and shops. The pastor's sermons and all the musical, dramatic, or comic performances that precede or follow his sermons[20] are filmed. Watching the TV screens during a service imparts the feel of participating in a live TV show that combines the talk show and talent performance genres. The Facebook page for this church is lively; it is updated on a daily basis and several times on Sundays. Much of the content reports on how an event or service went and what will be coming up next. There are many posts made by people who share their experience of a church event or service. On April 20, 2016, the Facebook page had 6,212 likes, which suggests that 70% of the members follow this site. There are over nine thousand members of this church, but every Sunday thousands of visitors attend the church services as well.

Olivier is particularly active on Twitter and has 7,957 followers,[21] which suggests that 80 percent of the members follow his tweets. His ministry and theology are summed up in his slogan "Life by Design." According to Olivier, Christians need to learn how to succeed in the workplace—with success also being measurable by a stylized, aesthetic presentation of one's life—and he gives continual tips on how to be more productive, proactive, or profitable at work so that one can achieve more success. He advocates working hard and offers much advice on how to manage one's time and remain focused on one's goal. By implementing these tips and motivational lessons, believers can "design" their own lives so that they can achieve all the goals they set for themselves. This message is couched in a broader Christian language, in which God will bless a believer's hard work and dedication with the success he or she is looking for.

Mediation of Experience

Where TV once brought religious experiences into the home, mobile phones, tablets, and computers now continuously bring religion into our immediate personal spaces. Social media such as Facebook, Instagram, and Twitter are all part of a new social media economy that is able to bring a message to its thousands, even millions, of followers within a few seconds.[22] It allows the follower to engage with the message and make their own comments for all to see and further discuss. In this section, I show that on the social media sites of these three churches, a specific vocabulary and structure has been established according to which people speak about past church events, advertise upcoming church events, and give testimonies about what happened at these events. These highly stylized discourses shape the way members reflect on and speak about their religious experiences. There is a certain uniformity across the three churches, which suggests that PCC social media is shaping the way people communicate, reflect on, and think about their faith experiences.

In interviews held with members of the marketing committees in all three churches, the following pattern emerged. These churches advertise only online and through social media. Their research suggests that their members (numbers of members in each church were given earlier) go online more than once a week, and that while only a small percentage engage in the social media "conversations" had on Twitter or Facebook, most members "like" these sites. They calculate that all their members have mobile phones and that this is the primary device they use to access church information. This echoes findings that in 2015 in South Africa the population was 51.8 million people and there were 66.1 million mobile phones in use. Only 15 percent of the population, overwhelmingly in remote rural areas, do not have mobile phones. The prepaid subscriber base is 83 percent, and just over 60 percent of all users use their phones to access the internet.[23] When I tracked the rate and time of response to posts, it became clear that there is not one particular time of the day when more people are active online. According to the members of the marketing committees at the churches, people's access to social media sites is affected by resources, such as whether they have money to buy air time on a particular day and also whether they have internet connectivity. In all three churches the emerging and established middle class had the resources to engage continually and actively on the social media sites. By focusing on the social media use in these churches, this study is examining a subgroup within these churches that is more actively engaged on social media than the working class or unemployed cohorts who often have more limited access to social media because of their constrained resources.

The pattern of the posts on the three sites is the same: the church, usually someone assigned to manage the communication of the church, posts a reminder of an upcoming event or service, which is then followed by a series of posts from followers who have attended the event or service and express how this has moved, blessed, or encouraged them. All three churches will post reminders about the upcoming services or events at least twice before the event takes place. After the event, there will be comments from followers who attended the event. On average GBC will have an average of 62 posts after an event, but the range can be anywhere from 3 posts to 125 posts.[24] If all the comments after a service are calculated as an average over the year April 2015–April 2016,

His People has an average of 21 posts and Rivers an average of 45 posts. The interviews with members of the marketing teams suggested that all comments are made by different people who attended an event and are not "staged" by the marketing team. The range of comments and the fact that neither the same number of people nor the same names post week after week supports the idea that a fair proportion of these posts are genuine.

Social media usage is key in creating an upbeat, positive ethos around church activities. Rivers advertises events often by telling followers how amazing the previous event was and how the next service will be just as fantastic: "Last night the guys had a fantastic I.AM.MAN meeting! We can't wait for Heroes Conference coming up 20–21 May 2016! Register today!"[25] On his Twitter account, Olivier often posts comments similar to this one, encouraging people to come to church: "I have a sense in my spirit that church will be a turning point for many tomorrow. Don't stay home wherever you are. God can shift your life" (@AndreGOlivier).[26] These posts do two things: they instruct people about the boisterous, go-getting attitude they should employ in reflecting on their experience at church, and they also communicate with followers who were not at a service or event that they have missed out on something "life changing."

The sites also serve as a platform for testimony giving, albeit refashioned in the new guise of contemporary PCC theology and practice. The majority of posts on the three Facebook pages were short fragments of testimonies relating to how an individual participant at a church service experienced the service. For example, one member posted to @BishopMosaSono, "Today's message was POWERFUL! The Service was Excellent as always."[27] Pralene Goss posted, "Brilliant service—well researched, and delivered. An excellent translation of the word to today's life. Truly felt the Easter spirit—thank you Rivers church for continuously growing me in each service."[28] Emoticons are frequently used to convey a sentiment. Another post directed to @BishopMosaSono stated, "The sessions have been life changing. Thank you Bishop for the Awesome vision."[29] These generic posts offer very little personal information; at most people will say that they are "struggling" or feeling "disconnected from God" or that their lives have been "barren." Duncan Stewart posted on Pearce's Facebook page on April 6, 2016, saying that "I still remember one evening arriving at HP bible school at Wits (years ago:-), feeling shattered from the day and I asked how you were and these words of yr response continue to encourage my heart . . . 'my brother, when I am weak God is strong'!"[30] Above all, the posts emphasize what a blessing the church or its pastor have been in congregants' lives, and how the person feels "restored," "blessed," "encouraged," or "renewed." This post by Miss Malebye on Bishop Sono's Twitter account reflects her experience being an usher at the GBC Easter Service: "Serving!!! What a great experience! I'm glad I answered the Call! @ BishopMosaSono ❤👐😊."[31]

Facebook and Twitter posts by church leaders and people's responses on these sites are highly stylized expressions of religious experience that further encourage the triumphal ethos of this type of spirituality. Giving testimonies during church services has long been a hallmark of older Pentecostal churches as well as newer PCC and has been a key factor in the movement's success in North America,[32] Latin America,[33] and Africa.[34] Testimonies in services have served as a way to convert people,[35] unpack Pentecostal theology,[36] explain spiritual manifestations like healing,[37] and establish a common rhetoric of what it means to be a Christian and a sense of Christian community cohesion.[38] These testimonies had three components to them: orientation, or explaining what the setting is; complication, or explaining the problem; and resolution, or explaining how God solved the problem, for example, bringing about healing in the believer's life.[39]

Anderson points out that in the prosperity gospel churches in South Africa, "human faith is placed above the sovereignty and grace of God" and "the strength of faith is measured by results."[40] His argument is that people no longer have to give testimonies to share their experiences of blessings; rather, their designer clothes and luxury cars are the "testimonies" of their faith and blessing—much as the trappings of a successful life are elevated to the status of religious symbol in Olivier's church. This change in the manner of testimonies—testimonies expressed through material symbols rather than speech—may go some way to explain why the practice of standing up before the church to give one's testimony has fallen away in the services at the three churches in this study. But I argue that they have not fallen out of the larger Christian practice and rhetoric; rather, they can be found, albeit in a highly condensed form, on new social media sites.

These electronically mediated testimonies serve to both reflect and reinforce several important elements about this type of PCC in its South African incarnation amid an emerging black middle class. The traditional component of a Pentecostal testimony that relates a period of sin, struggle, or discouragement is largely missing from these fragmented short posts. Thus, over the period of this analysis, no one posted that they were disappointed by a church event, further reinforcing the churches' slogan of triumph and success. It is not possible to know at this point if the church police or delete comments before they appear on the sites, and so at present this analysis is based solely on what appears on the sites. There was also not a single post from Rivers and His People directly referring to evil or the power of Satan, and very few such posts from GBC.

Thus, what members of the three churches in this study mention most frequently in their social media testimonies is that they have learnt something new about how to succeed in life and their faith, and that they have been "blessed," "motivated," and "strengthened" to continue with life's struggle to be successful. Furthermore, these testimonial tweets and posts package spiritual success in secular idioms. In almost all posts, a stylized language is used in which anything "irrational" like evil spirits or tongues—a mainstay of older Pentecostal testimony giving—is edited out. Being filled with the Holy Spirit is referred to as being "blessed," "strengthened," or "motivated," and dealing with evil spirits is referred to as being "burdened" or involved in a "struggle." This stylized language recodes the religious experiences of spirits, both good and bad, into the language of a more modern, "rational" discourse compatible with broader models of success in the nonreligious world. Furthermore, these testimonies have none of the depth, self-examination, and agony of the traditional testimonies given in services.[41] Rather, they are quick, immediate, and affirming of the goodness of God; whereas a traditional testimony given in a service could last ten or more minutes, these electronic testimonies are short, sharp soundbites about the life victorious. Where Paul in his letters to the early Christian churches spoke about the Christian life as a struggle (1 Cor 9:24; Eph 6:12; Col 2:1) that would ultimately be overcome only in death, these fragmented microtestimonies elaborate a Christian theology that expects the quick resolution of earthly challenges in the immediate here and now.

Mediating Faith and Giving Followers the Christians' Secret to Success

The churches in this study all used Facebook and Twitter as an important vehicle to develop and share how followers should live the good Christian life. In the social media posts sent out by leaders, as well as in comments by their followers, there is a reshaping of the tradition of printed devotionals, which were historically popular in so many types of Christianities.[42] In this section, I will examine the online style of devotionals that focus less on spiritual disciplines and rather offer readers tips on how to succeed in life, often but not always incorporating business wisdom.

Sono's Twitter account gives reminders of upcoming events but is primarily focused on teaching people how to live out their faith. In contrast to the triumphal tone of testimonies posted by followers of GBC, Sono's posts are very honest about the difficulties people face and focus on giving them hope to overcome the challenges of unemployment and poverty in South Africa. On Easter Sunday, Sono posted, "Some people's crosses are unemployment. Others it could be your children that have gone into wrong things. #GBCGoodFriday16 #TeamBishopSono."[43] The posts that get the most likes are the posts where Sono gives life lessons based on scripture. The larger message in these posts is that life is difficult but through God's grace and by living according to Godly principles that embrace hard work, fidelity, sobriety, and commitment to God, the Christian will have purpose, joy, and meaning in his or her life.

Olivier's tweets are prolific, and he often sends out five tweets in a day. His slogan is "Life by Design," and his tweets are thus about helping his followers design their own healthy, wealthy, happy, and blessed lives, just like his own. At least 60 percent of his tweets are focused on being successful in one's career. Very often he retweets things written by business leaders, underscoring the point that PCC spirituality in South Africa shares much common ground with the aspirations of secular society—as with this post of March 2, 2016, where he retweeted, "Cameron Morrissey @Managers Diary Mar 2. 5 Ways a Lack of Punctuality Can Kill Your Career."[44] There are then five posts that follow this outlining of the points. He also sends many tweets in which he quotes ideas from management experts, such as this tweet sent on February 24, 2016: "Andre Olivier @AndreGOlivier February 24, To be successful you need to have your business in your heart and your heart in your business. Thomas J Watson." At least a third of the tweets focused on business are his own thoughts, and he portrays himself as a business leader and life coach: "Andre Olivier @AndreGOlivier February 24, Self discipline leads to self esteem. Don't start with self esteem and no discipline—it leads to foolish overestimation of nothing."[45] In fact, about 70 percent of the tweets and retweets he sends focusing on business make no reference to God but give followers a continual stream of advice on how to become successful as a Christian in the world of work.

About 30 percent of Olivier's tweets give advice on how to cope with life, such as this post: "AndreOlivier @AndreGOlivier February19. 'Struggle' is life's way of sorting out strong from the weak. If u are born rich there's no struggle Born poor? Struggle then strengthens."[46] In these life-coaching type of tweets, he also emphasizes how Christians should live with other people and be known for a life of generosity and care; for example, "AndreOlivier Retweeted, Brian Houston @Brian-CHouston February 29, God promotes the lives of those who promote the lives of others."[47] Many of his tweets come from his book *Becoming a Person of Excellence*, such as this one: "Andre Olivier @AndreGOlivier Mar 11. 4 things build confidence: Discipline, righteous living, strong faith, knowing grace & love of God. Anytime any r lacking confidence erodes."[48] The overall message of these posts is that Christians should continually strive to be better and never stop implementing new habits and engaging new mindsets that will make them more effective, which will help them achieve more success in their careers, thus realizing their aspirational goals of upward mobility. His message completely ignores the structural, historical, and racial inequalities that most South Africans face, and his messages persistently maintain that through hard work and some help from God everyone can attain all they desire.

In contrast to Sono and Pearce, Olivier makes very few posts that directly reference the Bible or give explanations of a passage of scripture, and whereas people retweet his messages a lot, there are very few comments from his followers saying how his message affected them. This is very different from Sono's and Pearce's online communities, where followers regularly post comments on how their messages have impacted people's lives.

Pearce (His People) does not use Twitter, but he does use Facebook since its length is not as restricted as in Twitter. His focus and style are very different from that of the other two leaders. His Facebook posts are filled with pictures and stories from his own life, his family, and friends. By sharing his life with his followers, he actively models what a good Christian man, father, and husband looks like. His posts fall into three main themes: a) engagement with social and political issues, which will be discussed in the next section, b) life skills or life coaching messages that are inspirational but not directly focused on faith or scripture, and c) messages about how to live the Christian life by interpreting a passage of scripture or elaborating on a Christian doctrine. Both Sono and Pearce post many messages that are interpretations of scripture showing how they are relevant to people's lives today. These receive the most likes and shares. This particular message posted by Pearce on March 25, 2016, got 132 likes: "Mankind cannot, and I certainly cannot pull myself up by my own bootstraps. The nature and consequences of our sin can only be dealt with by a perfect lamb, a sinless substitute."[49] Over the one-year period of the study, messages like this got an average of 87 likes.

As is common with other PCC pastors throughout the world, Pearce's messages focus on how to apply a passage of scripture to one's everyday life. On March 17, 2016, he posted, "When men stay behind instead of going out to fulfill their calling they end up on the roof looking at their Bathsheba's: 'In the spring of the year, the time when kings go out to battle, David sent Joab . . . But David remained at Jerusalem' 2 Sam 11vi–5." Lance Bell responded, "Do all the things your [*sic*]supposed to do and theres [*sic*] no time to do what you shouldn't." Refilwe Matsei Lengana posted, "Ohhhhhhh wow!!!! I honestly get this . . . it is so true." This online dialogue is representative of how much people make comments on Pearce's posts. Those who comment are both black and white and, from the language, well educated. From the analysis of the content of comments, those responding to Pearce's posts are generally not people who are unemployed. The same pattern emerged with Olivier's and Sono's followers—those who comment on the posts or tweets appear to being working people with aspirations to improve their lives.

Mediating Political Response and Engagement

Research by Meyer and Moors[50] argues that PCC is embracing media and producing videos and other forms of technology to create a bottom-up spread of democratic ideas that reshape the cultural and political landscape of the countries they are located in. They thus argue that PCC media is at the forefront of a new democratic culture. In this section, I investigate how the churches in this study responded to social and political events and show that while we have seen greater involvement in politics by these adherents of PCC over the last ten years, they do not represent the grassroots, populist movement some have taken them to be. Moreover, far from confirming the narrative that new social media promote democratic subversion of the status quo, in fact the example of the media sites used by these three churches demonstrate that electronically mediated engagement in politics is still circumspect and usually, but not always, undertaken only when it promotes the churches' own popularity. It is on issues of political engagement that we see significant differences in the three churches in this study. These differences are somewhat reflective of the different socioeconomic groups in the country, but they also reveal a number of theological issues and the role these churches see themselves playing in the country.

To appreciate the political changes in these churches, we need to remind ourselves of the role of Christianity in politics over the last two decades. During the 1980s and early 1990s, mainline churches, but not PCC churches, were at the forefront of the struggle against apartheid.[51] After South Africa's first democratic elections in 1994, mainline churches withdrew from the public political arena and, for the next ten years, churches were not significantly involved in politics and little reference was made to Christianity in the political rhetoric. As Jacob Zuma began to rally support for his bid to oust President Thabo Mbeki from government in 2007, he turned to churches as a platform to garner political support. He particularly gained the support of Pentecostal Charismatic Churches.[52]

In the buildup to the 2014 presidential elections, GBC became more and more politically active in inviting government ministers and various political leaders—such as Mogoeng Mogoeng, South Africa's chief justice and ANC supporter, and Floyd Shivambu, the chief of staff of the Economic Freedom Fighters[53]—to address their congregation.[54] They sent out continual reminders to church members and followers that it was their Christian duty to vote, although the church at no time told people which party to vote for.[55] Posts to vote in the elections were particularly uncreative and gained less the twenty likes, showing that the GBC community were disinterested in the elections, at least on the social media platform.

Two issues that instantly gained traction—gaining over two hundred likes in the first few hours—were calls against violence and abuse. Between March 2014 and October 2015, GBC and Sono actively commented on a variety of political and civil issues. In 2014, both Bishop Sono's Twitter feeds and the GBC Facebook page were dominated by calls to #BringBackOurGirls and rescue the Nigerian girls held captive by Boko Haram, a militant Islamic group that abducted over two hundred girls in 2014. Following the attacks on foreigners in Johannesburg on April 16, 2015, GBC posted on its Facebook page, "We strongly condemn the Xenophobic attacks." This posting alone got 228 likes in one day.

During the second half of 2015, there was a marked change in the GBC's use of social media; its Facebook page became almost inactive after October 2015, whereas Bishop Sono's Twitter account, by contrast, virtually exploded with action. On any given Sunday in the latter half of 2015 and early 2016, the number of tweets from followers averaged around fifty-one (this does not include all the retweets), and from Bishop Sono there were generally twenty-four tweets per Sunday. Whereas the Facebook page had regularly made mention of social and political events, Bishop Sono's Twitter feeds in this period made comment about neither social nor political events. He was silent on the topic of the severe drought that gripped the country in late 2015, although this was a major media topic on TV news, phone-in radio stations, and in print media. Neither the GBC Facebook page nor Bishop Sono's Twitter feed alluded to the crisis in education or the civil uprising around #FEESMUSTFALL. Bishop Sono's Twitter feed also made no mention of Zuma's use of state funds to develop his homestead at Inkandla or Chief Justice Mogoeng ruling in March 2016 that Zuma had been in violation of the constitution. There was also no mention of South Africa's increasingly unstable economy or Zuma's disastrous shuffles of finance ministers in a short period of time at the end of 2015.

Given how politically active GBC had been in 2014 and the role it had claimed to be playing in the country's Moral Regeneration Campaign[56] during the first decade of the 2000s, this sudden silence was surprising. Part of the answer lies in GBC's theology, one underpinned by the idea that faith, hard work, and morally just living are the keys to personal success. Democracy and capitalism have been upheld as two of the primary pillars on which to build a free and fair South Africa, the primary vehicle through which the central goal of GBC theology—upward mobility on the part of the new black middle classes in a modernizing country—can be achieved. Aligning itself to the project of democracy in the 2014 elections and fighting for the fair treatment of abused girls and foreigners fitted into this framework. But since mid-2015, South Africa and its government, in particular, are perceived no longer as a success story but rather as increasingly subject to international and domestic criticism.[57] At present, political engagement does not strengthen or prove the church's message of success; it rather brings it into question. The current government, which GBC maintains was voted in by Christians and ordained by God, is corrupt, ineffectual, and spiraling into failure; therefore, the church must distance itself from the political arena or address difficult problems concerning the effectiveness or validity of its own theology.

Another part of the answer to GBC's silence lies in the makeup of the congregation. While 35 percent are middle class, the other 65 percent are from the aspirational working class and the unemployed—the vast majority of whom have traditionally been ANC supporters. The church therefore cannot be seen to be speaking against the ANC. Silence may denote different things; it can mean disinterest in or a desire to disengage from a topic or issue. In the case of GBC, its silence is arguably a desire to distance itself and even disengage from the ANC. This was most noticeable in the 2016 Easter rally at Orlando Stadium in Soweto. Sono and Ray McCauley were two of the keynote speakers, and Zuma attended the service. But Sono in his tweets made no mention of Zuma's participation, nor did GBC in its Facebook page. Over the two years from 2014 to 2016, we see how dynamic and fluid PCC theology and politics in South Africa has been. Key decisions about political engagement are not made by a church council that deliberates issues over several months or years; rather, engagement can change in a matter of days or weeks, according to the decisions taken by leaders.

In contrast, the membership at His People is by and large upwardly mobile and university educated. Their online discussions show much more political debate around ideas and concepts, echoing Mattes's findings.[58] This is a class that is moving from voting for the ANC because of its "struggle" credentials to questioning the political agenda of the country in general and political parties in particular.[59] The ethos of the church is to change the country by changing those in leadership—therefore to question who has power and what the powerful do with it.

Leading up to the 2014 elections, there was heated political engagement on the His People Facebook page about which party a Christian should vote for.[60] From the beginning of the #FEESMUSTFALL student campaign to end the payment of universities fees, Pearce was particularly active. On November 2, 2015, he released a formal statement supporting the campaign but condemning violence. There was a heated debate on social media about the role of the church speaking about a civil protest, and many members said that the church should not be involved in a struggle that had become violent. Pearce's rebuttal to this on November 3, 2015, was "In the first place, we as leaders are called to bring hope to people and speak life into situations. . . . Our stance was very clearly one of non-violence and non-intimidation. We don't believe in using unbiblical methods and condemn these methods. We understood that there's a chance that we would be associated with this, but sometimes you have to take risks."[61] Early in 2016, violent protests broke out on the University of Pretoria Campus (Tuks), and on February 23, 2016, His People and other students joined together to pray for the Tuks campus. Pearce tweeted several pictures in the following days showing Christian students united in prayers against violence and in support for the aims of the campaign. On February 27, 2016, he posted, "We have received a request from our campus ministry in the Free State to send a few leaders who can assist the church engage more deeply the issue of racial reconciliation."[62]

On the whole, Pearce's political comments are nuanced, often veiled, and measured. Below is an example of the type of comments his followers posted on his Faceboook page. Anne Achadinha posted this comment: "Our God hears as we all together praise His name above every other name. No weapon formed against us shall prosper in Jesus name. We are all standing in agreement for our nation South Africa."[63] Her comment was in response to the #FEESMUSTFALL and the #ZUMAMUSTFALL campaigns. This led to a series of posts from different people about the need for Christians to pray for truth and justice. On March 4, 2016, Pearce followed up the online conversation with this post: "Deep soul challenge for all in South Africa: 'He has told you, O man, what is good; and what does the Lord require of you, but to do justice, and to love mercy, and to walk humbly with your God?' Micah 6." This got 140 likes.

Why has this church become more politically active since 2015, whereas GBC has become less engaged? Part of the answer might lie in the content of the political debate. A significant proportion of His People members are university graduates who understand the burden of university debt. And in social, economic, and political terms, they are also a highly mobile group moving into the middle class and out of the unemployed and working class of their parents. Because neither the congregation nor the leadership has any particular ties to government, they are free to challenge the government and even openly support the #ZUMAMUSTFALL campaign to oust Zuma from government. In their social media, we see new channels opening up through which some Christians in the black middle classes are exercising a political voice outside the margins of the dominant political structures and breaking away from historic loyalty to the ANC as the party of the liberation movement. At present Pearce is shaping the church's political discourse around a theology of mercy and justice rather than prosperity and growth. In the coming months, we will see if this is a genuine shift in the church's broader theology or if it is gaining members' support only because they are invested in the particular issue at hand.

Rivers has never aligned itself to South African political parties nor shown an interest in shaping the moral or political life of the country. Under apartheid, this political nonengagement was seen as being apolitical, but there is arguably no such thing as being politically neutral—even silence voices a strong political message. The church does not engage with the merits or limitations of the government but continues to preach a message that through hard work, business skills, and faith people can achieve their aspirations—even in the face of a failing economy, corruption, and political unrest. A "life by design" is presented as entirely independent of the structure of the economy; Rivers is keeping an impossible dream alive for thousands of people.

Conclusion

We are left with an unpredictable space. GBC had been significantly involved in politics but in April 2015 was distancing itself from the political project of the country, the ramifications of which will likely be felt in the municipal elections to be held in August 2016. His People, which had never encouraged members to become political active, is now playing a significant role in the civil uprising around the #FEESMUSTFALL campaign. Although Rivers remains politically unengaged, we might be beginning to see a turn in South African PCC politics, in which a new voice critical of the corruption, maladministration, and economic crisis of the current regime is emerging—in large part through the outlets of social media sites.

In these churches, social media has opened up a new space for testimonies as people who have participated in these events stream their comments. These comments are stylized expressions of how, through the teaching at a particular event, the follower found peace, was encouraged, learned a new insight about life, or was given new hope. By clicking on and "liking" a testimony, followers engaged with each other and affirmed each other's comments, thus creating an engaged online community. Through in-depth analysis, it is possible to unpack the theology and worldview presented in the social media spaces used by these three churches and their followers. Whereas the two dominant rhetorical styles are about church events and motivational or devotional messages, these postings on social media create a mediated religious experience that encourages followers—many drawn from the country's emerging and highly aspirational black middle classes—to see themselves and their being-in-the-world through a particular lens focused on individual success. Through the immediacy of social media into people's personal space via a computer or handheld device, these online communities bring the religious into followers' lives on a continual basis.

Notes

1. The ability to pray in tongues was quickly understood as the sign that a believer was filled with the Holy Spirit, and this marked Pentecostal Christians as different from other Christians who do not see tongues as the sign that believers are filled with the Holy Spirit. Vinson Synan, *The Holiness-Pentecostal Tradition: Charismatic Movements in the Twentieth Century* (Grand Rapids, MI: W. B. Eerdmans, 1997); Gary McGee, "Latter Rain Falling in the East: Early Twentieth Century Pentecostalism in India and the Debate over Speaking in Tongues" *Church History* 68, no. 3 (1999): 648–65.

2. Although this market has remained relatively small in South Africa.

3. "How Big Is South Africa's Black Middle Class?," *Business Tech,* August 4, 2015, http://businesstech.co.za/news/wealth/94987/how-big-is-south-africas-black-middle-class/.

4. Robert Mattes, "South Africa's Emerging Black Middle Class: A Harbinger of Political Change?," *Journal of International Development* 27 (2015): 666.

5. Mattes, "South Africa's Emerging Black Middle Class," 665.

6. Ilana van Wyk, *The Universal Church of the Kingdom of God in South Africa: A Church of Strangers* (Cambridge: Cambridge University Press, 2014).

7. Soweto was created on the outskirts of Johannesburg during the apartheid regime as a "township" or area where only black people could live.

8. See Pauline Hope Cheong, Jessie P. H. Poon, Shirlena Huang, and Irene Casas, "The Internet Highway and Religious Communities: Mapping and Contesting Spaces in Religion-Online." *The Information Society* 25, no. 5 (2009): 291–302; Amanda Sturgill, "Scope and Purposes of Church Web Sites," *Journal of Religion and Media* 3, no. 3 (2004): 165–76; Buster Smith, Christopher P. Scheitle, and Christopher Bader, "The Ties that Bind: Network Overlap among Independent Congregations," *Social Science Computer Review* 30, no. 2 (2012): 259–73; Melissa M. Smith, "Nonprofit Religious Organization Web Sites: Underutilized Avenue of Communicating with Group Members," *Journal of Media and Religion* 6, no. 4 (2007): 273–90; Richard Waters, Christine S. Friedman, Brittney Mills, and Lei Zeng, "Applying Relationship Management Theory to Religious Organizations: An Assessment of Relationship Cultivation Online," *Journal of Communication and Religion* 34, no. 1 (2011): 88–104; Lynne M. Baab, "Portraits

of the Future Church: A Rhetorical Analysis of Congregational Websites," *Journal of Communication and Religion* 31, no. 2 (2008): 143–81.

9. Maria Frahm-Arp, "The Political Rhetoric in Sermons and Select Social Media in Three Pentecostal Charismatic Evangelical Churches Leading Up to the 2014 South African Election," *Journal for the Study of Religion* 28, no. 1 (2015): 115–41.

10. Smith, Scheitle, and Bader, "Ties That Bind."

11. John G. Wirtz, Prisca S. Ngondo, and Philip Poe, "Talking *with* Us or *at* Us: How U.S. Religious Denominations Use Organizational Web Sites to Communicate with Their Constituents," *Journal of Media and Religion* 12, no. 4 (2013): 165.

12. Maria Frahm-Arp, *Professional Women in South African Pentecostal Charismatic Churches* (Leiden: Brill, 2010).

13. See van Wyk, *Universal Church,* who shows that the Universal Church of the Kingdom of God is centered on praying for the exorcism of demons, which are believed to be the ones holding people in poverty, illness, or loneliness.

14. Grace Bible Church Facebook page, accessed April 18, 2016, https://www.facebook.com/Grace-Bible-Church-Soweto-490602324377798/likes.

15. Waters, Friedman, Mills, and Zeng, "Applying Relationship Management Theory."

16. Bishop Mosa Sono's Twitter page, https://twitter.com/BishopMosaSono.

17. For a more comprehensive overview of the history of this church, see Maria Frahm-Arp, "A History of Pentecostal Charismatic Christianity in South Africa," in *Global Renewal Christianity: Spirit-Empowered Movements Past, Present, and Future,* vol. 3, *Africa,* ed. Vinson Synan, Amos Yong, and J. Kwabena Asamoah-Gyadu (Lake Mary, FL: Charisma House, 2016).

18. Rivers of Joy website, accessed March 30, 2016, http://www.riverschurch.co.za/sandton/.

19. Ibid.

20. Olivier is the head pastor and preaches many of the sermons, but there is a team of other male pastors who also preach. At some conferences and at weekday services, Wilma, Olivier's wife, preaches.

21. Accessed on April 20, 2016.

22. Jeremy Stolow, "Religion and/as Media," *Theory Culture Society* 22, no. 4 (2005): 119–47.

23. "The Reality of Mobile Usage and Social Media Growth in South Africa," *Imagi-Social* (blog), November 2, 2014, http://www.imagi-social.co.za/reality-mobile-usage-social-media-growth-south-africa/.

24. This was received after the Easter Service on March 27, 2016.

25. Rivers Church Sandton Facebook post of April 8, 2016, http://www.facebook.com/RiversChurchSandton/.

26. Posted February 20, 2016.

27. Bono posted on April 17, 2016.

28. Rivers member posted on April 3, 2016

29. Posted March 8, 2016, by member of GBC.

30. Roger Pearce's Facebook page, accessed April 15, 2016, https://www.facebook.com/roger.pearce.16.

31. Posted March 27, 2016.

32. Vinson Synan, *The Holiness-Pentecostal Tradition: Charismatic Movements in the Twentieth Century* (Grand Rapids, MI: W. B. Eerdmans, 1997).

33. Marcel A. Chavan De Matviuk, "Latin American Pentecostal Growth: Culture, Orality and the Power of Testimonies," *Asian Journal of Pentecostal Studies* 5, no. 2 (2002): 205–22.

34. David Maxwell, *African Gifts of the Spirit: Pentecostalism and the Rise of a Zimbabwean Transnational Religious Movement* (Athens: Ohio University Press, 2006); Akoko Robert Mbe, "You Must Be Born-Again: The Pentecostalisation of the Presbyterian Church in Cameroon," *Journal of Contemporary African Studies* 25, no. 2 (2007): 299–315; Allan Anderson, "Pentecostal Approaches to Faith and Healing," *International Review of Mission* 91, no. 363 (2002): 527.

35. Mark Cartledge, *Testimony in the Spirit: Rescripting Ordinary Pentecostal Theology* (Aldershot: Ashgate, 2010).

36. Scott Ellington, "The Costly Loss of Testimony," *Journal of Pentecostal Theology* 16 (2000): 48–59; Ellington, "History, Story and Testimony: Locating Truth in a Pentecostal Hermeneutic," *PNEUMA: The Journal of the Society for Pentecostal Studies* 22, no. 2 (2001): 245–63.

37. Myung Soo Park, "Korean Pentecostal Spirituality as Manifested in the Testimonies of Believers of the Yoido Full Gospel Church," *Asian Journal of Pentecostal Studies* 7, no. 1 (2004): 35–56.

38. Wynand De Kock, "Pentecostal Power for a Pentecostal Task: Empowerment through Engagement in the South African Context," *Journal of Pentecostal Theology* 16 (2000): 102–16; J. Stephen Kroll-Smith, "The Testimony as Performance: The Relationship of an Expressive Event in the Belief of a Holiness Sect," *Journal for the Scientific Study of Religion* 19, no. 1 (1980): 16–25.

39. De Kock, "Pentecostal Power," 102.

40. Anderson, "Pentecostal Approaches," 529.

41. Ellington, "Costly Loss of Testimony," 246–47.

42. Richard Rambuss, *Closet Devotions* (Durham, NC: Duke University Press, 1998); Jan Blodgett, *Protestant Evangelical Literary Culture and Contemporary Society.* (Westport, CT: Greenwood Press, 1997); C. E. Hambrick-Stowe, *The Practice of Piety: Puritan Devotional Disciplines in the Seventeenth-Century New England* (Chapel Hill: University of North Carolina Press, 1982); Krista Lysack, "The Production of Time: Keble, Rossetti and Victorian Devotional Reading," *Victorian Studies* 55, no. 3 (2013): 451–70.

43. Posted March 27, 2016.

44. André Olivier's Twitter page, accessed April 2, 2016, https://twitter.com/AndreGOlivier.

45. Posted February 24, 2016.

46. Posted February 19, 2016.

47. Posted February 29, 2016.

48. Posted March 11, 2016.

49. Posted March 25, 2016.

50. Birgit Meyer and Annelies Moors, eds., *Media, Religion, and the Public Sphere* (Bloomington: Indiana University Press, 2005).

51. Anthony Balcomb, "From Apartheid to the New Dispensation: Evangelicals and the Democratization in South Africa," *Journal of Religion in Africa* 34 (2007): 7; Tracey Kuperus, "The Political Role and Democratic Contribution of Churches in Post-Apartheid South Africa," *Journal of Church and State* 53 (2011): 297.

52. Frahm-Arp, "Political Rhetoric in Sermons," 124–26.

53. The EFF are a relatively new political party started in 2013 by Julius Malema after he was ousted as the leader of the ANC Youth League. It is currently the third largest party in parliament. They hold a revolutionary socialist position and aim to nationalize big business in South Africa to distribute wealth to the black poor.

54. Itumeleng Mafisa, "Catholics Berate Kasrils for Election Stand," *The New Age*, April 13, 2014, http://www.thenewage.co.za/mobi/Detail.aspx?NewsID=123222&CatID=1007.

55. Frahm-Arp, "Political Rhetoric in Sermons." 126–31.

56. This project ran across government and police departments and aimed to end corruption in these institutions. GBC and Sono in particular played a significant advisory role in this project.

57. "South Africa Gets a Rating Downgrade," *Economist*, December 7, 2015, http://www.economist.com/news/middle-east-and-africa/21679693-mismanagement-and-magical-thinking-are-driving-rainbow-nation-debt.

58. Mattes, "South Africa's Emerging Black Middle Class."

59. Frahm-Arp, "Political Rhetoric in Sermons." 128.

60. Ibid.

61. http://everynationafrica.org/Rogers%20Blog/?p=314 (accessed 3 April 2016). This page has subsequently been deactivated.

62. Roger Pearce's Facebook post from February 27, 2016, https://www.facebook.com/roger.pearce.16.

63. Posted February 27, 2016.

Bibliography

Abdul-Razak, Idriss. "Alhaj Umar of Kete-Krachi: A Muslim Leader a Teacher a Poet and a Social Commentator of His Time." M.Phil thesis, University of Ghana-Legon, 1996.

Adama, Hamadou. "Islamic Communication and Mass Media in Cameroon." In *New Media and Religious Transformations in Africa,* edited by Rosalind I. J. Hackett and Benjamin Soares. Bloomington: Indiana University Press, 2015.

Adeboye, Enoch Adejare. *Open Heavens: A Daily Guide to Close Fellowship with God.* Vol. 12. Lagos: Open Heavens Publications, 2012.

Ahmed, Leila. *Women and Gender in Islam: Historical Roots of a Modern Debate.* New Haven: Yale University Press, 2011.

Akindayomi, Josiah O. *This Is My Story: An Authentic Posthumous Autobiography of Reverend Josiah O. Akindayomi.* Dallas, TX: One-Hour Books, 2010.

Almir, Ibric. *Das Bilderverbot im Islam.* Marburg: Tectum Verlag, 2004.

Amselle, Jean-Louis. "Le Wahabisme à Bamako (1945–1985)." *Canadian Journal of African Studies/Revue Canadienne des Etudes Africaines* 19, no. 2 (1985): 345–57.

Anderson, Allan. "Pentecostal Approaches to Faith and Healing." *International Review of Mission* 91, no. 363 (2002): 523–34.

Anderson, Benedict. *Imagined Communities: Reflections on the Origin and Spread of Nationalism.* London: Verso, 1991.

Anyanwu, K. C. "African Religious Experience." In *African Philosophy: An Introduction to the Main Philosophical Trends in Contemporary Africa,* edited by E. A. Ruch and K. C. Anyanwu, 161–76. Rome: Catholic Book Agency, 1981.

Arnoldi, Mary Jo. "Bamako, Mali: Monuments and Modernity in the Urban Imagination." *Africa Today* 54, no. 2 (2007): 3–24.

Asad, Talal. *Formations of the Secular: Christianity, Islam, Modernity.* Stanford: Stanford University Press, 2003.

———. "Two European Images of Non-European Rule." *Economy and Society* 2 (1973): 263–77.

Austen, Ralph, and Jan Jansen. "History, Oral Transmission and Structure in Ibn Khaldun's Chronology of Mali Rulers." *History in Africa* 23 (1996): 17–28.

Bâ, Amadou Hampâté. *The Fortunes of Wangrin.* Translated by Aina Pavolini Taylor. Bloomington: Indiana University Press, 1999.

Baab, Lynne M. "Portraits of the Future Church: A Rhetorical Analysis of Congregational Websites." *Journal of Communication and Religion* 31, no. 2 (2008): 143–81.

Bade, Klaus J. "Antisklavereibewegung in Deutschland und Kolonialkrieg in Deutsch-Ostafrika 1888–1890: Bismarck und Friedrich Fabri." *Geschichte und Gesellschaft* 3 (1977): 31–58.

———. *Friedrich Fabri und der Imperialismus in der Bismarckzeit: Revolution—Depression—Expansion.* 2nd internet edition. Osnabrück, no publisher (original Atlantis Verlag, Freiburg) 2005.

Badr, Hanan. "Limitations of the Social Media Euphoria in Communication Studies." *Egypte/Monde Arabe* 12 (2015): 177–93.

Bailleul, Charles. *Dictionnaire Bambara Français.* Bamako: Donniya, 1996.

Balcomb, Anthony. "From Apartheid to the New Dispensation: Evangelicals and the Democratization in South Africa." *Journal of Religion in Africa* 34 (2007): 5–38.

Bald, Detlef. *Deutsch-Ostafrika 1900–1914: Eine Studie über Verwaltung, Interessengruppen und Wirtschaftliche Erschließung.* Munich: Weltforum Verlag, 1970.

bana Hasani, Muhamadi. "Shairi la Majermani." In *Kala Shairi: German East Africa in Swahili Poems,* edited by Gudrun Miehe, Katrin Bromber, Said Khamis, Ralf Großerhode, and Hilke Meyer-Bahlburd, 369–71. Cologne: Rüdiger-Köppe-Verlag, 2002.

Barber, Karin. *The Anthropology of Texts, Persons and Publics: Oral and Written Culture in Africa and Beyond.* Cambridge: Cambridge University Press, 2007.

———. "Introduction: Hidden Innovators in Africa." In *Africa's Hidden Histories: Everyday Literacy and Making the Self,* edited by Karin Barber, 1–24. Bloomington: Indiana University Press, 2006.

———. "Preliminary Notes on Audiences in Africa." *Africa: Journal of the International African Institute* 67, no. 3 (1997): 347–62.

Barth, C. G. "Die ersten Lebensjahre unserer deutschen Schule in Tanga, Ostafrika." *Deutsche Kolonialzeitung* 8, no. 12 (23 March 1895): 90–93.

Bayart, Jean-François. *The Illusion of Cultural Identity.* Translated by Steven Rendell, Janet Roitman, and Jonathon Derrick. London: C. Hurst, 2005.

Becker, Carl Heinrich. "Karstedt's Islampolitische Aufsätze." *Der Islam* 5 (1914): 244–47.

Becker, Felicitas, and Jigal Beez, eds. *Der Maji-Maji-Krieg in Deutsch-Ostafrika 1905–1907.* Berlin: Ch. Links Verlag, 2005.

Becker, Felicitas. *Becoming Muslim in Mainland Tanzania, 1890–2000.* Oxford: Oxford University Press, 2008.

———. "Freeborn Villagers: Islam and the Local Uses of Cosmopolitan Connections in the Tanzanian Countryside." In *Cosmopolitans in Muslim Contexts: Perspectives from the Past,* edited by Derryl N. MacLean and Sikeena Karmali Ahmed, 10–30. Edinburgh: Edinburgh University Press, 2012.

———. "Remembering Nyerere: Political Rhetoric and Dissent in Contemporary Tanzania." *African Affairs* 112 (2013): 238–61.

Behrend, Heike. *Contesting Visibility: Photographic Practices on the East African Coast.* Bielefeld: Transcript, 2013.

———. *Resurrecting Cannibals: The Catholic Church, Witch-Hunts and the Production of Pagans in Western Uganda.* Oxford: James Currey, 2011.

———. "'The Terror of the Feast': Photography, Textiles and Memory in Weddings along the East African Coast." In *Photography in Africa: Ethnographic Perspectives,* edited by Richard Vokes, 229–40. Oxford: James Currey, 2012.

Behrend, Heike, and Tobias Wendl, eds. *9/11 and Its Remediations in Africa.* Berlin: Lit Verlag, 2015.

Bekaert, Stefan. *System and Repertoire in Sakata Medicine: Democratic Republic of Congo.* Uppsala Studies in Cultural Anthropology 31. Uppsala: S. Academiae Ubsaliensis, 2000.

Belting, Hans. *Das echte Bild: Bildfragen als Glaubensfragen.* Munich: C H Beck, 2005.

Bender, Courtney, and Ann Taves, eds. *What Matters? Ethnographies of Value in a Not So Secular Age.* New York: Columbia University Press, 2012.

Benjamin, Walter. "Ursprung des deutschen Trauerspiels." In *Gesammelte Schriften.* Vol. 1. Edited by Rolf Tiedemann and Hermann Schweppenhäuser, 203–429, 868–981. Frankfurt: Suhrkamp, 1974.

Berman, Bruce, Dickson Eyoh, and Will Kymlicka. *Ethnicity and Democracy in Africa.* Athens: Ohio University Press, 2004.

Besançon, Alain. *L'image interdite: Une histoire intellectuelle de l'iconoclasme.* Paris: Fayard, 1994.

Bible-Davids, Rebecca. *Enoch Adeboye: Father of Nations.* Charlotte, NC: Biblos Publishers, 2009.

Blakely, Thomas D., Walter E. A. van Beek, and Dennis L. Thomson, eds. *Religion in Africa: Experience & Expression.* Portsmouth, NH: Heinemann, 1994.

Blodgett, Jan. *Protestant Evangelical Literary Culture and Contemporary Society.* Westport, CT: Greenwood Press, 1997.

Bodjoko-Lilembu, J. P. *Développement de la radio catholique en République Démocratique du Congo.* Paris: L'Harmattan, 2011.

Bongard, Oscar. "Die Studienreise des Staatsekretärs Dernburg nach Deutsch-Ostafrika (Fortsetzung)." *Deutsche Kolonialzeitung* 24, no. 48 (30 November 1907): 490.

Bornhak, Conrad. "Das Recht der Eingeborenen in den deutschen Schutzgebieten." *Deutsche Kolonialzeitung* 4, no. 11 (October 17, 1891): 146.

Botte, Roger. "Pouvoir du Livre, pouvoir des hommes: La religion comme critère de distinction." *Journal des Africanistes* 60, no. 2 (1990): 37–52.

Bourdieu, Pierre, ed. *Eine illegitime Kunst: Die sozialen Gebrauchsweisen der Fotografie.* Frankfurt: Suhrkamp, 1981.

Bowen, John. *Islam, Law and Equality in Indonesia: An Anthropology of Public Reasoning.* Cambridge: Cambridge University Press, 2003.

Braimah, J. A., and J. R. Goody. *Salaga: The Struggle for Power.* London: Longmans, 1967.

Brebant, Emilie. "La Vierge, la guerre, la vérité: Approche anthropologique et transnationale des apparitions mariales rwandaises." PhD diss., ULB (Free University Brussels), 2011.

Brennan, James R. "Radio Cairo and the Decolonization of East Africa." In *Making a World after Empire: The Bandung Moment and Its Political Afterlives,* edited by Christopher Lee, 173–95. Athens: Ohio University Press, 2010.

Brenner, Louis. "Constructing Muslim Identities in Mali." In *Muslim Identity and Social Change in Sub-Saharan Africa,* edited by Louis Brenner, 57–78. London: Hurst, 1993.

———. *Controlling Knowledge: Religion, Power and Schooling in a West African Muslim Society.* Bloomington: Indiana University Press, 2001.

———. "Youth as Political Actors in Mali." In *Transitions in Africa: Expanding Political Spaces,* edited by Pearl T. Robinson, Catharine Newbury, and Mamadou Diouf. Unpublished, 2003.

Brielmaier, Isolde Anna. "'Picture Taking' and the Production of Urban Identities on the Kenyan Coast." PhD diss., Columbia University, New York, 2003.

Broqua, Christophe, and Anne Docquet. "Penser les masculinités en Afrique et au-delà." *Cahiers d'Etudes Africaines* 209–10 (2013): 9–41.

Brown, H. W. "Coins of East Africa: An Introductory Survey." *Yarmouk Numismatics* 5 (1993): 9–16.

Buckley, Liam. "Cine-Film, Film-Strips and the Devolution of Colonial Photography in the Gambia." In "Photography in Africa," edited by Sylvester Okwunodu Ogbechie and John Pfeffer. Special issue, *History of Photography* 34, no. 2 (2010): 147–57.

Bürgel, Johan Christoph. *The Feather of Simurgh: The "Licit Magic" of the Arts in Medieval Islam.* New York: NYU Press, 1988.

Burgess, G. Thomas, and Andrew Burton. Introduction to *Generations Past: Youth in East African History,* edited by Andrew Burton and Hélène Charton-Bigot, 1–24. Athens: Ohio University Press, 2010.

Cabrita, Joel. *Text and Authority in the South African Nazaretha Church.* Cambridge: Cambridge University Press, 2014.

———. "Texts, Authority and Community in the South African Ibandla lamaNazaretha ('Church of the Nazaretha'), 1910–1976." *Journal of Religion in Africa* 40, no. 1 (2010): 60–95.

Calmettes, Jean-Loup. "The Lumpa Sect: Rural Reconstruction, and Conflict." Master's thesis, University of Wales, 1978.

Cartledge, Mark. *Testimony in the Spirit: Rescripting Ordinary Pentecostal Theology.* Aldershot: Ashgate, 2010.

Casewit, Jane Fatima. "The Spiritual Significance of Marriage in Islam." In *Voices of Islam.* Vol. 3, *Voices of Life: Family, Home, and Society,* edited by Vincent Cornell and Virginia Gray Henry-Blakemore, 77–92. Westport, CT: Greenwood Publishing, 2007.

Castells, Manuel. *The Rise of the Network Society.* Oxford: Blackwell, 2000.

Chamberlin, John Weir. "The Development of Islamic Education in Kano City, Nigeria, with Emphasis on Legal Education in the 19th and 20th Centuries." PhD diss., Columbia University, 1975.

Chappatte, André. "Chinese Products, Social Mobility and Material Modernity in Bougouni, a Small but Fast-Growing Administrative Town of Southwest Mali." *African Studies* 73, no.1 (2014): 22–40.

———. "Night Life in Southern Mali: Being a Muslim Maquisard in Bougouni." *Journal of the Royal Anthropological Institute* 20, no. 3 (2014): 526–44.

Cheong, Pauline Hope, Jessie P. H. Poon, Shirlena Huang, and Irene Casas. "The Internet Highway and Religious Communities: Mapping and Contesting Spaces in Religion-Online." *The Information Society* 25, no. 5 (2009): 291–302.

Chidester, David. *Savage Systems: Colonialism and Comparative Religion in South Africa.* Charlottesville: University of Virginia Press, 1996.

Clifford, James. *Routes: Travel and Translation in the Late Twentieth Century.* Cambridge, MA: Harvard University Press, 1997.

Colleyn, Jean-Pierre, ed. *Bamana: The Art of Existence in Mali.* New York: Museum for African Art, 2001.

Comaroff, Jean. *Body of Power, Spirit of Resistance: The Culture and History of a South African People.* Chicago: University of Chicago Press, 1985.

Comaroff, Jean, and John L. Comaroff. "The Colonization of Consciousness in South Africa." *Economy and Society* 18 (1989): 267–96.

———. "Millennial Capitalism: First Thoughts on a Second Coming." *Public Culture* 12, no. 2 (2000): 291–343.

———. *Of Revelation and Revolution: Christianity, Colonialism and Consciousness in South Africa.* Vol. 1. Chicago: University of Chicago Press, 1991.

———. "Reflections on Youth: From the Past to the Postcolony." In *Makers and Breakers: Children and Youth in Postcolonial Africa,* edited by Alcinda Honwana and Filip De Boeck, 19–30. Oxford: James Currey, 2005.

Comoro, C., and J. Sivalon. "The Marian Faith Healing Ministry: An Expression of Popular Catholicicsm in Tanzania." In *East African Expressions of Christianity,* edited by T. Spear and I. N. Kimambo, 275–95. Athens: Ohio University Press, 1999.

Connell, R. W. *Masculinities.* Cambridge: Polity Press, 1995.

Connerton, Paul. *How Societies Remember.* Cambridge: Cambridge University Press, 1989.

Cook, Alexander C., ed. *Mao's Little Red Book: A Global History.* Cambridge: Cambridge University Press, 2014.

Cooper, Frederick, Thomas C. Holt, and Rebecca J. Scott. *Beyond Slavery: Explorations of Race, Labor, and Citizenship in Postemancipation Societies.* Chapel Hill: University of North Carolina Press, 2000.

Cooper, Frederick. *Africa since 1940: The Past of the Present.* Cambridge: Cambridge University Press, 2002.

Cowling, Lesley. "Building a Nation: The *Sowetan* and the Creation of a Black Reading Public." *Journal of Southern African Studies* 40, no. 2 (2014): 325–41.

Crary, Jonathan. *Suspension of Perception: Attention, Spectacle and Modern Culture.* Cambridge, MA: Harvard University Press, 1999.

De Boeck, Filip, and Alcinda Honwana. "Children and Youth in Africa: Agency, Identity and Place." In *Makers and Breakers: Children and Youth in Postcolonial Africa,* edited by Alcinda Honwana and Filip De Boeck, 1–18. Oxford: James Currey, 2005.

De Bruijn, Mirjam, Francis Nyanmjoh, and Inge Brinkman, eds. *Mobile Phones: The New Talking Drums of Everyday Africa.* Bamenda: Langaa RPCIG, 2009.

De Kock, Wynand. "Pentecostal Power for a Pentecostal Task: Empowerment through Engagement in the South African Context." *Journal of Pentecostal Theology* 16 (2000): 102–16.

De la Cruz, D. "Coincidence and Consequence: Marianism and the Mass Media in the Global Philippines." *Cultural Anthropology* 24, no. 3 (2009): 455–88.

De Lame, Danielle. "Flows and Forces: Once Contained, Now Detained? On Connections, Past and Present in Rwanda." In *The Social Life of Connectivity in Africa,* edited by Mirjam de Bruijn and Rijk van Dijk, 21–44. London: Palgrave Macmillan, 2012.

De Matviuk, Marcel A. Chavan. "Latin American Pentecostal Growth: Culture, Orality and the Power of Testimonies." *Asian Journal of Pentecostal Studies* 5 (2002): 205–22.

De Witte, Marleen. "Altar Media's *Living Word:* Televised Charismatic Christianity in Ghana." *Journal of Religion in Africa* 33, no. 2 (2003): 172–202.

———. "Media Afrikania: Styles and Strategies of Representing 'Afrikan Traditional Religion' in Ghana." In *New Media and Religious Transformations in Africa,* edited by Rosalind Hackett and Benjamin Soares, 207–26. Bloomington: Indiana University Press, 2015.

Delius, Peter, Laura Phillips, and Fiona Rankin-Smith, eds. *A Long Way Home: Migrant Worker Worlds 1800–2014.* Johannesburg: Wits University Press, 2014.

Diouf, Mamadou. "Engaging Postcolonial Cultures: African Youth and Public Space." *African Studies Review* 46, no. 2 (2003): 1–12.

Djebbare, Elina, and Emmanuelle Olivier. "Des 'religions du terroir' à l'Islam et *vice versa:* Politiques culturelles et pratiques artistiques croisées." In *Le Mali contemporain,* edited by Joseph Brunet-Jailly, Jacques Charmes, and Doulaye Konaté, 333–63. Bamako: Editions Tombouctou, 2014.

Dole, Christopher. *Healing Secular Life: Loss and Devotion in Turkey.* Philadelphia: University of Pennsylvania Press, 2012.

Drewal, Henry John. "Mami Wata: Arts for Water Spirits in Africa and Its Diasporas." *African Arts* 41, no. 2 (2008): 60–83.

Dudley, Sandra. "Material Visions: Dress and Textiles." In *Made to Be Seen: Perspectives on the History of Visual Anthropology,* edited by Marcus Banks and Jay Ruby, 45–73. Chicago: University of Chicago Press, 2011.

Durham, Deborah. "Disappearing Youth: Youth as Social Shifter in Botswana." *American Ethnologist* 31, no. 4 (2004): 589–605.

———. "Youth and the Social Imagination in Africa: Introduction to Parts 1 and 2." *Anthropological Quarterly* 73, no. 3 (2000): 113–20.

Eickelman, Dale F., and Jon W. Anderson, eds. *New Media in the Muslim World.* Bloomington: Indiana University Press, 1999.

———. "Redefining Muslim Publics." In *New Media in the Muslim World: The Emerging Public Sphere,* edited by Dale F. Eickelman and Jon W. Anderson, 1–18. Bloomington: Indiana University Press, 1999.

Eisenlohr, Patrick. "Media and Religious Diversity." *Annual Review of Anthropology* 41 (2012): 37–55.

Ellington, Scott. "The Costly Loss of Testimony." *Journal of Pentecostal Theology* 16 (2000): 48–59.

———. "History, Story and Testimony: Locating Truth in a Pentecostal Hermeneutic." *PNEUMA: Journal of the Society for Pentecostal Studies* 23 (2001): 245–63.

Ellis, Stephen, and Gerrie ter Haar. *Worlds of Power: Religious Thought and Political Practice in Africa.* London: C. Hurst, 2004.

Engelke, Matthew. *A Problem of Presence: Beyond Scripture in an African Church.* Berkeley: University of California Press, 2007.

Englund, Harri, ed. *Christianity and Public Culture in Africa.* Athens: Ohio University Press, 2011.

Erlank, Natasha. "'Brought into Manhood': Christianity and Male Initiation in South Africa in the Early Twentieth-Century." *Journal of Southern African Studies* 43, no. 2 (2017): 251–65.

Fabian, Johannes. *Remembering the Present: Painting and Popular History in Zaire.* Berkeley: University of California Press, 1996.

Fair, Laura. "Dressing Up: Clothing, Class and Gender in Post-Abolition Zanzibar." *Journal of African History* 39, no. 1 (1998): 63–94.

Faseke, Modupeolu. "From Redemption Camp to Redemption City: Mission Accomplished for Pastor Enoch Adejare Adeboye?" In *Enoch Adejare Adeboye at 70: The Story behind the Glory,* edited by Modupeolu Faseke, 231–44. Lagos: CIBN Press, 2011.

Fenrich, J., and T. E. Higgins. "Promise Unfulfilled: Law, Culture and Women's Inheritance Rights in Ghana." *Fordham International Law Journal* 25 (2001): 259–341.

Ferguson, Douglas E. "Nineteenth-Century Hausaland: Being a Description by Imam Imoru of the Land, Economy and Society of His People." PhD diss., University of California, Los Angeles, 1973.

Ferguson, James. *Global Shadows: Africa in the Neoliberal World Order.* Durham, NC: Duke University Press, 2006.

Fields, Karen. *Revival and Rebellion in Colonial Central Africa.* Princeton, NJ: Princeton University Press, 1985.

Fika, Adamu Mohameed. *The Kano Civil War and British Over-Rule 1882–1940.* Ibadan: Oxford University Press, 1978.

Fisher, Humphrey J. *Ahmadiyyah: A Study in Contemporary Islam on the West African Coast.* London: Oxford University Press for the Nigerian Institute of Social Research, 1963.

Flood, Gavin. "Dwelling on the Borders: Self, Text and World." In *Religion on the Borders: New Challenges in the Academic Study of Religion,* edited by

David Thurfjell and Peter Jackson, 25–57. Stockholm: Södertörn University, 2009.

Förster, Wilhelm. "Die christliche Mission und der Islam in den deutschen Kolonien." *Koloniale Zeitschrift* 9, Kriegsausgabe (11 August 1915): 2.

Frahm-Arp, Maria. "A History of Pentecostal Charismatic Christianity in South Africa." In *Global Renewal Christianity: Spirit-Empowered Movements Past, Present, and Future.* Vol. 3, *Africa,* edited by Vinson Synan, Amos Yong, and J. Kwabena Asamoah-Gyadu. Lake Mary, FL: Charisma House, 2016.

———. "The Political Rhetoric in Sermons and Select Social Media in Three Pentecostal Charismatic Evangelical Churches leading up to the 2014 South African Election." *Journal for the Study of Religion* 28, no. 1 (2015): 115–41.

———. *Professional Women in South African Pentecostal Charismatic Churches.* Leiden: Brill, 2010.

Freedberg, David. *The Power of Images: Studies in the History and Theory of Response.* Chicago: University of Chicago Press, 1989.

Freitag, Ulrike. "Researching 'Muslim Worlds': Regions and Disciplines." *ZMO Programmatic Text* 6 (2013): 1–10.

Gaffney, Patrick. *The Prophet's Pulpit: Islamic Preaching in Contemporary Egypt.* Berkeley: University of California Press, 1994.

Gandolfi, Stefania. "L'enseignement islamique en Afrique noire." *Cahiers d'Etudes Africaines* 43, no. 1–2 (2003): 261–77.

Gandy, Matthew. "Planning, Anti-Planning and the Infrastructure Crisis Facing Metropolitan Lagos." *Urban Studies* 43, no. 2 (2006): 371–96.

Gerber, Haim. *Islamic Law and Culture, 1600–1840.* Leiden: Brill, 1999.

Geschiere, Peter. "Sorcery and the State: Popular Modes of Action among the Maka of Southeast Cameroon." *Critique of Anthropology* 8, no. 1 (1988): 35–63.

Gibb, H. A. R, and J. H. Kramers. *Concise Encyclopedia of Islam.* Leiden: Brill Academic Publishers, 2001.

Giddens, Anthony. *Runaway World: How Globalization Is Reshaping Our Lives.* London: Profile, 1999.

Gifford, Paul. *Ghana's New Christianity.* Bloomington: Indiana University Press, 2004.

Ginsburg, Faye, Lila Abu-Lughod, and Brian Larkin, eds. *Media Worlds: Anthropology on New Terrain.* Berkeley: University of California Press, 2002.

Glassman, Jonathon. *Feasts and Riot: Revelry, Rebellion, and Popular Consciousness on the Swahili Coast, 1856–1888.* Portsmouth, NH: Heinemann, 1995.

Gledhill, Ruth. "How Reverse Missionaries Built the UK's Fastest-Growing Church." *Christianity Today,* June 5, 2014. http://www.christiantoday.com/article/how.reverse.missionaries.built.the.uks.fastest.growing.church/37894.htm.

Goliama, Castor. *Where Are You Africa? Church and Society in the Mobile Phone Age.* Bamenda: Langaa RPCIG, 2010.

Goody, Jack. *The Domestication of the Savage Mind.* Cambridge: Cambridge University Press, 1977.

———. *The Interface between the Written and the Oral.* Cambridge: Cambridge University Press, 1987.

———. *Representations and Contradictions: Ambivalence towards Images, Theatre, Fictions, Relics and Sexuality.* Oxford: Blackwell, 1997.

Gordon, David M. "Community of Suffering: Narratives of War and Exile in the Zambian Lumpa Church." In *Recasting the Past,* edited by Derek Peterson and Giacomo Macola, 191–209. Athens: Ohio University Press, 2009.

———. *Invisible Agents: Spirits in a Central African History.* Athens: Ohio University Press, 2012.

———. "Rebellion or Massacre: The UNIP-Lumpa Conflict Revisited." In *One Zambia, Many Histories: Towards a History of Post-Colonial Zambia,* edited by Jan-Bart Gewald, Giacomo Macola, and Marja Hinfelaar, 45–76. Leiden: Brill, 2008.

Grabar, Oleg. *Die Entstehung der Islamischen Kunst.* Cologne: Boehlau, 1977.

———. "The Story of Portraits of the Prophet Muhammad." *Studia Islamica* 96 (2003): 19–38, VI–IX.

Gunner, Elizabeth. "Jacob Zuma, the Social Body and the Unruly Power of Song." *African Affairs* 108, no. 430 (2009): 27–48.

———. *The Man of Heaven and the Beautiful Ones of God.* Leiden: Brill, 2002.

Gupta, Akhil. "Blurred Boundaries: The Discourse of Corruption, the Culture of Politics, and the Imagined State." *American Ethnologist* 22, no. 2 (1995): 375–402.

Gyanfosu, Samuel. "A Traditional Religion Reformed: Vincent Kwabena Damuah and the Afrikania Movement, 1982–2000." In *Christianity and the African Imagination: Essays in Honor of Adrian Hastings,* edited by David Maxwell and Ingrid Lawrie, 271–94. Leiden: Brill, 2013.

Habermas, Jürgen. *The Structural Transformation of the Public Sphere: An Enquiry into the Category of Bourgeois Society.* Cambridge, MA: MIT Press, 1991.

Habermas, Rebekka. "Debates on Islam in Imperial Germany." In *Islam and the European Empires,* edited by David Motadel, 231–53. Oxford: Oxford University Press, 2014.

Hackett, Rosalind J. "Charismatic/Pentecostal Appropriations of Media Technologies in Nigeria and Ghana." *Journal of Religion in Africa* 28, no. 3 (1998): 258–77.

———. "Mediated Religion in South Africa: Balancing Air-Time and Rights Claims." In *Religion, Media, and the Public Sphere,* edited by Birgit Meyer and Annelies Moors, 166–87. Bloomington: Indiana University Press, 2005.

Hall, Bruce. "An Early Tuareg Anti-Colonial Manifesto? A Local Critique of the French Occupation of the Niger Bend." In *Le temps des Oulèmas: Les manuscrits africains comme sources historiques,* edited by Seyni Moumouni and Viera Pawlikova-Vilhanova, 107–48. Niamey: Etudes Nigériennes, 2009.

———. *A History of Race in Muslim West Africa, 1600–1960*. New York: Cambridge University Press, 2011.

Hallaq, Wael B. *Authority, Continuity, and Change in Islamic Law*. Cambridge: Cambridge University Press, 2001.

———. "Model Shurūt Works and the Dialectic of Doctrine and Practice." *Islamic Law and Society* 2, no. 2 (1995): 109–34.

———. *Sharī'a: Theory, Practice, Transformations*. Cambridge: Cambridge University Press, 2009.

Hambrick-Stowe, C. E. *The Practice of Piety: Puritan Devotional Disciplines in Seventeenth-Century New England*. Chapel Hill: University of North Carolina Press, 1982.

Hanretta, Sean. *Islam and Social Change in French West Africa: History of an Emancipatory Community*. Cambridge: Cambridge University Press, 2009.

Hanson, John H. "Modernity, Religion and Development in Ghana: The Example of the Ahmadiyya Muslim Community." *Ghana Studies* 12–13 (2009–10): 55–75.

Harries, Patrick. "From Public History to Private Enterprise: The Politics of Memory in the New South Africa." In *Historical Memory in Africa: Dealing with the Past, Reaching for the Future in an Intercultural Context*, edited by Mamadou Diawara, Bernard Lategan, and Jörn Rüsen, 121–44. New York: Berghan, 2010.

———. "Missionaries, Magic, and Marxists: Power and the Politics of Literacy in South-East Africa." *Journal of Southern African Studies* 27, no. 3 (2001): 405–27.

Harrison, Christopher. *France and Islam in West Africa, 1860–1960*. Cambridge: Cambridge University Press, 1988.

Hart, Gillian. *Rethinking the South African Crisis: Nationalism, Populism, Hegemony*. Pietermaritzburg: University of KwaZulu-Natal Press, 2013.

Hartman, Wolfram, Jeremy Silvester, and Patricia Hayes, eds. *The Colonizing Camera: Photographs in the Making of Namibian History*. Cape Town: University of Cape Town Press, 1998.

Harvey, David. *A Brief History of Neoliberalism*. Oxford: Oxford University Press, 2005.

Hastings, Adrian. *African Christianity*. London: Geoffrey Chapman, 1976.

Hawkins, Sean. "'The Woman in Question': Marriage and Identity in the Colonial Courts of Northern Ghana, 1907–1954." In *Women in African Colonial Histories*, edited by Jean Allman, Susan Geiger, and Nakanyike Musisi, 116–43. Bloomington: Indiana University Press, 2002.

———. *Writing and Colonialism in Northern Ghana: The Encounter between the LoDagaa and "the World on Paper."* Toronto: University of Toronto Press, 2002.

Haydara, Yuusuf Mohamed, Ibirahima Sango, and Mahamman Tindirma. *Farang maka boote*. Bamako: EDIS, 2007.

———. *Tooya farru*. Bamako: EDIS, 2010.

Herrera, Linda, and Asef Bayat. "Conclusion: Knowing Muslim Youth." In *Being Young and Muslim: New Cultural Politics in the Global South and North,* 355–64. Oxford: Oxford University Press, 2010.

Hinfelaar, Hugo. *Bemba-Speaking Women of Zambia in a Century of Religious Change.* Leiden: Brill, 1994.

Hinfelaar, Marja. "Debating the Secular in Zambia: The Response of the Catholic Church to Scientific Socialism and Christian Nation, 1976–2006." In *Christianity and Public Culture in Africa,* edited by Harri Englund, 50–66. Athens: Ohio University Press, 2011.

Hirsch, Leo. "Arabische Weltanschauung." *Deutsche Kolonialzeitung* 5 (1 March 1890): 55.

Hirschkind, Charles. *The Ethical Soundscape: Cassette Sermons and Islamic Counterpublics.* New York: Columbia University Press, 2006.

Hiskett, Mervyn. "Commissioner of Police v. Musa Kommanda and Aspects of the Working of the Gold Coast Marriage of Mohammedans Ordinance." *Journal of African Law* 20, no. 2 (1976): 127–46.

———. *The Course of Islam in Africa.* Edinburgh: Edinburgh University Press, 1994.

———. *A History of Hausa Islamic Verse* London: SOAS, 1975.

Hofmeyr, Isabel. *The Portable Bunyan: A Transnational History of "The Pilgrim's Progress."* Princeton, NJ: Princeton University Press, 2004.

———. *"We Spend Our Years as a Tale that Is Told": Oral Historical Narrative in a South African Chiefdom.* Portsmouth, NH: Heinemann, 1994.

Holder, Gilles. "Chérif Ousmane Madani Haïdara et l'Association Islamique Ançar Dine: Un réformisme malien populaire en quête d'autonomie." *Cahiers d'Etudes Africaines* 2, no. 206–7 (2012): 389–425.

———. "'Maouloud 2006,' de Bamako à Tombouctou. Entre réislamisation de la nation et laïcité de l'etat: La construction d'un espace public religieux au Mali." In *L'Islam, nouvel espace public en Afrique,* edited by Gilles Holder, 237–89. Paris: Karthala, 2009.

———. "Un espace publique religieux: Pour une lecture contemporaine des enjeux politiques de l'Islam en Afrique." In *L'Islam, nouvel espace public en Afrique,* edited by Gilles Holder, 5–20. Paris: Karthala, 2009.

Hopkins, Anthony. "The New Economic History of Africa." *Journal of African History* 50 (2009): 155–77.

Horkheimer, Max, and Theodor Adorno. *Dialectic of Enlightenment.* London: Verso, 1986.

Hughes, Heather. *First President: A Life of John Dube, Founding President of the ANC.* Johannesburg: Jacana, 2011.

Hull, Matthew S. "Documents and Bureaucracy." *Annual Review of Anthropology* 41 (2012): 251–67.

Hunt, Nancy Rose. "Bicycles, Birth Certificates, and Clysters: Colonial Objects as Reproductive Debris in Mobutu's Zaire." In *Commodification: Things, Agency, and Identities (The Social Life of Things Revisited),* edited by Wim M. J. van Binsbergen and Peter Geschiere, 123–41. Münster: LIT Verlag, 2005.

Hunter, Emma. *Political Thought and the Public Sphere in Tanzania: Freedom, Democracy and Citizenship in the Era of Decolonization.* Cambridge: Cambridge University Press, 2015.

Hunwick, John O. *Arabic Literature in Africa.* Vol. 2, *Writings of Central Sudanic Africa.* Leiden: Brill, 1995.

———. "Falkeiana III: The Kitāb al-Tarsīl, An Anonymous Manual of Epistolatory and Notary Style." *Sudanic Africa* 5 (1994): 179–84.

Hydén, Göran, Michael Leslie, and Folu F. Ogundimu, eds. *Media and Democracy in Africa.* New Brunswick, NJ: Transaction Publishers, 2002.

Ibrahim, Mustapha. *Islamic Law of Marriage. Part One.* 5th ed. Accra: Sebewie Publishers, 2003.

Iliffe, John. *A Modern History of Tanganyika.* Cambridge: Cambridge University Press, 1979.

———. *Tanganyika under German Rule 1905–1912.* Cambridge: Cambridge University Press, 1969.

Illich, Ivan. *In the Vineyard of the Text: A Commentary to Hugh's* Didascalicon. Chicago: University of Chicago Press, 1993.

Izard, Michel. *Gens du Pouvoir, Gens de la Terre. Les institutions politiques de l'ancien royaume du Yatenga (Bassin de la Volta Blanche).* Paris: Editions de la Maison des sciences de l'Homme, 1985.

James, Deborah. *Money from Nothing: Indebtedness and Aspiration in South Africa.* Johannesburg: Wits University Press, 2014.

———. "Money-Go-Round: Personal Economics of Aspiration and Indebtedness." *Africa* 82, no. 1 (2012): 20–40.

Jansen, Jan. "The Sunjata Epic: The Ultimate Version." *Research in African Literatures* 32, no. 1 (2000): 14–46.

Janson, Marloes. *Islam, Youth, and Modernity in the Gambia: The Tablighi Jama'at.* Cambridge: Cambridge University Press, 2014.

Janson, Marloes, and Akintunde Akinleye. "The Spiritual Highway: Religious World Making in Megacity Lagos (Nigeria)." *Material Religion: The Journal of Objects, Art and Belief* 11 (2015): 549–62.

Jay, Martin. *Downcast Eyes: The Denigration of Vision in Twentieth-Century French Thought.* Berkeley: University of California Press, 1994.

Jewsiewicki, Bogumil. "Historical Memory and Representations of New Nations in Africa." In *Historical Memory in Africa: Dealing with the Past, Reaching for the Future in an Intercultural Context,* edited by Mamadou Diawara, Bernard Lategan, and Jörn Rüsen, 53–66. New York: Berghahn, 2010.

Kamara, Ousmane. "Les divisions statutaires des descendants d'esclaves au Fuuta Tooto mauritanien." *Journal des Africanistes* 70, no. 1–2 (2000): 265–89.

Kane, Cheikh Hamidou. *L'aventure ambiguë.* Paris: Julliard, 1961.

Keane, Webb. *Christian Moderns: Freedom and Fetish in the Mission Encounter.* Berkeley: University of California Press, 2007.

Kepel, Gilles. *The Revenge of God: The Resurgence of Islam, Christianity and Judaism in the Modern World.* Cambridge: Polity Press, 1994.

Kimberley, David. "Preaching to the Converted: Charismatic Leaders, Performances and Electronic Media in Contemporary Islamic Communities." Master's thesis, Concordia University, 2002.

Kirsch, Thomas G. *Spirits and Letters: Reading, Writing and Charisma in African Christianity.* New York: Berghahn, 2008.

Kitutu, L. Sabuni. "La notion de religion populaire appliquée au catholicisme en Afrique: Regard sur les conditions et les enjeux actuels de la piété populaire dans le champ religieux du continent africain." PhD diss., University of Strasbourg, 2011.

Klouwenberg, Fiona Klein, and Inge Butter. "African 'Youth' since Independence: Notes on a Bibliographic Overview, 1990–2005." *Africa Development* 36, no. 3–4 (2011): 55–66.

Kobo, Ousman Murzik. *Unveiling Modernity in Twentieth-Century West African Islamic Reforms.* Leiden: Brill, 2012.

Koolhaas, Rem. 2002. "Fragments of a Lecture on Lagos." In *Under Siege: Four African Cities: Freetown, Johannesburg, Kinshasa, Lagos,* edited by Okwui Enwezor, Carlos Basualdo, Ute Meta Bauer, Susanne Ghez, Sarat Maharaj, Mark Nash, and Octavio Zaya, 173–83. Kassel: Hatja Canz Publishers, 2002.

Koolhaas, Rem, Stefano Boeri, Sanford Kwinter, Nadine Tazi, and Hans Ulrich Obrist. "Lagos." In *Mutations: Harvard Project on the City.* Bordeaux: ACTAR, 2000.

Kounta, Albakaye Ousmane. *Contes de Tombouctou et Macina.* 2 vols. Paris: L'Harmattan, 2000.

Kramer, Fritz. "Praktiken der Imagination." In *Die Unvermeidlichkeit der Bilder,* edited by Gerhard von Graevenitz, Stefan Rieger, and Felix Thuerlemann, 17–29. Tübingen: Gunther Narr Verlag, 2001.

Krapf, Ludwig. *Travels, Researches and Missionary Labours.* London: Truebner, 1968.

Kroll-Smith, J. Stephen. "The Testimony as Performance: The Relationship of an Expressive Event in the Belief of a Holiness Sect." *Journal for the Scientific Study of Religion* 19 (1980): 16–25.

Kuperus, Tracey. "The Political Role and Democratic Contribution of Churches in Post-Apartheid South Africa." *Journal of Church and State* 53 (2011): 278–306.

Kustenbauder, Matthew. "Believing in the Black Messiah: The Legio Maria Church in an African Christian Landscape." *Nova Religio: Journal of Alternative and Emergent Religions* 13 (2009): 11–40.

Lambek, Michael. Introduction to *Ordinary Ethics: Anthropology, Language, and Action,* edited by Michael Lambek, 1–36. New York: Fordham University Press, 2010.

———. *Knowledge and Practice in Mayotte: Local Discourses of Islam, Sorcery and Spirit Possession.* Toronto: University of Toronto Press, 1993.

Landau, Paul. *The Realm of the Word: Language, Gender and Christianity in a South African Kingdom.* Portsmouth, NH: Heinemann, 1993.

———. "'Religion' and Christian Conversion in African History: A New Model." *Journal of Religious History* 23, no. 1 (1999): 8–30.

Latour, Bruno. "Visualisation and Cognition: Drawing Things Together." *Knowledge and Society* 6 (1986): 1–40.

Leblanc, Marie-Nathalie, and Muriel Gomez-Perez. "Jeunes musulmans et citoyenneté culturelle: Retour sur des expériences de recherche en Afrique de l'Ouest francophone." *Sociologie et Sociétés* 39, no. 2 (2007): 39–59.

Lee, Christopher, ed. *Making a World after Empire: The Bandung Moment and Its Political Afterlives.* Athens: Ohio University Press, 2010.

Leguy, Cécile. "Revitalizing the Oral Tradition: Stories Broadcast by Radio Parana (San, Mali)." *Research in African Literatures* 38, no. 3 (2007): 136–47.

Leue, August. "Vor dem Sturm." *Deutsche Kolonialzeitung* 23, no. 42 (20 October 1906): 410–11

Lewis, Martin. "The Vexatious History of Indo-European Studies." *GeoCurrents* 11–17 Dec., 2013. http://www.geocurrents.info/indo-european-origins/vexatious-history-indo-european-studies-part.

Lewison, Elsie. "Pentecostal Power and the Holy Spirit of Capitalism: Re-Imagining Modernity in the Charismatic Cosmology." *Symposia* 3, no. 1 (2011): 31–54.

Limb, Peter, ed. *The People's Paper: A Centenary History and Anthology of* Abantu Batho. Johannesburg: Wits University Press, 2013.

Lindhardt, Martin. "More than Just Money: The Faith Gospel and Occult Economies in Contemporary Tanzania." *Nova Religio: The Journal of Alternative and Emergent Religions* 13 (2009): 41–67.

Loimeier, Roman. *Between Social Skills and Marketable Skills: The Politics of Islamic Education in Twentieth-Century Zanzibar.* Leiden: Brill, 2009.

———. *Islamic Reform and Political Change in Northern Nigeria.* Evanston, IL: Northwestern University Press, 1997.

Lydon, Jane. *Eye Contact: Photographing Indigenous Australians.* Durham, NC: Duke University Press, 2005.

Lysack, Krista. "The Production of Time: Keble, Rossetti and Victorian Devotional Reading." *Victorian Studies* 55 (2013): 451–70.

Macpherson, Fergus, and W. V. Stone. "The Alice Movement in Northern Rhodesia." *Occasional Papers Issued by the Department of Mission Studies, London* (August 1958).

Mann, Gregory. "Old Soldiers, Young Men: Masculinity, Islam, and Military Veterans in Late 1950s Soudan Français (Mali)." In *Men and Masculinities in Modern Africa,* edited by Lisa A. Lindsay and Stephan Miescher, 69–87. Portsmouth, NH: Heinemann, 2003.

Marcuse, Herbert. *One-Dimensional Man: Studies in the Ideology of Advanced Industrial Society.* London: Sphere Books, 1968.

Marsden, Magnus, and Kostas Retsikas. Introduction to *Articulating Islam: Anthropological Approaches to Muslim Worlds,* edited by Magnus Marsden and Kostas Retsikas, 1–33. New York: Springer, 2013.

Marshall, Ruth. *Political Spiritualities: The Pentecostal Revolution in Nigeria.* Chicago: University of Chicago Press, 2009.

Martin, David. *Pentecostalism: The World Their Parish.* Oxford: Blackwell. 2002.

Marx, Karl. *Critique of Hegel's "Philosophy of Right."* Translated by Annette Jolin and Joseph O'Malley. Cambridge: Cambridge University Press, 1970.

Masquelier, Adeline. "Negotiating Futures: Islam, Youth and the State in Niger." In *Islam and Muslim Politics in Africa,* edited by Benjamin Soares and René Otayek, 243–63. New York: Palgrave Macmillan. 2007.

———. *Women and Islamic Revival in a West African Town.* Bloomington: Indiana University Press, 2009.

Matson, A. T. "Sewa Haji: A Note." *Tanzania Notes and Records* 65 (1966): 91–94.

Mattes, Robert. "South Africa's Emerging Black Middle Class: A Harbinger of Political Change?" *Journal of International Development* 27 (2015): 665–92.

Maxwell, David. *African Gifts of the Spirit: Pentecostalism and the Rise of a Zimbabwean Transnational Religious Movement.* Athens: Ohio University Press, 2006.

———. "Delivered from the Spirit of Poverty? Pentecostalism, Prosperity and Modernity in Zimbabwe." *Journal of Religion in Africa* 28 (1998): 350–73.

———. Introduction to *Christianity and the African Imagination: Essays in Honour of Adrian Hastings,* edited by David Maxwell, with Ingrid Lawrie. Leiden: Brill, 2002.

Mbe, Akoko Robert. "You Must Be Born-Again: The Pentecostalisation of the Presbyterian Church in Cameroon." *Journal of Contemporary African Studies* 25, no. 2 (2007): 299–315.

Mbembe, Achille. *On the Postcolony.* Berkeley: University of California Press, 2001.

McGee, Gary. "Latter Rain Falling in the East: Early Twentieth Century Pentecostalism in India and the Debate over Speaking in Tongues." *Church History* 68 (1999): 648–65.

Mchakula, Japhet. "Youth Participation in Radio Listening Clubs in Malawi." *Journal of Southern African Studies* 33, no. 2 (2007): 251–65.

McIntosh, Janet. *The Edge of Islam: Power, Personhood and Ethnoreligious Boundaries on the Kenyan Coast.* Durham, NC: Duke University Press, 2009.

McLaughlin, Fiona. "Islam and Popular Music in Senegal: The Emergence of a 'New Tradition.'" *Journal of the International African Institute* 67, no. 4 (1997): 560–81.

Meinecke, Gustav. "Die Lage in Ostafrika und die Araber." *Deutsche Kolonialzeitung* 1, no. 40 (October 6, 1888): 317.

———. "Wandlungen." *Deutsche Kolonialzeitung* 1, no. 7 (February 18, 1888): 49.

Merensky, Alexander. "Der mohammedanische Gegenstoß gegen christliche Einflüsse in Zentral-Afrika." *Deutsche Kolonialzeitung* 1, no. 17 (April 28, 1888): 129.

Meyer, Birgit. "Christianity in Africa: From African Independent to Pentecostal-Charismatic Churches." *Annual Review of Anthropology* 33 (2004): 447–74.

———. "Commodities and the Power of Prayer: Pentecostal Attitudes towards Consumption in Contemporary Ghana." *Development and Change* 29 (1998): 751–76.

———. "Impossible Representations: Pentecostalism, Vision, and Video Technology in Ghana." In *Religion, Media, and the Public Sphere,* edited by Birgit Meyer and Annelies Moors, 290–312. Bloomington: Indiana University Press, 2005.

———. "'Make a Complete Break with the Past': Memory and Post-colonial Modernity in Ghanaian Pentecostal Discourse." *Journal of Religion in Africa* 28 (1998): 316–49.

———. "'Praise the Lord': Popular Cinema and Pentecostalite Style in Ghana's New Public Sphere." *American Ethnologist* 31, no. 1 (2004): 92–110.

———. *Sensational Movies: Video, Vision and Christianity in Ghana.* Berkeley: University of California Press, 2015.

Meyer, Birgit, and Annelies Moors. Introduction to *Religion, Media, and the Public Sphere*, edited by Birgit Meyer and Annelies Moors, 1–25. Bloomington: Indiana University Press, 2005.

Michaels, Eric. "A Primer of Restrictions on Picture-Taking in Traditional Areas of Aboriginal Australia." *Visual Anthropology* 4 (1991): 259–75.

Middleton, John. *The World of the Swahili: An African Mercantile Civilization.* New Haven: Yale University Press, 1992.

Miescher, Stephan F., and Lisa A. Lindsay. "Introduction: Men and Masculinities in Modern African History." In *Men and Masculinities in Modern Africa,* edited by Lisa A. Lindsay and Stephan F. Miescher, 1–31. Portsmouth, NH: Heinemann, 2003.

Mitchell, Robert Cameron. "Religious Change and Modernization: The Aladura Churches among the Yoruba in Southwestern Nigeria." PhD diss., Northwestern University, Evanston, Illinois, 1970.

Mokoena, Hlonipha. *Magema Fuze: The Making of a Kholwa Intellectual.* Scottsville: University of KwaZulu-Natal Press, 2011.

Morgan, David. "The Ecology of the Image: Seeing and the Study of Religion." *Religion and Society: Advances in Research* 5 (2014): 83–105.

———. "Religion and Media: A Critical Review of Recent Developments." *Critical Research on Religion* 1 (2013): 347–56.

———. *The Sacred Gaze: Religious Visual Culture in Theory and Practice.* Berkeley: University of California Press, 2005.

Morton, Christopher, and Elizabeth Edwards, eds. *Photography, Anthropology and History: Expanding the Frame.* London: Ashgate, 2009.

Mudimbe, V. Y. *Tales of Faith: Religion as Political Performance in Central Africa.* London: Athlone Press, 1997.

Munyua, Alice Wanjira. "Women Entrepreneurs in Nairobi: Examining and Contextualizing Women's Choices." In *African Women and ICTs,* edited by Ineke Buskens and Anne Webb, 119–32. London: Zed Books, 2009.

Muoria-Sal, Wangari, Bodil Folke Frederiksen, John Lonsdale, and Derek Peterson, eds. *Writing for Kenya: The Life and Works of Henry Muoria.* Leiden: Brill, 2009.

Mutombo, M. Ngandu. *Femmes dans les mouvements chrétiens africain : Récits de vie à Lubumbashi (R-D Congo).* Paris: L'Harmattan, 1997.

Mwangi, Evan. "Queer Agency in Kenya's Digital Media." *African Studies Review* 57, no. 2 (2014): 93–113.

Naef, Silvia. *Y a-t-il une "question de l'image" en Islam?* Geneva: Tetraede, 2004.

Ndaywel è Nziem, Isidore. "Du Zaïre au Congo: La Vierge du Désarmement et la guerre de libération." *Canadian Journal of African Studies* 33, nos. 2–3 (1999): 500–529.

Neudörfl, Elisabeth. "Photography vs. Visibility: Seeing Unseen Aspects of a City." *Visual Resources: An International Journal of Documentation* 26 (2001): 13–29.

Nimtz, August H. *Islam and Politics in East Africa: The Sufi Order in Tanzania.* Minneapolis: University of Minnesota Press, 1980.

Nugent, Paul. *Africa since Independence: A Comparative History.* London: Palgrave Macmillan, 2012.

Nyamnjoh, Francis B. "Global and Local Trends in Media Ownership and Control: Implications for Cultural Creativity in Africa." In *Situating Globality: African Agency in the Appropriation of Global Culture,* edited by Wim van Binsbergen and Rijk van Dijk, 57–89. Leiden: Brill, 2004.

O'Brien, D. B. Cruise. *Symbolic Confrontations: Muslims Imagining the State in Africa.* London: Hurst, 2003.

Offei, William E. *Family Law in Ghana.* Accra: Sebewie Publishers, 1998.

Olaleru, Olanike. *The Seed in the Ground: The Story of the Founding of the Redeemed Christian Church of God.* Lagos: Father of Light Publishers, 2007.

Olivier, Emmanuelle. "Droits d'auteur vs usages locaux de l'autorité: Réflexion à partir d'une K7 de louanges." *Volume!* 10, no. 2 (2013): 151–72.

———. "Les louanges Islamiques au Mali: Un art de la filiation." In *Musiques au monde: La tradition au prisme de la création,* edited by Emmanuelle Olivier, 93–116. Paris: Sampzan Delatour, 2012.

———. "Musique et globalisation: 'Techno-logiques' de la création musicale." *Le Temps des Médias* 1, no. 22 (2014): 134–48.

Omoyajowo, Akinyele J. *Cherubim and Seraphim: The History of an African Independent Church.* New York: NOK Publishers International, 1982.

Osella, Filippo, and Caroline Osella. "Islamism and Social Reform in Kerala, South India." *Modern Asian Studies* 42, no. 2–3 (2007): 317–46.

Oshitelu, Gideon A. "Religion and Poverty Alleviation in Nigeria." Paper delivered at the Annual Religious Studies Conference, Department of Religious Studies, University of Ibadan, May 8–11, 2001.

Osinulu, Adedamola Olusegun. "City on Edge: Constructing Efficacious Pentecostal Sites in Lagos." PhD diss., University of California, Los Angeles, 2011.

Otayek, René, and Benjamin Soares. "Introduction: Islam and Muslim Politics in Africa." In *Islam and Muslim Politics in Africa,* edited by René Otayek and Benjamin F. Soares, 1–24. New York: Palgrave Macmillan. 2007.

Oyatambwe, W. *Église catholique et pouvoir politique au Congo-Zaïre.* Paris: L'Harmattan, 1997.

Paden, John N. *Religion and Political Culture in Kano.* Berkeley: University of California Press, 1973.

Paret, Rudi. "Textbelege zum islamischen Bilderverbot." In *Das Werk des Künstlers,* edited by Hans Fegers, 36–48. Stuttgart: Kohlhammer, 1960.

Park, Myung Soo. "Korean Pentecostal Spirituality as Manifested in the Testimonies of Believers of the Yoido Full Gospel Church." *Asian Journal of Pentecostal Studies* 7 (2004): 35–56.

Parkin, David. "Latticed Knowledge: Eradication and Dispersal of the Unpalatable in Islam, Medicine and Anthropological Theory." In *Counterworks: Managing the Diversity of Knowledge,* edited by Richard Fardon, 143–63. London: Routledge, 1995.

Parsitau, Damaris. "'Arise Oh Ye Daughters of Faith': Women, Pentecostalism, and Public Culture in Kenya." In *Christianity and Public Culture in Africa,* edited by Harri Englund, 131–48. Athens: Ohio University Press, 2011.

Passarge, Siegfried. "Mission oder Islam?" *Deutsche Kolonialzeitung* 8, no. 50 (14 December 1895): 394–95.

Peel, J. D. Y. *Aladura: A Religious Movement among the Yoruba.* London: International African Institute, 1968.

———. *Christianity, Islam, and Orisha Religion: Three Traditions in Comparison.* Oakland: University of California Press, 2016.

———. *Religious Encounter and the Making of the Yoruba.* Bloomington: Indiana University Press, 2000.

Peletz, Michael G. *Islamic Modern: Religious Courts and Cultural Politics in Malaysia.* Princeton: Princeton University Press, 2002.

———. "'Ordinary Muslims' and Muslim Resurgents in Contemporary Malaysia: Notes on an Ambivalent Relationship." In *Islam in an Era of Nation-States: Politics and Religious Renewal in Muslim Southeast Asia,* edited by R. W. Hefner and P. Horvatich, 208–31. Honolulu: University of Hawai'i Press, 1997.

Perret, T. "Médias et démocratie au Mali." *Politique Africaine* 97 (2005): 18–32.

Pesek, Michael. "Für Kaiser und Allah: Ostafrikas Muslime im Großen Krieg für die Zivilisation, 1914–1919." *SGMOIK Bulletin* 19 (2004): 9–18.

———. "Kreuz oder Halbmond: Die deutsche Kolonialpolitik zwischen Pragmatismus und Paranoia in Deutsch-Ostafrika 1908–1914." In *Mission und Gewalt. Der Umgang christlicher Missionen mit Gewalt und die Ausbreitung des Christentums in Afrika und Asien in der Zeit von 1792 bis 1918/19,* edited by Jürgen Becher and Ulrich van der Heyden, 97–112. Stuttgart: Franz Steiner, 2000.

———. "Sulayman B. Nasr Al-Lamki and German Colonial Policies towards Muslim Communities in German East Africa." In *Islam in Africa,* edited by Thomas Bierschenk and Georg Stauth, 211–29. Munster: Lit Verlag, 2002.

Peters, Carl. *Die Deutsche Emin-Pasha-Expedition.* Munich: R. Oldenbourg, 1891.

Peterson, Brian. *Islamization from Below: The Making of Muslim Communities in Rural French Sudan, 1880–1960.* New Haven: Yale University Press, 2011.

Peterson, Derek R. *Creative Writing: Translation, Bookkeeping and the Work of the Imagination in Colonial Kenya.* Portsmouth, NH: Heinemann, 2004.

———. *Ethnic Patriotism and the East African Revival: A History of Dissent, c. 1935–1972.* Cambridge: Cambridge University Press, 2012.

Peterson, Derek, and Giacomo Macola. "Homespun Historiography and the Academic Profession." In *Recasting the Past: History Writing and Political Work in Modern Africa,* edited by Derek Peterson and Giacomo Macola. Athens: Ohio University Press, 2009.

Peterson, Derek, Emma Hunter, and Stephanie Newell, eds. *African Print Cultures: Newspapers and Their Publics in the Twentieth Century.* Ann Arbor: University of Michigan Press, 2016.

Philips, John Edward. *Spurious Arabic: Hausa and Colonial Nigeria.* Madison: University of Wisconsin Press, 2000.

Pollock, Sheldon. "Cosmopolitan and Vernacular in History." *Public Culture* 12, no. 3 (2000): 591–625.

Premawardhana, Devaka. "Transformational Tithing Sacrifice and Reciprocity in a Neo-Pentecostal Church." *Nova Religio: The Journal of Alternative and Emergent Religions* 15 (2012): 85–109

Price, Frederick K. C. *Name It and Claim It!* Benin City: Christian Bookshop, 2005.

Prud'homme, Pierre. "Les 'griots d'Allah,' ou l'émergence d'une musique religieuse populaire." In *Le Mali contemporain,* edited by Joseph Brunet-Jailly, Jacques Charmes, and Doulaye Konaté, 317–32. Bamako: Editions Tombouctou, 2014.

Pype, Katrien. "The Liveliness of Pentecostal-Charismatic Christianity in Africa." In *Pentecostalism in Africa: Presence and Impact of Pneumatic Christianity in Postcolonial Societies,* edited by Martin Lindhardt, 345–78. Leiden: Brill, 2014.

———. *The Making of the Pentecostal Melodrama: Religion, Media, and Gender in Kinshasa.* Oxford: Berghahn Books, 2012.

———. "Media as Technologies of Enchantment. Initial Comparisons between Kimbanguist and Pentecostal Media Pedagogies." In *Simon Kimbangu: Le Prophète de la Libération de l'Homme Noir.* Vol. 2, edited by E. Mbokolo and K. Sabakinu, 135–59. Paris: L'Harmattan, 2014.

Qasim Zaman, Muhammad. *The Ulama in Contemporary Islam: Custodians of Change.* Princeton: Princeton University Press, 2002.

Quaas, Anna D. *Transnationale Pfingstkirchen: Christ Apostolic Church und Redeemed Christian Church of God.* Frankfurt am Main: Verlag Otto Lembert, 2011.

Radley, Alan. "What People Do with Pictures." *Visual Studies* 25, no. 3 (2010): 269–79.

Rambuss, Richard. *Closet Devotions.* Durham, NC: Duke University Press, 1998.

Ramirez, Francis, and Christian Rolot. *Histoire du cinéma colonial au Zaïre, au Rwanda et au Burundi.* Tervuren: Musée Royal de l'Afrique Centrale, 1985.

Ranger, Terence. "Missionaries, Migrants and the Manyika: The Invention of Ethnicity in Zimbabwe." In *Creation of Tribalism in Southern Africa,* edited by Leroy Vail, 118–50. Berkeley: University of California Press, 1991.

———. "Religious Movements and Politics in Sub-Saharan Africa." *African Studies Review* 29, no. 2 (1986): 1–69.

———. "Scotland Yard in the Bush: Medicine Murders, Child Witches and the Construction of the Occult: A Literature Review." *AFRICA* 77, no. 2 (2007): 272–83.

Rasmussen, Susan J. "Between Several Worlds: Images of Youth and Age in Tuareg Popular Performances." *Anthropological Quarterly* 73, no. 3 (2000): 133–44.

Raum, Johannes. "Von den Missionsfeldern: Die mohammedanische Gefahr in Deutsch-Ostafrika." *Koloniale Zeitschrift* 11, no. 31 (16 September 1910): 572–74.

Reefe, Thomas. *The Rainbow and the Kings: A History of the Luba Empire to 1891.* Berkeley: University of California Press, 1981.

Reese, Scott S. *The Transmission of Learning in Islamic Africa.* Leiden: Brill, 2004.

Reichard, Paul. "Die Bedeutung von Tabora für Deutsch-Ostafrika." *Deutsche Kolonialzeitung* 3, no. 6 (March 15, 1890): 67–68.

———. "Vorschläge zu einer praktisch-kolonisatorischen Inangriffnahme ostafrikanischer Besitzungen (Schluß)." *Deutsche Kolonialzeitung* 2, no. 11 (March 16, 1889): 83–85.

Reisman, Paul. *Société et liberté chez les Peul Djelgôbé de Haute-Volta: Essai d'anthropologie introspective.* Paris: Mouton, 1994.

Richelman, Georg. "Wie mir Ostafrika nach langer Trennung erscheint." *Deutsche Kolonialzeitung* 25, no. 41 (10 October 1908): 727–28.

Rillon, Ophélie. "Féminités et masculinités à l'épreuve de la contestation: Le genre des luttes sociales et politiques au Mali (1954–1993)." PhD diss., Université Panthéon Sorbonne, 2013.

Roberts, Allan F., and Mary Nooter Roberts. *Memory: Luba Art and the Making of History.* New York: Museum for African Art, 1996.

———. *A Saint in the City: Sufi Arts of Urban Senegal.* Los Angeles: University of California Fowler Museum of Cultural History, 2003.

Robinson, David. *The Holy War of Umar Tal: The Western Sudan in the Mid-Nineteenth Century.* New York: Oxford University Press, 1985.

———. "The Umarian Emigration of the Late Nineteenth Century." *International Journal of African Historical Studies* 20 (1987): 245–70.

Robinson, David, and Jean-Louis Triaud, eds. *Le temps des marabouts: Itinéraires et stratégies islamiques en Afrique occidentale française, v. 1880–1960.* Paris: Karthala, 1997.

Rudolph, Susanne Hoeber, and James Piscatori, eds. *Transnational Religion and Fading States.* Oxford: Westview Press, 1997.

Sachau, Eduard. *Muhammedanisches Recht nach schafiitischer Lehre.* Lehrbücher des Seminars für orientalische Sprachen zu Berlin, XVII. Stuttgart: W. Spemann, 1897.

Safaian, Dorna. "After the Machine: The Economy of Innovation and the Iconotechnics of Islam." In *Medium Religion: Faith, Geopolitics, Art,* edited by Boris Groys and Peter Weibel, 68–77. Cologne: Walther Koenig, 2009.

Sassen, Saskia, ed. *Global Networks, Linked Cities.* London: Routledge, 2002.

Scheele, Judith. *Smugglers and Saints of the Sahara: Regional Connectivity in the Twentieth Century.* New York: Cambridge University Press, 2012.

Schielke, Samuli. "Pious Fun at Saints Festivals in Modern Egypt." *ISIM Newsletter* 7, no. 1 (2001): 23.

Schimmel, Annemarie. *Deciphering the Signs of God.* Edinburgh: Edinburgh University Press, 1994.

———. *Mystical Dimensions of Islam.* Chapel Hill: University of North Carolina Press, 1976.

Schmidt, Rochus. *Geschichte des Araberaufstandes in Ost-Afrika.* Frankfurt a. Oder: Verlag der Königlichen Hofdruckerei Trowitsch & Sohn, 1892.

Schnee, Heinrich, ed. *Deutsches Kolonial-Lexikon.* Leipzig: Quelle & Meyer, 1920.

Schöfert, Arne. "Übersicht der wichtigen Kolonialzeitungen und–Zeitschriften." Accessed May 30, 2017. http://www.traditionsverband.de/magazin/kolonialpresse/kolonialpresse.html.

Schulz, Dorothea. "'Charisma and Brotherhood' Revisited: Mass-Mediated Forms of Spirituality in Urban Mali." *Journal of Religion in Africa* 33, no. 2 (2003): 146–71.

———. "Evoking Moral Community, Fragmenting Muslim Discourses: Sermon Audio Recording and the Reconfiguration of Public Debate in Mali." *Journal for Islamic Studies* 27 (2007): 39–72.

———. "A Fractured Soundscape of the Divine: Female 'Preachers,' Radio Sermons and Religious Place-making in Urban Mali." In *Prayer in the City. The Making of Muslim Sacred Places and Urban Life,* edited by Patrick Desplat and Dorothea Schulz, 239–64. Bielefeld: Transcript Verlag, 2012.

———. "Morality, Community, Publicness: Shifting Terms of Public Debate in Mali." In *Religion, Media, and the Public Sphere,* edited by Birgit Meyer and Annelies Moors, 132–51. Bloomington: Indiana University Press, 2005.

———. *Muslims and New Media in West Africa: Pathways to God.* Bloomington: Indiana University Press, 2012.

———. "Praise without Enchantment: Griots, Broadcast Media, and the Politics of Tradition in Mali." *Africa Today* 44, no. 4 (1997): 443–64.

———. "Promises of (Im)mediate Salvation: Islam, Broadcast Media, and the Remaking of Religious Experience in Mali." *American Ethnologist* 33, no. 2 (2006): 210–19.

Seesemann, Rüdiger. "Kenyan Muslims, the Aftermath of 9/11, and the 'War on Terror'." In *Islam and Muslim Politics in Africa,* edited by Benjamin F. Soares and René Otoyek, 157–76. New York: Palgrave, 2007.

Shembe, Johannes Galilee. *Izihlabelelo zamaNazaretha.* Durban: W. H. Shepherd, 1940.

Sissoko, Mamadou. *Odyssée héroïque, cinquante ans d'action de l'homme El Hadji Abdoulaye Koné Ladji-Blen: Belles lettres, connaissance mystique, morale politique; La palme du martyr, aventures, critiques sociales et religieuses: Une mission suicide.* Bamako: Editions Jamana, 2007.

Sitas, Ari. *The Mandela Decade 1990–2000: Labour, Culture and Society in Post-Apartheid South Africa.* Pretoria: Unisa Press, 2010.

Smith, Buster, Christopher P. Scheitle, and Christopher Bader. "The Ties That Bind: Network Overlap among Independent Congregations." *Social Science Computer Review* 30, no. 2 (2012): 259–73.

Smith, Melissa M. "Nonprofit Religious Organization Web Sites: Underutilized Avenue of Communicating with Group Members." *Journal of Media and Religion* 6, no. 4 (2007): 273–90.

Smith, M. G., *Government in Kano, 1350–1950.* Boulder, CO: Westview Press, 1997.

Smith, Zeric Kay. "From Demons to Democrats: Mali's Student Mouvement 1991–1996," *Review of African Political Economy* 72 (1997): 249–63.

Soares, Benjamin. "The Historiography of Islam in West Africa: An Anthropologist's View." *The Journal of African History* 55, no. 1 (2014): 27–36.

———. "Islam and Public Piety in Mali." In *Public Islam and the Common Good,* edited by Armando Salvatore and Dale F. Eickelman, 205–27. Brill: Leiden, 2004.

———. *Islam and the Prayer Economy: History and Authority in a Malian Town.* London: Edinburgh University Press, 2005.

———. "Islam in Mali in the Neoliberal Era." *African Affaires* 105/418 (2005): 77–95.

———, ed. *Muslim-Christian Encounters in Africa.* Leiden: Brill, 2006.

———. "Notes on the Anthropological Study of Islam and Muslim Societies in Africa." *Culture and Religion* 1, no. 2 (2000): 277–85.

———. "'Rasta' Sufi and Muslim Youth Culture in Mali." In *Being Young and Muslim: New Cultural Politics in the Global South and North,* edited by Linda Herrera and Asef Bayat, 241–57. Oxford: Oxford University Press, 2010.

———. "Saint and Sufi in Contemporary Mali." In *Sufism and the "Modern" in Islam,* edited by Martin Van Bruinessen and Julia Day Howell, 76–92. London: I. B. Tauris, 2007.

Soares, Benjamin, and R. Launay. "The Formation of an 'Islamic Sphere' in French Colonial West Africa." *Economy and Society* 28, no. 4 (1999): 497–519.

Spitulnik, Debra. "Alternative Small Media and Communicative Spaces." In *Media and Democracy in Africa,* edited by Göran Hydén, Michael Leslie, and Folu F. Ogundimu, 177–205. New Brunswick, NJ: Transaction, 2002.

Spyer, Patricia. "In and Out of the Picture: Photography, Ritual, and Modernity in Aru, Indonesia." In *Photographies East,* edited by Rosalind Morris, 161–83. Durham, NC: Duke University Press, 2001.

Sreberny-Mohammadi, Annabelle, and Ali Mohammadi. *Small Media, Big Revolution: Communication, Culture, and the Iranian Revolution.* Minneapolis: University of Minnesota Press, 1994.

———. "Small Media and Revolutionary Change: A New Model." In *Media in Global Context: A Reader,* edited by Annabelle Sreberny-Mohammadi, Dwayne Winseck, Jim McKenna, and Oliver Boyd-Barrett. London: Arnold, 1997.

Starrett, Gregory. "The Varieties of Secular Experience." *Comparative Studies in Society and History* 52, no. 3 (2010): 626–51.

Stewart, Charles C., and Bruce S. Hall. "The 'Core Curriculum' and Book Market in West Africa." In *The Trans-Saharan Book Trade: Manuscript Culture, Arabic Literacy and Intellectual History in Muslim Africa,* edited by Graziano Krätli and Ghislaine Lydon. Leiden: Brill, 2011.

Stewart, Charles C. "Southern Saharan Scholarship and the Bilad al-Sudan." *Journal of African History* 17 (1976), 73–93.

Stoler, Ann Laura. "Colonial Archives and the Arts of Governance: On the Content in the Form." In *Refiguring the Archive,* edited by Carolyn Hamilton, Verne Harris, Jane Taylor, Michele Pickover, Graeme Reid, and Razia Saleh, 82–101. Cape Town: Kluwer, 2000.

Stolow, Jeremy. "Religion and/as Media." *Culture and Society* 22, no. 4 (2005): 119–45.

Strassler, Karen. *Refracted Visions: Popular Photography and National Modernity in Java.* Durham, NC: Duke University Press, 2010.

Sturgill, Amanda. "Scope and Purposes of Church Web Sites." *Journal of Religion and Media* 3, no. 3 (2004): 165–76.

Sturmer, Martin. *The Media History of Tanzania.* Ndanda: Ndanda Mission Press, 1998.

Switzer, Les, ed. *South Africa's Alternative Press: Voices of Protest and Resistance: 1880–1960.* Cambridge: Cambridge University Press, 1997.

Synan, Vinson. *The Holiness-Pentecostal Tradition: Charismatic Movements in the Twentieth Century.* Grand Rapids, MI: W. B. Eerdmans, 1997.

Taussig, Michael. *Defacement: Public Secrecy and the Labor of the Negative.* Stanford: Stanford University Press, 1999.

Traoré, B. "Islam et politique à Bobo-Dioulasso de 1940 à 2002." In *L'Islam politique au sud du Sahara: Discours et enjeux,* edited by Muriel Gomez-Perez, 417–47. Paris: Karthala, 2005.

Traoré, Oumar Seydou. *Qui est Chérif Ousmane Madani Haïdara?* Bamako: Oumar Seydou Traoré, 2007.

Triaud, Jean-Louis. "Bamako, la ville aux deux cents mosquées, ou la victoire du 'secteur informel' islamique." *Islam et Sociétés au Sud du Sahara* 2 (1988): 166–77.

Tumwaka, B. Kipanza. "Le ministère de guérison en Afrique: Chance et défi pour l'Église." *Nouvelle Revue Théologique* 122 (2000): 416–30.

Ukah, Asonzeh. "The Deregulation of Piety in the Context of neoliberal Globalization: African Pentecostalism in the Twenty-First Century." In *Global Renewal Christianity: Spirit-Empowered Movements Past, Present, and Future.* Vol. 3, *Africa,* edited by Vinson Synan, Amos Yong, and J. Kwabena Asamoah-Gyadu, 213–21. Lake Mary, FL: Charisma House, 2016.

———. "Die Welt erobern, um das Himmelreich zu errichten: Pfingstkirchen, Prayer Camps und Stadtenwicklung in Lagos." In *Urban Prayers: Neue religiöse Bewegungen in der globalen Stadt,* edited by metroZone, 109–27. Berlin: Assoziation A und metroZone, 2011.

———. "God Unlimited: Economic Transformations of Contemporary Nigerian Pentecostalism." In *Economics of Religion: Anthropological Approaches,* edited by Lionel Obadia and Donald C. Wood. Research in Economic Anthropology Series 31, 187–216. Bingley, UK: Emerald Group, 2011.

———. "Managing Miracles: Law, Authority and the Regulation of Religious Broadcasting in Nigeria." In *New Media and Religious Transformations in Africa,* 245–65. Bloomington: Indiana University Press, 2014.

———. *A New Paradigm of Pentecostal Power: A Study of the Redeemed Christian Church of God in Nigeria.* New Jersey: Africa World Press, 2008.

———. "Roadside Pentecostalism: Religious Advertising in Nigeria and the Marketing of Charisma." *Critical Interventions: Journal of African Art History and Visual Culture* 2 (2008): 125–41.

———. "Seeing Is More Than Believing: Posters and Proselytization in Nigeria." In *Proselytization Revisited: Rights Talk, Free Markets and Culture Wars,* edited by Rosalind I. J. Hackett,167–98. London: Equinox Publishing Limited, 2008.

———. "'Those Who Trade with God Never Lose': The Economics of Pentecostal Activism in Nigeria." In *Christianity and Social Change in Africa: Essays in Honor of J. D. Y. Peel,* edited by Toyin Falola, 251–74. Durham, NC: Carolina Academic Press, 2005.

Umar, Muhammad S. *Islam and Colonialism: Intellectual Responses of Muslims of Northern Nigeria to British Colonial Rule* Leiden: Brill, 2006.

Van Dijk, Richard. "Young Puritan Preachers in Post-Independent Malawi." *Africa* 62 (1992): 152–81.

van Wyk, Ilana. *The Universal Church of the Kingdom of God in South Africa: A Church of Strangers.* Cambridge: Cambridge University Press, 2014.

Vellut, J.-L. "Quelle profondeur historique pour l'image de la Vierge Marie au Congo?" *Canadian Journal of African Studies* 33, no. 2–3 (1999): 530–47.

Velten, Carl. *Desturi za wasuaheli na khabari za desturi za sheri"a za wasuaheli.* Göttingen: Vandenhoeck & Ruprecht, 1903.

Villalón, Leonardo A. *Islamic Society and State Power in Senegal: Disciples and Citizens in Fatick.* Cambridge: Cambridge University Press, 1995.

———. "Rethinking Education in the Sahel: Democracy, Religious Change, and the Politics of Reform." In *Governing Africa's Changing Societies: Dynamics of Reform,* edited by Ellen Lust and Stephen Ndegwa, 177–202. Boulder, CO: Westview Press, 2012.

Vismann, Cornelia. *Files: Law and Media Technology.* Translated by Geoffrey Winthrop-Young. Stanford: Stanford University Press, 2008.

Vokes, Richard. *Ghosts of Kanungu: Fertility, Secrecy & Exchange in the Great Lakes of East Africa.* Woodbridge, UK: James Currey, 2009.

von Stengel, Karl. "Muhammedanisches Recht." *Deutsche Kolonialzeitung* 11, no. 39 (29 September 1898): 349.

von Wissmann, Herrmann. "Die Bedeutung der Emin Pascha-Expedition für die Erschließung von Afrika." *Deutsche Kolonialzeitung* 1, no. 39 (29 September 1888): 310.

Vreede-de Stuers, C. "Churi: The Fragile Position of Women in Muslim Marriage in North India." *Bijdragen tot de Taal-, Land- en Volkenkunde* 148, no. 2 (1992): 274.

Waggoner, Diane. "Photographic Amusement, 1888–1919." In *The Art of the American Snapshot, 1888–1978: The Collection of Robert E. Jackson*, edited by Sarah Greenough, Diane Waggoner, Sarah Kennel, and Matthew S. Witkovsky, 7–45. Washington, DC: National Gallery of Art, 2007.

Ware, Rudolph T. *The Walking Qur'an: Islamic Education, Embodied Knowledge and History in West Africa.* Chapel Hill: University of North Carolina Press, 2014.

Wariboko, Nimi. *Nigerian Pentecostalism.* Rochester: University of Rochester Press, 2014.

Warm, Richard L. "Merchants, Muslims, and Wahhabiyya: The Elaboration of Islamic Identity in Sikasso, Mali." *Canadian Journal of African Studies* 26, no. 3 (1992): 485–507.

Warner, Michael. "Publics and Counterpublics." *Public Culture* 14, no. 1 (2002): 49–90.

Wasserman, Herman. *Tabloid Journalism in South Africa: True Story!* Bloomington: Indiana University Press, 2010.

Waters, Richard, Christine S. Friedman, Brittney Mills, and Lei Zeng. "Applying Relationship Management Theory to Religious Organizations: An Assessment of Relationship ultivation Online." *Journal of Communication and Religion* 34, no. 1 (2011): 88–104.

Weber, Max. *The Theory of Social and Economic Organizations.* Translated by A. M. Henderson and Talcott Parsons. New York: Free Press, 1947.

Weidmann, Conrad. *Deutsche Männer in Afrika: Lexicon der hervorragendsten deutschen Afrika-Forscher, Missionare etc.* Lübeck: Verlagsbuchhandlung Bernhard Nöhring, 1894.

Werner, Jean-François. "Photographies and Modernities in Africa." In "Photographies and Modernities in Africa," edited by Heike Behrend and Jean-François Werner. Special issue, *Visual Anthropology Review* 14, no. 3 (2001): 241–42.

———. "Photography and Individualization in Contemporary Africa: An Ivorian Case-Study." In "Photographies and Modernities in Africa," edited by Heike Behrend and Jean-François Werner. Special issue, *Visual Anthropology* 14, no. 3 (2001): 251–68.

Westerlund, David. *Ujamaa na Dini: A Study of Some Aspects of Society and Religion in Tanzania, 1961–1977.* Stockholm: Almquist and Wiksell International, 1980.

White, Landeg. *Magomero: Portrait of an African Village.* Cambridge: Cambridge University Press, 1997.

Wilkens, K. "Mary and the Demons: Marian Devotion and Ritual Healing in Tanzania." *Journal of Religion in Africa* 39, no. 3 (2009): 295–318.

Willis, Justin. *Mombasa, the Swahili and the Making of the Mijikenda.* Oxford: Blackwell, 1993.

Wimmelbücker, Ludger. *Mtoro Bin Mwinyi Bakari (c. 1869–1927). Swahili Lecturer and Author in Germany.* Dar es Salaam: Mkuku ny Nyota Publishers, 2009.

Wirtz, John G., Prisca S. Ngondo, and Philip Poe. "Talking *with* Us or *at* Us: How U.S. Religious Denominations Use Organizational Web Sites to Communicate with Their Constituents." *Journal of Media and Religion* 12, no. 4 (2013): 165–80.

Woodman, Gordon R. "Ghana Reforms the Law of Intestate Succession." *Journal of African Law* 29, no. 2 (1985): 118–28.

Wright, Marcia. *Strategies of Slaves and Women: Life-Stories from East/Central Africa.* New York: Lilian Barber, 1993.

Yankah, Kwesi. "Power and the Circuit of Formal Talk." In *Power, Marginality and African Oral Literature,* edited by Graham Furniss and Liz Gunner, 211–24. Cambridge: Cambridge University Press, 2008.

Yates, Joanne. *Control through Communication: The Rise of System in American Management.* Rev. ed. Baltimore: Johns Hopkins University Press, 1993.

Zache, Hans. "Koloniale Eingeborenenpolitik (Fortsetzung)." *Koloniale Zeitschrift* 6, no. 15 (20 July 1905).

Zomeño, Amalia. "Abandoned Wives and Their Possibility for Divorce in al-Andalus: The Evidence of the Wathā'iq Works." Translated by Harry J. Bone. In *Writing the Feminine: Women in Arab Sources,* edited by Manuela Marin and Randi Deguilhem, 111–26. London: I. B. Tauris, 2002.

Contributors

FELICITAS BECKER is professor of African history at Gent University and a specialist in the modern history of East Africa. Her research interests focus on the history of Islam in continental East Africa, Islamic reform and protest, rural poverty and development, and the aftermath of slavery. Her publications include *Becoming Muslim in Mainland Tanzania* (Oxford University Press, 2008), and articles in *Journal of African History, Journal of Global History, African Affairs, Journal of Religion in Africa,* and *African Studies Review,* among others. She has recently completed a book manuscript on the dynamics of forced optimism and victim-blaming in rural development, and is now working on a study of Muslim preachers.

HEIKE BEHREND is a professor emerita of anthropology at the Institute of African Studies of the University of Cologne. She has conducted intensive ethnographic research in Kenya and Uganda in the field of violence, war, and religion as well as in media anthropology. Since the early 1990s, she has been working together with popular photographers in Kenya and Uganda. She has published extensively on photographic practices in Eastern Africa and worked as a curator. Her latest publication is *"Contesting Visibility": Photographic Practices along the East African Coast* (Transcript, 2013). She lives in Berlin.

JOEL CABRITA is a lecturer in the Faculty of Divinity at the University of Cambridge. Her research focuses on the history of Christianity in Southern Africa in the modern period. Her publications include *Text and Authority in the South African Nazaretha Church* (Cambridge University Press, 2014) and *Relocating World Christianity: Interdisciplinary Studies in Universal and Local Expressions of Christianity* (Brill, 2017), with David Maxwell and Emma Wild-Wood. Her forthcoming book on the transatlantic Zionist Church (*The People's Zion: South Africa, the United States and a Transatlantic Faith-Healing Movement*) will be published by Harvard University Press in 2018.

ANDRÉ CHAPPATTE graduated from SOAS in 2013. He is a research fellow of the research group on Cities as Laboratories of Change at Leibniz-Zentrum Moderner Orient in Berlin. His postdoctoral interests are the socio-sensory unfolding of a Muslim life in relation to public morality, secrecy and desire at night in provincial towns of the West African savanna as well as the growth of border towns in southern Mali and northern Côte d'Ivoire.

MARIA FRAHM-ARP is an associate professor in religion studies and vice dean in the Faculty of Humanities at the University of Johannesburg. She is the author of *Professional Women in Pentecostal Charismatic Churches in South Africa* (Brill, 2010). She has published widely on women, gender, and politics in contemporary Pentecostal Charismatic Churches in South Africa.

DAVID M. GORDON's research focuses on the history of southern and central Africa over the last two centuries. He has published four books, including a monograph that considers how central African and Christian spirituality influenced human agency in Northern Zambia, *Invisible Agents: Spirits in a Central African History* (Ohio University Press, 2012). His many articles on African history and Africanist historiography appear in journals such as the *Journal of African History, Slavery and Abolition, Comparative Studies in Society and History, William and Mary Quarterly,* and *Past & Present.*

LIZ GUNNER is professor and researcher at the School of Languages at the University of Johannesburg. Her many book publications include *Politics and Performance: Theatre, Poetry and Song in Southern Africa,* and *Power, Marginality and African Oral Literature* (with Graham Furniss). Liz has a forthcoming book on radio in South Africa with the International African Library monograph series, to be published by Cambridge University Press. She has extensively published articles on various aspects of Southern African popular culture, literature, and religion, including in the journals *African Affairs, Journal of Southern African Studies,* and *Research in African Literatures.*

BRUCE S. HALL is an associate professor in the Department of History at the University of California, Berkeley. He obtained his PhD in

African history from the University of Illinois at Urbana-Champaign in 2005. His research has focused on the intellectual and social history of Muslim West Africa. He has previously taught at Duke University, University at Buffalo (SUNY), and the Johns Hopkins University.

SEAN HANRETTA (PhD Wisconsin) is currently an associate professor in the Department of History at Northwestern University. His book, *Islam and Social Change in French West Africa: History of an Emancipatory Community*, was published by Cambridge University Press in 2009 and his shorter works have appeared in the *Journal of African History, Comparative Studies in Society and History, Past & Present, The Oxford Handbook of Modern African History*, and other volumes.

JÖRG HAUSTEIN is Senior Lecturer in Religions in Africa at the School of Oriental and African Studies in London. His two main fields of research are Pentecostalism in Africa (especially in Ethiopia) and the history of both Christianity and Islam in colonial Africa. He is currently working on a book about colonial perceptions and discussions of Islam in German East Africa.

KATRIEN PYPE, a social and cultural anthropologist, studies media cultures in Kinshasa. She is a research professor at the Institute for Anthropological Research in Africa at KU Leuven University (Belgium), and a research fellow with the Department of African Studies and Anthopology at the University of Birmingham (UK). Her publications include a monograph on the production of evangelizing television serials in Kinshasa (Berghahn Books, 2012). Articles have appeared in journals such as *Journal of the Royal Anthropological Institute, Ethnos, Africa: Journal of the International Institute, Journal of Religion in Africa*, and *Journal of African Cultural Studies.*

MARIE RODET is Senior Lecturer in African History at the School of Oriental and African Studies, University of London. Her principal research interests lie in the field of migration history, gender studies, and the history of slavery in the West African Sahel in the nineteenth and twentieth centuries. Her publications analyze how slave resistance, rebellions, and mobility disrupted supposedly fixed relations of gender and power hierarchies, leading to complex renegotiations for kinship, marriage, religious practices, and, more generally, for notions of belonging in Mali and Senegal. She is the author of *Les migrantes ignorées du Haut-Sénégal (1900–1946)* (Paris, 2009) and director of *The Diambourou: Slavery and Emancipation in Kayes–Mali* (DVD, London, 2014). She is currently working on her second monograph on resistance against slavery in Kayes, Mali.

ASONZEH UKAH is a sociologist/historian of religion affiliated to the Department of Religious Studies, University of Cape Town. He is the Director of Research Institute on Christianity and Society in Africa (RICSA), University of Cape Town, South Africa, and Affiliated Senior Fellow of Bayreuth International Graduate School of African Studies (BIGSAS), University of Bayreuth, Germany, and also the author of *A New Paradigm of Pentecostal Power* (AWP, 2008) and coeditor (with Magnus Echtler) of *Bourdieu in Africa* (Brill, 2016).

Index

Note: Page numbers followed by n indicate an endnote with relevant number; page numbers in italic refer to illustrations